DANCING WISDOM

YVONNE DANIEL

Dancing
Wisdom

*Embodied Knowledge
in Haitian Vodou,
Cuban Yoruba, and
Bahian Candomblé*

UNIVERSITY OF ILLINOIS PRESS

URBANA AND CHICAGO

Frontispiece: Yvonne Daniel. © Frank Ward Photo.
Reprinted by permission.

Publication of this book was funded in part
by the Sophia Smith Fund of Smith College.

⊚ This book is printed on acid-free paper.

Library of Congress Cataloging-in-Publication Data
Daniel, Yvonne, 1940–
Dancing wisdom : embodied knowledge in Haitian Vodou,
Cuban Yoruba, and Bahian Candomblé / Yvonne Daniel.
p.   cm.
Includes bibliographical references and index.
ISBN 978-0-252-02966-0 (hardcover : alk. paper)
ISBN 978-0-252-07207-9 (pbk. : alk. paper)
1. Dance—Religious aspects. 2. Africa, Sub-Saharan—Religion.
3. African Americans—Religion. 4. Orishas. 5. Yoruba (African
people)—Cuba—Religion. 6. Voodooism. 7. Candombli
(Religion)—Brazil—Bahia (State) I. Title.
BL605.D28   2004
299.6'097—dc22   2004017210

To my ancestors:
Orixá ure saul laxé, Orixá ure oberi o ma

To future generations of
African Diaspora scholars.

For my grandchildren Tatiana, Dominique,
Berenz, Jasmine, T.J., Martina, Isabella,
Marbella, Ava, and T. Ashley:

Axé, Aché, and Ayi bobo

CONTENTS

ILLUSTRATIONS

FIGURES

Illustrated by Leah Smith and Cleveland Bellow

CHARTS

ACKNOWLEDGMENTS

This has been a mammoth project, and there are many who must share in my joy at the book's completion. First, I wish to thank the editors and staff of the University of Illinois Press, particularly Associate Director and Editor-in-Chief Joan Catapano, for supporting this project. Second, I thank Smith College for funding two sabbaticals and numerous trips to each site over eight years. By extension, I am grateful to the teachers who substituted for me and who carried a heavier burden with my students while I was doing the research. Also, I thank my family and my neighbors for enduring the even longer years of my inquiry and, as a result, my absence and their hardships on my behalf.

For my discussions of Haiti, I am indebted to Katherine Dunham and the late Lavinia Yarborough for their early work and personal kindnesses. Many thanks go to three colleagues whose works I cite often, but who were willing discussants for parts of chapters 4 and 6. I am particularly thankful for Gerdès Fleurant's song and music check, for Leslie Desmangles's Kreyol check, and for Joan Burroughs's dance critiques and friendship. Also, I am forever grateful for assistance from two Haitian dance masters, Jean Léon Destiné and Louinis Louinis. *Ayi bobo.*

For assistance with chapter 7 and my work on Bahia generally, I am also indebted to dancers and anthropologists. To Isaura Oliveira I am particularly thankful for her own spirituality and for sharing it along with her dance experiences with me. Augusto Soledade also has made considerable contributions to my thinking on the Bahian materials. I am grateful to him for bringing Pai

Carlinhos to his home, since I profited from Carlinhos's patient dialogue for two years while I was revising the manuscript. I also profited greatly from the comments and guidance of J. Lorand Matory and Julio Caesar de Tavares, two brilliant colleagues who guided my inquiries deeper with their questions. And, of course, my friendship with Gracinha de Santana Rodrigué over many years has given me so many opportunities to participate in Candomblé that it is hard to express thanks. I am most proud of her publication on Candomblé and hope that our incredible conversations were as much a part of her book as they are in mine. *Axé.*

It is almost impossible to thank all of the people I need to thank for their assistance with chapter 8. Relations have always been colored by the economic situation of the moment and the ever-changing political climate between the United States and Cuba; thus I value the genuine friendships I have been able to maintain: *muchíssimas gracias a Samuel y Amparito.* Still other individuals and groups made my life full over seventeen years of fieldwork and visiting, which permitted my contact and entry into a Cuban spiritual world. I thank the Ministry of Culture staffs of Havana, Santiago, Camagüey, and Matanzas. I thank my friends and colleagues in my ritual family: Ana Perez, Dolores Perez, Paula Perez, Sulima X, Franciso Minini Zamora, Vereál, Ogan Oswaldo, Teresa Pedroso, Baba Pedroso, and Yurien, Dalia, Sandi, and Enrique Perez. I give thanks to Ernesto El Gato Gatell, Harold Muñiz, Tobaji Stewart and Nadhiyr Velez for adding to my charts and lists, making them more correct. It is my hope that one day this book will be translated so that my Cuban families can read what I have been talking to them about all these years. I hope they will see themselves in the context of the Diaspora as well. *Aché.*

I thank Nelson Graburn at the University of California at Berkeley for giving me the idea of a comparative study as we fathomed my switch from Haitian to Cuban concentration. I thank the thoughtful unidentified readers who critiqued my manuscript. I thank the undergraduate students in my spirituality seminar in 2003, especially Leeanne Atkins, who used her experiences within the Yoruba religion and in Portuguese to clarify my writing on Bahia. I am grateful to my student assistant Candice Taylor for her careful work on the bibliography. I am particularly grateful for the concern of my Kreyol translators in chapters 1 and 6, Sara Quessa and Joanne Violin, both of whom were indispensable at a time when I was desperate in rendering the material authentic and artistic. And I am forever grateful to my friend and artist Cleveland Bellow and graphic designer Leah Smith for taking on the visualization of my central ideas and making the verbal visible.

Thanks are given to the following authors and their publishers, which permitted quotations: Olabiyi Yai (Rowman and Littlefield Publishers), Morton Marks (Universal Press), Karen McCarthy Brown (University of California Press), Robert Voeks (University of Texas Press), Zora Neale Hurston (J. P. Lippincott Publishers), Lavinia Yarborough (CORD Publishing), Moreau de St. Méry (Princeton Books, Dance Horizons), David Eltis and David Richardson (*Slavery and Abolition Journal*), John Mason (Yoruba Theological Archministry), Paul Connerton (Cambridge University Press), Katherine Dunham (Center for African American Studies, UCLA), Laënnec Hurbon (Harry N. Abrams Co.), and Rachel Harding (Indiana University Press). I am indebted to both Rowman and Littlefield and the University of Florida Press for allowing me to quote from my own work in their publications.

Several individuals have gone beyond the help of others and have arduously persevered by my side. To Sheila Walker I send *aché* for all the inspiration that her intellect and her travel analyses have given me. I could never answer all of her meticulous questions, but the attempt has fortified and amplified the final version of this work, and I am deeply grateful. Alice Horner, another anthropologist and friend since our Berkeley days, and dance historian and friend for even longer, Sharon Arslanian, also deserve this public note of appreciation. I value their consistent support over the years, especially for reading parts of the manuscript on quick notice. I offer my deepest thanks to my friends Isabel Cryer, Naima Lewis, Babalawo John Fagbemi Turpin, Lou Potter, Q. R. Hand, and Bunseki Fu-Kiau, who have come to my rescue in multiple ways and who, unknowingly and knowingly, have helped this finished product immeasurably.

ORTHOGRAPHIC NOTE

During the course of writing this book, I have tried to accommodate the most recent determinations of the Haitian Kreyol, Spanish, Portuguese, and ritual Yoruba languages. The present written form of Kreyol is still dynamic and has inconsistencies, but I have tried to be consistent within common usage. For the Haitian material, however, I have used the French spelling for place-names: Bois Cayman, Port-au-Prince, Sucrie Danasch, and Cap-Haïtien, for example—in order to avoid using the word "Haytian" repeatedly in English.

I have used the spelling for Yoruba divinities in accordance with the linguistic conventions of the home country on which I am writing. In other words, when I discuss Bahia, Brazil, I say "Xangó," and when I discuss Cuba I say "Changó"; in English I say "Shango." On the African continent among Yoruba peoples, the same word is spelled "Şango" and pronounced the same in English and Portuguese. Another example of different spellings for Yoruba-based words is the use of n, m, or ũ, as in Brazilian Ogun, Ogum, or Ogũ and Cuba's Ogún; this is contrasted with the Haitian versions, Ogou or Ogoun. I distinguish Ogun, Ogún, and Ogou for Bahia, Cuba, and Haiti, respectively.

The spelling of the word "Congo" usually refers to the Congo River and two countries: the Republic of the Congo and the Democratic Republic of the Congo, which have been carved out and fought over in contemporary West Central Africa. Since the 1990s, "Kongo" refers to the peoples of that region, the BaKongo being only one of these, although some nonethnic BaKongo peoples from the area around the Congo River have been called "Congos" as well. The term "Kongo" also refers to cultural behaviors of the region or Kongo culture; the term "Kongo-Angola" includes the entire cultural region.

In the Haitian and Cuban dance and music literature, however, the cultural legacies of West Central Africa are called "Congo" and sometimes "Bantu" (referring to the Bantu language family of neighboring peoples in West Central Africa) up through the 1980s. In Cuba, a similar spelling, "conga," is used for the barrel-shaped drum and for a dance form, both of which have Kongo-Angola roots. I use the term "Kongo-Angola" to refer to the peoples and related cultures of this huge West Central African region, except in the Haitian case where I have noted their usage preference of "Congo" for referencing dance/music terms.

DANCING WISDOM

ONE

Deciphering
Diaspora Dances

*Their Origin Nations and
Belief Systems*

I am fascinated by belief systems that rely heavily on dance behavior. While dance and music behaviors are not immediately associated with religious, sociopolitical, or politico-economic issues, they can reveal intriguing nonaesthetic information. In the following chapters I show how dance/music data make significant contributions to African Diaspora studies. In three African-derived religious systems of the Americas, dance performances are categorized by means of "spirit families," African "nations," or cosmic forces, called *lwas* in Haiti, and *orichas* and *orixás* in Cuba and Brazil, respectively. I refer to these spiritual entities as "divinities" so that I can speak of the religions jointly and avoid the use of the terms "gods and goddesses," which is misleading when we are trying to understand how worshipers understand. The divinities of these African American religions receive dance/music offerings within religious rites and come to dance with the believing community. For ritual community members, the dance/music performances suggest myths and retell cultural stories, but most important, they charter and encourage social behavior in present everyday lives.

The word "religion" in contemporary English is derived from the Latin, *religare,* meaning "to bind back," "retie," "bond," or "fasten," and it is the human world that is fastened to the spiritual world in my three examples of African American ritual practice. Whether worshipers believe in sacred stone tablets, a virgin conception, enlightenment through silent meditation, or a higher consciousness through dance and drum rituals, religious beliefs tie most humans to a spiritual world. For the communities I study, Haitian Vodou and Cuban Yoruba in the Caribbean and Bahian Candomblé in South America, it is most often the dance/music behavior within ritual behavior that continually reties the worshipping community to its spiritual affinity.

Fundamentally, "religion" refers to the union of humans with either an omnipotent nonhuman or several suprahuman spiritual entities (de Santana Rodrigué 2001). In these three religions, the fastening of the human world to a spiritual world, and thereby the bonding of differing spheres of existence, occurs *through or as a result of* dance performance *and/or* music practices.

There are similarities among the religious and dance/music systems that I study. For example, during my research I found that African ethnic groups such as the Fon and Yoruba meshed and intertwined their religious practices in the Americas. Even more intriguingly, I found that their origins in what are now the Republic of Benin and Nigeria are replete with mixing, exchange, and interaction over centuries, rather than the discrete national units about which we are often conditioned to think. Similarly, the many African ethnic groups of the Kongo-Angola region in Central Africa have lived as neighbors and shared cultures beyond what the geopolitical boundaries of any particular contemporary African nation might suggest.

Such proximity and sharing have resulted in meshed belief systems. For example, one of the Yoruba spiritual entities, Elegba, is found among both Fon and Yoruba religions; also Ogou, another spiritual entity in Fon culture is called Ogún in Yoruba culture. Fon and Yoruba divining systems are shared as well, called Fa in Fon culture and Ifa in Yoruba culture. As Olabiyi Yai, a Yoruba linguist from Benin, has said, well before coming to the Americas, continental Africans were accustomed to having dual or multiple religious loyalties, in addition to dual or multiple cultural allegiances (Yai 2001:244–55). This has made the study of American contexts difficult when searching out origins and distinctions.

My recent travel to the Yoruba and Fon areas of Benin has underscored for me an understanding of the consequences within a history of double or multiple religious loyalties. Many ethnic groups on the African continent have shared religious beliefs and practices as a result of trade, intermarriages, and conditions of war and enslavement. Distinct but similar belief systems have resulted, and often worshipers have professed double religious loyalties, such as in the story of the Yoruba and Fon wedding where the new bride brought her Yoruba divinities to add to the groom's Fon pantheon. Accordingly, worshipers could express affinity with either Fon or Yoruba religion or Fon or Yoruba national identity.

I have repeatedly found this tendency toward multiple loyalties in the Americas. Despite what friends and associates might say at first, their behaviors have demonstrated religious mixtures. Today, the three religions that I discuss are complex, plural, and multidimensional amalgams that exhibit *intra-African syncretism* at their roots (Walker 1980:32–36; Daniel 1995:36; see also chapter 3 of this volume). For example, the Fon word *vodun* (spirits or gods) became the name of the Fon-derived Vodou religion in Haiti (Herskovits 1975 [1937]:140), but Haitian "spirits" are called *lwas, mistès* (mysteries), *invisibles* (invisibles), or *ley mo* (the dead [ancestors]), and not *voduns.* The term *lwa* comes from the Yoruba *o loua,* meaning "spiritual master." The usage of the terms *vodun* and *lwas* indicates the influence of two neighboring cultures on each other and their continued meshing within religious culture of the Americas.

Another example of intra-African syncretism is found in the name for one of the Afro-Brazilian religions, Candomblé, a Yoruba-based religious practice that is also called Nago/Ketu for the prominence of particular types of Yoruba peoples, those of the Nago and Ketu nations. The word "Candomblé," however, comes from Bantu language origins in Central Africa, and not from the heavy West African religious core of the belief system. Thus, a West African religion came to be known by a Central African title.

Both examples suggest intimate and profound exchange among African ethnic and regional groups upon their arrival in the Americas. These instances of intra-African syncretism continue a long tradition of similar exchange in ancient kingdoms and among varied regional groups on the continent. These also suggest different notions regarding nationhood.

Again, Yai's important African data help to explain why numerical dominance, as opposed to cultural and ethnic allegiance, was not always the major criterion for the name that Africans in the Americas chose. He relates, for example, that Fon-related peoples who landed in Brazil chose the name of a small and politically weak group within their region of Africa, the Jêje nation. In so doing, Africans were articulating different values from the European model of "size and power yields name." Rather, Yai hypothesizes, the Jêje may have been the first Fon-related group to establish a Vodou religion or temple in the new environment; their language was mutually intelligible and they shared the same divinities (2001:251–52). Thus expressing nationhood in the Americas was dependent on several characteristics, religion being one. Careful consideration of intra-African syncretism implies that each of these religions contains beliefs and practices that were more often shared and not always original to any one ethnic group or religious community.

My study analyzes the Fon-based case in Haiti and two Yoruba-based cases, one in Cuba and the other in Bahia, Brazil. Haitian Vodou, Cuban Yoruba, and Bahian Candomblé utilize dance performance and music-making as primary vehicles for religious and spiritual transformation. They concur on divination systems in order to receive information from and communicate with a Supreme Being and his/her emissaries. The religions uphold life and death realms that constitute an ongoing vital universe and that involve funereal practices, spiritual manifestations, and animal sacrifices, which systematize relations among humans, divinities, and the Supreme Divinity.

Through mounting numbers of worshipping practitioners, visual documentaries, and written analyses, more consideration of African American religions, as opposed to their previous "cult" descriptor, is emerging (e.g., Deren 1983, 1953; Dunham 1969; Courlander 1973; Laguerre 1980; Kramer 1981, 1985, 1988; Thompson 1983; Rolando 1988, 1999, 2001; Murphy 1988, 1994; Barnes 1989; Bolívar 1990; Brown 1991; Desmangles 1992; Brandon 1993; Canizares 1999; Matory 2001a, 2001b; Harding 2000; Vega 2000; de Santana Rodrigué 2001; Murphy and Sanford 2001).

Now through analysis of ritual music and dance, even more knowledge about the significance of these religious traditions is available. In this study, I am transposing the often silent, nonverbal information that is embodied within lively and dynamic dance performances to make it at least partially explicit. In addition to dance and music analysis, I offer other explanations that come from cultural interpretation based on ethnographic field research within the three regions. My theme, therefore, is the shared and pivotal activity of three Diaspora religions—their dance/music behavior. I see the three religions as dance-dependent ritual structures with dance-initiating objectives that have captivated the interests of different populations around the world.

Ultimately I am also concerned with how this behavior informs and challenges the notion of hierarchical types of knowledge. Embodied knowledge—that is, knowledge found within the body, within the dancing and drumming body—is rich and viable and should be referenced among other

4

kinds of knowledge. In performance, and as my analyses show, Haitian, Cuban, and Bahian practitioners reveal and reference history, philosophy, religion, physiology, psychology, botany, and mathematics in addition to music and dance. These disciplines are among what the body articulates as it grows in spiritual practice over a lifetime.

The "praise performance" that results from African belief systems makes these and other African-derived communities able to contend with contemporary society in the Americas. As practitioners perform divinity, they ultimately receive social medicine; in performing the music and dance and embodying the *lwas, orichas,* and *orixás* repeatedly, dancing worshipers grow in individual esteem and dignity. They become involved in ritual community service and display social decency. Dancing in repetitive ceremonial practice feeds the physical and social body.

Embodied knowledge in African Diaspora communities has been revered and developed; it can reveal what the body knows, what it is capable of, and, recalling Foucault, what—what it does—does. Through resilient and exciting ritual performance, dance and music embody memory and perseverance and, in the end, inspire and support survival.

Three African American Dance Rituals

A Haitian Vodou Ritual, 1974

It wasn't going to be my first trip to Haiti, but it would be my first trip alone in Haiti. I had received an unexpected gift from my recently deceased father, a small amount of money, and amid my sad and joyful tears, I immediately decided to risk it all. I would go to that intriguing island of Haiti. I knew that I was running away from intense stress and that I needed a break; I also realized that the monetary gift could afford me the opportunity to do further research on the Haitian Vodou dances that I had witnessed earlier.

Prior to receiving the check late in the day, I had had only ten dollars to my name, with no balance in my checking account, and it was the Christmas season. I had fallen asleep with quiet tears the night before, totally frustrated and fatigued, wondering how I could manage a decent holiday season for my four sons and finish both choreographing my dance concert and writing my master's thesis in the next three months. My rationale then was that if I went to Haiti, my sons could continue to celebrate with their father, who had taken them on an extended camping and skiing trip in a huge luxurious trailer. They would not have to face my harsh realities and mounting depression, and I could concentrate for one month on my thesis work. I wrote a letter of explanation to them all, my ex and the boys, as to the length and focus of my travel. I hoped that they would understand.

A week later, I was settled in a pension in Port-au-Prince with an elderly lady from Haiti's governing elite as hostess. My room was modest and comfortable with a firm double bed, beautiful white lace curtains, and a small, private bath, all within a converted "gingerbread house," a large home in the French planter architectural style with a lovely tropical garden surrounding the entire structure. My seven-dollars-a-day accommodations included two meals with other boarders. Each day I spotted my silver napkin holder with an engraved #12—my room number—at the same table with the English speakers. I tried to change places, at least after coffee, to meet and get to know other travelers, but it was obvious that I was breaking the rules of the house.

Madame found this slightly irritating, but she was also a bit fascinated. For her, I was a young, seemingly intelligent and educated North American woman who was unusually interested in Haitian peasants and their dancing. Even though she had known Katherine Dunham decades earlier and was currently acquainted with several international dance students of Lavinia Williams Yarborough, she still marveled at our fascination with peasant dance culture.[1] Madame Lavinia was well known in Port-au-Prince and, like Dunham, was an American who had made her home in Haiti for more than forty years. She had been in the original Katherine Dunham Dance Company and while teaching dance in Haiti became an investigator of Haitian dance culture. Everyone knew Mesdames Lavinia and Katherine, as the customs and immigration officers told me when I arrived at Port-au-Prince.

I spent my mornings walking Haiti's steep dirt roads to Madame Lavinia's dance studio and taking classes—technique, folklore, and private instruction in the dances of Vodou. (Madame Dunham was not in Haiti that December.) I studied *yanvalu, mayi, zépòl, zarenyen, Nago, Petwo, Ibo, Congo,*[2] *juba, Affranchi,* and *banda,* learning each dance's nuance but also sensing the style of a genuine Haitian collective as compared with U.S. Afro-American versions of Haitian style. I had been studying Haitian dance in the States, where the stylization seemed rather theatrical; at least that is what I surmised after I witnessed and experienced the native island style on my first visit.

During that trip to Haiti, I attended a prepared Vodou service for tourists, and its dance style intrigued me so much that I was determined to compare

6

Haitian styles on my next trip. I observed cultural presentations of the same dances again and again at Hotels Ibo Lélé, Oloffson, La Belle Créole, and a few others. Two dance companies performed Vodou dances at the main hotels, alternating between nights. The soloists were especially fluid and dynamic in their dancing; they executed body rolls and undulations—the most typical movement pattern of Haitian Vodou—with more flexibility than I had seen up until that moment. They made me eager to see dancing in the ritual setting.

Eventually I began to spend my evenings in ritual ceremonies, watching the dances performed in their original context. My first genuine Vodou service was in La Saline, a district of Port-au-Prince, where I witnessed some of the preparations before the ceremony began at a temple or *ounfo*. It was a celebration that would install a new *oungan,* a Vodou priest, healer, and family leader. A childhood friend and a Haitian Jesuit, both doctoral candidates in anthropology, invited me to accompany them to a Vodou community. They were surprised at my particularized knowledge of Haitian cultural symbols— for example, recognizing the artistic representations or *veves* for particular *lwas,* who were also called *espri* or *mistè nan Vodou,* the spirits or mysteries of Vodou. Considering that I was not a trained anthropologist then and knew mainly Euro-American classical music, American modern dance, and only a few Haitian dances, they seemed pleased that I knew some of the roles within the community. I had studied Dunham technique for about five years in the States before I visited Haiti for the first time. On that trip, five years before this one, I had absorbed my deep attraction to Haiti and had become conscious of the richness in its dances through brief but intense dance sessions with Madame Lavinia.

I was introduced to the officiating *oungan* and to the man who was to be initiated as a new *oungan.* I watched the blessing of statues, candles, and other altar objects as both *oungans* cleaned and prepared the space and everything in it. I noticed the young boys who took turns practicing rhythms with sticks on the drums in the corner, and I observed the numerous entrances of community members passing in and out of various doors that led off the open-air, thatched-roofed ceremonial space. For two or three hours, until the sun was down fully, community members brought in foods of various sorts, cases of soft drinks, clothing, candles, flowers, and covered packages; they laughed and talked casually with each other.

I was startled and excited when three men suddenly started to drum loudly and continuously and another struck the *agogo* or iron gong repeatedly as the Vodou *ceremòni* started in earnest. Community members stopped passing to and fro and congregated in a semicircle with specific sections. The drummers who completed the circle were the focus of interest. The area next to them was filled with a twenty-to-thirty-member chorus and its female lead singer or *oungenikon*. The remaining congregation stood or sat on benches around the rest of the circle. An imposing wooden pole, the *potomitan*, the center-post that connected the spirit and human worlds, was sunk deep in the earthen floor at the center of the veranda-like *tonnel* (a covered porch) and extended about twenty feet up to the apex of a sloped ceiling. Most of the members of the community were dressed in white skirts or pants and headscarves; some had other colored clothing as well.

As more community members arrived, some came through several doors off the one wall of the ceremonial space, and others came in from the street or adjoining fields, filling the space with lots of noise and excitement. The crowding caused everyone to lean from side to side for a glimpse of whatever ritual behavior was going on around the *potomitan*. The singing was very strong, lots of loud and vibrant voices answering the solitary intonations of the leader over the insistent drum rhythms. Sometimes there was particular zest in the vocal response, as when everyone knew all the words and apparently loved what they meant. At other times, the lead singer commented with some disgust that community members failed to sing the appropriate words, did not come in singing on the correct beat, or perhaps did not give sufficient energy in their response.

From the little Haitian Kreyol that I understood from my French studies, I sensed that the *oungenikon* was upset and in frequent dialogue with the officiating *oungan*. Every time that I positioned my small, still camera on the chorus, she covered her face or turned her back. Once she stopped the singing, and immediately a big discussion ensued among the officiating *oungan*, the lead female singer, and my Haitian anthropologist friend. I felt sure that the *oungenikon* was disturbed by my presence; she did not seem to react to my colleagues at all. I was told that even though we had previously been given permission to take still photographs and to record the audio portions of the ceremony, she (and perhaps others) objected now, and we should not photograph. (There was no video then.) My utter excitation from being in attendance at a ritual event kept me poised; I was not disappointed or offended.

We spent several more hours dancing, singing, and praying. Community members "marked time," that is, they moved from side to side in time to the drums. Their rhythm called for the dance, *yanvalu*, the "dance of the snake" that was dedicated to Papa Dambala, a Haitian spiritual force, called *lwa* or

8

spirit. The dance term *yanvalu* means "I beg of you," and dancers bowed their heads low in supplication as they danced. Other community members greeted one another with ritual bows and turns and passed through the space with lighted candles and other ritual objects. I was happy to see the dances that I had studied in California with Ruth Beckford, known as Miss B, another Katherine Dunham dancer in Oakland, and those I was currently studying with Madame Lavinia.

The Haitian doctoral student queried me about what was occurring and what was about to happen. I believe he was testing me. At first I did not know for sure which type of spirits were presenting, *lwas* or *ley mo,* but I learned that only *lwas* were invoked during the public ceremonies. When the student was satisfied that I could differentiate among several of the *lwas* who manifested in human bodies and that I could recognize the main ritual personnel, he alerted me to intriguing particulars. For example, he made me aware of the Catholic prayers that were recited among the Kreyol songs and chants. The *pre savann* or "bush priest" led the Lord's Prayer and Hail Mary in Latin and French, respectively. The student pointed to the *oungans* who were manipulating a sacred gourd with bells, the *asson.* He showed me how the *asson* rang at particular times to signal different sections in the continuing service, and he told me to carefully watch the *oungenikon* who led the singing and the *laplas* who danced with a sword at the beginning of the ceremony. They both seemed knowledgeable; they observed the lead *oungan* almost constantly and would lurch in anticipation of something that might help the lead *oungan* as he conducted the ceremony. I learned later that they were prepared to take the *oungan*'s place if necessary.

The center space became so crowded that it was impossible to see everything. It seemed like everyone focused on those individuals who were affected by the performance excitation and were overwhelmed by the ritual stimulation. First one man and quickly thereafter a woman bounded forcefully through and about the space in apparent oblivion to others. This was the manifesting of spirit, in Haiti called *monte chwal le,* which involves the *lwas* who "mount" their human "horses." The *lwas* often give instructions to their horses, the human vessels that are not aware of the *lwa* presence during the "ride," and additionally to the community, with the phrase, "tell my horse. . . ." This suggests that the human horse needs to be told later about the advice and commentary that have taken place, since s/he is usually unaware of what transpires while s/he is mounted. The arrival of *lwas* is marked by sudden movement in the human body and signifies the fierce presence of the spirits who have come from in front or behind, but through the center-post, "*de potomitan lwa monte chwal devan-deye.*"

I was curious about the arrival of the spirits, but I was also a bit fearful the first time I witnessed Haitian faith in action. From my place at the back, I stretched my neck to glimpse what I had longed to see, the embodiment of a *lwa,* only to cringe and grab hold of my friends at my first sighting. Previously most worshipers were dressed in white for the ceremony, but when the *lwas* arrived within some of them, those worshipers were given bright-colored pants or dresses as well as implements that were symbolic of the character each *lwa* presented. For example, I saw a yellow satin blouse and a bottle of perfume for a *lwa* called Ezili and a peacock-blue waistcoat and a machete for a *lwa* called Ogou.

The power of the spiritual entrance was intriguing. The individuals, who had been dancing and singing vigorously only a few moments before, now had distorted facial expressions. They hopped on one foot, twisted their waists from side to side, separating the upper and lower torso, and then slumped their bodies against members of the congregation or leaned along the one wall with the altar room doors. One worshiper even rolled on the floor. They were alternately erratic and swift or lethargic and heavy as they moved, and those who were close by supported the dancers' weight but did not touch or comfort the seemingly tortured bodies. Only after their explosive, sporadic episodes, which lasted just a few seconds each, did the enraptured dancers go limp and community members encircle their bodies and support them out of the outdoor *tonnel* space and into the inner recesses, called the *peristil* of the *ounfo* or temple. When these dramatic episodes punctuated the ritual service, louder and more animated responses came from the chorus, as well as from the congregation.

The whole scene reminded me of some of my oldest memories of visiting my great-grandparents in Florida: when we picked up an aunt at a tent service (even though we were staunch Episcopalians), I was thrilled to hear the music and joyous celebration, but simultaneously I was tense when trying to figure out why there was shouting and flailing of bodies as the Holy Ghost arrived incorporated.

The physical space in Haiti was packed with sweating, rhythmic bodies. Community members continued to enter the ceremony, including three Catholic priests. The Vodou specialists gave the Catholic priests particular greetings, handshakes with finger snapping and laughs—as if in jest about the hand signals. Rum bottles were passed around good-naturedly for both specialists and guests to drink. One priest, who had entered and then retreated to the back of the congregation with my anthropology friends and me, was introduced to me especially because our names sounded the same in French, Yvonne and (Father) Ivan. He was suddenly given a bottle of rum by a small group of elders. I watched him take the bottle, wipe off the top with his palm, pour a bit of rum on the ground, make the sign of the cross with the bottle as he lifted it in the air, and drink a quick swallow. Just as suddenly, the *oungenikon* who had seemed to be upset with me earlier came across the room, took hold of the bottle, and pressed it toward me.

I looked inside. There was a handful of assorted leaves and lots of other things, and I feared the drinking. Watching me, Father Ivan nodded, assuring me, and I repeated his gestures and swallowed a small amount of *kleren,* the raw white rum that is used in Haitian ritual settings. Community members cheered approvingly; the *oungenikon* even laughed pointedly at me. Drinking from the rum bottle with assorted unknowns felt important to me later, like a profound conquest of my lingering tendency to exoticize "the Other" or my fear of the Vodou religion. Partaking of the assorted unknowns became symbolic of my reconciliation with Vodou and Haitian belief.

As each *lwa* revealed her/himself in the bodies of community believers, other participants laughed and talked with the specially dressed spirits. Some yelled salutations from across the room and others spoke pointedly as the *lwa* came close. The *lwas* danced and deported themselves in an independent and demanding manner, some apparently taking over the ritual happenings. I gathered that the *lwas* called for things that had to be brought from behind the several doors that lined the one wall of the ceremonial space. Cigars, perfume, liquor, and food were brought to the *lwas* at frequent intervals from small altar rooms behind the doors.

The *lwas* greeted one another and participants by taking the hand of a person to turn her/him around in ritualized movement or *virés*. Haitian ritual greetings were generally turning salutations: three steps to the right while turning, then a little dip or bow, followed by three steps turning to the left with a dip, followed by three more steps turning to the right to complete three sets for a salutation pattern. Often specialists greeted or blessed participants with a ritual spraying of a mouthful of rum. During breaks in the drumming, community members received sodas, which were dispensed from cases—usually Coca-Cola and a Caribbean orange drink. These drinks, as well as rum, were all appreciated because of the heat and the heavy humidity of the night air in addition to the exertion of dancing. It was soothing to have a swallow of anything during the intervals between rites.

More dancing followed; different *lwas* were received—an Ezili, Kuzen Zaka, and several Ogous (see other *lwas* in chart 4)—and the ritual community deepened its focus on the particular rite of ascendance: a new *oungan* was being presented to the public congregation. He displayed some of the new knowledge of his status with and for the other *oungans*, gesturing with the *asson* in multiple patterns toward them.

Despite my pleas to remain until the end, my hosts insisted that I leave with them, along with the Catholic priests. They said the service was essentially over and that what would transpire later would not be significantly different from what we had witnessed so far. I was disappointed and surprised that their fieldwork techniques did not include staying to the end. Now I understand that perhaps they had already seen enough Vodou rituals, and I know their primary interest was not, like mine, in the continuous dancing. I was also exhausted after the eight to ten hours of dancing and singing. And yes, I too was tired of watching the participants laugh, gossip, pray dutifully and dedicatedly, and argue to set things "ritually right."

With my first genuine *ceremòni* in 1974 as my main reference and subsequently more than twenty-five years of attending public ceremonies (and private ceremonies, generally those without dancing and music), I have come to understand the underlying structure of Vodou dance rituals in Haiti. I found early on that I could anticipate opening libations and invocations for the *lwas;* salutations with a sword to the drums, to the *potomitan,* to the doors, and to the major personnel in attendance; salutations, drumming, songs, and praise dancing for ancient African spirits; prayers without drumming, singing, or dancing and then resumption of dance ceremony; and finally bidding the *lwas* goodbye. There was always lots of socializing with neighbors and community members throughout the services (see chart 7 in chapter 5).

During that first ceremony I realized how much I had learned from dancing in Haitian dance classes. I recognized and understood a great deal about Haitian religion just from the process of learning the dances. I knew that the dance ritual's ultimate purpose was to bring transformation of the believing community, such that particular spirits would appear in the bodies of ritual believers. I was aware of the Haitian history I had learned when I realized that I could follow the ceremonial order according to the dances. The names for the dances were often the names of African ethnic groups (e.g., Mahí and Ibo),

African local or regional groups (e.g., Allada and Congo), as well as evolved names for African groups in the Americas (e.g., Nago, Gédé, and Petwo). The major Haitian nations or *nasyons* are now called Rada, Mahí, Nago, Ibo, Congo, Petwo, and Gédé (see charts 2 and 3 in chapter 3).

Although the Haitian services managed specific religious goals—to honor one *lwa* in particular, to initiate new members into the religious family, to install officials, or to bury the dead—they simultaneously recognized different African *nasyons* by differing dance styles. Even though there are several types of nation dances and even more stylistic dance variations in Haitian Vodou ceremonies, African *nasyons* represent families of spirits, *fanmis,* hence "nation families" in a liturgical series (e.g., the Rada family of spirits, the Nago family, the Gédé family). Each *nasyon*'s opening song is an invocation for the ancestor and cosmic *lwa* of that family. A gradual accumulation of specialists, ritual acts, prayers, and dance/music results in bringing the *lwa* from Haiti's historic, spiritual, and legendary past to contemporary circumstances and to the present generation. Overall, the spirits of a particular nation family are invoked, danced, and then sent away (Métraux 1972 [1959]; Deren 1983, 1953; Fleurant 1996:27–28, 30).

What is peculiar to Haiti is that several of the dances—*yanvalu, mayí,* and *zépòl,* for example—are performed for many different *lwas* (Fleurant 1996:24–33). This rather pan-African dance practice does not occur in the Cuban or Brazilian cases, where there is more direct correlation between rhythms that are reserved for one particular divinity. Wait—I am fast-forwarding and comparing too soon; let's stick to Haitian dance ritual first.

Haitian Vodouists believe that the *lwas* enter the head, and as another anthropologist Sheila Walker told me once, "one of the nicest expressions I ever heard [in Haitian Kreyol] was something like, '*lwa ap danse nan tèt mwen,*'" meaning "the *lwa* dances in my head" (personal communication). By this time on that full and festive night in Haiti, thoughts of the *lwas* and Vodou were "washing through my head." This expression about "washing the head" comes from the name of one of the first initiation processes of Vodou, *lavé tèt.* In other words, I was deepening physically, mentally, emotionally, and spiritually into my core, as *lwas,* believers, and other participants danced in praise all night. At that time, I was a musician and dancer only, with no anthropological training. Still, I had questions. I sensed more than I understood, and I wanted to know more. Vodou dance rituals made me feel as if I were in the presence of veiled information, and I planned to return in order to learn and experience more.

A Cuban Yoruba Ritual, 1987

My Cuban friend and I had heard the night before that a ceremony would be held for Oyá, also called Yansán, the next morning. It would be in the "ritual house" of a *santero* (in Yoruba-based terminology, *babaloricha,* a priest, healer, or ritual leader) named Chucho, around eleven o'clock in the morning. A "house" in Cuba can be both a living space and at times a prepared religious space, and Chucho's *casa* in Matanzas was large enough to be a worship space year-round. Not only was his space ample, but he also boasted of hundreds of godchildren, including non-Cubans, whom he had initiated.

My friend Ana and I were running, something that Cubans rarely do except in sports, on a particularly burning sunlit morning in February. We had planned to participate in the ceremony together and record the beautiful chants for Oyá that were bound to be sung. We were running because we had heard the singing start as we climbed the cobblestone streets from the Matanzas marina to the higher ground: *calle Daoez, calle Compostela, calle San Carlo.* As we approached the tile steps in front of the house, I saw the familiar faces of three *batá* drummers at the center of the farthest wall. Their hourglass-shaped *batá* drums were strapped horizontally across their knees so that they could play a total of six drumheads for the liturgical order.

I discovered that, like in Haiti, the African legacies in Cuba had meshed, but in Cuba the resulting nations (*naciones)* formed rather separate cultural, religious, and performance units as compared with Haiti's *nasyons,* all of which combined within one religious organization (see charts 2 and 3 in chapter 3). In Cuba, the cultural heritages of many African nations coalesced into four major amalgam groups: Kongo-Angola, Arará, Carabalí, and Yoruba.[3] Most Cubans and academics call them collectively "Afro-Cuban religions," since they do not have an umbrella name, such as "Vodou" is for Haiti. The four legacies represent major African ethnic and regional groups, differing belief systems, and distinct stylistic performance practices. The *nación* performing in front of me that morning in the rectangular room was Yoruba, identified primarily by the particular drums that were being played.

As I listened more carefully upon entering the house, I heard the beginning rhythms that unfold the *Regla de Ocha* (The Rule or Order of the *Orichas*), also known as *Regla de Eya Aranla* or *Oru de Cantos* (Order of the Highest Spiritual Calling or Order of Chants). All three terms indicate a semipublic Cuban Yoruba ritual, where worshipers and their invited guests dance and sing to three sacred Yoruba *batá* drums in honor of divinities or cosmic powers called *orichas*, not spirits.

Cubans and Brazilians use the word "spirit" differently from Haitians; Cuban and Brazilian usage refers specifically to spirits of dead people. Haitian spirits can be cosmic divinities associated with nature, as well as both deified ancestors and recently deceased ancestors. In either case and in order to understand both generally and specifically how worship is constructed in terms of sacred dance/music performance, I again refer to the English term, "divinities." Whether spirits of dead ancestors or cosmic forces, they are revered and periodically honored in song, dance, and drumming.

I thought the *oru seco* (literally, the "dry order," meaning the private solemn drum presentation without chants, also called *oru de igbodu*, the order of the altar room), which is only for close ritual members, had already finished. A small group of about twelve were already singing and dancing. As Ana joined in the *coro* or chorus, I noticed community members acknowledging her presence because of her coloratura-like voice, crystal clear above the drums. She was acknowledged with nods and kisses, and I received the warmth extended to a now-familiar friend, *socia* or *compañera* of a renowned community member. I gave kisses to all around the room, as would any respectful community member, and we joined in the song with dance movement. Many more community members came in gradually, some ritual practitioners who had undergone specific rites of initiation to secure their membership, and others who participated or observed as uninitiated community members and guests. Eventually we were a group of about seventy ritual practitioners and community participants.

It was so wonderful to be at a ceremony with my friend and mentor who, as an experienced Cuban dancer, could swiftly indicate to me in gesture and stance which *oricha* we were honoring through dance and music. I loved the sensual sequences and subtle dynamics of the Yoruba *nación* movements, but even then, after living in Cuba and dancing the *oricha* dances often for about six months, I could not always, or quickly, distinguish the rhythms according to a given divinity and begin dancing confidently on my own. There, unlike in Haiti, more specific information guides each dance performance; that is, the personality and domain of each divinity. In addition, I was learning Cuba's immense movement repertoire—not just Yoruba dances, but also Arará, Palo, and Carabalí religious traditions—each musical complex with an ample dance vocabulary. The Cuban Yoruba *nación* alone had more than nine codified dances as compared with Haiti's thirteen main dances for several *nasyons* (see charts 4 and 5 in chapter 4). Knowing the liturgical order eventually helped, but it was very complex.

I could not dance the same dance for several *orichas* as I could for several Haitian *lwas*. In Haiti, usually one to three dances were performed for each *nasyon*. I had studied these Haitian dances for four or five years before going to a Haitian ritual. On the other hand, in the Cuban ceremony, I needed help from the chants and cues from a lead dancer's first movement phrases to secure proper form. Also, at that time I knew very few chants, which are the real guides to the order of a ceremony. While I knew the movements and the style well enough to follow, these were not sufficient to know when to initiate the proper step within a specific rhythmic pattern. Sometimes I was on target with both the rhythm and the correct identification of the *oricha*, but several times I had to correct myself as I caught up with other ritual dancers.

I was learning like an eager child, mainly by imitation, not with detailed deconstruction, and it was wondrous and thrilling. The super-attentive process of imitation, intuition, repetitive practice, and finally intensification and improvisation (a kinesthetic learning process) enlivened all my senses. More important, this process connected me to others. We became a dancing, drumming, singing whole.[4]

My thoughts, however, drifted back to my earliest dancing in Cuba. As a U.S. professor of dance and a doctoral candidate in anthropology, I did not automatically require instruction, from the Cuban point of view, when I arrived in 1986. Rather, I was expected to "catch on and catch up," or perhaps they gave me a proficiency test by just watching me acquire the movements. There was some kind of expectation, since I looked Cuban or *Latina* as opposed to their stereotypical image of a North American, and community members presumed that I would be able to dance well like most Cubans. As a guest of the Havana Ministry of Culture who had been assigned to the Conjunto Folklórico Nacional de Cuba, the Cuban National Folkloric Company, for my fieldwork, I had the unique opportunity to dance among some of the greatest interpreters of Cuban style, the disciples of *la última*, the late Nieves Fresneda.

I dutifully took my place (North American style) in the back row of the female dancers in the national company. I figured that I could see the dancers in the first row, practice diminutively in place with the next few rows, and move with the slightly subtle execution of the older ladies in the last rows. These ladies—for example, Concha, Margarita Ugarte, Ilda Calle, and Zanaida Armenteros (Librada Quesada and Sylvina Fabars were not considered elders then)—did not speak or try to correct me but demonstrated and kinestheti-cally pulled me into the movements and their qualitative expression. On a few occasions I even had nonverbal coaching from some of the male dancers (Juan de Dios, Johannes Garcia, Domingo Pau, Pablito, Alfredo O'Farril, and especially Juan "Petit" Ortiz). At the end of class, Domingo or Petit would dance a particular step close to my side and watch as I imitated their model-ing. As the year went by I also received pointed commentary from the male singers (Felipe Alfonso, Cándido, and Lázaro Ros). Singers sat on a raised stage as the company practiced, and they could see my diligent, but less comfort-able, performance clearly amid the precision in form and style of the masters. Felipe in particular took time to encourage me and arranged to give me a tape of him singing for my home practice.

Little did I know then that my modest self-placement at the back of the class actually put me among the stars of the company, the legendary dancers and singers; it proved to be a true gift. Regular practice, literally surrounded by Cuban dance masters, made me feel as if I were inside a huge band of Cuban stylistic energy. I also felt a tremendous saturation in Africanity, since the Cu-ban masters represented each of the four distinct African *nación* dance/music traditions.

After about three months of dancing seven hours a day for six days a week, they told me how good they thought I was, how my sense of rhythm and phrasing were very musical, and how my style was definitely better than they had expected for an outsider, *extranjera* (stranger), even a professional dancer *extranjera*. They praised my dedication and accomplishments; after all, I was keeping up with some of the nation's strongest and most skilled dancers. Still, my ability to dance the Yoruba liturgy was dependent on being in an ensemble of knowledgeable singers and drummers and following a lead dancer.

Because of this extended kinesthetic contact, I gradually developed my personal dance style toward a recognizable Cuban version. When I arrived in Cuba, I had been dancing Haitian style for a little over twenty years (studying since 1965 with Miss B in Oakland and teaching since 1973), and my Cuban immersion—even with the best of the best—did not give me adequate confi-dence in Cuban stylization quickly. With Ana in a crowded Matanzas ritual setting at the end of five months, I thought I could practice what I had learned in Havana. More important, I thought I could relax and access the movements and style of the "ordinary community members."

Yet these "ordinary" Cubans were from Matanzas, and their profound and admired style throughout Cuba was slightly different from that of the

Havana dance specialists with whom I had been practicing. Even though I had been dancing in Havana's representative style, I had not had Matanzas style demonstrated pointedly. Matanzas, more than Havana, contains and is influenced by all four African cultural heritages of Cuba. Most Cubans consider Matanzas *el alma,* the "soul" of Cuba and distinguish it as the historic and more African periphery from the metropolitan center of Havana.

Matanzeros follow a slightly different order for the ritual liturgy, and almost always their style involves or suggests changes in rhythm and tempo in comparison to Havana style. (*Santiaguero* style from the eastern end of Cuba is closer to Matanzas than to Havana styles, although it is differentiated by a more prominent Kongo-Angola influence than Yoruba influence.) While within a fairly standardized Yoruba liturgical order in Cuba, there is a distinction in the sequence of certain songs and dances, creating Havana and Matanzas regional variants in the liturgical order. In spite of these regional and stylistic differences, however, most Cubans dance the Yoruba *nación* rhythms in a recognizable and precise style. That morning it was a Yoruba *nación* dance/music *wemilere* or *toque* ("sacred drum/dance ceremony" in Yoruba, and "drum/dance ceremony" or "drum party" in Spanish) in honor of Oyá (see chart 8 in chapter 5).

Back in Chucho's house, participants were seeking a kind of individualized unison within the Matanzas ritual order. While each dancer danced the same gestures and locomotive patterns, each dancer also displayed individuality. The entire congregation repeatedly performed a common denominator of codified steps. They meshed in uniform rhythm and built a collaborative energy in order to honor each *oricha*. As the chants of each *oricha* were sung, those practitioners who were ritually affiliated with or dedicated to that particular *oricha* came forward and placed money in the small gourd in front of the drums and then returned to their dance and singing places. (Within a Yoruba religious ceremony, individuals usually make a small donation in the name of an *oricha* with whom they may have or are developing a relationship.)

A set of chants and dances was first sung and performed for the *oricha* Elegba. Just as Papa Legba is the first spirit to be honored in a Haitian Vodou service, his Cuban counterpart, called by several names (Eleguá, Elegba, Elegbara, Exú, or Echú), begins the ceremonies in Cuba, making a direct structural relationship to another African American liturgical order. (And we will soon discover a similar relationship with regard to Elegba/Exu in Bahian practices of Brazil.) Elegba in Cuba, like Papa Legba in Haiti, is a dimension of one whole, the powerful intermediary of deific proportion who begins and ends each *wemilere*. He is responsible for efficient transport of messages between humans and the *orichas*, the initiates as well as those who want to communicate with the *orichas* but who are not initiated. Elegba in Cuba is revered; he is the symbol of change, of openings and closures, of chance and opportunity, of unpredictability and creative surprise; he is welcomed and admired as an old and wise man, and he is feted and adored as a mischievous child.

Next, two distinct sets of chants and dances were sung and danced, for the *oricha* Ogún and the *oricha* Ochosi. Each musical set contained a thorough, danced examination of the myriad ways that the *orichas* might behave. For example, Elegba has both mischievous running and spying steps, as well as measured walking and rocking steps; both Ogún and Ochosi have sharp, aggressive patterns that signal their statuses as hunter/warriors, as well as smooth loping steps when they are courting their wives.

Within each set of chants, there was distinct tempo acceleration from slow to faster speeds. The organization of time within each set seemed to introduce and then reinforce a characteristic mood through a series of gestures that identified the elements associated with an *oricha*. Even with the chants of Obatalá, who is the judge and aged father of the *orichas* and who dances very slowly, there was an increase in tempo as he completed his cycle of chants or *tratao* (see chart 12 in chapter 8). As the pace quickened, an intensification of both the quality of movement and the amalgam of mythic symbols in gesture and sung lyrics deepened the physical, mental, emotional, and spiritual atmosphere toward a composite experience. The kinesthetic accumulation, both within each individual dancer and among the similar energies of other community members in the shared space and at the same time, yielded a body experience for performing participants. What resulted was a set, a repeated cycle of hypnotic, rhythmic, melodic, and kinesthetic dynamics for the distinctive temperament of each *oricha*. Each *oricha*'s section, while a musical and danced entity within itself, was part of an accumulating, larger event.

Oricha performance is complex, and I sensed the dynamics of "multiples of multiples." I felt a hidden dimension of certain rhythms that built power, some mathematical formula perhaps. Also I had a familiar artistic understanding of manipulated dynamics and their affect within community observers and dancing participants.

That morning, a few *orichas* seemed to want to enter the bodies of believers, but repeatedly community members quickly and firmly led the entranced believers away from the room. Some dancing worshipers, who shuddered, bent their knees, and then leaned into the arms of those next to them, moved outside onto the street for fresh air or into the back rooms at the edge of the ceremonial room. When their bodies sensed the presence or aura of an *oricha,* entranced participants shook their heads as if saying "no." They wrinkled their brows in disturbing frowns, only to return to the collective song prayers and community dancing. Each affected individual was literally trying to shake off the spiritual energy that had been generated thus far. Each individual's harbored divinity or *oricha* seemed to recognize his or her appropriate rhythms; but each participant was postponing the special effect, staying the overwhelming emotion.

It appeared to me then that despite the zeal and enthusiasm of multiplying rhythms, each *oricha* had to be honored in song and drumming before any one *oricha* came.[5] The rule of respect remained for the proper acknowledgment in singing and drumming for all the *orichas,* before settling on the dedicated section for any one. The congregation continued the honorific praise salutations in dance, drumming, and ancient poetry set to music, both to and for several *orichas:* Babaluayé, Obatalá, Ibedys, Changó, Obba, Oyá, Yemayá, and Ochún, among others to whom they only sang and drummed (e.g., Oricha Oko, Inle, Dadá, Oggué, Agayú, Yeggua, and Orunla [see chart 11 in chapter 5]). Then they returned to singing and dancing only those chants and movements that were dedicated to Oyá, expressing the specific order and common form of a Cuban Yoruba *nación* dance ritual (cf. chart 8 in chapter 5 with drum, chant, dance composites in chapter 8).

By now the afternoon sun was hot, and the fifteen-by-twenty-foot room was filled with dancing worshipers. The ritual space was packed, except for a small area immediately in front of the drums where a few lead dancers and sometimes Chucho placed themselves. It felt like everyone in Matanzas had come to the service for Oyá. Community members stood outside the windows and peered in, and others crowded the stairs and doorway at the front of the house. Just about everyone was singing in call-and-response form. One or two singers alternated as lead singers or *akpwones* (also called *akupwones*) and were answered primarily by a small chorus standing to one side of the centered drummers, and by the entire dancing congregation. The lead singers elaborated their verses melodically and rhythmically, while the congregation sang a repetitive and less ornate response. Just as Haitian Vodou had its *oungenikon* and chorus, in Cuban Yoruba the *akpwon* sang her/his statement and the chorus sang its answer, a parallel musical and personnel structure. Everyone inside was dancing and performing the identifying *oricha* gestures together, sensitively, above the changing but repetitive foot patterns. Just like in Haiti, despite the densely crowded space, no one stepped on anyone's toes!

The strongest and most popular dancers of the ritual community danced in the front and center because of their full and apparent expressiveness, but also in order to lead the congregation in the dance ritual sequence. They faced the drummers and the *akpwon*. Occasionally other dancing worshipers came to the front to dance with big gestures and decided commitment, but without manifesting their *orichas*.

Dancers and singers crowded in within a semicircular pattern, perhaps seven to ten dancers across, in perhaps eight rows. Every inch of the room had dancing bodies, which incredibly opened and closed ranks intermittently. Sometimes, as in Haiti, the crowded space parted for various individuals, an energetic dancing elder or a particular community member with an association to the *oricha* that was being honored at present. It was as if the dancer had an electric field that surrounded her/him, and as s/he traveled, other worshipers could feel or sense the electricity nearby. In this way, the individual community member was given space and traveled while dancing to the front in order to be highlighted and to lead the congregational practice. There was no call, cue movement, or chant that directed community worshipers to adjust to the traveling dancer; only a concentrated kinesthetic sense could account for the ripple effect.

Similarly, at the far end of the space with drummers and singers packed solidly, a different voice started to lead a new chant or another verse of the same chant. The voice of the new *akpwon* overlapped the voice of the former *akpwon,* and, simultaneously, the other singers gave way to the new leader. Not only did they relinquish the song or chant to the new song leader, but they also parted their space to give room toward the front for the new lead singer to assume the lead space.

Everyone knew most of the chanted lyrics and expressed delight with vigorous voices as each consecutive chant began. Some of the chants created even more noticeable excitement among the congregation; community members sang the words clearly, enunciating emphatically and, at one point, laughing full-out. I asked Ana about the words and why community members were laughing within such a serious event.

She laughed even harder and said that the *akpwon* was challenging Oyá. He was trying to ensure that she would come to the ceremony through the words of the song, but people laughed because Oyá was not an *oricha* to "play with" as one could do with other *orichas*, almost insulting them in songs (called *puyas* and sung especially for Ochún). Usually *akpwones* sang *puyas* with suggestive and risqué language to irritate the *oricha* enough so that s/he would move toward the ceremony quickly. This *akpwon* used strong, improvised phrases to suggest that Oyá should come now, and eventually that is what happened: Oyá arrived.

Suddenly there were two Oyás presenting, manifesting, *bajando* (coming down) into the bodies of believers. While Cuban Yoruba worshipers talk about the *orichas montando* or "riding" them, just as the Haitians describe the arrival of the *lwas* in their bodies, more often Cubans speak of the *orichas "bajando (o descendiendo) a bailar o subiendo a la cabeza de sus 'hijos'"* (coming down [or descending] to dance or rising to the heads of their "sons and daughters"). Their terminology is predicated on the belief that the *orichas* live in Orun, the world of the *orichas,* which is either an expansive realm "above" or in the deepest depths across all the oceans "below," creating a plane of cosmic energy above and below the human realm. Also the term *subiendo* reflects the learned initiates' experience of receiving *oricha* energy as it begins to displace ordinary consciousness and travels as a tingling seed or an exceedingly cold energy shaft from their feet up through their spines to their heads (Milta in Cuba, personal communication). Those worshipers and observers who view the *oricha* incorporated within a human body see it and speak of it either as the initiate "presenting an *oricha*" (*presentando un oricha*) or the *oricha* "manifesting him- or herself" (*manifestandose*).

Two men began to twist their upper torsos to alternate sides, raising their arms irregularly in space. One stopped abruptly and proceeded to lift and drop his shoulders rapidly as he closed his eyes and held his hands together in prayer. In addition, his upper body bent forward slowly and then leaned backward, only to bend forward again. The other man almost marched around the room with knees high, still twisting at the waist from side to side, and making short, high-pitched cries with each effort. Each fell, in his own time, against a group of dancers, leaned on one foot, stretched out his arms and a nonsupporting leg, and cried out in a succession of guttural or muffled sounds, sort of like "aiyee, aiyee." Both men manifested their Oyá energy in tandem, but definitely as independent sources of force in erratic time.

I recognized one of the men as one of the singers who had gone outside earlier for fresh air and to regain his stable condition. He had been one of those whose bodies would tremble periodically at the beginning of the ceremony, trying to contain the *oricha* energy. He was tall and muscular, and his large body now alternated with rapid vibratory motion, hops, and dashing runs that ended as he leaned against a couple of worshipers. He was sweating profusely, moaning, and making cries. His shoes were taken off by a *iawo* or special ritual assistant whose major duty is to attend to the manifested *orichas,* since s/he never receives divinity her/himself.[6]

The man was now considered "female," since he was incorporating a female *oricha.* Both men and women can alter gender in this way. Women, if they receive male *oricha* energy, manifest maleness and are treated ritually as males. Likewise, men who manifest female *oricha* energy are treated as women in the ritual setting. This is also the case in Haitian Vodou where gender is situational and flexible (for Nigerian Yoruba gender and manifestation, see Matory 1994).

Oyá was given a black fly whisk, called an *íruke,* made of long horsehair. Also, she was handed an additional implement: a long, thin, dried locust bean pod that contained seeds. She rattled the bean pod rhythmically and waved the *íruke* high in the air. Then she rushed toward the space in front of the drums, resting the whisk high on her head and waving the singing pod-shaker forcefully for all to hear. She began to dance the same steps we had all been dancing before while shaking her head cockily, but her forceful energy and highly coordinated execution were greater than even the popular lead dancers. I couldn't take my eyes away from her as she danced.

My eyes shifted away only when the other Oyá came into view, dancing strongly also. They both stayed in the front and center for some time and were attended to by two *santeras* who were dressed in white,[7] except for their noticeable multicolored bead necklaces. These *collares* aligned them through symbolic colors with their protective guiding "mothers" and "fathers," the *orichas.* Most of the Cuban ritual community dressed in white whenever ritual activity was planned; however, not everyone could, because of the social and economic demands of the Cuban environment. In those moments of *oricha* arrival and participation, the *santeras,* in their white dresses and headscarves, contrasted sharply with the community participants who were in their "Sunday best," but in a range of colors.

After a short time, ritual assistants took both Oyás separately to the back rooms beyond the ceremony. The muffled shouts and cries of the Oyás continued every once in a while. I stood amid the wandering, resting practitioners, who had wiped their foreheads, necks, and hands with the soothing fragrance of the *orichas,* a lavender cologne called *agua florida* or "flower water" (often called "Florida water" in English). It was usually offered to everyone at the beginning of a ceremony (when it was available), but I noticed its smell most when the drifting practitioners wandered around the space on the drum breaks.

The drummers returned. Some changed places, new drummers replaced two of the first three, and the ritual music began again. I noticed that dancers also changed places. Some from the rear of the room and from outside came inside and toward the front, trying to maximize their dance space as the ritual continued. One of these was a special friend of mine, Danilo. Many community members were excited that he had entered near the front, mainly because he is such a fantastic dancer. On that day, the excitement extended to the fact that Danilo had brought a female partner. Much of the community understood Danilo to be a young gay man, and to see him attentive (in a courting manner) to a woman was causing more than casual discussion. He introduced me to his friend quickly and started dancing.

The music began again at a relatively slow pace and had the grace of a melodious breeze, a connection to Oyá as the wind. A few community members drank swallows of rum when a bottle appeared and was passed along. Even though the rum added to the feelings of extreme heat (both from dancing and drumming so long and from the tropical February climate), it was considered a good thing to drink the ritual rum, called *aguardiente* or *malafó* (Spanish and Yoruba for non-aged white rum in Cuba). With sweat-soaked handkerchiefs and added zeal from the *aguardiente,* community members resumed the repetitive intensification of Oyá's foot pattern, marking Oyá as a breeze with their hands waving high over their heads.

One Oyá returned, dressed in multicolored skirts and dancing. These were symbolic colors and held the powerful number of Oyá. Oyá was supposed to wear nine vivid colors—all the colors of the other *orichas,* which ritually connected her importance to them as well as identified her: white of Obatalá, red and white of Changó, dark blue of Yemayá, green, black, and light purple of Ogún, turquoise of Ochosi, golden yellow of Ochún, red-orange of Obba, deep purple of Babaluayé, and black and red of Eleguá (see chart 1 in chapter 2). Her own color is ochre, a brownish red, but she is dressed with and identified by multicolors, places of multiple activities (like the marketplace), at the crux of crucial times (such as dawn and dusk, the first and last day of the year, at births), and especially at times of death. The multiple colors and her appearance in a morning ceremony were actually part of a larger ceremony for the Eguns that day, the spirits of the dead, the elevated ancestors in Cuban Yoruba (and Bahian Yoruba, but called Egunguns among continental Yorubas). Oyá, among all the *orichas,* is invoked and supported for her association with the cemetery and the dead in general, and she is the only *oricha* who comes in the vicinity of the Eguns.

Meanwhile, participants sang to Oyá. The ritual family seemed so pleased with her arrival. Each community member went to her and formally greeted her. Depending on the gender of their own guardian *oricha,* they executed the ritual movement phrases of respect and greeting, the *dobale:* either they lay prostrate on the floor for male *oricha* recognition and acknowledgment, or they lay on one side and an elbow, the female *oricha* position of respect.

Everyone gave space, one after another in a ripple effect, as each worshiper greeted Oyá. To my eyes, this was as if worshipers were aware of a compositional technique called "canon" in the academic dance world, which is the repetition of a short sequence of movements among different performers who stagger their beginning, creating a ripple effect of the same movements.

Oyá would stop dancing to wait for them to complete their *dobale* from the floor and then return their salute with open arms, despite the continuing music. She gave and received the ritualized Cuban Yoruba salutation, which is distinct from the Haitian *viré* or turning salutation, but a parallel movement structure in that Cuban Yoruba *dobale* and Haitian Vodou *viré* are elaborately and repeatedly performed and in the same situations. She raised each successive ritual greeter into her arms and kissed her/him on each side of the face as participants rose up to embrace her vigorously. Then she went back to dancing intensely. Dancing worshipers matched the forceful drum energy and followed Oyá as the turbulent wind. She led them with galloping feet and slashing arms, but she departed abruptly. With high steps, she ran out of the room. Some community members went outside for air when the drummers took a break, presuming that she would return after a while. Others went to the back room where an Oyá stood staring and making sporadic squealing sounds just past the doorway.

After a short respite, the drummers sounded out rhythmic demands that accelerated very quickly, and the ritual passed to Oyá as the epitome of the tornado. (It is one of the most enjoyable of the dance movements for Oyá, but also a complex dance step and musical rhythm, both called *tuitui.*) As everyone in the room came toward the unison expression of *tuitui,* the identifiable scream of yet another Oyá sounded. It did not come from the back rooms, however, but from in front of the drums. It was Danilo's friend who lent her body for Oyá's manifestation. She grimaced and fell against dancing members and began to swirl and run around the room as Oyá was incorporated into the present.

This young, dark-skinned woman housed a powerful Oyá, who put her hands on her hips, took bold high steps, and galloped in spurts. She was short and muscular, and her strong body churned the air in the packed room. When community members gave her the horsetail and wrapped her hips and legs in a multicolored skirt, she whipped the air in circles and spun around fiercely. Community members made space for her exquisite execution; they supported her dance performance with strong, full-out energy in their own movements and bright, clear, and enthusiastic voices in praise songs. Some community members even doubled with the drums and clapped out the basic rhythm or *clave*. Electricity was in the air and within each one of us.

As the drums continued to play, Oyá then greeted everyone in the room. Sometimes she simply embraced the person she faced, and sometimes she gave herself to another typical Cuban Yoruba salutation of crossing both arms across the chest and touching alternate shoulder to shoulder, ending with the kissing of each cheek. At other times, she wiped the sweat from her brow and spread it on the person's face, neck, and shoulders. I received the warm stroking of my face, neck, and shoulders several times, as Oyá murmured and stared into my eyes. Ana told me later that it was a good sign, a blessing from Oyá to me, her intended child.

Many community members, however, were guarded as she approached them, standing still and stiff. A few exited the room swiftly as she drew near. Perhaps they were in awe of her high status, or they may have tried to avoid contact with her because it might mean that they would have to comply with any demands she might make. (There is always reciprocity in the African American religions that I have studied, as I will detail later.) She was awesome. I was now accustomed to the rapid, periodic force of movement that each *oricha* (or *lwa*) performed, and I marveled at their vigor and their beauty.

The ceremony continued with more praise—more dancing, singing, and drumming—until I noticed Chucho and another community member passing through the crowded rows with a bucket of water. They went toward the drums, perhaps after other ritual behaviors that I could not see among all the dancing and singing community members. Then they proceeded toward the door through which Ana and I had entered early that morning. Chucho watched at the door as his female assistant went outside to the street and poured the water into the gutter, watching it flow away. The water had symbolically collected all the negativities that might have surfaced within the ceremonial process. These were thrown away to flow and dissipate, leaving the family, the ritual community, cleansed and refreshed.

Chucho and his assistant both reentered the ceremonial space and faced the drums. She began to dance, and the congregation cleared a diagonal space from the door to the drums, a path for her to dance the empty bucket back to the drums. Everyone on either side of the woman faced the opposite side and danced a sequence that repeatedly advanced toward the door and regressed toward the drums. The woman retreated up the diagonal space in front of the drums; after a moment or two more of dancing in synchrony with the three drums, she turned the empty bucket upside down and slammed it to the floor. The drums stopped and the ceremony ended.

Community members drifted away gradually after five or six hours of dancing, drumming, and singing in the heat of the afternoon sun. Most left after commentary on events within the event (like Danilo's interest in a woman). They shared all sorts of gossip and community information and tried to determine if later that night there would be a *bembé* (a more party-like ritual, with secular drums, but with the same type of chants and dancing). Ana and I left after eating delicious *congrí* (mixed rice and black beans) and a few pieces of scrumptious lamb. About six community members remained in the room. Two drummers were drinking cold beers, a couple talked romantically in a corner, one community member stood in the corridor off the ceremonial space shouting to others in the back, while the other remaining member in sight began mopping the ceremonial floor.

I exited in a state of unusual excitement, filled with multiple layers of dance, music, and ritual. An early breeze awaited me, soft and warm from the Caribbean Sea beyond Matanzas Bay. I walked silently with Ana back down the cobblestone streets to the marina end of *calle Daoez* for a much-needed rest. My head was full of details, many from my now-advanced training in anthropology and also from my keen familiarity with African Diaspora cultures. I also had questions.

For example, I wondered how an Oyá could give advice, like the other *orichas,* if she only shrieked, moaned gently, and did not talk openly. A ceremony was supposed to contain a time when the *orichas* gave counsel to those in need or to anyone they felt warranted a piece of advice. How did this happen with Oyá? Did I miss it? And I also had some answers.

Since I was a trained observer by this time, I could clearly scope the generalities and commonalities within differing ritual events. I had a Yoruba ritual for comparison to not only other Yoruba rituals I had seen in Cuba but for comparison to other African American dance ceremonies, like those in Haiti. The similarities were great: each ritual community performs music and dance ceremonies in order to invoke spiritual entities, and it does so through a similar embodiment process in which spiritual entities displace ordinary human consciousness, shift gender on occasion, and reveal themselves in communal celebrations. Drumming, singing, and dancing are prayerful acts that feed into a reciprocal relationship between humans and categories of spiritual beings, mainly called *lwas* and *ley mo* in Haiti and *orichas* and Eguns in Cuba. Both Haitian Vodou and Cuban Yoruba communities view and treat humans and spiritual beings alike as family and extended family members, consanguineous and fictive kin. The members of both ritual communities routinely perform physical movement phrases of greeting and respect to honor the powerful life force in everyone and to greet, salute, and confirm the embodiment of wisdom and knowledge that ritual officials conserve and that result from the teachings of their *lwas* and *orichas,* respectively.

As I reflected on the Haitian and Cuban cases, I found some peculiarities: Cuban Yoruba dance ceremonies occur more often indoors during the late afternoon and early evening, while Haitian Vodou ceremonies occur more often outdoors and very late at night; there were several dances that were repeatedly performed for many Haitian *lwas*, while in Cuba generally each divinity had its own dance; and Haiti had over a dozen *nasyons* and Cuba had only four; Cuban Yoruba worshipers have a *wemilere* for Oyá within their Egun ceremonies for the dead, while Haitians separate ritual activities for their *lwas* and *ley mo.*

Multiple layers of information swam in my head that evening along with lyrics and steps for Oyá, *batá* rhythms, the smells of *aguardiente* and Florida water-soaked handkerchiefs—ritual comparisons and ritual uniqueness, and in addition, inexplicable pleasure. I sensed that more understandings and information were within the ceremony and, as always, my curiosity caused me to want to know more.

A Bahian Candomblé Ritual, 1991

It was Wednesday, *quarta-feira,* the day of Xangó in Bahia.[8] (Actually, in this case, Bahia is the nickname for the capital city, Salvador da Bahia, of the Brazilian state also named Bahia.) I was at Axé Opô Afonjá, the Candomblé compound and temple of Mãe Stela, with my friend Gracinha and with all my Cuban paraphernalia for the *orixás.* I had hoped to return to Cuba to complete

28

an initiation ceremony into the Yoruba religion that I had begun during my fieldwork. I had had difficulties entering Cuba that year, having discovered late that it could take up to three months for my visa approval. My Cuban family and I had planned the culminating ceremony for June 1991, yet by May I had not received confirmation of my license and visa from the U.S. Department of the Treasury and Immigration Services, respectively. It was now June, and my travel time was running out.

Because I did not want to enter Cuba illegally from Mexico or Canada, I shifted my focus to Bahia with its Yoruba religion resources as a possible site for the completion of my initiation ceremony. I was trying to complete a Yoruba initiation between two countries, having started and completed the beginning phase in Cuba with my adopted ritual family and presuming that I could do the remaining rituals to close the initiation procedures in Bahia with yet another adopted ritual family. I had wanted to return to Cuba to continue what was started in June of 1987. I had wanted to have the blessing and presence of the eldest Oyá in my Cuban ritual family, Tomasa, with whom I had a wonderful attachment and who was almost ninety years old then. I also needed to accommodate my friend Ana's professional touring schedule, which was not meshing with the summer months in which I was free to travel. In addition, the excessive bureaucracy that permeates Cuban-U.S. relations prevailed.

By now, seventeen years after my first Haitian ceremony and four years after the Cuban Oyá ceremony I just described, Ana had become my god-mother or the ritual specialist who was responsible for and supportive of my spiritual growth. I had not had my guardian *oricha,* my "mother," as dancing worshipers would say, firmly planted in my head. Therefore, in Cuban Yoruba terms, I was *media sentada* or "half seated"; that is, ritually I remained in limbo, without the requisite conclusion of blessings and protection. While my Cuban ritual family did not encourage such a status (nor would any ritual family encourage more than the usual few days, possibly weeks, of this status), neither they nor I had been able to secure both sufficient time and necessary resources to complete the ceremony in the normal manner. We were desperate with the coming of yet another June.

Finally, unable to make the trip to Cuba, I set out to visit my next closest and wisest friend within a Yoruba practice, Gracinha of Bahia. This was signifi-cant in terms of the manner in which I have accessed certain knowledge and the kind of knowledge I could access among my three sites. My experiences in Haiti were primarily as a dance and music researcher. My experiences in

Cuba were decidedly as an anthropologist; my focus was on expressive culture, dance and music performance. My experiences in Bahia, on the other hand, were made possible first and foremost through friendships and informal rather than professional relations. These took place in religious enclaves, however, and certainly had dance and music as important emphases.

Gracinha practiced the Yoruba belief system that is widespread in Brazil and generally called Candomblé.[9] She called it then by the nation name of its specific heritage, *nacão Ketu* or Ketu nation; now (in 2003) she prefers to call it Orixá religion. Her practice involved the same Yoruba entities or *orixás,* the cosmic powers that I had been introduced to in Cuba.

I was aware of slight differences between Cuban Yoruba religion and Bahian Candomblé. For example, Cubans generally practice in their homes, *casas,* while Bahians practice in temples, *terreiros;* Cubans do not have many initiates who are connected to Ochosi, while Bahians have major connections to Oxossi. I viewed these differences as variations, and I hoped under the impossible travel situation that I could complete my initiation in Brazil. Gracinha and I went to her ritual godmother to determine what I might do.

Gracinha and I arrived before nine o'clock in the morning and joined about six Brazilians who were seated in the waiting room of Axé Opô Afonjá, which I called "a Candomblé cathedral." (I use the English word "cathedral" because of my impression of the largesse and profundity of this religious community, and to suggest how extensive, formal, and historic this compound has been.) It was a huge *terreiro* or ritual compound that included small and large *iles* or houses for each of the *orixás,* living quarters for many participants of the religious community, and sprawling *roça* or unfettered land. I had witnessed many U.S. Americans journeying to the ritual centers of Bahia since my first trip in 1980, and I had talked with several researchers in the Caribbean who knew these centers well. We all seemed to have been directed to the oldest, most entrenched, and tremendously populated Yoruba religious centers: Casa Branca, Gantois, and Axé Opô Afonjá. (Casa Branca has become a national landmark as the oldest *terreiro* in Bahia and the other two are related "daughter" *terreiros* or "houses.") Also, as I read the literature on Candomblé in Bahia, I found that these three were the research foci of several authors, probably because these centers are the oldest in the region and most continuously connected to Nigerian Yoruba practice (Landes 1947 [1994]; Verger 1957; Harding 2000). The three *terreiros* were and still are major sites of Yoruba influence in the Americas.

That morning, *iawos (awon iawo)* and *ebomis* in their long colorful skirts greeted Gracinha and others with kisses and big hugs. (*Iawo* is Yoruba for "wife of the *orixás*," also known as *iya awo*, "mother of secrets"; the same expression in Portuguese is *filho/a de santo*, meaning "son or daughter of the saints or *orixás*." Both terms refer to those ritual community members who have completed the first stage of initiation into the religion; the related term, *ebomi*, refers to those who have completed their seven-year commitment as a fully initiated member of the religion.) These *iawos* and *ebomis* were stunning in their gorgeous white lace headscarves and blouses.

I watched as several of them dropped to the floor in the ritual greeting of respect toward some senior members of the community. As they lay on their stomachs, they pressed their arms along their bodies, and then they brought their stacked fists under their foreheads. Next, they came to their feet, kissing the hand of the gray-haired elder, embracing her twice with face to both sides, and lastly kissing both of her cheeks. (This was the male *orixá* greeting, meaning that the women had male guardian *orixás*.)

Gracinha introduced me to a few very senior women (at least seventy-five years old) dressed in vibrant colors, and they watched my Cuban version of the appropriate female guardian salutation, which was similar to the Bahian gestures in that we drop to the floor and kiss the ground, roll over onto the right hip, pull the wrist to the hip, and alternate these moves on the left side. As we come to standing, we place crossed arms over the chest and touch shoulders. Of course these greetings and honorific behaviors resonate in Nigeria and the Republic of Benin to this day (cf. Ajayi 1998:52, 54).

Gracinha then took me into a small room, gave me a red-print skirt to wear in place of my white pants, and left me to wait with the others in the front waiting room. Many people entered the waiting room and abruptly paused and breathed heavily in the contrast of outside heat and inside coolness of the shaded white plaster house with a red door. It was Xangó's shrine house or *ile* and where the consultations took place.

There were couples, single men, older grandmother types accompanied by little children, and small family groups. They eventually left the waiting room to have their consultations in another room, while I sat dutifully on a bench against a cool white wall. They left the room by a small door and occasionally I could see them taking off their shoes beyond the entrance. What I noticed early while waiting, as community members passed through the room's three entrances, was how often they dropped to the floor and repeated the ritual salutation. It did not seem to matter that the chronological age of the lowered bodies was higher than the standing or receiving greeter. Age in the religion is calculated beyond chronological or biological age and relates to total years of initiation. By day's end, I noticed how much time I (and many others) had spent on the floor, bending in humility and honoring the knowledge and higher consciousness of ritual elders.

On *quarta-feira* each week, Mãe Stela, the *iyalorixá* or "mother of the Orixás" in charge of the *terreiro*, received in consultation those with questions regarding their spiritual relationships and their physical and material well-being. The *terreiro* was dedicated to Xangó since he was the patron divinity of the first founding *iyalorixá* of the *terreiro*. Wednesday is Xangó's day and Mãe Stela's consultation day, and I was considered a daughter of Yansan (Oyá) who shared the same day. I thought this was a propitious set of circumstances in the eyes of practitioners and hopefully in terms of the *orixás!*

As Gracinha left the waiting room, we said "good-bye" in English. A man who was also waiting in the room then spoke to me in English and identified himself as a New Yorker. He was a Puerto Rican artist with a fifteen-year connection to the Gantois *terreiro*. He wondered where I was from and upon hearing that I, too, was a New Yorker by birth, he related that he was paying his respect to the Candomblé *terreiro* and to Mãe Stela. He was deliberate in his emphasis on the Brazilian practice as a strong and continuous Yoruba practice in comparison to the Cuban practice, which he felt had changed due to the lack of periodic, fresh African influence that Bahia had had. He wished me well as he finished his salutation to a ritual member who led him toward Mãe Stela and his consultation. It was he who first indicated to me that the Yoruba systems of Brazil and Cuba were more distinct than I had imagined.

I would have begun to be bored after waiting most of the early morning with nothing to read were it not for the surprise entrance of two U.S. friends just before the peak of the afternoon. Both of them had anticipated a trip to Bahia that summer and, incredibly, both arrived separately that same afternoon. Just as I finished explaining my relationship (friend to one and professor to the other) to both of them, I was called for my consultation. I left them waiting on "my" bench in the waiting room. I include this coincidence to show how things flow into place when matters of the *orixás* take precedence and as a reminder to myself that when the way is clear and right, everything that is meant to be will be.

I went through the doorway and took off my shoes. Gracinha ushered me from a hallway into a shaded altar room where she instructed me to greet Xangó. Then she brought me into the consultation room where I proceeded to talk with Mãe Stela and her and to show them my ritual objects. I asked Mãe Stela to help me complete my initiation ceremony and explained the Cuban impasse. She suggested that we do a cowry divination, but she first wanted to examine the ritual objects I had with me.

When I opened my elaborately wrapped ritual objects, she saw that I had the material items for an initiate and the identifiable symbols of several *orixás:* beaded necklaces (my *collares*), cowries, statuettes and little pots with miniature implements (my *guerreros*), and particularly Oyá's stone (an *otan*). She sat back abruptly—staring at the objects and seemingly thinking. Gradually, she shifted toward one side and put her elbow on the arm of the chair with her chin resting in her hand. After an even longer pause, she started talking rapidly in Portuguese to Gracinha and suddenly in English to me (she and I had been speaking in Spanish and Portuguese until then).

She told me in clearly enunciated emphatic terms that I needed to take everything to Gracinha's house and spend time cleaning each element in a particular way. She advised me to talk to the *orixás,* that is, to talk out loud, sincerely, intimately, and quite openly (to pray), as I cleaned and wrapped their implements in fresh cloth. She instructed me to take a ritual bath, which Gracinha would prepare, and to return the next day—*quinta-feira,* Thursday, *Oxossi*'s day.

Gracinha led me from the consultation room back to the waiting room. I put my shoes back on and entered another public room of Xangó's house—a dining and kitchen area for the big meal of the day. My friends had left a message that they would be fine together, that I should not feel responsible for them, and that I should concentrate on my project and ritual requirements.

The rooms beyond the quiet altar and consultation rooms were teeming with twenty or more women and a few men, who were talking and arranging a large table with foods and drink. Each day many from the large compound ate together, preparing and sharing the specific foods of the day's dedicated *orixá.* Highly seasoned rice abounded with a strange (for me) type of very long, stringy beans, wild and hot *malagueta* peppers, and several dishes that I could only describe from their delicious tastes. Some dishes were covered with a sauce that, upon keen examination, contained teeny granules of dried shrimp, which I do not eat knowingly, and also flecks of savory condiments and intriguing textures. Gracinha quietly identified one dish as *amalá,* the okra and white cornmeal favorite of Xangó. After volunteering to clear the table, I helped Gracinha and others wash the dishes, which was a larger task than I had estimated (due to the constantly augmenting numbers of ritual members who frequented the imperceptibly huge interior of the main house). Then we returned to Gracinha's home.

That night we prepared supper and talked as usual for a while. When her husband retired for the evening, Gracinha guided me first toward the shower. She had prepared a special mixture of leaves and herbs in a five-gallon bucket and she left me to bathe with the infused waters. The leaf particles, trace minerals, and perfumed aromas were both stimulating and soothing. As I entered my room later, I discovered that Gracinha had laid out my white gown and white head-wrap on the bed. I dressed in the indicated clothes and joined her in the kitchen. I unwrapped all my ritual paraphernalia and washed each piece separately with oil, salt, or water, as required by custom. We did not talk beyond occasional instructions until each piece was safely rewrapped, now in bright colors instead of in white, as the Cuban practice had dictated.

I think the major reason for this difference was due to differing economic situations between the two countries. The Cuban practice has changed over time to adapt to situations of scarcity. In the process, a less elaborate and more uniform behavior or item, like white cloth, was selected for the outer wrapping of most ritual implements. The Brazilians had access to varied world trade and resourceful exchange; therefore the specific colors of each *orixá* graced even the outer wrappings. I went to bed feeling fresh and relaxed with instructions to remember my dreams.

The next visit to the Candomblé compound and Mãe Stela was swifter than the first. I met with her in a bedroom of her home on the compound. She examined my objects with her eyes, never touching them. It seemed to me that my Elegba mesmerized her. In Cuba, Elegba is constantly addressed; initiates wear his red and black beads often; and he is considered powerful, necessary, and a constant companion. In Bahia, he is always kept outside the house; people rarely wear his beads in public; and he is regarded (avoided and perhaps feared) as the powerful, unpredictable Exu. Gracinha told me later that neither she nor Mãe Stela had seen such a miniature stone Elegba as I had.

Mãe Stela just stared at my Elegba. Then she shifted to my Oyá stone and began to whisper seriously, profusely, and incomprehensibly to it. She slowed her speech and asked me to describe my initiation in detail and to tell her of my spiritual instruction. Finally she told me that according to the ritual objects I showed her, what I described of my ritual, and her deep understanding of Yoruba belief and Bahian practice, I was or should have been fully initiated already. She quickly added, however, that I did not fully demonstrate the commensurate knowledge of language, plants, and herbs of an initiated practitioner.

She reiterated the careful and pronounced connection of Brazilian practice to the Yoruba practice of Nigeria. I wondered if that implied that Cuban Yoruba worshipers were allowing changes within the rituals. She did caution me, as a person from the United States who was too intensely engaged in my academic time schedule, to adhere to the guiding principles of Bahian practice. She expressed concern and openly explored how Bahians from the *terreiros* would resolve the interruption of an initiation ceremony and how they would insist on a quick conclusion. I emphasized that the length of my *media sentada* status was not a common occurrence in Cuba.

Then she threw the cowries in order to hear the advice of the *orixás*. The divination system, she explained, offered me a choice, but it would be a difficult decision. If I proceeded according to one of the choices, it would mean that I could complete my initiation in Brazil, but in the process I would have to symbolically sever the relationship with my Cuban ritual family, which she knew was sincere and long-standing. If I proceeded with the other choice, I would continue in my ambiguous status. The decision was mine, and I chose to remain *media sentada,* and to wait for the possibility of completing my initiation in the traditional Yoruba manner (both Cuban and Brazilian), with the godparents with whom I began my instructions. I needed to respect those who had welcomed me into their family, those who had shared with me the knowledge of their grandparents and great-grandparents. They had spent precious time and, most persuasively, had shared meager resources with me. I could not sever such a relationship because of my impatience. I was the one who had had to leave Cuba and did not have more time to complete the ceremony. Cuban ritual practice should not be blamed for Cuba's insufficient resource supply, nor for my academic and personal time limits.

I spent the rest of my time in Bahia investigating Bahian Yoruba practice. What I noticed most was the vast knowledge of plants and herbs and their uses that my friends in the *terreiro* exhibited repeatedly. It seemed that plants and herbs were as important in Bahia as the dance and music ceremonies. I felt the need to know more about the relationship between plants and herbs and music and dance, both in Cuba and in Bahia.

Gracinha and I were fascinated by the events of the consultation and, perhaps also for her own reasons and enlarging knowledge, she agreed that I should call my *madrina,* my ritual godmother in Cuba, and relate what had happened so far in Brazil. After I had recounted events from my point of view, Gracinha took the telephone and began to talk to Ana both in ritual Yoruba and in Spanish. They laughed and deliberated comfortably for quite some time on the commonalities and the distinctiveness of their Yoruba practices.

When the call ended, Gracinha told me how much both Mãe Stela and she admired the respect and loyalty I had demonstrated in my willingness to follow the precepts and advice of my ritual godmother in Cuba, even though they had concerns for me. They felt that I was ritually open to both positive and negative energies, not fully protected by the *orixás*. Still, they agreed with two *babalawos* with whom I have consulted since then that apparently I have wonderful relationships with the *orixás* as I am.

Both Cuban and Brazilian Yoruba practices rely heavily on respect for the wisdom of aged family members and for loyalty within the family. After conversing with Ana, Gracinha told me that she understood the development of Cuban practice better and that she was more convinced of Ana's sincere faith and careful knowledge than before speaking with her directly. She explained to me that I had been treated as if I were a Cuban child, born into that family, and was given all the ritual material culture that I would need as if I were to grow up from then on in that Cuban household. The presumption was that I would learn more about everything I had been given over time, and what was implied was that I would be in constant connection with ritual family members. My problem was that I had not continued to stay in a Cuban household and had not remained subject to the daily lessons of Cuban ritual incorporation.

Gracinha then told me of an impending ceremony at the *terreiro* for Oxun, which we could attend together the following week. On the night of the ceremony, however, I attended alone; Gracinha was not feeling well and sent me early in the morning to spend the entire day and evening.

At the *terreiro,* Mãe Stela and certain *ebomis* led the ritual singing and dance movement in front of the *iles*. I watched the ritual blessing of the *iles* of Ogun, Oxalá, and Oxun and the quiet, veiled eating of sacrificial chicken, guinea hen, beef, and lamb. After an hour or so, a few *ebomis* and other worshipers among the crowd received their *orixás* and entered the *iles*. Inside, there was an altar that contained scores of ritual implements. These were the personal ritual paraphernalia (like my warrior pots, implements, and stone for Oyá) of each person who had been initiated at this *terreiro*. Occasionally, ritual objects of long-term guests were included in the ample display. In other words, the Bahian practice was to keep the ritual objects of the initiates at the *terreiro,* in contrast to the Cuban situation where each initiate kept her/his ritual materials at home.

Most of the participants remained outside singing and clapping occasionally with prayers, or waiting. Some *ebomis* and *ekedis,* female assistants in the *terreiro* organization who, as in Cuba, do not receive the *orixás,* went to members within the crowd to distribute offerings and sacrifices. After these rites, the crowd disbanded for the afternoon to make preparations for the evening *xirê* or *festa,* a music/dance ceremony. Bahians, like Haitians and Cubans, have ritual parties in order to give thanks for the blessings that the divinities have given.

I noticed that the chanting was the only musical stimulus for the arrival of the *orixás* in the bodies of *terreiro* members that morning, which reminded me of similar experiences of manifesting divinities in Haiti and in Cuba without drumming and dancing. I was struck also by the reverence of all of the people within the *roça,* the natural and unmodified grounds of the compound beyond the *iles.*[10] The faithful stood outside in the blazing sun for hours, praying, witnessing, and observing in ritual participation. Many famous Brazilian movie stars, directors, and musicians were among the crowd. Later, compound members were preparing elegant ritual clothing for the evening ceremony; the cloths were made of lace, some woven and some "cut-lace."

Again there was heavy emphasis on the plants that were utilized from the compound grounds. Plants and lots of fresh herbs were used in the foods I ate that afternoon, as well as in communal meals. Plants and herbs were used for medicinal and ritual baths as well. As I noticed these things, I began to remember similar plant practices in Cuba: the regularity of distinct plants at the door of many Cuban households, the infused baths that community members talked about and made for me, and the various boiled leaf teas that were offered for specific ailments. Previously, I had been struck by the incessant drinking of coffee in Cuba, and I had not reflected on the Cuban use of teas as plants and herbs until this Brazilian experience. It reminded me of the "many unknowns," leaves, roots, and so forth, in the bottles of Haitian rum within both ritual and preritual settings that I had grown accustomed to over the years. I had neglected these observations in the past, but my Bahian Candomblé experiences that summer kept paralleling the Cuban and Haitian reliance on plant knowledge.

I had time between the morning and early afternoon rituals and the evening service to look around the physical space of the *terreiro.* It was located outside the center of the city within a suburban tropical setting (at least two blocks square). The nine or ten *iles* were grouped casually together within its walls. Oxalá's house, a long dormitory-like white building, was the largest *ile;* it was used to accommodate initiates and visiting guests. Of course ritual responsibilities for Oxalá, the father of the *orixás,* were its primary function.

Xangó's house was the next largest *ile,* with the waiting room, altar room, and consultation and dining rooms, as well as, on a lower level, a museum for interested visitors. Its museum space contained important historical documentation that showed the way in which the religious membership conveyed its own story to the public with pictures of its *iyalorixás* of old. The other *iles* were small, and each contained an altar with many ritual objects for its *orixá,* and sometimes a chair or bench along the walls.

The *barracão* or dance space was a separate large building that functioned as the ceremonial space for the invocation and presence of the dancing *orixás.* It was only busy when a *xirê* occurred. There were other buildings, however, about fifteen to twenty small homes on the compound site, where some families of the ritual community resided. I was not privy to all of the interior spaces of either the *iles* or the domiciles, but I did have my meals that day in a two-story home with a man, his wife (an *ekedi*), and their children. If the other interiors were similar, they were very modest and comfortable two- or three-bedroom homes with kitchen and bath.

The ceremony began around sunset in the largest structure of the compound, the *barracão.* As I entered, I was surprised and excited by the setting; it did not resemble any other type of ceremonial space that I had experienced— either in Haiti or Cuba. There was no thatched roof outside over an earthen floor, which is common for dancing space in a Haitian ceremony. This was not a large room of a house that was packed with people in concentric semicircles, where the dancing would occur in Cuba. I felt like I was entering an amphitheater with a roof, a theater-in-the-round space, a huge earthen rectangular floor space with steep (raked) seating around an immense "stage."

I chose my seat near the musicians, so I situated myself in the fourth row from the bottom, near the middle of the wall space. As it turned out, I could see the entrances and exits of *iawos* from that vantage point, and I could witness most of the major ceremonial events clearly. In fact, the circular dance formations in the interior space allowed everyone to see *as* they participated, that is, as attendees sang and observed in their seats. It quickly became obvious that the Bahian practice was to permit only the initiated members of the hosting ritual family to dance, while even initiated practitioners from other neighboring *terreiros* were seated as participating attendees.

This really made an indelible impression on me. I had presumed the Haitian and Cuban sense of open welcome in public ceremonies, as well as the "democratic" nature of divinity manifestation such that anyone can receive a divinity, initiated or noninitiated, ritual family member or stranger (see Courlander 1973; Daniel 1980, 1989). The Cuban and Haitian dance spaces seemed to generate more solidarity in the moment, as all members of the society who were present generally danced and sang together in their ritual performances.

Gracinha told me later that the reason for exclusivity within the Bahian *terreiro* was to protect and produce the appropriate energy or vitality for the ceremony. Other *terreiro* worshipers might interrupt (or ruin) what the hosting ritual family had prepared and was activating. Several other Bahian ritual members reiterated that their *terreiros* also maintained this ideal, and that their leaders were particularly reluctant to aid the arrival of *orixás* within strangers to the *terreiro*. Casa Branca, Gantois, and Axé Opô Afonjá have only a few ceremonies in which "outsiders" can dance in the circle at the center—for example, during the *aguas de* Oxalá and at *axêxê* or funereal ceremonies. Those who have completed their first obligations, who are initiated as *iawos;* sons and daughters of the *orixás,* or *ekedis* who do not receive *orixás* but who take care of them during the ceremonies; and *ebomis,* who have completed all obligations, are the three categories of persons who are permitted to dance in the circle of hosting members. Often all categories are jointly spoken of as *iawos,* referring to both male and female initiates.

There is also a separation between "insiders" and "outsiders" in Cuba and Haiti, but in practice everyone dances and sings. In Cuba, with the exception of Yemayá's dances, which take place in a counterclockwise circle, everyone dances as a mass in front of the drums, sometimes in lines or semicircles, and generally ritual leaders and prestigious members dance closer to the drums at the front. In Haiti, ritual leaders and important ritual members dance close to and around the *potomitan,* while everyone is free to dance on the periphery.

In Haiti and Cuba, there is joint participation of many *ounfos* and many *casas.* With this joint temple or house participation, sometimes there are personal clashes, disruptions over temple procedures, and discrepancies in ritual practices between houses. In Bahia, the separation between those who have pledged family ties to a *terreiro* or a compound leader and those who are visiting the ceremony is more defined, and, accordingly, Bahia's ideal temple practice is quite efficient in this regard.

With the sounding of three *atabaque* drums or the Candomblé instrumental ensemble, a group of mainly teenage girls entered and crowded around the musicians. The young people sang vigorously from perhaps four or five rows above the *alebês* or Candomblé drummers. There were three *alebês* with one cone-shaped drum each, and an *agogô* or metal gong/bell player, very similar to the Haitian ritual ensemble in terms of the three elongated drum shapes and the metal *agogô*. The drummers were seated on a raised platform within the raked rows, where they could see the focal space of Mãe Stela who was seated in a chair on the earthen floor at the far end of the huge space. As she and the *iyakekere,* the deputy or "little mother" (*Mãe pequena*) of the *terreiro,* watched from their chairs, all of the *iawos* entered from the opposite side, the entrance to the *barracão.*

Each female dancer was elaborately dressed in grand, bouffant skirts made of yards and yards of vivid white lace cloth and with several white underskirts; males wore white pants and shirts. The white headscarf with a long white lace blouse and skirt visually signals spiritual connection to the Afro-Brazilian religion of Bahia. Members wear long bead necklaces to align them with spiritual protection that is associated with the different colors of each *orixá.* That night, all the female *iawos* wore their gorgeous lace blouses falling loosely from their shoulders to their hips, and everyone was adorned with layers and layers of long bead necklaces hanging down to their navels. Each necklace had only one or two colors, which made the ensemble effect lush in multicolors.

Bahian necklaces shared one attribute with Haiti and a different one with Cuba. In Cuba, the initiates wear seven to ten bead necklaces close to their necks, but still on their upper chests, and their necklaces are relatively short. Bahian practice is much the same except their beads are longer, and sometimes they use more necklaces at one time than is the custom of Cuba. (Some say that Bahianas can wear up to eighty necklaces at once.) In Haiti, male and female ritual officials, *oungans* and *manbos,* respectively, wear only two bead necklaces. Each one is worn over the head and one shoulder, making a huge *X* in beads across their chests and lower abdomens. Bahian practice for leaders of *terreiros* and their assistants, *ogans* (like deacons, literally "big man"), follows Haiti in this regard. Bahian male worshipers wear beads diagonally sometimes. Haitian worshipers do not display beads prominently in ritual dress, although bead necklaces are worn sometimes. Haiti's economic isolation throughout the nineteenth century reduced its access to glass beads; over time Haitian beads were strung and painted coffee beans.[11]

The gorgeous *iawos* in all of their *orixá* finery were the sole sources of interest for about three to five hundred practitioners and observers who had completely filled the ten rows of seats on each wall. At first, the twenty or thirty dancing worshipers were in a procession of serene white—headdresses, blouses, petticoats, overskirts, pants, and shirts—topped with a spray of colors from the beads. After this procession, there was gradual animation in the singing and intensification in the dancing. *Iawo* eyes were downcast and their faces were serious, as they repeated their dance behavior. Gradually, they gave in to their spiritual mothers and fathers. The *iawos* were seeking to display their *orixá* affinity and to assist the community by bringing the cosmic *orixás* to the temple compound.

For most viewers without a performance background, I am sure that this part of the ceremony would have been assessed as an intimate spiritual experience. While I shared that view, I also perceived another view as a dance performer. I saw a theatrical space and presentational floor pattern on the ritual stage, yet the body orientation of the *iawos*, their stance, was *not* uplifted, presentational, or theatrical. They were presenting themselves publicly, but not in presentational style. Rather, they were initiates dancing in small individual circles as they traveled in a circular path around the periphery of a huge dance floor. Their differing arm gestures over a repetitive and uniform foot pattern projected individual characterizations or personalities (cf. Ajayi 1998:35–36).

Their performance gathered fullness and conviction as they intentionally drew their energy inward, deliberately deepening their connection to the movements, drumming, and the chants and allowing their spiritual mothers and fathers to use their bodies. Many chants were sung and many circles were completed as the ritual practitioners danced in a counterclockwise direction all together.

I tried to identify the *orixá* of each dancer among many performers during the first of two parts of the ceremony. All of the *siete potencies* (seven powers) from the Cuban Yoruba religion were represented; in fact, there were several representative colors for each *oricha*: Ogún, Ochosi, Ochún, Oyá, Yemayá, Obatalá, and Changó. (Elegba and Babaluayé are very important, but not included when the term *siete potencias* is used in Cuba). I could detect the nine major *orixás* of Brazil by the bead colors. In Bahia, iridescent blue and green or crystal is for Yemanja; golden yellow for Oxun; dark blue for Ogun; turquoise blue for Oxossi; red and white for Xangó; reddish brown or ochre for Yansan; purple for Nana; red, black, and white or black and white for Omolu

(Obaluayé or Babaluayé); and white for Oxalá. The doubled representatives of a given *orixá* were interspersed in the long line of circling dancers (see chart 1 in chapter 2).

In Cuba, Elegba would have been included in such an array of representation, but the propitiations for Bahia's Exu had been completed previously, both in a separate ceremony and as part of the morning rituals of preparation.

The dancers all performed for the *orixás* in this part of the *xirê*, but they did not dance as a uniform rhythmic ensemble; they seemed to accent different parts of the rhythmic phrase. They were all doing the same step, but often at different times. No one seemed to mind the irregularity that I perceived as a trained dancer, but it was perplexing to me, considering the exactness of performance practice I had witnessed in Haiti and Cuba. It was not simply that Bahian ritual community members danced to the alternate half of the rhythmic phrase—that is, on the one and three of a four-beat pattern (as they do occasionally in Haiti and Cuba)—but apparently in Bahia it was still good form to start the dance pattern on any of the four beats. As long as the dancers were performing the appropriate steps, including foot pattern and hand gesture, it seemed as though it was all right to do so on any beat! There was certainly enough space for everyone to do her/his own thing, and I saw this rhythmic freedom throughout Bahia. Other Brazilian dancers have reported the same inconsistency and irregularity among Bahian ritual performers. The custom is imprecise rhythmically but acceptable spiritually.

After a time, some of the *iawos* lurched and the second part of the *xirê* commenced, wherein the dancers performed as the *orixás*. They began to make guttural calls, which alerted the *ekedis* to come to their aid one by one, unwrap their headscarves, take off their shoes and eyeglasses, and guide them outside of the main dance space. Every once in a while, a dancer shimmied, stopped in place, and bent from the waist with her/his hands pulled around to rest on the back at waist level. This stance and behavior, called *jika* or *sarará,* shuddering shoulders over bobbing knees, was unique to Brazil when compared with the full-bodied and demanding expressions of *lwa* arrival in Haitian Vodou or the upright lurching of *oricha* arrival in Cuban Yoruba worship. In Bahian Candomblé, *iawos* stand in one place most often and shake or vibrate their shoulders; they bob up and down from their waists as the *orixás* enter their bodies and make their identifying cry. (Each *orixá* has a particular cry or *grito*.)

High around the *barracão* walls, the observing attendees roared with excitement at each manifestation and, like in Haiti and in Cuba, the singers sang with more force and volume. An *ekedi* came from the performance circle to escort an entranced dancer out of the dance space. I saw a beautiful Oxun manifest and later a Yansan, an Oxossi, and another Oxun, ending with the arrival of two Oguns.

The dancing was exquisite that night, as were the singing and drumming. One entranced dancer reentered the space dressed as Oxun and danced a sweet and sensual solo in front of the drummers, while Mãe Stela and her *iyakekere* watched nearby. The singers and drummers quickened the pace slightly and sang what seemed to be encouraging phrases, laughing and even clapping when the dancing Oxun was particularly demonstrative. This Oxun was calm and demure as she exited with her *ekedi* at the end of a set of songs.

Suddenly there was a commotion, and a male dancer in dark blue pants ran across the entire space and somersaulted over and over on the ground. An Ogun, one of the hunter *orixás,* was manifesting. An *ekedi* gave him a sword, and he began dancing toward Mãe Stela. Then, across the room, as the drummers and singers began the songs for Ogun, a man in the sixth or seventh row began to gesticulate and throw his body from side to side, responding also to the chants for Ogun. This was a strong manifestation, one that in Cuba or Haiti would be incorporated into ritual priorities. He was brought down from the observation spaces of attendees, however, and taken forcibly outside the *barracão,* under apparent protest, as were a few other audience-participants later when they also began to show signs of manifestation.

Ritual practitioners and observers sat through all the dancing for several hours. Most often these practitioners sang with the youthful chorus, and occasionally they stood up when a particularly well-known set of lyrics was being sung or when a dancing *orixá* became noticeably active or intense. We all watched the acrobatic movements of the dancing Ogun in the center. He was fighting something or someone that we could not see and fiercely slashing his small sword. The sword was nowhere near the size of Ogún's steel machete in Cuba, or Ogou's in Haiti. At times he looked like he was demonstrating fencing movements; at other times he was somersaulting furiously on the ground, only to stand rapidly and flip or leap to another side.

Another Ogun was escorted into the center. He, too, carried a small sword. The two Oguns danced and "fought" on separate sides; still both were in front of Mãe Stela and the *iyakekere.* They advanced and retreated sporadically and lunged downward to place their swords into an invisible opponent. They also acknowledged the musicians and singers by dancing toward and in front of the music section; it was the only other focused space in performance than that for Mãe Stela.

I had hoped to see Mãe Stela's Oxossi, but he did not manifest in her that night. The ceremony ended when the Oguns were both led out and the musicians stopped playing. Each *iawo* had danced for the "mothers" and "fathers," "masters" and "mistresses," of her/his head and then exited. The next section involved the dancing *orixás* and then their exit. It was a series of heightened performances in the center preceded by processional dances of invocation.

Participants from the seated area began to file out into the night breeze. Slight as the breeze was, it was cooling and fresh after four or five hours of singing in the *barracão*. Everyone was quick to depart; some had been at the compound since dawn for the early preparations, as I had been—probably a total of sixteen hours. Most participants said their good-byes with hugs and kisses; some compound members retreated either to the house of Xangó or to their homes in the *terreiro*. I left in a truck with a couple that was recruited for me by Mãe Stela, ending a day and a night of Bahian Candomblé ceremony.

With this experience during a Brazilian visit of two months and a total of five field trips of one to two months each, I was merely scratching the surface of Bahian belief. Here I have described only one type of Bahian ritual practice, the Yoruba-based Nago/Ketu form of Candomblé, but I discovered several other forms during my fieldwork that were noticeably diverse. There seemed to be so many forms of Bahian (and Afro-Brazilian) religious worship that I was often confounded until I began to isolate the commonalities of certain Bahian practices and simultaneously to think in terms of African nations across the Diaspora. When I began to fathom the complexities of Haiti, Cuba, and Bahia in terms of nations, the dance performance data revealed clear relationships among the religions. Another way of looking at the African Diaspora emerged beyond common stereotyped "possession rituals." I could not dismiss the notion of "nation," or "what—what the dance does—does" (spinning the words of Foucault). I was explicitly concerned with how significant the dance performance was beyond music and dancing, what dancing and music-making does, and what African American religious rituals mean. I set out to document and compare the social significance of African American religions through analysis of these three Diaspora sites.

Foundations

Over time, the three Diaspora belief systems that I have just briefly described have generated a great deal of public curiosity and academic interest. Haitian Vodou, Cuban Yoruba, and Bahian Candomblé—with their dance/music performances—are now overflowing their traditional geographic boundaries. Due to a series of coups in recent Haitian history, the Cuban Revolution, and increasing Brazilian migration, many worshipers have brought their beliefs to new American sites. Often their beliefs and practices have been displayed as part of cultural presentations, both in international tourism and on televised folk programming. The African-derived religions have been a source for spiritual quests within contemporary social life throughout the Diaspora.

Despite the seeming growth and mounting popularity of these religions, the elite classes of Haiti, Cuba, and Brazil have generally snubbed them. The Haitian connection between politics and Vodou, particularly in the regime of "Papa Doc" Duvalier, has characterized the Haitian Vodou religion as the ultimate stereotype of superstition. Before and at the beginning of the Cuban Revolution, most rites and practices of Cuban Yoruba were performed in secret and carried the weight of ridicule and prejudice. Brazil's struggle with contemporary understanding of African religions has ranged from police raids of *terreiros* to dismissive and pejorative references. In Brazilian novelist Jorge Amado's widely acclaimed books and films, Candomblé belief has been referenced in intriguing and informed ways, but also with humor and disbelief as the main lens, as, for example, in *Dona Flor and Her Two Husbands*. And for the last century, Hollywood and the world film industry have served up Haitian "voodoo" images of zombies sticking pins in dolls and "wild frenzied possession dancing" to international moviegoers, for example, in the unfortunate promotion of the film version of *Serpent and the Rainbow* (see Davis 1985 for an alternate view). Audiences are encouraged to believe the worst about African-based religions, such as the Cuban example in *Believers*, which reduces African philosophy to witchcraft.

With the dispersion of Haitians, Brazilians, and Cubans (particularly after the Mariel expulsions in 1984), and, importantly, also with the spread of information technology, Haitian, Afro-Cuban, and Afro-Brazilian religions have come out into the public arena in newspaper and Internet articles. In fact, an increasing literature in several languages has given current validity and interest to the general field of African American religions. Bold declarations of membership by lay community members, augmented by popular artists and academics, have made reticent religious communities more vocal. Notably the popular success of Karen McCarthy Brown's study of a Brooklyn Vodouist (1991) has assisted the promotion of insider accounts over the last decade, such as the works of Raul Canizares (1999) and Marta Vega (2000) in English, the writings of *Iyalorixá* Graça de Santana Rodrigué (2001) in Portuguese, and the work of Natalia Bolívar in Spanish (1990). Native scholars have also championed the responsibility to describe and analyze African cultural legacies outside of their demeaning stereotypes; examples include Gerdès Fleurant (1996) and Leslie Desmangles (1992) from Haiti. The formal recognition of African American religions as cultural heritage in Cuba and Haiti's recent declaration of Vodou as an official religion (April 4, 2003) have both lessened the pejorative views that they have borne for centuries. The result is that the academic investigations of African American religious organization have had to include the centrality of spiritual belief across the Diaspora and the critical analyses of scholars from within the Diaspora community.

Important to the continued spread of interest and membership for the religions has been the influence of Caribbean music in popular culture (e.g., Averill 1997; Manuel et al. 1995; Behague 1994; Hill 1993; Manuel 1991; Hebdige 1987; Appleby 1983). Through popular music, the music and dance from within African religious practices have acted as performance ambassadors and have traveled to and influenced many cultures, nationalities, and ethnicities: for example, the roots or *razin* music of Haiti in Boukman Eksperyans, the *Afoxé* music of Bahia, and the flood of Cuban *oricha* music from classic Celia Cruz and Lázaro Ros to contemporary artistry of Síntesis and Santíssimo. Recorded music and dance traditions (both audio and video) have introduced the belief systems to Canada, France, Germany, Japan, Finland, and across the United States (Miami, New York, Los Angeles, Detroit, Chicago, Bloomington, Salt Lake City, Sonoma, and Oakland, to mention a few places). Within the music, dancing divinities or spiritual forces form vibrant images of cosmic strength and power and, accordingly, shape the social, in addition to the religious, behavior of women and men.

Accordingly, the geographical area on which I concentrate for this study is the Caribbean Basin and northeast South America, where there are strong African legacies, particularly from the Bight of Benin and the Kongo-Angola regions. My focus on these sites is important to cultures across North America as well as to nations of Central and South America since these territories also share some of the cultural characteristics that I discuss (Williams 1984

[1970]; Knight 1978 [1990]; contributors in Pescatello 1975; contributors in Walker 2001). In the Caribbean as well as in parts of North, Central, and South America, mixtures of African and European, African and Native American, or African, European, and Native American elements have permeated and then presided over Native and European mixtures or what is generally called *mestizo* culture. In these territories, *mulatto* culture (European and African mixtures) is a class phenomenon that is not always factored into cultural or national identity. The Americas are filled with such combinations,[12] and all North, Central, and South Americans have significant African roots and legacies within their national cultures that have been minimized or unacknowledged until recently. For now, I concentrate on religions within African and European cultural mixtures that have been continuous since contact in the 1500s and are characteristic in most of the Americas.

I focus on belief systems from two islands with national identities that are closely tied to their African-derived religions, popularly called Haitian Vodou and Cuban Santería. They both have had revolutions that have had an impact on the shaping of their religions. The Haitian Revolution in 1791 consolidated different versions of both African religions and Catholic practices. These stabilized during the early years of Haiti's independence when it was politically and economically isolated from the rest of the world, really until 1860 (Desmangles 1992).

On the other hand, Cuba's revolution in 1959 served to distinguish and further separate differing African religious practices, as the new nation looked inward for its identity. During the early days of restructuring a new society, African religions were highlighted as proof of Cuba's Afro-Latin, rather than simply Hispanic, identity. While actual religious behavior was repressed within Cuba's early communist/atheistic ideology, cultural representations from its African religious history were promoted as such in educational and tourist settings (Daniel 1996).

Candomblé belief and practice in Bahia is exemplary of the heavy dose of Africanity that presides over other cultural elements in the majority nation of South America. This religious practice is within and beyond the largest concentration of Africans outside of Africa. The state of Bahia in the northeast, particularly in the capital city of Salvador da Bahia, has produced distinctive variants of Brazilian culture, and it has much in common with Haitian and Cuban religious life. In Bahia, African forms are prevalent because of the high percentage of Africans who were deposited there as a result of the transatlantic slave trade and the concentration of specific ethnic groups, namely, Kongo-

Angola, Fon, and various Yoruba peoples, who were placed in the northeastern port of Bahia. In addition, the longevity of an active Brazilian slave trade from the early sixteenth century until very late in the nineteenth century made a continuous and sustained entry of African customs. Both high population concentration over time and the late arrival of fresh African cultures account for the density of the region's African-derived culture.[13]

I must mention also that many forms of religious worship are practiced within Haiti, Cuba, and Brazil, beyond the three discussed here. The African Americas contain orthodox and reform variants of Catholicism, Islam, Hinduism, Judaism, Protestantism, and Kardecian Espiritismo, as well as other African-derived religions such as Winti of Suriname; Rastafari, Nyabingi, Obeah, Pocomania, and Cumina of Jamaica; Caboclo and Umbanda of Brazil; and Espiritismo of Puerto Rico, Cuba, and Brazil. Most of the African-derived religions have distinct praise dance or specific liturgical movement within their worship practice.

I have chosen Vodou of Haiti and the Yoruba religions of Cuba and Bahia in order to examine "dancing religions." They became the focus of my research as I studied music and dance in the African Diaspora. It was impossible to ignore the African religions, however. I discovered Haitian Vodou as a dancer and musician in the late 1960s and concentrated on Haiti until the late 1970s; I returned to Haiti after twelve years in 1991. I focused on Cuban Yoruba from 1985 to the present as a part of but mostly after I had finished training as an anthropologist. I have had intermittent but profound contact with Bahian Candomblé since 1980, as a dancer first and then as an anthropologist. So I entered the three sites differently, and my knowledge has different emphases as a result.

Beyond my personal preferences, these three belief systems demonstrate fundamental ideas for understanding the African Diaspora. I selected them also because of their prominence in the documented literature of the African Diaspora and their significance and development in terms of varied, but parallel, African influence in the Americas. They are indicative of major surviving African nations in the Americas (Taylor 2001; de Santana Rodrigué 2001; cf. Matory 2001a:36–43).

When I refer to "nations," I do not mean geopolitical nations. I am referring to continental loyalties and legacies based on heritage, marriage, adoption, and allegiances that were understood in Africa as "ethnic group identity" (Yai 2001). I also include those congregations that were created by the experience of enslavement—that is, those who were captured and dispersed in the

Americas and who, as a result, were named by their captors or named themselves (see Matory 1999:82–88). Both African and African American groups solidified in terms of allegiances and notions of group identity.

As Yai states:

> Religions based on Orishas and/or Voduns were freely borrowed from one state to the other throughout the area, and the introduction of the transatlantic slave trade intensified this tradition of exchange of ideas, worldviews, and institutions. One important religious feature or practice that has not received the critical attention it deserves, and that is relevant to the understanding of the concept of nation in the area and understanding its instantiations in the New World Diaspora, is *the existence, permanence, and indeed cultivation of the phenomenon of double or multiple religious and cultural loyalties—across geopolitical entities. . . .*

> [T]he Orisha and Vodun communities have, as a rule, consistently functioned, in today's parlance, as *forces of transnational [religious] civil society,* countering the hegemonic state policies that tended to promote unconditional allegiance to one state [or one religion]. This explains why, strictly speaking there were no European style nation-states in the area. (2001:246, 248 [my emphases])

Through analyses of dance and music traditions, I have found that Caribbean and Latin American descendents of enslaved populations reveal and continue to rely on a sensed and remembered notion of "nations," nations of old in contemporary situations (see also Taylor 2001:1–13). Three amalgam nations surface repeatedly in the dance and music data.

First, the Abomey Kingdom of the Fon people in the current Republic of Benin in West Africa produced the Haitian Rada and Brazilian Jêje rites within Haitian Vodou and Bahian Candomblé, respectively. In Cuba, the same Fon nation was responsible for the religious system called Arará. Next, the Yoruba peoples from Anago, Ijesa, Ketu, Oyo, and Abeokuta were and still are represented in Haiti within Nago rites, in Cuba within Lucumí and Iyesa rites, and in Brazil within Nago/Ketu rites. And thirdly, the Kongo, Lemba, Teke, Suku, and many other peoples of the Kongo-Angola region in West Central Africa produced religious rites in Haiti, Cuba, and Brazil, called Haitian Congo/Petwo, Cuban Palo Monte or Palo Mayumbe, and Brazilian Angola rites, respectively. These dance data propose that the three religious practices under study display the persistent sociocultural organization around African nation legacies in the Diaspora.[14]

The results of my research are ultimately for my anthropology colleagues and those other eager minds who want to know how and why African religious practices continue in the midst of global technology and contemporary science. My study is also for my people—African Americans, young and old. I hope that African American community members will understand more of our African cultural, but mainly spiritual, legacies through reading these data, their analyses, and the stories behind them. The totality of enslaved Africans' history and their contributions to American and European contemporary societies are important. Few elders, now more than seventy years old, have acquired the knowledge that is found in the dance performances and music practices of African religions within their general education. Few travelers have traveled consciously and analyzed the Diaspora connections, and youngsters have little concept of what is missing from the history they are learning. Thus here, I attempt to pass on some danced knowledge through the written word. African dance/music performance has been embodied and transformed over centuries by wise women and wise men within the African Diaspora.

Although I emphasize religion and belief systems, I also decipher performance material. Dance/music performance resonates more deeply for audiences who know something about the sites and values of origin from which the performance comes. By examining specific dance/music traditions, I am able to present performance data in terms of the physiology, psychology, philosophy and religion, history, botany, mathematics, ethics, and aesthetics that they contain. I open dance/music traditions as windows that allow the viewer/reader to visually and mentally luxuriate in the stored body knowledge to which the performances give access.

I am suggesting also that we all, especially anthropologists, should treat dance behavior not only as a particular kind of knowledge but also as a particularly rewarding mode of access to knowledge. I write thinking of those of any cultural background who wish to learn about African-derived dance/music material. My words are dedicated also to those who take on the values and time concepts that are associated with learning in cultural enclaves like the ritual communities I describe and thereby give themselves to the beauty, elegance, and power of sacred performance or, in other terms, praise dance.

TWO

Body Knowledge
at the Crossroads

My orientation to the research data is through an "African Diaspora Dance Perspective."[1] In this perspective, dance movement and music are central to a description and an understanding of African American life; dance movement and music interconnect and reference other dimensions beyond the social arena; and dance movement and music are pivotal to spirituality and spiritual development in Diaspora cultures. With this approach, the manner in which information is communicated is exceedingly important and distinctly categorized: not only are expressive modes noted, but also body materials are canvassed, assessed, and included among other empirical data; and a comparative assessment within the African Diaspora is most profitably required before determining the meaning of dance behavior.

Dance behavior is central because it is a constant in most African American religious practices, as well as in many social, secular settings. African American forms of worship among many contemporary Baptists, Methodists, Pentecostals, and even Episcopalians are noted for shaping services to include pronounced body movement and active physicality. This tendency, however, is not universal—in African American Catholicism and Presbyterianism, for example. In the Caribbean and Brazilian ritual environments discussed here, however, dance movements have specific, identifiable features that combine with music, spatial considerations, color, food, and time constraints, and that allow worshipping participants access to different types of specialized, context-linked knowledge. The dances and their musical components influence both ritual members and participating observers through energy centers of the body.

I see ritual dance performances as "choreographed improvisations" because they utilize movement sequences, much of which are improvised artistic materials, but in a conscious organization. Unlike other contemporary choreography, however, the performances are not primarily concerned with the entertainment value of the movement behavior. Patterns of movement and body rhythms are organized and integrated formulaically with specific instrumentation and call-and-response singing. Performance spaces are washed, decorated, and blessed—often with chalked or painted artistic lines or circular configurations that are drawn on objects, on earthen floors, or in the air. The performances vibrate with both spiritual and social ideals.

In African American contexts, particularly ritual ones, dance performance is interconnected so that its aesthetic dimension can also signal a relationship to the political, the economic, the religious, and the social arenas of African Diaspora life; these arenas are infused within performance. Dance historians Katrina Hazzard-Gordon (1990) and Brenda Dixon Gottschild (1996) have given clear examples of the economic and political dimensions of African-derived dance in the United States (both popular and concert forms) and have drawn prominent lines joining the aesthetic and political domains. The discipline of anthropology widens the perspective, so to speak, in order to examine multiple levels of meaning.

As Anya Royce has clarified for dance performance (applying Victor Turner's useful terminology) and extending it to music performance as well, African Diaspora dance and music are multivocalic (Royce 1977; Daniel 1995). Dance and music communicate through multiple sensory channels and thereby contain, symbolize, and emit many levels of meaning. The search for meaning reaches from the visions of the creators and intentions of the performers to the content and context of the performance, to the participants or audience members, and usually to the entire social community. Different meanings can be found at every level of analysis (movement and symbolic levels, individual and societal levels, choreographer/dancer and audience levels, etc.), and multiple channels of sensory stimuli are activated for use in exploring and explaining meaning.

Dance ethnologist Allegra Snyder encourages the investigation of several interpretive levels to assess meaning within dance performance, looking first at the dancing body, the choreography, the affiliated dimensions of performance (music, costume, props, sets, etc.), and then the social environment (the stage audience, the locale, the times, etc.) in order to contend with meanings for differentiated members of the society (1981:213–24). Anthropologist Judith Hanna discusses how dance performance is perceived cross-culturally and urges the examination of its contexts as well as its properties in order to determine what dance performance means in varied cultures with diverse values and attitudes (1979:17–56). Her recommended analysis is based on dance as a nonverbal communication system, and linguistic modes of analysis are preferenced.

While my data evaluation process relies heavily on most of Snyder's and Hanna's concerns, it assumes the formidable line of other dance anthropology and cultural studies that have solidified the field (e.g., Kealiinohomoku 1976; Schieffelin 1976; Kaeppler 1967; Royce 1977; Williams 1997; Novack 1990; Cowan 1990; Ness 1994; Browning 1995; Savigliano 1995). I have also found assistance within the study of African researcher Omofolabo Ajayi (1998).

In her analysis of both historical and contemporary dance performance among the Yoruba peoples on the continent, Ajayi draws attention to two markers within the body (1998:27–42). These markers, the concepts of "beauty" and "body image," impact meaning in continental Yoruba societies and also affect my study. Ajayi discusses the Yoruba emphasis on "*stance*—the inner quality of an individual" as opposed to outward signs of beauty and "*body language* [which] frequently replaces verbal communication as a more compactly subtle and dynamic form" (1998:29–30; my emphases). Her work demonstrates that to discover meaning in normal communication, Yorubas concentrate on keen scrutiny of the body.[2]

My work confirms Ajayi's emphasis on the inner inquiry of the dancing African-derived body and stresses that Yoruba-derived and Fon-derived Americans regularly sense and adjudicate the meanings of the dancing body. It also augments the studies of Hazzard-Gordon and Gottschild by providing pivotal understanding of "Black Dance" within the Diasporic Americas. My study marks the inclusion of Caribbean and Latin American sacred dance forms among comparative studies of the Diaspora. In fact, my study includes an essential component to the, until now, Anglophone-privileged studies of African Diaspora dance. It adds a consideration of the Hispanic and Francophone Caribbean, in addition to a view of the majority African and only Lusophone population of the Americas.

Additionally, my study shows the several meanings within a given performance, since dance (and other aesthetic systems) crosscuts the full range of social organization. With detailed examination and analysis, dance researchers can discover and reveal a wide display of information. In the particular religious communities I have selected, I am trying to break some additional ground and focus on those ritual dances and music that spill over into social activity and social interaction, within the wider society as well as the cosmos. For these communities, there is little separation between such universes. For these worshipers, dance rituals create religious, social, and galactic harmony (see figure 1).

Within an African Diaspora Dance Perspective, an analyst augments understanding when s/he considers the spiritual dimension of performance. Even if the dance/music behaviors appear to be social and secular, a neglect of the spiritual dimension can limit understanding. Spirituality in dance and music-making accommodates a balance among three realms of existence: the human, animal and plant realm; the ancestral realm; and the cosmic realm. The ancestral and cosmic realms are differentiated from each other in Vodou, Cuban Yoruba, and Bahian Candomblé understanding, as well as in other African Diaspora belief systems.

Over time, some ancestors who have been deified because of esteem during their lifetimes have become part of a cosmic family of divinities. This results in differentiation among "the dead." Some ancestors are classified as those who have passed on and exist in the ancestral realm. In Haiti these are called *ley mo* or "the living dead"; in Cuba and Bahia, *Equns* or the "dead." Others ancestors have been deified and thereby exist in the cosmic realm.

Figure 1

The Crosscutting Domain: Aesthetics and Expressive Culture (developed with William A. Shack 1977)

These and other cosmic entities are called *lwas* in Haiti, *orichas* in Cuba, and *orixás* in Bahia.

In the process of dance/music performances in Haitian Vodou, Cuban Yoruba, and Bahian Candomblé, social cohesion results among the living, the ancestors, and the cosmological divinities. Ritual performances are filled with what I call "social medicine": power, authority, and community relations are affected, rearranged, or affirmed; social wounds are healed; each community member is accounted for; and the ritual community continues with strong bonds. The spiritual dimension of performance is connected to the social well-being of individuals and to the solidarity of a social community. Regular, repetitive ceremonial performances function as holistic medicine for community members.

Worshipers in the religions I study generally view ritual or ceremonial dance/music performances as a series of sacred offerings. The congregation performs the dances until specialists in divine manifestation emerge. These lead and intensify the performance, moving the ritual forward from extraordinary activity (ritual behavior) through transcendence or transformation (spiritual behavior). From the worshipers' perspective, the performances are presented simultaneously to the human and divinity communities in hope of transformations that will bring dancing divinities from the spiritual world to the worshipping community. Thus, an African Diaspora Dance Perspective often presumes the knowledge of and practices for an expanded sense of "life" and "living"; namely, the three realms of existence. It is precisely the dance/music, the ritual performance, that integrates these varied domains.

In an African Diaspora Dance Perspective, multiple modes of communication are canvassed. Written, theoretical communication, in home manuals and public libraries, for example, is not privileged but is weighed with other sources of communication, including nonverbal expressions of the body and the multiple meanings that are found in music/dance analysis. Regardless of the mode in which information is relayed, attention and due respect are given to many channels of communication. Thus oral histories and time-revered body behaviors count in Haitian Vodou, Cuban Yoruba, and Bahian Candomblé; they are the bases of teaching in all three religious systems.

With serious investigation, the fundamental understandings and commonalities among Haitian Vodou, Cuban Yoruba, and Bahian Candomblé can be seen as resilient patterns of human thought and time-tested human behaviors. They are also the result of politico-economic circumstances that have changed over time from their beginnings in the colonial period to the present. When enslaved Africans reached American shores, their memories and behaviors gradually refashioned whole liturgical orders (Herskovits 1941; Bascom 1951, 1980; Mintz and Price 1976; Bastide 1978:126–42; Raboteau 1978; Brandon 1993:126–57; Dayan 1995:65–74; cf. Drewal et al. 1989; Blier 1995). Reformulated in a new environment, West and West Central African ethnic group differences coalesced. Later, under the constraints of several competing belief practices—Roman Catholicism (Desmangles 1992), Protestantism, and Spiritism, for example (Thomas 1987; Glazier 1991; LaRuffa 1971; Taylor 2001)—worship practices again shifted, adapted, and reconfigured in new forms. The new ritual procedures echoed the resonating core of Fon, Yoruba, and Kongo-Angola religious practices. African American belief systems utilized the survival structures of ancient performance practices. When permitted, but also clandestinely, Africans and African Americans danced, sang, and drummed ancient knowledge to the present (Ortiz 1951; Verger 1957; Yarborough 1958; Emery 1972 [1985]; Thurman 1967). They searched for guidance, requested advice, and received sustenance to endure and strength to transcend temporal difficulties. They received advice through proverbs and divination practices, but they also received nonverbal guidance within dance/music performance.

For five centuries in new environments, artistic performances, aesthetic expressions, spiritual behaviors, oral discourses, joking subtexts, ordinary speech, and both ordinary and extraordinary body movements have been performed and received as worthy, informative, and valid modes of communication. In addition, written and visual forms of communication (books and journals, television and the Internet, etc.) have been included as other knowledge sources and competent media of investigation. Again the latter are not privileged. Body knowledge is given its fair hearing.

Foremost in an African Diaspora Dance Perspective is the need for a comparative assessment of seemingly different but related behaviors across Diaspora cultures. Often similar values and similar underlying attitudes emerge in African Diaspora comparisons, reflecting the double consciousness of, within, and among African Diaspora cultures (Walker 2001; Daniel 2002b:179–82; McDaniel 1998; cf. Gilroy 1993; Du Bois 1969:43–53, 221–22, 274–78). The African Diaspora Dance Perspective encourages a reappraisal of definitions and definitive findings of the past, as researchers release our coercive (and often Eurocentric) training in order to think more clearly and comparatively, thus "Afrogenically," about African-derived cultures (Walker 2001:7–13). With a more thorough collection and critical examination of all the facts, African American behaviors can be fully understood on their own terms.

Disembodied Knowledge

Intellectual knowledge without concomitant integration of somatic, intuitive understanding and the spiritual wisdom their combination yields is "disembodied" knowledge. From the period of enslavement through to the present, disembodied knowledge has dominated the Americas as a valued social paradigm (cf. Harrison 1991; Marglin and Marglin 1996). The lay public, including ritual community members, students, and others, has been encouraged to think of scientific theoretical knowledge as superior to, rather than equal to, practical, experiential, or kinesthetic knowledge (Gardener and Hatch 1988; Boggeman et al. 1996). Institutions such as schools, churches, government, and the modern family have stressed the importance of specialization and compartmentalization. Certainly the performing and plastic arts (dance, music, sculpture, painting, architecture, and theater) are given importance in these institutions, but usually as subsidiary units of the "important" or "real" knowledge; that is, theoretical and scientific knowledge. Rarely do institutional administrators expect or examine the theories and science within the dancing body.

Performance, the arts, and spirituality operate to correct and adjust disembodied knowledge. Over time and through extraordinary effort, performance, the arts, and spirituality may assist in transforming disembodied knowledge into embodied knowledge. Performance practices offer both individual and societal benefits. The intellectual, compartmentalized-only model of knowledge has deficiencies, which appear in narrow and inflexible perspectives. We can find their consequences ultimately in disruptive social behaviors and debilitating states of self-worth. Embodied knowledge is acknowledged only rarely outside the discipline of dance (cf. Sklar 1994; Graham 1991). When it is recognized, it is critiqued mainly for its lack of quantitative or empirical proof and its reliance on qualitative evidence. Limitations within both models should not suggest an "either/or" policy, either exclusively mainstream, partitioned specialization, or exclusively traditional, holistic integration of knowledge.

The ritual communities that I study have encouraged the utility of both cognitive—theoretical and kinesthetic—embodied knowledges. Because they do not subscribe to European and American mind/body dualism, which emphasizes the mental and theoretical over the experiential and kinesthetic, African American ritual communities do not reject science and theoretical knowledge for experiential knowledge. Rather, they incorporate all sorts of knowledge within bodily and ritual practice. In fact, some ritual leaders say their belief systems and practices are forms of "science."

Anthropologist Sheila Walker reports on two Candomblé authorities:

> Iyalorisha Stela of Ochossi asserts that there are various levels on which the Candomblé must be understood. . . . The Candomblé, in addition to being a religious system, is also a science, according to the priestess. The African ancestors who created this system of understanding and interacting with the forces of the universe had obviously figured out the complex interrelationships between human beings and these natural elements and had determined how humans could enter into conscious contact with and influence nature for their own purposes. These ancestors also created both exoteric and esoteric levels of explanation corresponding to the roles and responsibilities of the various actors in the system. . . .

> Afro-Bahian philosopher Edson Nunes da Silva analyzes the Candomblé as a religious system, the foundation of which is a complex science of life and nature . . . [some of which] . . . is still an unknown to present day science. (In Walker 1990:125–26)

In my fieldwork also, leaders refer to an understanding of the forces of the universe as *orichas, orixás,* or *lwas* like the understanding of quantum physics, waves, vibrations, and so on (Mãe Stela 1985: personal communication; Casquelourds 1991: personal communication; Fagbemi 1995: personal communication; Pai Carlinhos 2001: personal communication; Fleurant 2002: personal communication).

Throughout the Americas, contemporary African Diaspora communities occasionally integrate their knowledge of religion into schools and education systems—for example, schools for Catholics, Episcopalians, Lutherans, or Muslims. There are two African American educational institutions that deserve mention: the Yoruba religious instruction at the Oyotunji Oyo settlement in South Carolina and the Candomblé school at Axé Opô Afonjá in Bahia. Both are institutions of Yoruba-centered religious instruction within a European American education model; that is, alternative schools in their respective communities.

The religious institutions of the Diaspora have historically been paramount as sites of leadership, social advocacy, and economic power. The spiritual temples and houses of Haitian Vodou, Cuban Yoruba, and Bahian Candomblé, as well as the Black Christian church and the Black Muslim mosque, serve as recognized architectural monuments for healthy African American communities across the African Diaspora. They point to the reliance on spirituality as a necessary part of healthy social communities. The presence of temples, churches, and ritual houses in so many African American enclaves is a symbolic statement against disembodied knowledge, despite the fact that members of these communities are also subject to the infiltration and influence of mainstream notions of specialization and compartmentalization of knowledge.

Embodied Knowledges

Only minutely—perhaps during Mardi Gras in the South, in a St. Patrick's Day parade in the Northeast, at a Cinco de Mayo celebration in the Southwest, or a Gay Pride festivity in the West—do North Americans in the United States have an idea of the power in the dancing and music-making communities that I study! I see the same power in the images of Hawaiian, Samoan, and Papua New Guinean traditional dances, where unison movement is augmented exponentially in hundreds of performers. A more accessible example for a layperson would be the chorus finale in the Broadway play *A Chorus Line,* where the power of unison movement is vivid, chilling, and extreme. I want that understanding to double, maybe triple or quadruple, in order that readers understand the powerful aesthetic, emotional, physical, spiritual, and mental consequences of a unified ritual community with huge numbers of performers performing in unison.

In the ritual contexts of Haiti, Cuba, and Bahia, strong belief systems initiate regular, routine ceremonial performances among African Americans.[3] The ceremonies that have developed concentrate heavily on either the human or the suprahuman body; that is, a human body that has been transformed by a spiritual incorporation. The communities meet according to a ritual calendar, and whenever they come together, they are a mass of dancing bodies. Perhaps because of the packed spaces of their rituals, the dances look like crowd displays, performing a series of dances with literally fifty to a few hundred performers (depending on the size of the ritual space). They are expressive dancing bodies in the same space at the same time performing the same movements to the same rhythms. The dancing bodies accumulate spirit, display power, and enact as well as disseminate knowledge. Worshipping performers reenact what they have learned, what they have been told, what they feel, and what they imagine. They re-present feelings, ideas, understandings, and knowledges (see figure 2).

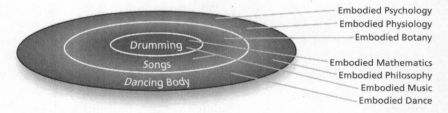

Embodied Psychology
Embodied Physiology
Embodied Botany

Embodied Mathematics
Embodied Philosophy
Embodied Music
Embodied Dance

Drumming
Songs
Dancing Body

Figure 2

Embodied Knowledges

Despite the incredible labor demands and resulting physical drain on the African-derived population during enslavement and the post-emancipation period, dancing and music-making have offered some relief, potential rejuvenation, and the promise of ecstasy or transcendence. In the Americas, the dancing body allowed temporary escape from the extraordinary hardships of enslavement and continued as a primary vehicle for spiritual communication and for both spiritual and artistic expression. In the Americas today, the dancing body still functions within ritual communities as a source of spiritual communication, aesthetic expression, and the site of extraordinary transformations. The communities dance and support the transformation of a few for the benefit of many.

A suprahuman body is the result of spiritual transformation, when the worshipping, believing, and dancing human body is prepared for or overwhelmed by the arrival of spiritual force. The dancing human body proceeds to unfold spiritual energy, or, in believers' understanding, to present or manifest divinities, who are aspects of a Supreme Divinity (see also chapter 8). Beauty salon operators and truck drivers, as well as journalists and lawyers, are transformed in the ritual setting into suprahuman bodies; they dance beautifully and forcefully in order to give expression to spiritual forces, which then give advice to the community. One example of an extraordinary transformation was told to me about a woman who weighed around three hundred pounds who entered the *peristil* in Haiti with great pain and suffering from arthritis, but after receiving her *lwa*, "danced as light as a fairy" for the rest of the ceremony (Beckford 1976: personal communication).

Another enduring image of transformation that I witnessed was of a Brazilian *babalorixá* who received and manifested the aged and wise Oxalá. Oxalá moved slowly with very small but exacting gestures. He whispered occasionally in a labored manner and could hardly dance, although he tried. He visited with every participant patiently and gently for about two hours. Afterward, that same *babalorixá* was transformed again and became a wild, boisterous little character, an *ere*, who gorged on chocolates and fruits incessantly for about twenty more minutes. Within his little-boy speech and as he scampered around playing with other children, he made sense seemingly without realizing it; that is, he gave pertinent advice to other worshipers.

In a Cuban transformation that I witnessed, a girl about fourteen years old was being brushed with leaves as everyone had been brushed in a closing ritual. Suddenly she started to tremble violently and uncontrollably. She registered fear and started to scream and cry profusely while holding onto her grandmother. Abruptly she lifted her legs and, in an exaggerated march, tore loose from her grandmother, stomped across the room, and then began to dance and spin furiously. This occurred at the close of a spiritual mass or *misa,* where mediums relate communications from spirits of the dead and where *orichas* rarely appear. After an hour or more of her vacillations between a frightened, humble, young girl and an audacious and fiery dancing *oricha,* those who were officiating concluded that she had received her first transformation. She had received suprahuman, spiritual energy without preparation, called a *bozal,* or un-baptized, "African" manifestation.

Such incredible dance transformations have stimulated the development of African American ritual dance performance over centuries. This huge category, African American ritual dance, exhibits two tendencies. While there is a reliance on gestures and movement sequences that come from a codified ethnic group heritage (Fon, Yoruba, Kongo-Angola, or other African legacies), there is also a reliance on abstract expression within the dancing body, both of which constitute meaning (cf. Ajayi for dance, 1998:27–106; Wilson for music-making, 1974, 1983). Ritual performance involves movement vocabulary that is structured; particular gestures and movement phrases occur with the sounding of specific rhythms and have a specific cultural or religious meaning.

For example, in African communities with "talking drums," dancers and musicians can relate stories, parables, and myths from their understanding of the drums in combination with specific movement sequences and their relationship to tonal languages. This is possible because the tones of the talking drums relate to linguistic structures and replicate speech patterns. Yet an alternative practice of abstract or noncodified movement and nontalking drums is also part of African heritage (e.g., Nketia 1965; Blum 1973; Bebey 1975; Chernoff 1979; Kubik 1954, 1979; Wilson 1992; Ajayi 1998; Kisliuk 1998). Both kinds of drumming practices and both kinds of movement sequences can lead dancers to convey aspects of myth, history, and narrative.

Religious and secular settings place dancers and musicians together in deep, improvisational performance, such as in the familiar case of instrumental jazz music. In the instance of a jazz song played by a quartet (piano, bass, drums, and a saxophone soloist, for example), meaning is accrued not only from a specific musical organization or form (e.g., three-part ABA song form), or only from the melodic relationship to its harmony and rhythm, but also from the melody (a given theme, a stated or declared known) and its development and transformations (its abstraction and elaboration).

Likewise, meaning in African American dance performance is accrued not only from specific, codified gestures and rhythmic sequences, although a few outstanding cues or signals might be employed, but also from the elaborate development of movement. For example, jazz dance partakes of a theme in sound and movement, an overarching series of rhythms, an accumulating series of movements, and changing and projected emotional states, all of which are abstracted and combined to constitute meaning.

So too, in Haitian Vodou, Cuban Yoruba, and Bahian Candomblé, some gestures and movement sequences signal a literal meaning, but more often the social circumstances of performers have created a deep reliance on the abstracted expressiveness of the dancing body and on nonverbal communication procedures. Often what makes a performance deepen and intensify with meaning is visually projected in the breath that accompanies specific movements or in newly discovered and performed dynamics within the repetition. Meaning registers within visceral responses to kinesthetic and musical affect. Meaning, realizations, and knowledge have often been abstractly embodied.

Most of the movement sequences and motifs for the divinities conform to identifiable patterns that are recognizable across the African Diaspora. The dance for Ogún is a good example of this because it contains both explicit, literal meanings and implied, abstracted meanings that are common in all three ritual communities. In all three sites, the dance's movement patterns denote a fierce male entity that fights as he dances with a sword or machete. With slight variation, this dance is performed in Haitian Vodou as the dance for the *lwa,* Ogou; in Cuban Yoruba as the dance of the *oricha,* Ogún; and in Bahian Candomblé as the dance of the *orixá,* Ogun. It is also performed in Nigeria as the dance of the orișa, Ogùn, and in Benin as the dance for the vodun, Gu. This example demonstrates the reliance on the dancing body continuously over time and across space, while also expressing the human need to dance and make music.

In each community, the dance for Ogou, Ogún, or Ogun involves aggressive warrior stances, rigorous traveling movement sequences, and an emphasis on slicing or cutting with a sword or some sort of metal. The codified gestures within the dance performance show a warrior traveling through impeded areas, kicking and fighting an opponent, chopping with and cleaning his sword, and reigning triumphant. The abstracted meanings converge within the image of a warrior/hunter archetype and are drawn from symbolic colors, forceful body movements with closed fists, argumentative grunts and growls, intimidating facial expression, stories and myths about a powerful warrior whose force is as impenetrable as iron, richly animated song melodies, thickly textured drumming patterns, percussive actions, accents, and outbursts. Performance elements combine and result in cultural understandings not only about the performance and the performer but also about his/her relationship to the viewer. The total performance embodies power and protection and forces the Haitian, Cuban, and Bahian worshiper toward strength and right action.

Over time, Africans in the Americas re-created dance/music and ritual sequences and created new forms in response to what they experienced. We have to conclude that they believed their dancing and music-making were linked to both survival and salvation. They needed to dance and play music in order to save and protect their individual spirits, their dignity as humans, and their sense of a cosmic family. Ritual dance performance was a repository of remembered movements and musical components but also a repository of complementary legends, beliefs, and attitudes, with contrasting and alternative resolutions for temporal problems. These repositories held responses to and possibilities for many social situations. Accordingly, the dance and music forms "housed" not only physical information about the human body in dance mode but also theoretical, emotional, aesthetic, and spiritual information. These data became blueprints with choices for possible action. When or if circumstances changed, ritual believers could choose from their repository of wisdom among differently powerful divinities and adjust appropriately, giving power and relevance to many social circumstances.

Under desperate and unfavorable conditions, even in spite of the loss of language and often the loss of meaning of many ritual elements, African Diaspora community members have guarded ritual choreographies, mainly teaching and performing them among ritual families. Ritual families—Haitian *fanmis,* Cuban and Bahian *familias de santo*—are extended families that are re-created in the image of a consanguine and religious ideal.[4] In the countryside of both Haiti and Cuba, a head-of-household usually serves as ritual leader, healer, and diviner for his/her blood relatives and a few honorific, or adopted, extended members of the family. In urban areas, Haitians and Cubans tend to combine several biologically related and unrelated individuals in an extended family form. In Bahia, several consanguine families may live and worship together on *terreiro* grounds; however, there are also many adopted members who augment the family form, making huge ritual families. It is within the ritual family, small or large, that proper performance instruction takes place.

In each of my three ritual examples, dancing worshipers display ritual dance, drumming, and song materials and demonstrate knowledge of omnipotent energy. In the first descriptive example, dancing Haitian worshipers displayed the communal goal, to release ordinary apprehensions and accumulate extraordinary spiritual belief as transformed and manifested energy, as they greeted their *lwas*. Dancing worshipers in the Cuban example recognized differing life realms as they invoked and greeted Oyá from the cosmos; they danced and sang to acknowledge her energy and then performed the required modes of behavior in order to receive her blessings. Dancing worshipers in Bahia witnessed spiritual connections, spiritual transcendence, and thereby affirmed their religious convictions, rededicated themselves through participation in the communal rites that are affiliated with the *terreiro* community. In all settings, the presence of the suprahuman divinities was and is the essence of and key to ceremonial events (cf. Bascom 1950:64–68).

While dancing with exquisite virtuosity and immense spiritual expression, worshipers simultaneously reach for acknowledgment within the universe, the community, and the self. Some performers sense their bodies' intricate execution as they perform ritual sequences; some can sense parts of their performance:

> I feel ice in my feet when Baba [the *oricha* Babaluayé] starts to come and even though I try to keep the rhythm, I can see my feet don't do it. Then I try to make my arms go forward and back like they should, and I see my hands—but the ice is coming, and then I don't remember. . . . All I remember is me trying to make my feet and arms do the steps right, and cold ice coming up from my feet to my back. (Cuba 2001: personal communication).

Some remember nothing but the aftereffects: "I don't know. You tell me what she (Oxun) did. I just wake up tired, very tired" (Brazil 1996: personal communication).

Most follow the popular Haitian priestess in Karen Brown's book, *Mama Lola*:

> When the spirit going to come in you head, you feel very light, light like a piece of paper . . . very light in your head. You feel dizzy in your head. Then after, you pass out. But the spirit come, and he talk to people, and he look at the table you make for him . . . you know. Then he leaves and . . . and you come from very, very, very far. But when the spirit in your body, in your head, you don't know nothing. They have to tell you what the spirit say, what message he leave for you. (Alourdes in Brown 1991:352–53).

As worshipers perform, they sense and learn. And as they continue to perform over time, in the process of music-making and dance performance, embodied knowledge is constantly consulted. It is a dynamic, practical referencing that can mean different things within a lifetime. Some ritual performers are only concerned with the musical and dance product that yields transformation. Others are interested in what the transformation means, the related embodied knowledge that usually has to do with healing the self and the community, balancing relationships between the cosmos and the ritual community (Daniel 2001:352–61; Sklar 1994).

The community feels the immense loss of such knowledge when a great dancer or musician passes on—a "library" of information, of embodied knowledge, is "burned," according to Amadou Hampâté Bâ from Mali at a 1960 UNESCO meeting (in Jessica Harris 2001:169) and according to Rogelio Martinez Furé from Cuba in several public lectures (1986, 1987, and personal communication). I concur because of results from my dance analysis and cultural interpretation. Over time, performers become consciously aware of the knowledge that exists within sacred performance.

Embodied Botany

Robert Voeks, an ethnobotanist working on Brazilian plant and human interaction, has highlighted the importance of historical environmental commonalities between parts of the African continent and the Americas, but he has emphasized more the effects of human intervention and "disturbed" forests and flora (1997). His historical recounting of the early physical continental development places Africa and South America together with a common forested landscape. For estranged captives during the transatlantic slave trade, languages and social situations were harsh and volatile, but the physical environment may not have been as strange, despite countless changes in the physical terrain over centuries. In addition, colonial exploration and settlement patterns included an exchange of food crops and plants that was extensive, such that recognized and familiar leaves were available for medicinal and herbal practices for both European and African populations. Voeks's work on Brazil suggests that Africans could not reinstate medicinal systems and herbal practices per se, but that their knowledge of forests and flora was combined with indigenous and European plant knowledge as well.

> Bahia's flora has come to resemble that of many other tropical forest regions: an ocean of homogeneous agricultural crop plants and their associated weeds, punctuated by the occasional island-like stand of pre-Columbian

flora. The divisive forces that yanked apart the Cretaceous African–South American biome have been counteracted by five centuries of human-induced floristic reconciliation, as close to a continental reunion as Africa and South America will ever witness. Thus, the floristic landscape that Africans encountered in Brazil, dominated by sugar, cacao, oil palm, coffee, and a host of pasture grasses, was pretty much what they had left behind in Africa. The major botanical differences, found mainly in the old-growth forests, dwindled as deforestation progressed. Afro-Brazilian ethnobotany would never be based on knowledge of the jungle. Their understanding of plants, particularly the healing flora, would be assimilated from indigenous sources, picked up from their European masters, and, ultimately, blended with the traditional knowledge of their ancestors. (Voeks 1997:32).

The histories and ecologies of Haiti and Cuba are substantially different from that of Bahia in that what Voeks relies on for Brazil is contact between indigenous Americans and both Europeans and Africans, in terms of learning about the new environment.[5] With the decimation and ultimate annihilation of native populations in Haiti and Cuba, indigenous plant knowledge was not available for long (Pérez 1995:14–30; Knight 1978:28–29; Horowitz 1971:24–25). In Haiti and Cuba, researchers estimate a slow decline of indigenous influence from fifteen to fifty years after initial contact early in the sixteenth century. They also point out the high gender ratio of European males to females and imply sexual contact among early male colonists and indigenous females. Some researchers do note the interaction between runaway Africans and African Americans or maroons as the major source for Native American cultural impact (Knight 1978: 15–16; Deren 1953:64–67). Even if early Catholic missionaries, sailors, and settlers, as well as African maroons, used indigenous American botanical knowledge in Haiti and Cuba, that knowledge was not as consistently integrated into centuries of religious and liturgical evolution as in Bahia. For the cultural development of the two islands, interaction of European and African knowledge of forests and flora was more pronounced.[6]

Within all three religious community sites, plant knowledge of African or African American herbalists and healers became community knowledge within liturgical and medicinal practices. Pierre Verger, a recognized authority on Yoruba plant knowledge, stated that over the forty years that he studied as a *babalawo* (Yoruba diviner), he observed the close configuration of plants, medicines, and the power of the "*odù*, or sign of Ifá under which [these are] classified," but he was also impressed by the knowledge "transmitted by *babalawo* to *omo awo* (from master to disciple) through short sentences based on the rhythm of breathing" (1995:14–15). Through incantations, Yoruba healers maximized the effect of combined leaves and plants, and, accordingly, in an oral tradition the incantations became significant parts of the remedies. Verger also emphasized that "in those incantations the names of the plants are accompanied by two or three stanzas describing their specific qualities" (1995:19).

With the detailed botanical studies of Pierre Verger (1995) for Bahia and Lydia Cabrera (1983 [1954]) for Cuba and with the detailed folk-medicine study of Michel Laguerre (1987) for Haiti, we have strong evidence that within the role of priest/diviner/healer, plant knowledge and medicinal procedures were conserved over time. The enunciation and preservation of verbal expressions were compounded, however, by multiple meanings of African language words and phrases, which made the job of ritual leader complicated, as s/he fathomed exact meanings. For my purposes, these researchers show the reliance on plant knowledge, memory, and active oral tradition to conserve not only plant knowledge but also the associated cultural knowledge that often permeated ritual performance.

Verbal communication is, of course, the main method of passing on knowledge and belief, and through regular ritual performances, whole texts of ritual prose and poetry were passed on in Haitian Vodou, Cuban Yoruba, and Bahian Candomblé ceremonies. An oral tradition conserved much through singing and praying, even as some understandings were lost. In Haiti, chants and songs of African nations were isolated in the new black republic by the end of the eighteenth century. In Cuba and Bahia, chant versions were influenced by a series of events.

With the proclaimed ending of the transatlantic slave trade in 1807 by the British, some Africans were returned to Freetown in Sierra Leone, educated, and eventually repatriated to Lagos, Nigeria. There, as educated civil servants and often missionaries, these Saro peoples (according to native pronunciation of Sierra Leone) were involved, more often than others, with the translation of the Bible. Under British colonialism in Africa, these educated Christians translated "into a language that Oyo, Egba, Ijesa, Ekiti, Ondo, Ijebu, Egbabdo, and Nago could all understand . . . [and] produced for the first time a standard language, a language that thereby reified the ethnic unity of these peoples and named that unity by a term previously reserved for the Oyo, that is Yoruba" (Matory 1999:85; see also Law 1977:25–44; Brandon 1993:18–31, 55–59; Matory 2001b).

Researchers also report the intermittent but continuous contact over centuries between Africa and the Diaspora (Verger 1957; Matory 1999:36–43).

Africans and African Americans experienced economic interchange over centuries, particularly between the Bay of All Saints in Bahia and the Bight of Benin in West Africa on the coasts of Nigeria and Benin. In addition, individual Africans in the Americas were sent to the continent for religious and ritual study and returned: Martiniano de Bomfim from Bahia and Adechina from Cuba, for example (Landes 1947 [1994]:22–34; Brown 1989:94). Such contact affected the continuity of ritual texts and chants. The need for an African *lingua franca* in commercial ventures and religious/cultural exchanges emerged and solidified in the nineteenth century.

Concurrently, many practitioners in the Americas did not understand African languages entirely, having been forced to take on the languages of the colonizers (in my three case studies, speakers of French, Spanish, and Portuguese). Thus, the continuous replenishment of the African enslaved population up through the end of the nineteenth century in both Cuba and Bahia brought a more uniform ritual language and influenced ritual procedures (Matory 1999:72–103).

Considering the ecological, historical, and cultural conditions of the three sites, it is amazing that there is such a wealth of songs, chants, and refrains that continue in African languages within danced and sung liturgies (Laguerre 1980; Mason 1992). It is a testament to religious faith and to the notion of cultural identity that worshipers retain specific word concepts, remember whole religious texts, and adapt practices that are associated with the words, although perhaps in new contextual orders and occasionally with new meanings. It is significant that some of these texts contain important botanical information.

Embedded in the nineteenth-century African languages of ritual chants and in the actual social interaction, there were references to behaviors, characteristics, and preferences of cosmic divinities. The sung references kept history and mythology alive and reinforced modes of behavior. One example is the requisite order of Papa Legba or Elegba as first in the liturgy with his several invocations. Here are some chants that are commonly used:

HAITIAN VODOU CHANT FOR LEGBA

Attibon Legba ouvri bayè pou'moin ago!
Ou wè Attibon Legba ouvri bayè
    pou' moin ouvri bayè!
M'apé rentré quand ma tourné
Ma salut loa yo!

Translation:

Attibon Legba, open the gate for me, ago!
You see, Attibon Legba, open the gate for me,
    open the gate!
I will enter when I return,
I salute the loa! (Courlander 1973:77)
(When I return [from Vilokan], I will salute
    the *lwas,* in Desmangles 1992:99.)

CUBAN YORUBA CHANT FOR ELEGBA

(Yoruba as given orally and transcribed in Cuba.)

I bara ago; moyuba (two times)
Omode koni ko sibara ago
Ago moyuba
Elegba e chulonna.

Translation:

Homage to the relative of the Club (the power
    and authority object of Elegba).
Give way, I pay homage.
Child who teaches the doctrine of paying
    homage to the Club.
Make way;
I pay homage to the Owner of Vital Force.
(English translation from Mason 1992:58; see also
chapter 8 in this text)

BAHIAN CANDOMBLÉ CHANT FOR ELEGBARA

Ena, Ena mojuba E,
Ena mojuba.
Ena, Ena mojuba E,
Ena mojuba.
Ena koroba E,
Ena koroba.
Ena koroba
Ena koroba E.

Translation:

Ena is another name for Elegbara, and means "two parts." When
Elegbara uses the name of Ena, it specifically refers to the dual
complements of Elegbara's character. Here he says repeatedly,
"Hello to the World from my two parts. Accept my two parts and

Greetings." (From Yoruba to Portuguese to English by Pai Carlinhos and Yvonne Daniel)

In the sets of chants, Elegba is the first divinity that is called as the ceremony begins. It is that divinity, called by similar names (Elegba, Legba, Elegbara, Papa Legba, Eshu, Echu, Exu, or Ena), who is responsible for opening communication between the human and suprahuman worlds in both Fon-derived (Legba) and Yoruba-derived (Eshu) religious communities. The clear emphasis on Elegba in all three communities is a result of the religious loyalties and shared religious practices among Fon and Yoruba descendents that I discussed earlier. The importance of Papa Legba/Elegba/Exu is also the result of his cosmic position at the intersection of physical reality and metaphysical concern. Elegba as *oricha* or as *lwa* is basically associated with the crossroads or the gates and requires appeal so that the prayers, praises, and requests of the ritual community will be heard, whether in Haiti, Cuba, or Brazil. He is at the crossroads to signify choices and opportunities, and he is considered the dynamic force of the universe that makes potential energy into kinetic energy, according to researcher Juana Elbein dos Santos (1998).

The chants and songs not only gave requisite behavior models, but they contained knowledge for well-being and health, in that they referenced botanical information. Chant texts that referenced plant names and usages ultimately maintained knowledge that provided healing and curing practices; the chants also functioned as initiators to forward the progress of the service or ceremony.

In Haiti, plant usage is plentiful in teas and for baths. One Vodou chant shows the reliance on leaves and their reference to specific and related *lwas:*

> Twa fey, twa rasin-o,
> Jete bliye, ramase sonje
> Mwen gen basen lwa mwen
> Twa fey tonbe ladann
> Jete bliye, ramase sonje
> Eskalye Bumba, twa fey tonbe, Eskalye Bumba
> Lan basen mwen, Langaj-o.
> Twa fey tonbe lan basen mwen, Zila Moyo,
> Twa fey tonbe lan basen mwen, Langaj-o
> Twa fey tonbe lan basen mwen.

Translation:
Three leaves, three roots.
Cast away forgets, pick it up remembers.

In the *Iwa's* bath tub,
Three leaves fell into it.
Cast away forgets, pick it up remembers.
Eskalye Bumba, three leaves have fallen
In my bathtub, Langaj-o.
Three leaves have fallen in my bathtub, Zila Moyo.
Three leaves have fallen in my bathtub, Langaj-o.
Three leaves have fallen in my bathtub.
(Translated by Gerdès Fleurant)

The song is sung in a context of healing, a major function of all Haitian Vodou (Brown 1991:4–5, 10).

The investigations of Lydia Cabrera in Cuba, documented in her thorough account, *El Monte* (1983 [1954]), and as analyzed by ethnomusicologist Morton Marks, relay a quantity of medicinal knowledge among ritual practitioners:

> A complete botanical entry in *El Monte* thus consists of a Spanish common name, a scientific classification, the plant's Yoruba and Kongo names, and an *orisha* "owner."

> It is possible to re-order all the entries and arrange them into two groups, one that would place them in their scientific families (*Acanthaceae, Agavaceae,* etc.), the other in their *orisha* family. In the latter, Elegua "owns" red bay (*Tabernaemontana citrifolia* in the Dogbane family), fowl foot (*Eleusine indica* in the Grass family), *espuela de caballero* (*Jacquinia aculeata* in the *Theophrastaceae* family), and many others. (Marks 1987:228)

Plant knowledge yielded associated spiritual knowledge:

> Afro-Cuban herbalists knew the *orisha* owners, ritual applications, and curative powers of hundreds of trees, roots, barks, grasses, herbs, vines and flowers. In their exploration and classification of the Cuban forests and savannas, they were undoubtedly guided by the cognitive categories anthropomorphized as the "*orishas,*" which could comprise philosophical, aesthetic, anatomical, botanic and even chemical dimensions. Particular leaves might belong to a certain deity on the basis of mythological associations. (Marks 1987:229)

This type of knowledge is guarded also in chants for Brazil's Ossein, master of forest leaves and herbal and medicinal plants. Bahian *Pai de santo* Antonio Carlos Silva Encarnação sang the following chants in response to my questions about the knowledge of plants and healing for Candomblé practitioners:

OSSEIN CHANT

E abb mi boua abb mi bou
E abb abb mi boua abb mi boua e abb. (two times)

Translation:

The Earth gave me my *abb* (Ossein's leaf)
Abb is my life and my death.
(Translation from Yoruba to Portuguese and then to English
        by Pai Carlinhos and Augusto Soledade)

Ya dacouro oju ewe adacouro oju o bogum.

Translation:

The Mother's leaf cures the eyes of the blind.
The eyes of the son, Bogum.
(Translation by Pai Carlinhos and Augusto Soledade;
        see also Verger 1995)

Accordingly, for a bath in Bahia certain leaves are used, and these are associated with particular *orixás.* One that I was given used large *majoram* for Yemanja, small *majoram* for Oxalá and Odudua, *macasá* for Oxun, *nacizú* for Oxaguian, and *sange lavo* and *agua elevanchi* for Yansan. (This bath was for general health and well-being for me, a child of Yansan/Oyá, and for my entrance into the temple grounds of Ogun.) The bath was prepared by singing chants for the named *orixás* as the leaves were shredded, rubbed, and dispersed in bathwater. These are purposeful preparations that suggest that the singing of chants was a way of invoking specific divinities and their powers with regard to plants, embodying and activating the powers of the plants.

The texts of the sung chants in each of the three religions made botanical information declarative and forceful, enough to be remembered and potentially effective. The dance ceremonies and ritual practices "housed" scientific references, the botany or botanical knowledge of Bahia's and Cuba's Yoruba inhabitants (Cabrera 1983 [1954], 1970 [1958]; Bascom 1950; Edwards and Mason 1986: 40–65; Marks 1987: 227–45; Verger 1995; Voeks 1997). Africans observed and experimented with plants in the Americas, applied the botanical understanding from within remembered ritual practices to social situations, and then related these to their African American descendents. The mysteries and scientifically proven validity of medicinal plants (folk wisdom regarding the properties of leaves) became a base for accumulating and transposing knowledge. Over time, ritual officials categorized the flora of the Americas, and ritual communities savored the fruits of their plant and seasoning knowledge in nourishing Africanized food preparations (Jessica Harris 1988, 2001:169–82). Each divinity had particular preferences for plants and animals that were also part of the preventive medicines that ritual practitioners employed. The song texts embodied botanical information within their sacred mission; that is, the texts embodied plant wisdom. The setting changed and so did some details, but the vehicle, in this case the chants and their dances, did not change essentially.

Embodied Physiology and Psychology

Within religious concepts of the Diaspora, the body is mapped by the divinities themselves, and the specialized tissue of a given part of the body, with its associated internal organs, is understood in terms of its anatomical and resulting physiological function. In Haitian Vodou, for example, a particular body part is associated with one of the *lwas* and often with one of the *nasyons* or nations. Madame Lavinia stated that in teaching the dances of Vodou, she discovered that

> the feet are dedicated to the god of war, Ogoun Féraille; the hips to the Congo's spirits of beauty and love; the chest to the brave warriors, the Ogouns [and Ibo spirits; 1970: personal communication];[7] the spine to the snake god, the water god and the rainbow goddess, Papa Damballah, Maitre Agwe, and Maitress Ayida Wedo respectively. The hands are dedicated to the spider spirit, Ghede Zarien. (Yarborough in Aschenbrenner 1980:159)

Within Madame Lavinia's designations of body-part associations, most of the African ethnic nations are displayed. Ogoun Féraille is from Yoruba heritage. Madame Lavinia's reference to the Congos is a signal of Kongo influence in the Haitian context. Dambala, Met Agwé, and Metres Ayida Wèdo are Haitian Vodou divinities that are well known as Dā divinity relations in the region of Ouidah in the Republic of Benin. They represent the Rada *nasyon* with Dambala, the snake, as its major *lwa*. The temple of the sacred python still exists in the city of Ouidah in the Republic of Benin; the *hueda* or snake (and dancers would say the snakelike movement) connects them to Haitian Vodou, especially considering that there were few snakes native to Haiti and yet snake rituals abound (see figure 3.).

In the Cuban context, the mapping of the *orichas* on the body gets more complicated. The warrior Ogún is associated mainly with the legs, but also with the heart. Ochún, the divinity of river water and femininity, is associated

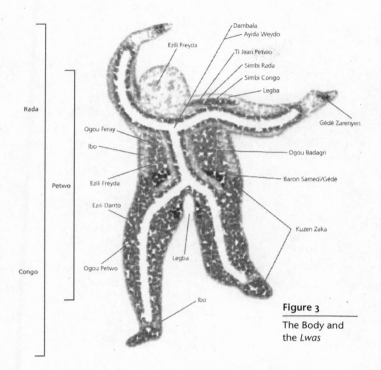

Figure 3

The Body and
the *Lwas*

with the lower abdomen, female groin area, and female genitalia, in addition
to the blood vessels throughout the body and going to the heart. Yemayá,
the divinity aligned with nurturing, the mother of all—including mother
of the other divinities—is associated with the breasts, the upper abdomen,
and the buttocks. Changó is often associated with the tongue and the penis.
Obatalá governs the head generally (although each worshiper has a guardian divinity that resides in the head as well). Ochosi is often associated with
mental processes and thereby is close to Obatalá and the head. Ochosi is also
associated with the eyes, the left leg, and the left hand; in Cuba, he is called
the "left-handed hunter." Elegba governs the feet, and Obba governs the ears.
Oyá governs the lungs and the back in general. The twins or Ibedys govern
the fingers and toes. And Babaluayé guards the skin (see figure 4).

In the Bahian Candomblé, the Yoruba mapping of the body is different
from Cuban Yoruba. First, different body parts are associated with *orixás* depending on whether the worshiper is concerned with healing or offerings (de
Santana Rodrigué 1995: personal communication; Pai Carlinhos 2001: personal communication, 2002: personal communication). Generally, however,
Yemanja and Oxalá govern the head as ultimate mother and father, as well

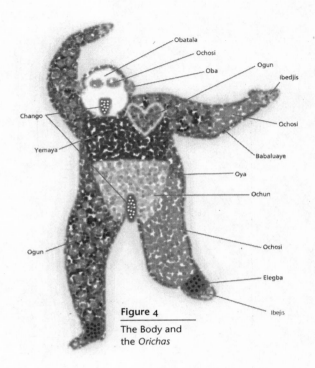

Figure 4

The Body and
the *Orichas*

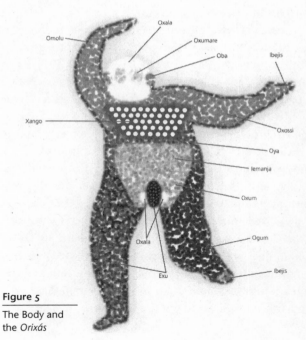

Figure 5

The Body and
the *Orixás*

as ova and sperm; Xangó governs the chest; Yansan governs the ribs; Oxun governs the stomach and female genitalia; and Exu governs the penis. The legs are divided between Ogun, who governs the left leg, and Exu, who governs the right leg. Omolu or Babaluayé governs the skin, and Oxumare governs the eyes. Oba governs the ears, and Oxossi governs the arms (see figure 5).

The dances of a particular *lwa, oricha,* or *orixá* utilize the dancing body as a whole, but they also emphasize particular body parts that are identified with a divinity. For example, in Haiti, the constant whole-body undulation (in the torso and pelvis, in the rippling of the back, and the lift and fall of the chest) emphasizes the stories and importance of the snake, Papa Dambala. In Haiti, the snake is coded with notions of ongoing and profound life: the snake is found in low levels on the ground, which gives life in the form of plants and nourishment for humans. It is also found in the high levels of trees. Being high and near the sky is akin to the notion of infinity and ongoing life in Vodou ritual. The snake also eats eggs, another symbol of life. Two snakes together, Dambala and his wife Ayida Wèdo, make an alliance and, in an arch, cover and protect the world; their typical movements reference copulation and life. The Vodou life notion is codified in the visual undulation of the torso and back, and its performance coincides with associated *lwas* in Haitian Vodou.

In Cuba, arm gestures indicate and identify most of the divinities. In Ochún's dance, for example, she splashes and spreads water (or honey) with her arms and hands. She strokes all over her body and emphasizes her lower abdomen, linking her also to all blood vessels throughout the body. In Bahia, Yansan's hands and arms—waving in the air, beating the air as if in a storm—characterize the dance. She also uses alternating rib and hip shifts over a fast-paced foot pattern, activating the area with which she is identified in Bahia. The accompanying chants, stories, and life histories of the divinities directly reveal associated body parts. One of the most well-known of these is the story about Oba and her loss of an ear due to Oxun's strategic (deceiving) ways. As a consequence, in Oba's dance she holds one ear at all times.

Beyond understanding body systems (respiratory, digestive, muscular, skeletal, and psychological), personality characteristics and psychology are understood in terms of the associated divinities in the dancing religions of the Americas. In the era of enslavement, this type of psycho-physiological knowledge, in addition to knowledge of medicinal plants, kept both the African and European populations in relative good health, since enslaved Africans were often the health caretakers for entire plantations (Barnet 1961; Patterson 1969; Sandoval 1989; Raboteau 1978; Fontenot 1994).

The ceremonial structure of Haitian Vodou, Cuban Yoruba, and Bahian Candomblé reveals deep knowledge of the body, emotional states, and social psychology and its functioning. Dance ceremonies are carefully constructed sets of deeply engaging, visual, rhythmic, sensory stimulation that result in specific emotional and physical behaviors. While unfolding religious liturgies and sacred orders of chants, drumming, and dancing, the ceremonies also compound and layer physiological principles that result in ecstatic experiences, both conscious and unconscious (Walker 1972; Bourguignon 1968, 1976). Concentration on specific body parts and also on the whole dancing body implies knowledge about what occurs inside the human body within repetitious, improvisational dance behavior. For my dancer audience, which generally associates improvised performance with little or no structure, I emphasize the fact that these rhythmic movement sequences are not random events, although they are heavily injected with improvisation. They are structured events that have been calculated over time to reach the full range of the body's physiological and psychological capacities and that stimulate affect. What results is what I described in chapter 1 when the *lwas, orichas,* or *orixás* manifest: suprahuman performance. These dance behaviors display embodied physiology and psychology within ritual contexts of Haiti, Cuba, and Bahia.[8]

Chart 1. Divinities, the Body, and Colors

Haiti

Legba	penis, spine, shoulders	white
Dambala	spine	white
Ayida Wèdo	spine	white
Ogou Feray	feet, chest	red
Ogou Badagri	chest	red
Ogou Petwo	shoulders, legs	red
Ezili Freyda	eyes, hands, shoulders	pink
Ezili Danto	shoulders, hips	red
Kuzen Zaka	feet, hips	denim blue
Simbi Rada		light blue
Simbi Congo	shoulders, hips	red
Ibo	back, feet	red and yellow
Ti Jean Petwo	shoulders	red
Gédé Zarenyen	genitals, buttocks, hands	black
Baron Sanmedi/Gédé	genitals, pelvis, heart	black

Chart 1, cont.

Cuba

Elegba	feet	black and red
Ogún	legs, heart	green, black, purple
Ochosi	eyes, left leg & hand	turquoise blue
Yemayá	breasts, upper abdomen	dark blue
Obatalá	head	white
Babaluayé	skin	purple
Ochún	lower abdomen, female genitals	golden yellow
Oyá	ribs, back	ochre, rainbow
Changó	tongue, male genitals	red and white
Obba	ear	yellow and red
Ibedys	fingers, toes	multicolors

Bahia

Exu	penis, right leg	black and red
Ogun	legs	dark blue
Oxossi	arms	turquoise
Yemanja	head, ova	crystal, translucent blue
Oxalá	head, sperm	white
Omolu	skin	black and white
Oxun	abdomen, female genitals	golden yellow
Yansan/Oya	ribs, back	ochre
Xangó	chest	red and white
Oba	ears	yellow and red
Ibejis	fingers, toes	multicolors
Oxumare	eyes	rainbow/opaque
Nana		purple

Embodied Philosophy

Within the danced ceremonies, there are also assumptions regarding nature and the universe and understandings regarding the nature of human beings. An order of precepts and commitments is encoded within the ceremonies, and also within the social organization of the ritual community, whether familial by blood, association, or ritual adoption. Both human and suprahuman actions are examined and interpreted in Haitian Vodou through the specific roles of priests/healers/leaders, called *oungans, manbos,* and mediums (Price-Mars 1983; Herskovits 1938; Maximilien 1945; Rigaud 1953; Deren 1953; Métraux 1972 [1959]; Laguerre 1980; Desmangles 1992). *Oungans* and *manbos* apprentice through various levels of training, but the main level involves those who display their readiness and knowledge by "going through fire" or *canzo.* The highest level among the roles, *pri je* (literally "prize of the eyes," meaning "giving the utmost ability to the eyes"), allows the highest level of *oungans* or *manbos* to see into the future, to be clairvoyant.

I am told this can occur without dancing; however, *oungans* and *manbos* of lesser rank most often interpret and divine when they are "mounted" by their *lwas*. Particularly through the arrival of Legba, Vodouists believe that the keys to the universe and destiny are available and that he assists the Supreme Being, Bondye, in setting and sealing the destinies of each worshiper. Also, *oungans* and *manbos* can divine for ritual and nonritual members as they stare into a stream of water or at a candle, when they read cards or tea leaves, or as they examine the palms of clients' hands.[9]

Another philosophical force in Haiti is found within stories that outline relationships among the *lwas* and also in folk literature: tales, proverbs, and riddles. These set the moral tone of the community and teach lessons of good and evil, life and death. Folk characters foster the attributes of the good-natured, generous, and hospitable ordinary peasant, called *Bouki* or those of the trickster and manipulator, called *Ti malice* (see Courlander 1973).

Human and suprahuman actions in both the Cuban Yoruba and Bahian Candomblé are mainly interpreted through the divining system, Ifa, after the practice in Yorubaland (Bascom 1951, 1969 [1991], 1980; Verger 1957; Bastide 1978; Abimbola 1975, 1977; Drewal 1994). Priestesses and priests/leaders/healers (*iyalorichas* and *babalorichas* or *santeras* and *santeros* in Cuba, and *iyalorixás* and *babalorixás* or *mães* and *pais de santo* in Bahia) can divine through coconut shells and cowries (*dilogun,* divination with sixteen cowries). The priestly role of *babalawo,* trained and reliable diviner, exists in Cuba quite regularly but is rare in Bahia. On the other hand, the role of *ogan,* an assistant to the "masters" (who organize the ritual slaughter of animals and are often financially responsible for the *terreiro*) is more prominent in Bahia than in Cuba. The lead drummers are called *olubatá* in Cuba and *alebê* in Bahia.

In all three sites, official functionaries of divination interpret events and actions through the rules and lessons learned in creation stories and the life stories of the divinities—that is, how the spiritual and material worlds were created and how their inhabitants function. These understandings are spelled out in religious ideology through parables (folktales in Haiti, *patakines* in Cuba, *histórias de odus* or *orikis* in Bahia) and memorized philosophical texts (*odus* in Cuba and Bahia) and have been celebrated and preserved across generations to the present (see William Bascom's major volumes 1969 [1991] for Ifa in Nigeria and 1980 for divination in the Americas; also Drewal et al. 1989).

In Haitian Vodou, Cuban Yoruba, and Bahian Candomblé, the pyramid of hierarchy exists (with a Supreme Being and divinities at the top, a priestly cast of leaders and initiated elders in the middle, and younger initiates and other humans, animals, and plants at the bottom), but it is overshadowed by other perceptions that influence structure. Rather, individual worshipers augment their understanding of religious belief through devotional practice and, as they accumulate ritual knowledge, become involved in an ever-widening circle of relationships (Laguerre 1974; Daniel 1980). Their ultimate understanding of where they are placed is within a huge, cosmic, spatial organization. Their worldviews enlarge over time with accumulated knowledge and, accordingly, they acquire strategic power and choice.

The believer is first at the center of a circle of informed family and ritual community members, a circle that intersects several planes of existence in the believer's worldview. Religious understanding at this point replicates a dynamic curvilinear set of spiraling circles that gyrate among different planes of existence. In Haiti, ritual practice surrounds the *potomitan* or center-post. As understanding grows, worshipers dance closer to the center and leave former positions that were circling on the periphery. In Cuba, the rectangular space contains a circular display of interacting vibrations. Crowds of dancers and singers, all trying to face the drums and drummers, create semicircular rows of performers that connect with the semicircular rows of drummers and singers. Overall, it is a circle of dance and music. (Particularly when dancing for Yemayá in Cuba, initiates make the same circle that Haitians do, around an implied center-post.) In Bahia, there is a revered spot at the centermost point of a *terreiro* where initiates circle while dancing.[10] Dancing takes place in a counterclockwise circle with the circling performers encircled by family and community guests or visitors. The ritual community is a site of energetic spirit or life force, called *espri* (or *nam,* "soul") in Haiti, *aché* in Cuba, or *axé* in Bahia.

THE IMPORTANCE OF THE CIRCLE Two-dimensional concentric circles can indicate the interrelationship among three realms of existence, basically shared realms of existence in the three religions I examine, since concentric circles share the same center or core (see figure 6).

The three realms can be expressed also as a three-dimensional sphere, an imagined celestial orange with one plane on the horizontal or the horizontal plane, dividing top and bottom, another on the vertical or sagittal plane, dividing right and left, and the last on the frontal or coronal plane, dividing front and back (see figure 7).

Figure 6

Planes of Existence as
Three Concentric Circles

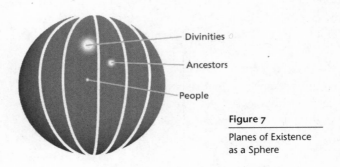

Divinities

Ancestors

People

Figure 7

Planes of Existence
as a Sphere

The circle is not only the two-dimensional, bounded space that visual or plastic arts often present; nor is it only the three-dimensional, bounded perspective just described as a sphere. The circle can be transformed, multiplied in number, and augmented or diminished in space so that we can envision a dynamic, rotating, revolving, three-dimensional spiral, like a tornado in space. As we come to understand the function of the dancing divinities, understanding the circle becomes more important (cf. Balandier 1968; Stuckey 1994).

THE IMPORTANCE OF THE SPIRAL The spiral is a continuous curvilinear line that travels away from or closer to the center and as such is the traveling, circular path between the concentric realms of existence that the divinities and dance performance can access. The spiral cuts through multiple realms within the planes of existence: the horizontal plane of living things—humans, animals, and plants; the sagittal plane of the ancestors, the powerful "living dead"; and the coronal plane of eternal essences—infinite cosmic energy of the *lwas, orichas,* and *orixás* (see figure 8).

The spiraling, circling path of the dancing divinities focuses in ritual performance, eventually permitting access to all three planes of existence. When at least two realms of existence interact, either the ancestral and human realms

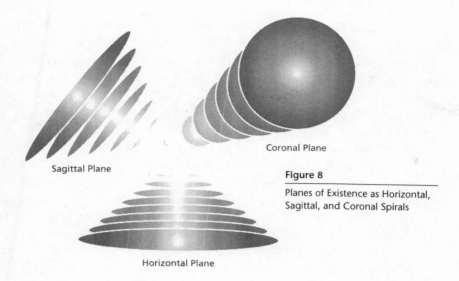

Sagittal Plane

Coronal Plane

Horizontal Plane

Figure 8

Planes of Existence as Horizontal, Sagittal, and Coronal Spirals

or the cosmic and human realms, dancing divinities can emerge. Because of a dancing human body that energizes energy around it, suprahuman entities can make their arrival known. The spiraling path of energies has touched a divinity, one of the guardians of a particular arena of social life, and affects all aspects of personal interest for ritual community members.

As I have come to understand the Haitian experience, the *gwo bonanj* (literally "big good angel" of an individual, i.e., the soul, psyche, or character essence energy) interacts with the *ti bonanj* ("little good angel," meaning conscience, impersonal self-energy). Both parts of the self are generally united in a circular energy path that engulfs each part in alternation and makes for the integrated whole of the individual. Within dance performance at the moment of the arrival of divinity, the *gwo bonanj* separates to create interaction with the divinities, *lwas* (distilled or exceedingly refined *gwo bonanjs*).

Each *lwa* has become a divinity because of dominion, strength, and knowledge (*konesanz*) in particular arenas of social life during her/his lifetime on earth ages ago. These are identified with the attributes of the families and *nasyons* of known *lwas*. At the earthly passing on of revered relatives and wise elders, family members acknowledged the wisdom and power their lives exemplified and enacted rituals that sent particularly knowledgeable, powerful, and distinctive *gwo bonanjs* to rest for a year and a day among the African dead in a place they call "Guinen."

In the cognitive mapping of Vodouists, "Guinen" has been the African continent, a place "on the other side," "under the seas" of the early African captives' world. There also, very select *gwo bonanjs* were "re-Africanized" after earthly death. They were able to return to the living as distilled character essence or *lwas* by means of required rituals. Today, this concept continues so that rituals can retrieve the souls of the living dead, which are placed in a jar or *govi* ("ouete mò nan ba dlo" or "retirer d'en le mort bas de l'eau"). The remembering family or *ounfo* community still enact such rituals.[11]

If we track a path within the Haitian dancing worshiper, spiraling planes emerge also. Circling energy on the horizontal plane within the believer (dividing the body between top and bottom) first connects the *gwo bonanj* (soul energy, life source from Bondye or the Supreme Being, consciousness from which the breath and heartbeat are set in motion) and the *ti bonanj* (conscience, moral being, personality energy). As the circling energy rotates on a spiraling axis, it is able to separate the two, the *ti bonanj* remaining on the horizontal plane and the *gwo bonanj* moving toward either the sagittal plane of the ancestors (dividing the body between right and left sides) or the coronal plane of the *lwas* (dividing the body between front and back).

Human *gwo bonanj* energy converges with and is replaced by distilled *lwa* energy when, as Haitian Vodouists say, "lwa monte chwal" or the "*lwa*/rider mounts his devotee/horse." Two realms of existence are then in simultaneous interaction. For example, the coronal plane of ancient African spirits, the most powerful *lwa nasyons,* connects with the horizontal plane of human energy, and different *lwas* manifest. The spiral encircles both qualities of energy, alternating between them (*debatment,* alternation between *gwo bonanj* and *lwa* energies), which is seen in the first moments of manifestation as the human horse bucks and shakes. The rider or *lwa* energy soars across time and space, ultimately arriving in the present within the dancing human body. Those who are able to serve their communities in this way, by accessing the spiritual realm with regularity, are said to have powerful *nam* or *espri,* strong vital energy or spirit.

In the Yoruba thought of Cuba and Brazil, the dance performances invoke and maintain *aché* or *axé,* the divine energy and vital power within all life (the divine life force). Dance and music performances bring the essence of the *orichas* and *orixás* to the present time and the ritual family in order to give wisdom and advice. The divinities usually emerge by means of prepared and initiated individuals who embody the character of the *orichas,* personify their associated natural elements, and project knowledge concerning a specialized arena of social life.

The divinities culminate within the widest band on the coronal plane, in my terms, and are understood, on one level, as many identified aspects of an ultimate supreme reality that encompasses the totality of the universe, the Supreme Divinity (Olofi), the source of *aché* or *axé*. The dancing divinities, as segmented but powerful *aché* or *axé*, speak through the baptized, initiated, and prepared bodies of worshipers, who also have *aché* or *axé*. When this happens, two planes of existence interact simultaneously, the coronal or cosmic plane and the horizontal plane of human existence, which is similar to the Haitian case. At the time of connection, the circling and spiraling energy is at its narrowest and most focused point, and the manifestation of *oricha* or *orixá* results. As Cuban and Bahian Yoruba thought that is projected three-dimensionally in space, the spiraling *aché/axé* does not allow the circle to close completely. As it shifts on its axis from plane to plane, it widens and narrows but never closes fully before it permeates a new dimension of another plane (see figure 8).

With the spiral as my image for the dance and movement of ritual transformation, I attempt to visually trace the ways in which Vodouists and Cuban Yoruba and Candomblé worshipers understand spiritual energy that they say "mounts," "manifests," or "incorporates" within the dancing human body. The dancing body articulates its own and other energies in space. The energy forces they call *nam, espri, aché,* or *axé* metamorphose within a dance performance to yield wisdom and knowledge that affects all types of social behavior.

Dancing worshipers in the three ritual sites have continued to believe in African philosophies and have relied on dance performance as one dynamic way to synthesize philosophy and direct behavior, truly another type of theoretical knowledge (see Horton 1993; Horton and Finnegan 1973; Mosley 1995). Praise dance produced philosophical paths of integration for human communities and spiritual paths of intersection between the visible and the invisible. The spiral of living dynamic energy, of divine power, has been routinely activated for the moral integrity of the community. As an image of generating and inclusive force, the spiral incorporates the understandings of the spiritual universe for Haitian, Cuban, and Bahian worshipers. These worshipers have looked to the dancing body as an embodiment of philosophy for centuries.

Embodied "Mathematics" of Drum Performance

Another type of knowledge that is found within ritual dance performance is mathematical at its essence in that pitches or tones are sounded as numerical relationships in particular patterns of time. While numerical relationships are not always mathematics, as, for example, not all combinations of words, phrases, and sentences are poetry, some numerical patterns result in lovely musical mathematics. Such are the melodies and rhythms of the drum liturgies of Haitian Vodou, Cuban Yoruba, and Bahian Candomblé. These pitches and rhythmic relationships are caressed and polished numerical relationships, not unlike the beauty of poetry or of a mathematical equation. Most sensitized listeners who hear a battery of three ritual drums play a codified drum service without singing or dancing would find it hard to challenge my meaning when I say, for example, that there is mathematics within Cuban *batá* drum performance. I must say "sensitized," meaning at least briefly introduced to musical regard for drum playing, since the drums are so maligned as "noise" in much of European and Euro-American cultures.

Musicians and musicologists commonly talk about music in mathematical, numerical relationships. They might explain that music is a series of pitches or tones, sounded within a rhythmic structure on a wide and changing continuum of dynamics. They would also place music into a sense of time. They would tell us that a given rhythmic pattern (for example, in duple or triple meter—4/4 or 3/4 time signatures, respectively) predicts tendencies and rules for melodic and harmonic organization. While those who perform music often use numerical designations for relationships between pitches, they rarely discuss the mathematical implications, inferences, and principles within the sound phenomena. For example, ritual drummers rarely discuss the multiple rhythmic relationships within ritual drumming as a display of mathematical principles. Further, ritual drummers do not generally discuss the relationship of those mathematical principles with regard to affect in the human body. What I have heard them discuss and marvel at more often is the effect of their playing on the dancing worshiper. They long for the appearance of a familiar and splendid effect within the dancing body, rather than the dissection of their formulas. Yet Haitian, Cuban, and Bahian ritual drummers rely on implicit, timed relationships within the mathematics of the music they produce; they manipulate mathematical knowledge that they have embodied as music.

Academically trained musicians the world over usually discuss pitches of sound in terms of numerical, intervallic (mathematical) relationships, between a beginning sound and succeeding sounds or a determined tonal center.[12] Fragments of melodies, series of pitches, or short melodic riffs are heard within ritual drumming patterns, but more so, rhythmic relationships are sounded out and result in patterns. These rhythmic patterns can be transposed to mathematics, a series of numerical relationships.

Over time, specific Haitian, Cuban, and Bahian rhythms have become codified due to their sounded rhythmical satisfaction, but also due to the affective or psychosomatic responses they generate. Much of ritual drumming in those locales assumes a progression of emotive patterns as rhythms are sounded, repeated, and intensified. As rhythmic drumming is augmented in terms of speed and intensity, the dancing body is affected. Fon and Yoruba worshipers of the past and worshipers in Haitian, Cuban, and Bahian ritual communities came to understand that with repetition, certain rhythmic patterns in specific sequences were able to produce physical, emotional, and spiritual transformations within the human body. Their repeated sequencing of specific rhythmic patterns corresponded to articulated emotional changes. This drum music steadily initiated and supported a growing intensity within the dancing body, which eventually created other states of consciousness. Over time, musicians appreciated, savored, and exclusively rendered the formulas of power and efficacy in ceremonial repetition. Without verbal articulation, they played out the mathematical underpinnings of music in a codified order within dance/music ceremonies.

Today, master drum musicians understand this type of knowledge as drum traditions and maintain and share with their apprentices the sequenced mathematical rhythms (Fleurant 1996; Garcia 1987, 2000: personal communication; Alfonso 1993: personal communication). In the example of a Haitian ritual in chapter 1, the drummers' eyes canvassed the mass of dancing worshipers constantly, looking for those whose dance behavior needed deeper, fuller, richer support in multiples of multiplying rhythms. In the Cuban Matanzas example, the drummers watched dancing worshipers closely, noting if and when they might shift to a contrasting and/or faster rhythm to assist Oyá's arrival. In Bahia also, the drummers attentively followed each Ogun, after also watching and supporting a long line of *terreiro* community members with distinctive emotive changes and thereby distinctive sets of rhythms.

Master drummers are highly respected within ritual communities by wise leaders, and also by intuitive worshipers. The ritual communities thank them publicly with words of praise and financially with hefty tips within the ceremonies. The community is grateful for the layering of correct, properly timed musical relationships that produce particular states of consciousness and unconsciousness. Master musicians are invited to routinely reproduce particular knowledge through musical sound. In predetermined sequences, musicians display a "buried mathematics" within the dance/music liturgy in order to facilitate human dancing and suprahuman transformation.

In the Haitian context, the musical sound that facilitates transformation is the *kasé* or "break," which disrupts the established pattern of rhythms and is heard above the formulated sequence of chants and songs (Fleurant 1996:34–48). The codified patterns of drum rhythms from the customary three-drum ensemble of Haiti—the *manman,* the *segon,* and the *boula*—are interspersed with *kasés,* as a call to stimulate the dancer and invoke a *lwa.* When there are insistent *kasés,* it is an indication that a drummer has recognized a dancer whose movements have intensified such that the body will "open" within the style of the dance to receive the *lwa* and manifest spirit. When the dancing body is open, the extremities are spread apart and the central core of the trunk is usually extended or exposed in what in dance parlance is called a *feint.* Often the worshipping performer hops on one foot, then arches the back, and exposes the entire body, as in the undulating character of a *yanvalu* dance, or percussively, as in the character of a *mayí* dance. The incessant *kasés* "summon the *lwa* . . . break the dancer's concentration and propel him or her to a new plane" (Fleurant 1996:39).

In the Cuban and Brazilian contexts, the drummers support and attempt to initiate transformations. The *iya* (the mother or lead drum), *okónkolo,* and *itótole* in Cuba and the *rum, rumpi,* and *le* in Bahia, again three drums, are employed in ritual practice of the codified musico-mathematical series in a parallel form and with a parallel function.

Master drummers revere the established patterns and their efficacy. They are often hard-pressed to join current popular performance styles that imitate but do not replicate the traditional patterns. Some popular bands use the sacred rhythms, and the results are enticing to lay audiences. Examples include Síntesis from Cuba, Santísimo in the United States, and Olodúm from Bahia. At times—in tourist settings, for example—Haitian ritual drummers condense the intermeshing of the three-drum ritual patterns into a semblance of their resultant rhythms (e.g., Fleurant 1996:45–46). A complex standard of mathematical relationships from three-drum synchrony is imitated through similar but other rhythmic patterns. No *lwas* appear because the proper formula of rhythms is not played; those that are played do not have a similar or sufficient effect for spirit arrival, or the drums and/or performers themselves are not prepared for such transformation (Fleurant 1996:39).

In Cuba and Bahia, the mathematical relationship between sounded drumheads is crucial, although not expressed or discussed in numerical terms. What are important to drummers are the intervallic relationships of the drumhead pitches, so that affect can be effectively produced. For example, in Cuban *batá* or the two-headed (hourglass-shaped) drum battery,

> each individual performance differs in terms of absolute pitch range according to where individual drums sound best, how the drums sound in relationship to each other, and problems relating to skin heads reacting to changes in humidity. Although there is no ideal pitch that each skin should be tuned to, there is an ideal pitch relationship within the ensemble. The *enu* [mouth or large drumhead] of the *okonkolo* should be identical in pitch with the *chacha* [butt or small drumhead] of the *itotole*. Likewise, the *enu* of the *itotole* should be identical with the *chacha* of the *iya*. (Amira and Cornelius 1992:17)

The investigations of Cuban ethnologist Fernando Ortiz also featured the understandings of Cuban *batá* musicians in the 1940s and 1950s. What they understood about how the drums should be played in order to display proper musical rhythm and to stimulate affect is captured in their intricate explanations:

> When in 1937 we took the *bata* to a public concert for the first time in Havana, the Maestro Gilberto Valdez handed us the following data, which we inserted into our conference [paper]. "Even though it may appear incredible, the *bata* drums are tuned by the note la [the sixth], as with any musical instrument. This note, la, from the 4th octave on the piano, is carried on the small membrane of the *iya* drum. Then the [bass] grave or large skin of the *iya* is tuned until the 2nd fa of the piano is found. Once the *iya* drum is tuned, the *itotole,* or medium drum, is then tuned by taking each skin a half tone higher than those of the *iya*. The large skin of the *itotole* will then be in the 3rd octave, which is one seventh above the fa of the large one of the *iya,* while the acute or small one will be at sol, sustained in the same octave, thus forming a third major [sic] between the one and the other note at a distance and at the same time, a diminished ninth from the superior skin of the *iya*. Then, based on the now tuned *itotole,* the tuning of the *okonkolo* is done, with the same note carried on both skins, the natural si of the 3rd octave, at one fifth higher than the large skin of the *itotole*." We must add that according to Valdes the *okonkolo* and the *itotole* form a perfect harmony of major mi, and this constant pluritonality exists always in the *bata* drums.

... The investigations recently realized under the direction of *Maest[r]o* Gaspar Aguero ... have given us other experiences that we are going to relate. As a whole, the *bata* give eight tonalities, or seven notes, some repeated on different membranes, and only one *ruido* [sound].

... According to what the *Maestros* Gaspar Aguero and Argeliers Leon advised us, said notes of these *bata* form a harmony of diminished fifth, first inversion with the third strengthened [double, tripled]. (Ortiz 1950:374–75, translation by Turpin and Martinez 1980)

Attention is also given to other aspects of pitch in these drums: "The *iyá* should have a ring of clay called *ida* or *fardela* molded onto the *enu* head. The *ida* works to darken the drum's timbre by dampening overtones and lowering the pitch" (Amira and Cornelius 1992:18).

Worshipping performers dance to the rhythms, to the codified mathematical relationships of sound, because they induce transcendence, transformation, and spiritual performance. Emotional responses have been associated with particular pitches, intervals, and chords from all over the world (e.g., within Indian *ragas*; within analyses of key signatures in the music of European, Euro-American, and African American composers; cf. Gutheil et al. 1952; Meyer 1956; Robinson 1997). Particular tones, in their analysis, have demonstrated a tendency toward or range of certain emotional responses. Today, European and American psychologists agree that music, single tones and pitches in vast combinations, is capable of shifting or swinging moods in individuals (Jordan and Allen 1993; Chua 1999).

In African-derived cultures across the Diaspora, this has been an assumption for centuries (Nketia 1962; Chernoff 1979; DjeDje 1999). In Haitian Vodou, Cuban Yoruba, and Bahian Candomblé, distinct rhythms have been associated over time with the emotional characters of particular divinities and are played in both an accelerating and differentiated series (Fleurant 1996; Ortiz 1951 [1985]; Behague 1994). Divinities can come to the dancing community at different times within the codified rhythmic sequences. Whenever they start to appear within the dancing bodies of worshipers, they are supported with additional effort, dynamics, and multiplying rhythms. The same rhythm that is being played is played faster; drummers proceed to the next rhythm of the given sequence; or the divinity's special prayer chant is sung over one of the fastest rhythms (see chart 12 in chapter 8).

After hearing an entire musical order from one of the three religions, a sensitized listener can point to a formidable corpus of musical knowledge. I contend that this music is predicated also on a corpus of mathematical knowledge. The knowledge of music and mathematics is linked in ritual performance, and that musico-mathematical knowledge has been maintained over centuries within the human body—mostly in the minds of particularly skilled musicians but also in the bodies of dancing worshipers. The knowledge of music and its underlying mathematical implications demonstrates nonverbal, symbolic knowledge (music) that embodies still another type of symbolic knowledge (mathematics). The transposition of theoretical mathematical knowledge to aesthetic knowledge, as well as the transposition of artistic understanding to ritual performance, occurs within the body in regular, repetitive ceremonial practice. It is self-conscious to the extent that master musicians guide apprentices toward intervallic and rhythmic perfection in order to achieve efficacious spiritual performance.

Embodiment

Within the five hundred years of enslavement, colonization, and postcolonial dominion of the Americas, there have been periods when the drums were outlawed and ritual paraphernalia were destroyed. For example, this was the case in Haiti due to the *Codes noires* of the seventeenth century (Métraux 1972 [1959]:31–35, 177–78). In Cuba during the eighteenth and nineteenth centuries, some of the enslaved communities were permitted to dance and drum, but only during daylight hours and with white supervision (Knight 1970:127–29). Just after the triumph of the Revolution in 1959 and up until 1984, the Cuban government resumed consistent control over African religious ceremonies. Religious gatherings were outlawed, and the playing of drums at a limited number of ceremonies was controlled by the police (Moore 1988:99–101, 300–305). In Bahia, the police had a history of raiding Candomblé *terreiros* throughout the nineteenth century (Harding 2000:132–39). Prejudice and repression were rampant against African-derived religious practice, but the ritual systems continued in each of these three sites.

The dancing and music-making body held forth, reenunciating Fon, Yoruba, and Kongo perspectives and displaying African American embodied responses. When the drums were outlawed, for example, Cubans used body percussion, tools, implements, and furniture to sound out rhythms; they remembered. During most of the past five hundred years, "disembodied knowledge" has reigned over the Americas. As the social paradigm for "true" intelligence, esteemed knowledge, and/or outstanding critical thinking, it often marginalized musical knowledge, especially drumming.

Also, during this long period, there were times and spaces in Haitian, Cuban, and Bahian ritual communities where dancing and drum playing were encouraged. These were times when cultural distinctions were flaunted as well as shared, as in the legendary Bois Caymon beginnings of Haitian Vodou, and in the *Dia de los reyes* celebrations of sixteenth- to eighteenth-century Cuba, and more recently in *Carnaval* parading of twentieth-century Bahia. Throughout the same five hundred years, embodied knowledge has been practiced, referenced, and expressed in historical ritual, praise performances. In praise performance, the knowledge of the dancing worshiper has played a significant role in both displaying embodied knowledge and resisting disembodied knowledge. There, the dancing worshiper has reinforced memory and cultural continuity within ceremonial repetition amid rhythmic, musical, and body movement display. There, the dancing worshiper has encouraged interchange, interaction, integration, and interdisciplinary reconciliation over time and across the Diaspora.

Many Africans in the Americas and their descendents did not entirely forget their multiple African heritages. They resisted mainstream education and miseducation by means of distinctive forms of dance, drumming, and singing, which alluded to and reinforced characteristic interests, propensities, and values from their African heritages. Where and when specific chants and songs, particular sets of rhythms, and distinct, repeatable gestures were maintained, distinctive cultural traditions were possible. Dancing worshipers replayed specialized muscular movement, motor behavior over and over, as "muscle memory" in sacred dance/music ceremonies, as well as in other nonritual dance/music events. They retained cultural knowledge as heritage and legacy by means of oral history, storytelling, folk-medicine practices, proverbs, naming patterns, food traditions, body decorations, basketry, carvings, weavings, and fabrics. They repeated ritual dance performances that referenced and maintained beliefs, attitudes, and ideas about a sense of family, treatment of the dead, and belief in their ability to have an impact on supernatural forces. Their muscle memory and cultural heritage, truly their deep culture, sustained an ongoing belief in the spiritual and galactic consequences of rhythmic and dynamic intensity, especially within the dancing body (Graham 1991; Chipaumire 2000).[13]

The total wisdom within African American chanting, drumming, and dancing can be viewed as an accumulation and transposition of many kinds of knowledge. African-derived performance is easily a transposing of philosophy, religion, or belief, as well as natural, technological, and social sciences into the aesthetic and artistic arena of primarily nonverbal, communicative forms. Embodied botany is revealed in an open state within the sacred chant texts that survived in the minds and healed the bodies of African and African American performers. Embodied physiology is revealed in the associations of divinities with particular parts of the human body, and embodied psychology emerges from within a history of skilled and effective performance. Embodied philosophy is read within the performance behaviors of worshipers and reveals cultural understanding of a suprahuman and interactive world within ritual performance. Embodied mathematical knowledge is buried and assumed within codified drum orchestrations. Dance performances of Haitian Vodou, Cuban Yoruba, and Bahian Candomblé are more than music and dance; in these religions, more than singing, drumming, and dancing are present. Praise performance practices have guarded embodied knowledges for centuries.

THREE

Days of Remembrance

for it is well established that if a memory is
great enough, other memories will cluster about it, and
those in turn will bring their suites of memories to gather
about this focal point, because perhaps, they are all
scattered parts of the one thing.

—Zora Neale Hurston

"Daughter, go and tell it! Direct yourself to the highest of the high, to the bottom of the ocean and the center of the earth, to each corner of the world. Let the path be clear! Open the sacred dialogue where the three roads come together. Start here with what is accessible and make this understandable through what is known on the other side of the gate."

Liturgical orders that have persisted over centuries mark the respect and acknowledgment of a community. African American liturgical orders have continued as recognized dance and music structures. Whether in Haitian Vodou, Cuban Yoruba, or Bahian Candomblé, the first step in the liturgical order is at the crossroad, at the gate between the human world and the spiritual world, between the known and the unknown, between the visible and the invisible.

Elegba, Exu, Papa Legba: The First Guards at the Entrance

"I stand at the door in red and black, watching and scrutinizing all who pass by. I guard each roadway in each direction. I facilitate messages, prayers, understandings, wants and desires on their route to the divinities and the Divine. I protect the divinities as well as you, in measuring how much and what sort of dialogue goes in any direction. My power is so great that wearing my colored beads openly in Bahia can be dangerous; people get so anxious. I am so necessary that my red and black beads are the first received in Cuba. I hold the cowry shells of each practitioner. I speak directly with Orúnmila and Ifá. My attributes and offerings affect the opening of doors and the closing of chapters, the ending of relationships and the beginning of transitions. My energy, my espri or my nam, my aché or my axé, is strong, universally needed, and generative; it provides chance and opportunity.

"Over time I have looked at these African Americans and wondered why some of them reject the physical appearance of their bodies—their dark and darker skin, their curly and nappy hair, their ample hips and wide spread noses. Why is the body hated so?

"The church goers—Baptists, African Methodist Episcopalians (AME), Pentecostals, and Catholics too—often find fault with the dancing body of any color, in its visual and spiritual power. The body for them is "the flesh" and "sinful." It is opposed to 'goodness.' For some, the black body and the dancing body of any hue, while normal on the one hand, are negative, problematic, and sources of trouble, shame, or embarrassment.

"I, Elegba, Vital Force, Owner of Vital Force, Vital Force who appears far and wide, take all who come to me and show them both sides of the coin and its singular source in the body. I walk with them on the red side and confound them when they see only the black of my other side. Perhaps you and they will be more empathetic and open-minded, with clear vision from all sides. Perhaps you and they will accept the apparent and seeming contradictions—of the body, of life, and of relationships."

"Okay, Elegba, I begin as you say with one view and then another: a nation view of religious organizations and a historical view of praise performances. In order to fully grasp African ritual liturgies in their contemporary African American communities, I focus first in this chapter on the development of African American religious systems and their references to specific African contexts. In the next chapter, I examine the wealth of dance and music materials that became pertinent. In the process, I must contend with the history of two huge geographical regions (the African continent and the Americas) and three histories of sacred ritual performance. I am concerned with both the days of remembrance and the dances of memory that forged three liturgical practices and that featured dance and music performance so prominently."

"Good. Now your path is clear."

Nation Religions in the Diaspora

African history reminds American historians that the mixing and blending, or creolization, of European and African cultures in the Americas was not the first fusion or syncretism of African religions. At the time of contact with Europeans, trading, marriage, slaving (primarily from prisoners of war and violators of social laws), diplomacy, expansionism, population pressures, and the like within West and West Central Africa had resulted in the fusion of neighboring and local as well as distant religious practices. Likewise, Africans in the Americas wedded the ideals of Fon, Adja, Ewe, Efik, Ejagham, Popo, and so on to those of Yoruba derivation, such as the Iyeshas, Ketus, Sabes, Oyos, Abeokutas, Anagos, Ijebu, and Egbas, as well as to many differing Congo basin cultures, such as Kongo, Lemba, Teke, Suku, and Yaka. Hundreds of African cultures were thrust through an American cultural sieve. Ethnic groups from what are now called Senegal, Guinea, Sierra Leone, Liberia, Côte d'Ivoire, Ghana, Togo, Benin, and Nigeria, as well as from what are now Cameroon, Gabon, Republic of the Congo, Democratic Republic of Congo, and Angola were affected (Herskovits 1938:22–32; Tempels 1959; Brandon 1993; MacGaffey 1986; Inikori and Engerman 1992; Thornton 1998; de Souza 2000; Joseph Harris 2001). Ethnic groups from many regions were impacted as people were stolen from their homelands along a zone of fear and greed in West and Central sub-Saharan Africa that stretched for thousands of miles, first at the coasts, then spreading hundreds of miles inland.

The most notable and important ethnic and regional groupings for this study are the Fon, the Yoruba, and the Kongo-Angola, who continued to blend both beliefs and practices in the Americas (Thompson 1983:163–67; Yai 2001:244–55). The dance performance data that I present here suggest that these three ethnic amalgams solidified in the Americas and were distinguished as nation groups and nation identities. None of these ethnic groupings are "pure." Each was reconfigured in the Americas and was a susceptible cultural structure to both continuity and change. For example, anthropologist J. Lorand Matory shows how the Cuban and Bahian Yoruba grouping emerged as

"Yoruba" only after the American enslavement period and due to changes on the continent (2001b:171–214). He cites the different Yoruba ethnic groups who were in close proximity and points out a traveling Yoruba elite (e.g., seamen, tradesmen and businessmen, missionaries) that initiated a kind of nationhood and superiority that did not exist previously in the territories of the Bight of Benin (see also Brandon 1993:20–21, 30, 56; Matory 1999:72–103). By extension, in Cuba and Bahia particularly, the Yoruba became a recognized social group and represented the cluster of related Yoruba speakers. Similarly, many ethnic groupings within what are now Benin and Nigeria were enjoined in the Rada rites of Haitian Vodou, including Fon, Ewe, Mahí, Ibo, and Nago.

I want to emphasize the Kongo peoples, in order to extend my discussion of African nations in the Americas, and discuss their relationship to the Fon and the Yoruba. The name "Kongo" came to represent several ethnic groups from West Central Africa, the Kongo-Angola region, in that they represented not only the history of the great Kongo Kingdom but also the many peoples who were captured and who left via the Congo River. The names of those peoples from the current geopolitical Congos and the state of Angola have been given to this tremendously large territory and to the major cultural influence from West Central Africa in the Americas over centuries. Demographers find that over time, the highest numbers of enslaved populations to enter the Americas were from the nations of West Central Africa, what I refer to in music/dance performance as the Kongo-Angola nation (see Curtin 1969; Eltis and Richardson 1997). Their influence on African American religious behavior is fundamental to what I have discussed so far in terms of the Fon and Yoruba: Kongo-Angolans replicated their cultural beliefs and practices in the three sites of this study within a similar intra-African syncretism.

> Mariwo yeyeye! Mariwo Yeye Ogún ala wede;
> Mariwo yeyeye! Mariwo Yeye Ogún ala wede;
> Eni mowoniwo eni mowoniwo Ogún ala wede.

My, my! This is to my advantage in explaining histories and days of remembrance. Ogún has arrived; apparently, he has more to say about his history. After all, he was there in all three places. He has seen it all unfold:

"Nasyon yo te vinn melanje pou fè twa patie tout twa te bay twa groupman; los grupos africanos se mezclaron en una olla americana; os africanos se juntaron nas Américas. African nations became amalgams in each place you are talking about—Haiti, Cuba, and Bahia!! They had to communicate with each other; they

had to interrelate; and then they had to reconcile their differences. They expressed their differences in terms of African nations. In the process, three rites or three divisions were born. In Haiti, the Fon and Yoruba nations claimed the 'Rada' or 'Arada' rites; the Kongo nation claimed their Congo rites; and heavy mixtures of Kongo, Fon, and Yoruba nations were responsible for the Petwo rites—all within Vodou.

"In Cuba, Fon and Yoruba nations continued in 'Arará' rites and two varied, but related Yoruba rites: Iyesa and Yoruba. And the Kongo-Angola nations represented their cultures in 'Palo' rites.

"In Brazil, the pattern was more like Haiti: the Fon nations became 'Jêje'; and the 'Ketu' or 'Nago/Ketu' nations secured the Yoruba rites; the Kongo-Angola nations became 'Angola.' In Brazil, all of these—Jêje, Nago/Ketu, and Angola—were 'Candomblé.' I have drawn you charts."

"Isn't that interesting, Ogún, how in Haiti all nations took an overarching name with separated 'rites,' but in Cuba, the divisions remained distinct and, with one additional religious orientation, Carabalí (Abakuá or Ñañigo). In Cuba these have been regarded as relatively separate religious orientations. I think this was because on the island of Cuba, the *cabildo* organizations, the

Chart 2. Selected African Nations in the Americas

	Haiti	Cuba	Bahia
Fon	(A)Rada	Arará Vodú	Jêje
Yoruba	Nago	Yoruba Iyesa	Nago/Ketu
Kongo-Angola	Congo	Kongo Angola Bantu	Angola
Combined	Petwo		
Other Nations	Mahí Ibo Gédé	Carabalí	

Chart 3. Selected African American Religions

Haiti:	Vodou (Rada, Congo, Petwo)
Cuba:	Arará, Vodú, Yoruba, Palo, Abakuá
Bahia:	Candomblé (Jêje, Nago/Ketu, Angola)

guildlike associations of the Catholic Church, held enslaved peoples together specifically as regional and nation groups. This was similar to the Bahian case in which enslaved Africans were divided into *irmandades* or brotherhoods and sisterhoods (Reis 1977:7–33). These were lay organizations, certainly still attached to the Catholic Church, but organized by nations that offered mutual aid to members; in fact they differentiated among African and Creole groups as well. They used an umbrella term for all of their amalgams, 'Candomblé'—which was Kongo-Angola in origin, doing exactly as the Haitians did for a different population base (Fon) to acknowledge the earliest African ethnic groups."[1]

"*Yes, when they came to the Americas, Africans called the religion by different names. The Fon-derived beliefs, Rada (or Arada), Arará, and Jêje are related to Allada and the Fon Kingdoms from Gangnihessou in the late sixteenth century to Agoliagbo at the turn of the twentieth century. These were also known as the Kingdom of Dahomey. Today, this cultural center is found in the city of Abomey, Benin. Haiti received many ethnic groups from this region before its Revolution, since these were the main groups to be enslaved from the sixteenth to the eighteenth centuries. The Fon predomination up through the eighteenth century in Haiti is recognized by the usage of the Fon term 'voduns,' which means 'spirits,' for the entire religion. And after the Revolution, Haiti received four thousand Dahomeans into the police force during the reign of President Henri Christophe*" (Matory 1999:73; Métraux 1972 [1959]:360).

"*Yoruba belief from Nigeria and Benin became Nago nasyon in Haiti, and Yoruba, Lucumí, or Santería in Cuba. In Brazil, it is nação Nago, Ketu, or Nago/Ketu. These names call forth many related Yoruba nations, the 'Lucumís'[2] or 'neighbors,' who were bound together later by the glory of Yoruba cities, like Ile Ife, Oyo, and Ilesha.*

"*Also, the Kongo-Angola religions of Central Africa became Congo, Petwo, Petwo-Lemba, or Mundungo in Haiti; Kongo, Bantu, Palo, or Palo Monte in Cuba; and Angola in Brazil.*"

"Yes, Ogún, African Americans wedded African religious amalgams to the resources and conditions of a new environment. In the adjustments and reconciliation, African belief systems continued in the Americas in similar ways to each other, yet as distinct forms."[3]

"*The knowledge of tens of thousands of wise women and wise men was not lost. Even when several belief systems challenged one another, the wisdom continued*" (see Herskovits 1941:295–98; cf. Matory 1999).

"One belief that explains how adjustments were made and how mixtures resulted on the African continent, and could be easily projected in the Americas, is found in a similar story that I mentioned before. In this version, the Fon divinity for iron, Gu, married a Yoruba woman. At the time of the wedding, the story says that she brought her *orişas,* her divinities, to join his *voduns* (Abomey 2001: personal communication). The joining of practices to adore and maintain both *orişas* and *voduns* reveals the reliance and borrowings within both religious systems."

"You can believe that Yoruba influence on Haitian Vodou is plenty! In Vodou, I am Ogou Feray or Ogou Badagri—very, very important lwas. The Ogou fanmi of Haiti has the Yoruba divinity of iron and war, because you see, Ogou Badagri gets his name from Badagri, a town in Yorubaland."

"I know that Ogou in Haiti cannot simply reflect the Yoruba Ogún but must also echo the Fon divinity for iron, Gu. Ogou in Haiti is another result of recurrent Yoruba/Fon contact, both in Africa and the Americas (see Barnes 1989). That contact resulted in specific dances and musical rhythms called by the Fon name, *voduns,* within Vodou's religious practice."

"Yes. African history is very long and complex, and complicated by Europeans and slavery. Here you need to talk about Kongo-Angola cultures specifically."

"Thank you Ogún. Kongo-Angola influence was immense in the Americas. Several scholars have shown how pervasive Kongo-Angola influence has been, basing their studies on their numerical significance in the slave trade over most of the fifteenth to nineteenth centuries" (MacGaffey 1991, 2000; Thompson and Cornet 1981; Heusch 2000; Janzen and MacGaffey 1974; Biebuyck 1973; Thompson 1983; cf. Crowell 2002:11–20).

"Kongo-Angola nations were so important that they gave Central African names to West African religions. Look, Candomblé is a Bantu name for a Yoruba religion. You see Kongo-Angola influence in other Yoruba culture, like dende from the Bantu, 'ndende,' for the red oil from the oil palm tree (Elais guineensis in Jessica Harris 2001:171) and kizila (another Bantu-derived word for food taboos within the Yoruba religion). Like you say, this is a result of their early arrival and significant numbers during the Afro-Atlantic crossing. In the end, the story of African American religions is dependent on three big nations: Kongo-Angola, Fon, and Yoruba nations."

"These examples point out continuous influence and ultimately syncretism among these African nation groups in the Americas (see Walker 1980:32–36; Daniel 1995:36–37), but they also remind me that we haven't addressed the more familiar example of syncretism, between Roman Catholic practices and African beliefs, which is customarily used to explain African American religions. For a time, many were satisfied with an explanation for African religious continuity in the Americas with the 'umbrella' relationship of the Roman Catholic Church to the African religions 'beneath.' Anthropologist Melville Herskovits was working on African connections in the Americas before much field research was completed in Africa, and which was then still under colonial rule. He wisely promoted research in the early decades of the twentieth century about African continuities and syncretism in the Americas (1975 [1937], 1941). At that time, investigators understood African divinities, called *lwas* and *orichas/orixás* by practitioners, as 'saints' under the guise of Catholicism.[4]

"Of course in Cuba, the Yoruba religion is called 'Santería' for that exact connection between the saints of Roman Catholicism and the *orichas* of the Yoruba faith (Gonzalez-Wippler 1973; Murphy 1988; Canizares 1999). Also in Bahia,[5] worshipers are called 'daughters and sons of the saints,' *filhas/os de santo.* Over time, however, specific ritual procedures, beyond concepts of the saints, connected African and Catholic practices and made the Catholic Church necessary for proper African American religious practice. First, baptism in the Catholic Church is usually a prerequisite for the initiates of Haiti and Cuba, and often, Catholic priests have comfortable relations with *oungans, manbos,* and *santeros,* respectively.[6]

"And now there are sections of the ritual that demand Catholic contact. For example, the Haitian *pre savann* or 'bush priest' regularly recites Catholic prayers within many Vodou ceremonies. And in Yoruba practice of Cuba and Bahia, worshipers must go to Catholic Mass at intervals and have the Catholic priests bless saint statues that for them represent the *orichas* and *orixás*.

"Historically and perhaps unwittingly, the Catholic Church has helped the African American religions. I have witnessed practical examples of contact and integration of Catholicism and Vodou in Port-au-Prince and also Sucrie Danash in 1991. I filmed Haitian Vodou ceremonies in which Catholic prayers were recited as a specific part of a public Vodou ceremony (see also Deren 1953; Desmangles 1992; Fleurant 1996). And in Cuba in 1987, I was instructed several times to go to Mass and to dedicate a Mass for one of my ancestors in order to complete segments of my ritual obligations. In Cachoeira, an old city of Bahia, I witnessed Candomblé participants in procession to the Catholic Church, where the worshipers were met outside on the steps of the church by the priest and where all were welcomed to celebrate Mass.

"Sometimes priests caution worshipers about bringing the *orixás* inside the church because, as it has also been fictionalized in movies and books, some worshipers manifest divinities within the Catholic service" (e.g., Jorge

Amado's *Dona Flor and Her Two Husbands,* 1975, and Geovanni Brewer's video, *Bahia: Africa in the Americas,* 1988).

"Hmmm, even if the Catholic Church is found in the practice of Vodou, Cuban Yoruba, and Bahian Candomblé, it does NOT have the strong or central role that your terms 'Santería' or 'syncretism' suggest. Many wise and knowledgeable leaders reject all Catholic additions to the rituals, for example, in Bahia's Axé Opô Afonjá and in your country, Oyotunji Village in South Carolina. These communities concentrate on the requirements of traditional Africa. While some of their practices are parallel to some Catholic rites, African religions are based in divination rites, stones, and spirit-raising dancing and, therefore, are not compatible with Catholic practice" (de Azevedo Santos 1982; Adefunmi 1982; Métraux 1972 [1959]:323–58; Edwards and Mason 1986:iii–vi, 1–7; Murphy 1988:26–36; Bastide 1978:109–25; Desmangles 1992; de Santana Rodrigué 2000: personal communication).

"I agree, Ogún. The Saint/Orisha relationship, while it clearly exists as Catholic/African syncretism, is an incomplete analysis. Coercive baptisms in the enslavement period and national politico-religious hegemony reinforced the Catholic presence in colonial times and predicted its influence in postcolonial periods. These conditions in a context of African religious enclaves have resulted in the integration of important Catholic phases and phrases within the African American religions (Brandon 1993:45–55, 74–78; Desmangles 1992:17–59). This is not, however, a syncretism that adheres to a deeper analysis of religious ideas, practices, or spiritual understanding."

"I know my words are harsh, but I am correct. All the terms—Catholic/African syncretism, dissimulation, symbiosis, and intra-African syncretism—are extensions of our African religions over time. You know of our concept of change: it is like the river that runs deep and swiftly between two banks. Water that is near the shore takes things from the banks and carries these for a time, and perhaps even mixes additions into the main flow. The core of the river, however, rarely changes. It continues forcefully and resiliently."

"We talk of this in terms of 'culture,' Ogún. While the practices of Haitian Vodou, Cuban Yoruba, and Bahian Candomblé are distinct, there are also evident dynamic continuities within them. Continuity in Diaspora situations was based in commonalities that revolved around similar perspectives and understandings of the universe; highly structured initiation, divining, and funereal procedures; a richly textured sound, visual, and gesture complex; and a supporting social kinship organization. Today, devotional communities are called *temples des mystères, ounfos du Vodou, casas de Lucumí, casas de Yoruba, casas de Palo, templos de Kongo, terreiros* or *casas de Candomblé, Oricha* or *Ocha houses, casas Africanas,* or simply African religious houses. So far, they are found mainly in the Caribbean and South America, as well as in significant pockets across the United States.

"And the dances of the *lwas, orichas,* and *orixás* illuminate a vigorous social process of endurance and resistance. A formulaic array of sensory elements (sounds, images, smells, tastes, touches, and movements) combine in order to activate communal belief, to access sacred ritual and embodied knowledge, and, as dancers would say, 'to make the body remember what its ancestral soul already knows.' The dance/music performances delineate liturgical orders from Haitian Vodou, Cuban Yoruba, and Bahian Candomblé that are based in performed memory and recognized history. As anthropologist Zora Neale Hurston said in the epigraph at the beginning of this chapter, and as I would have us all remember, they are 'scattered parts of the one thing'" (Hurston 1938:140).

"*You have it now. I am going.*"

"Thank you for your help, Ogún; *Olorún modupé.*"

"*Aché.*"

FOUR

Dances of Memory

Haitians acknowledge this quality of memory more directly.
Whereas we are anxious that our history not be false, their anxiety
centers on the possibility that their history might become lifeless or
be forgotten. Whereas in our eyes truthfulness is the paramount virtue
of any historical account, in theirs what matters most is relevance and
liveliness. We write history books to remember our ancestors, and the
Haitians call on Gédé, the playful trickster who is the spirit of the dead
[to dance]. Mercurial Gédé appears in many forms and speaks
through many voices. His special talent lies in viewing
the facts of life from refreshing new perspectives.

—Karen McCarthy Brown

What I have presented so far serves the ultimate goal of understanding African American religious ritual. My analyses have sketched ritual performances and revealed the basic tendencies of syncretism in terms of belief, both in Africa and in the Americas. In the Fon-based ritual style of Haitian Rada, Cuban Arará, and Brazilian Jêje, the most characteristic performance style is seen in constant shoulder action—circling or thrusting of the shoulders, and in small rhythmic undulations that involve the pelvis and torso. The performers dress in uniform, relatively simple, even ordinary clothing: skirts, pants, blouses, headscarves, and so on. In the Yoruba-based ritual style of Haitian Nago, Cuban Yoruba, and Bahian Nago/Ketu nations of Candomblé, ritual performance style is seen in exaggerated verti-cal undulation of the entire body, sometimes subtle and low and sometimes percussive and fast, with elaborate, extraordinary, and regal costuming. In the Kongo-Angola ritual style of Haitian Congo/Petwo, Cuban Palo, and Ba-hian Angola, the most characteristic movement is seen in forceful, rhythmic jumping or aerial steps, often full stride and running steps beneath constant rhythmic body-part isolation.

For a better understanding of ritual performance style for each of the three religions, I turn now to their historical dance vocabularies. The following sec-tion reviews history from a fresh perspective. It is limited to a discussion of the distinct dance and music materials that were used in the development of what currently comprises African American praise performance. I start with Haitian ritual dance formation because of Haiti's historical importance and influence as the first independent nation south of the United States, the first black republic in the Americas (1804), and the first nation to end slavery in the Americas. Then I survey the diversity of Cuban ritual performance, and, lastly, I comment on the unequal documentation of Bahian praise performance.

Haiti's Nation Dance Mélange

Every time I start to think about Haitian dance history, I am reminded of its intimate connection to political history (e.g., Laguerre 1974, 1989; Trouillot 1990, 1995; Dayan 1995). After repeated European contact in the last decade of the fifteenth century, most of Haiti's original inhabitants were decimated early in the sixteenth century. Colonialists observed and documented their contact with native peoples—mainly Taino, Arawak, and Carib—primarily in the hope of finding the sources of their gold ornaments and body decoration. Within a few years, however, native ethnic groups were exploited for labor in mining, in building Catholic missions and outposts, and in exploration of the lush tropical terrain of Hispaniola (Santo Domingo) and other neighboring islands. With the defeat of the Spaniards by the French and Spanish expan-sion to mainland territories, what are now Haiti and the Dominican Republic became known as Saint Domingue and was controlled by the French. Interest-ingly, some dance descriptions have survived from the early Spanish contact period, but not specifically for the island of Hispaniola. The dance descriptions appear dispersed within reports to the Spanish Crown, written by Fernandez de Oviedo and other Catholic colonials and missionaries (Las FAR 1971).

Most of Haiti's documented dance history begins during the eighteenth century with the descriptive reports of a Creole from Martinique, Médéric Louis Elie Moreau de St. Méry (1976 [1796]).[1] This early traveler went from Martinique to Saint Domingue, writing a detailed account or ethnography of the activities he observed and experienced as he journeyed. His interest was decidedly piqued by the dance performances he witnessed, and his carefully written details give some of the most reliable descriptions of dance and music in the colonial period. He devoted a major section of his journal to *Danse*.

What Moreau de St. Méry describes is the performance practice of European colonists and both freed and enslaved peoples of African descent within the development of what was becoming Haitian society. From his writings we can conclude that Europeans (Spanish, French, and briefly also the British, depending on who was in control and who frequented the island over time) brought court and folk forms. These were heavily influenced by the opulence of the sixteenth- and seventeenth-century French court (cf. Labat 1724; Emery 1972 [1985]). Even when the dance forms were performed in farmer, merchant, or upper-class style, imitation of court configurations, dress and costume, musical accompaniment, and gestures were apparent as an ideal. Also, Moreau de St. Méry's descriptions show that enslaved peoples continued some of their nation traditions as part of their separate plantation social life and as part of social displays for Europeans. He even reports on the spiritual dances, *le don Pedre* and *vaudoux*, for example, in which the enslaved desperately tried to "fly away," to transcend immediate circumstances, and to escape (see Moreau de St. Méry 1976 [1796]:56–59).[2]

European Dance Practices in Haiti

Moreau de St. Méry describes several European dance forms that both Europeans and Creoles performed (1976 [1796]:37–41). Court forms from the sixteenth and seventeenth centuries that included the *pavane, gaillard, courante, minuet, gigue,* and so forth were performed, as were other European favorites from the eighteenth and nineteenth centuries, such as the *polonaise* and the waltz. Mask dancing was known among the French, Spanish, and English colonists, but the Creoles of the Americas were fonder of dancing than any of the European national groups. Their versions of court forms, as well as less formal folk forms, were part of social events.

European dance practices were performed not only in social settings but also in religious contexts, since it was the Europeans who brought the forceful institution of the Roman Catholic Church to the island. Catholic observances included processions inside the church as well as parading in the streets for the saints of the Church calendar and in honor of the patron saints of townships and religious fraternal orders. Later, *Mardi Gras* or Carnival procession dances were associated with the pre-Lenten season just before Easter. Carnival bands featured African "Kings" and "Queens" or *majordomos* who led the dancing parade, while most colonists were spectators. Similar festive parading was associated with Christmastime and the Three Kings Day, when Europeans gave the parading enslaved population gifts and replaced their annual work clothing. These Christian occasions of merrymaking provided the inclusion of dance and music-making within European Catholic culture.

Moreau de St. Méry also reports that dance events sometimes involved Europeans and Creoles performing the line dance configurations of European dance practice in the style of Africa. Apparently after a minuet that started the evening of dances, the dances were arranged informally with "*Allemandes, Anglaises,* and (interestingly) the *Congo Minuet,*"[3] which followed (Moreau de St. Méry 1976 [1796]:39). (This type of minuet was most probably part of the African stylized *affranchi* that I describe below.) As Moreau de St. Méry's remarks suggest, Europeans brought court dance forms to American social events, and they participated in the Americanization of those forms through a gradually shifting stylization based on European forms, but in addition to the early borrowing of African movement and/or music (cf. Gottschild 1996). Moreau de St. Méry describes the European elite dancing court forms, but also what other researchers later called *affranchis* (Dunham 1983; Honorat 1955; Yarborough 1958).

To trace European heritage, however, I look first at structure and then at style, and *affranchi* dances involved European court patterns and European fashion. Within European spatial configurations, European performers employed upright body orientation and added rhythmic emphases either in music or dance performance style from the African-influenced environment. St. Méry's mention of the Congo minuet, performed by the European elite, implies early African imitation of court dance forms. Equally, however, his descriptions verify European performance of *affranchi* formations.

Dance anthropologist Katherine Dunham also attended to European dance forms in her published master's thesis on Haitian dance (1947). Dunham's research was based on professional fieldwork in Haiti, Jamaica, and

Martinique in 1932–33 (although she continued to visit Haiti regularly until the late 1960s and has commented publicly on those experiences and understandings over the years). She described and categorized many types of Haitian dances (1983:9–11, 57), relying on a range of cultural interpretations by farmworkers, housemaids, bourgeois teachers, and elite diplomats.

Dunham notes that European court forms were practiced throughout the colonial period and influenced Haitian dance practices up through the twentieth century. She describes the main social dance of European origin, the *contredanse* or *carabinien,* as Haitians of the 1930s and 1940s referred to it (1983:46). *Contredanse* was a form that included set dances in two lines, men and women facing one another, with string and wind instruments as musical accompaniment. The later popular set dance was distinctive because of its *quadrille* formation. Four couples danced set configurations, often alternating as two couples.

African *Nasyon* Practices in Haiti

Moreau de St. Méry enjoyed the idiosyncratic style of Africans and Creole Africans in dance performance: "When they resist their unfortunate tendency to imitate, Negroes have charming dances, all their own, coming originally from Africa as they do . . ." (1976 [1796]:50–51).

He describes two African dance forms in particular. One involved partnered performers in a circle dance form, called *calenda.* In his description, both male and female dancers dance in a circle and meticulously turn and circle each other, differentiating the *calenda* from other circle forms (Moreau de St. Méry 1976 [1796]:52–56). He was struck by the rigorous and intricate patterns of the dancing partners. As they danced together, the man moved his arm and elbow to accent his movements, and the woman held her skirt at its edges or waved a handkerchief. The dancers did not touch.[4]

The other dance Moreau de St. Méry describes in detail is called the *chica* with its particular rhythm. Like the *calenda,* it demonstrated a couple form in a circle dance, but it emphasized the female's lower torso movement and the male's bursting advances and quick retreats (cf. Honorat 1955:23–26 and Daniel 1995:64). The *chica* in Haiti was apparently adopted by both white and black Creoles and was performed at balls. Later it was prohibited among whites, but it continued within the African-derived population (Moreau de St. Méry 1976 [1796]:60–73; Honorat 1955:26–27). Thus, we note the importance of reviewing both European and African practices in order to understand either European or African dance formation.

In describing the dance performances of freed and enslaved Africans of the eighteenth century, Moreau de St. Méry also relates that their public dancing of European forms was prohibited; however, a freed African or freed Creole African could publicly dance the European steps s/he had seen and perhaps imitated (1976 [1796]:45–46). These were the *affranchi* dances where African creativity was applied to European music and dance structure. They were improvised and developed most in sectors populated by freed Africans.

Lavinia Yarborough, writing in the 1950s, reported that the "African spice" that was added to European court dance designs was overt hip move- ment (1958:26–27; 1970: personal communication). Haitians taught her during her forty years of residence that *affranchi* movements were less restrained in African contexts and allowed more abandon within the same European floor patterns and spatial figures. Her investigations show that *affranchi* variation and development were often added as an ending section to a structured Euro- pean dance form. Also the drums replaced the strings and wind instruments or were added to the musical ensemble when in African settings. The dances were varied and creative (Emery 1972 [1985]:98–101; cf. Gerstin for Martinican *bélé* 1998; Olivera Chirimini for Uruguayan *candombe* 2001:256–74).

As they appear in descriptions and performances through the twentieth century, *affranchi* dances also suggest vestiges of African royalty within the assumed European configurations and upright body orientation of perform- ers. Looking through a Diaspora lens, a student of dance can easily imagine enslaved Africans borrowing occasions of elite parading and bowing gestures to reference their own historical kings and queens or other esteemed person- ages who also required formal processions and bows in music and dance. *Affranchi* dances that I witnessed in the 1970s in Haiti (and in similar forms such as Cuban *tumba francesa* in the 1980s and in *bélé* forms on Martinique and Trinidad in the 1990s) included lines or couples of African-derived men and women in elegant long or short dresses and long-sleeved, open-neck shirts and pants. They performed intricate floor designs and processional patterns, usually with a gliding or very short walking step throughout. Inevitably one man with at least two women would dance virtuoso foot patterns while turn- ing his female partners on either side of him or while passing the women alternately in front of him and from side to side. Often this solo male waved handkerchiefs or scarves in both his hands above his head, while the females complemented his bravado with demure and supportive rhythmic motion. A woman was often introduced in addition, as the leader/Queen of the en- semble in other related activities beyond the dance, in the parading prior to performance or in the festive feasting after dance performance, for example. These significant variations to the set configurations of couples or lines of Diaspora dancers help to document a history of two-way influence among Europeans and Africans in the Americas.

Moreau de St. Méry states, "The African peoples . . . are sensitive to this pleasure [dancing] with the same intensity they show for food and for life itself . . . a love so strong that though exhausted by work they find the strength to dance, and even to walk several miles to and from the place of this delight" (1976 [1796]:51–52).

Like many other Europeans, Moreau de St. Méry still saw the dances of enslaved Africans as wild, exotic episodes of frenzy or unacceptable and alarming sexuality. He spells out what many Europeans of the period thought as they watched exciting displays of physical virtuosity, playful sensuality, and powerful spirituality.

Away from watchful colonial eyes, Africans danced the dances of their homeland allegiances, their nations. They danced to generate a spiritual connection with their African ancestors and to experience moments of physical and emotional freedom, even though short-lived. The dances within their Vodou ceremonies, which developed clandestinely, were organized around and demonstrated an array of African nations (mainly (A)Rada, Nago, Mahí, Ibo, Congo, Petwo, and Gédé *nasyons*)[5] (Herskovits 1975 [1937]; Métraux 1972 [1959]; Deren 1983 [1953]:83–84; Courlander 1973:317–31; Laguerre 1980; Desmangles 1992:15, 36, 94–95; Murphy 1994:15–16; Burroughs 1995:5).

At the celebration of two hundred years of Vodou in 1991, Haitians talked to me of twenty-one (or seventeen) originating *nasyons* that were recognized within ritual ceremonies. Which nations were acknowledged for ritual inclusion, however, depended on the remembered dances and their music. Those dances survived that had musicians and dancers who could perform the *nasyon* allegiances, *nasyon* memory, and *nasyon* history; those nations survived that were able to direct the path of transcendence for worshipers. Even as early as the 1930s and 1940s, during Dunham's fieldwork she reported that "very often the older people indicated that they remembered dances no longer known to the community, but they were unable to execute them because there was no one to play the rhythms or sing the songs to accompany them" (1983:21).

I do not emphasize the importance of dance just because I am a dancer, but because the research indicates that the dance and music traditions in these cultures (in Haiti as well as in Cuba and Bahia) were and are pivotal. The dancing body contains a fantastic muscle memory system, which helps to encode history. For example, during my first dance lessons in Haiti, I was taught *yanvalu, zépòl, mayi, agwé,* and *banda* as the main dances for the Rada nation. I was taught one dance, *Nago,* that represented the entire Nago nation, but I was told of others—perhaps variations (*Nago gran cou* and *Nago cho*). I was told that the dances *Congo, Congo payet,* and *Congo fran* represented the Congo nation and that one dance, *Ibo,* represented the Ibo nation. I was taught one Petwo dance but was told that *bambula* and *kita* were from this nation and that the *juba* and the *Martinique* could be performed during a Petwo rite.

I understand now that I was taught which nations were important to Haitians; which dances were important to Haiti; and that in signaling the names, musical characteristics, and movements of distinct African ethnic groups, Haitian history was encoded within the dancing body over time. The most celebrated nations came to comprise sections or rites in the Vodou religion: Rada, Congo, and Petwo rites (Yarborough 1958:12–14, 27–29, 1969: personal communication; Dunham 1983:9–11, 57; Fleurant 1996). These are the performance distinctions that the dance data reveal regularly. Herskovits and Courlander state clearly that there are two main African heritages, West (Rada) and Central (Kongo-Angola/Petwo) African: "Only one of the lists specifically assigned gods to other than the Rada and Petro categories" (Herskovits 1975 [1937]:314, 310–13). "In general, Congo and Petro tend to 'march' together" (Courlander 1973:217).

Drawing on research in the Kongo-Angola region, Belgian scholar Luc de Heusch more recently presses the inclusion of Petwo rites into Kongo-Angola or West Central African heritage, rather than a separate grouping of Petwo *lwas* and rites (2000:327–88). The dance data indicate a close relationship, but also a clear distinction between Congo and Petwo.

Haitian ritual dances have some names of specific *lwas,* but they mainly reference the nations or transnational groupings of Africans in the colonial period. Unlike the Cuban Yoruba and Bahian Candomblé cases, Haitian dances are not always named for the divinities. The dance names, when not nation names, emphasize a basic concept in the belief system or direct the worshiper in particular ways of worship.

For example, Haitian *yanvalu* is considered the ultimate dance of Haitian Vodou ceremonies by worshipers and others, since it references the servant of Papa Dambala, the snake of Fon worship in Ouidah, Benin, and its omnipotent power over all other *lwas* in the Rada rites (Hurston 1938:141–43). *Yanvalu* means "I beg of you," in the Fon language (Fleurant 2002: personal communication) and is danced with head bowed and knees very close to the ground while the back is undulating continuously. In *yanvalu,* dancers allow the entire body to simultaneously relax and work; the dance movement follows the normal inhalation and exhalation of breathing, but expands the breath movement throughout the entire body toward a series of undulations on a vertical axis. When the rhythms mark a more animated and less smooth pattern, the body movement is curtailed from full body undulations and concentrates within specific body-part isolations. *Yanvalu's* mood is the utmost of supplication. It is danced to or for the most important spiritual entities: Papa Dambala, Metres Ayida Wèdo, Ezili,[6] and for members of the Gédé family.

Zépòl, meaning "shoulders" (that is, "work the shoulders" from the French, *les épaules,)* is the Vodou dance of the Rada rite that features continuous shoulder movement. *Zépòl* is the rapid thrusting of the shoulders—that is, shifts in direction either from forward to back as swiftly as possible or in a rapid and constantly repetitive pattern: forward, back, forward, and rotate around. It is also danced for many *lwas.*

Mayí, on the other hand, is a quick-paced, foot-slapping, agriculturally rooted dance within Rada rituals and is immensely important in Haiti's agricultural society. The *mayí* rhythms and songs come from the Mahí nation, a neighboring group of the Fon. Their dance in Haiti usually announces the arrival of Kuzen Zaka or Azaka, the *lwa* of agriculture and guardian of farmworkers and their families. His dance has four variations: *mayí simple, mayí derial, mayí ciyé,* and *mayí d'été.* The basic *mayí* foot pattern is a step back, forward, together and then lift to alternate; *derial* is a definitive planting step; *ciyé* is a circling turn to a particular ascending pitch in the drums; and *d'été* is a carnival-like rocking horse step (Yarborough 1958, 1970: personal communication). Dancers who invoke Kuzen and receive him within their bodies are required "to bend low in the movements of planting and hoeing. Sometimes they will embrace the ground. Their movements are always awkward and crude to typify mountain people working in the fields. . . . They are immediately dressed in the garb of the mountain peasant—hat, smock and knapsack—and their behavior requires that they be treated as Cousin" (Dunham 1983:52).

In *mayí,* the concentration is on the feet in a fast-paced, three-step pattern that uses a fourth beat to suspend the third step off the ground, which alternates the pattern from one foot to another.

In the Rada rite, the trilogy of *yanvalu, zépòl,* and *mayí* corresponds to a set order of songs and rhythms (see chart 4 in this chapter; also Fleurant 1996; Daniel video, 1997b). When I danced *zépòl* and *mayí* in ritual and social occasions on my trip to Benin, people quickly saw a connection between what they danced and what I was dancing from Haiti. From my limited exposure to Benin dance culture, the Rada trilogy exemplifies some of the significant regional dance forms there as well.

One dance in the Rada *nasyon* is named for the divinity for whom it is danced, Agwé, the *lwa* of the sea. In agwé, movements of the arms suggest the motion of the sea. Flowing movements of the arms (going forward and back above the head, up and down, and side to side) symbolize the waves and make connections between the dance and the *lwa,* Agwé.

Ibo dance performance, from the eastern neighbors of the Yoruba on the continent, is an important dance in Haitian Vodou today. It reinforces the reputation of defiant and courageous Ibo ancestors, now Haitian *lwas.* The dance emphasizes a high chest lift, strong kicks, and tightly closed fists—held prominently. Haitian worshipers believe that enslaved Ibo danced these particular movements so that bullets could bounce off their chests and so that they would not only be protected but also would be returned to their ancestors in a process of transformation (Honorat 1955:88; Yarborough 1970, 1974: personal communication; Dunham 1976, 1989: personal communication).

Haiti's Congo dances reference Congo nationhood, generally emphasizing the essence of Kongo-Angola sociability and congeniality, as well as fertility, male/female challenge, and seduction. Haitian Congo dances employ playful advances and retreats between male and female dancers. The main step involves hip circling for both male and female performers, while stabilizing the upper torso. The supporting foot pattern either alternates on one flat foot and the toe or ball of the other foot or adheres to a simple walk.

The reliance on hip circling and hip swinging made Congo dance quickly recognizable and probably accounted for much condemnation of African "lascivious" behavior; however, it is characteristic movement within Kongo-Angola heritage and is performed within both secular and sacred settings. The Congo hip circling step and playful seduction became identified with the parading Kings and Queens in Carnival displays, in Christmas processions, within most popular dance on social occasions, as well as within the Congo *nasyon* of Vodou ceremonies. Even though other African ethnic amalgams have ample use of hip movement, the heritage from the Kongo-Angola region that was transported to the Americas saturated new dance formations and became a characteristic legacy.

The Petwo rite of Vodou introduces a different character of dance material and new *lwas.* Both were identified with the hard-fought revolution on the island of Haiti. Petwo dances symbolize the blood that was spilled on Haitian land and new *lwas* who support both a historic, independent black republic and the religious rites within a constantly developing Vodou belief system.

The dances for the Petwo *lwas* are explicitly powerful. When compared to Rada and Congo rite dances, even in comparison to the Nago *nasyon* dances (the most overtly forceful within the Rada rite), Petwo dances flirt with actual violence. The Nago *nasyon* steps involve thrusting the chest fiercely and lifting the legs high, all over a powerful hypnotic and propelling rhythm. The Petwo dance steps, however, shift the body orientation from organic relaxation or balanced readiness to tense irregular stances (for fighting, for war, for gathering and carrying ammunition) to fast-paced jumping, vibrating, sometimes jerking and stilted steps. These movements are performed over a relentless and complex set of pulsating rhythms. Some say Petwo foot patterns are based on the chains of slavery (Yarborough 1970: personal communication; Destiné 1989: personal communication). More so, the Petwo dances are not reverent or social in the manner of Rada or Congo rite dances; they have a stubborn and fiercely defiant ambiance.

The Gédé *nasyon* is also prominent in Haiti, with its concerns about sex and the potential of life as well as death. The Gédé family members are associated with the cemetery and manage a relationship with all Vodou *nasyons*. The Gédés usually come at the end of a service but frequently interrupt at unexpected times. They are comical and risqué, yet they command great respect. Haitian ethnologist Laënnec Hurbon has said that "the Gédé represent an ethnic group conquered by the royal family of Abomey, many of whom were shipped to Saint Domingue as slaves. Having disappeared in Benin, in Haiti they became the *lwa* of death" (1995:74–75).

The Haitian *nasyons* are ultimately amalgams; each is a creation from other African amalgams, resulting today in Rada/Petwo or Congo/Petwo rites. The nation dances and nation drum rhythms provided ways for Africans to respectfully recognize *nasyons* within the new American environment. The Fon-derived Rada rite utilized the many West African nations of its origins within its liturgy, namely, the Allada, Mahí, Nago, Ibo, and Gédé nations. Their *nasyon* dances, songs, and rhythms were placed in a generalized but flexible liturgical order, a *regleman,* according to local family traditions and regional practices within a *fet* or *dans,* more commonly called a Haitian service or dance *ceremòni.* Other dances, like Congo and Petwo *nasyon* dances, were placed separately after the *yanvalu, zépòl,* and *mayí* dances of the predominant Fon neighbors.

As each of the *nasyons* performs its dances and chants, its *lwas* arrive, and they are greeted with a series of salutations. A salutation consists of three choreographed bows or bending the knees between three steps to the right, three steps to the left, and three steps to the right. These movements are understood by ritual officials as mirroring the inversion that exists between the spiritual and material worlds (Desmangles 1992:102–8).

Among the *nasyon* dances, there is playful and almost comedic dance. All that is visually playful and seemingly recreational, however, can also be spiritually serious (see spontaneous ceremony in video, Daniel 1997b). For example, a *mazone* dance is used to release the tensions that the sacred dance and music liturgy regularly build up. Normally, *mazone* is a slightly virtuoso dance, with feet flying in complex patterns and bodies dancing close to one another. The dance is often explicitly sexual, even though in a sacred setting.

On instruction from a *manbo* or *oungan,* the *mazone* is performed with its *grouyad* or *gouilleé,* hip-twisting and hip-circling step (like wynin'/whining/wining in the Anglophone Caribbean) from Kongo-Angola-influenced social dance forms. In the social setting, it can be performed in a suggestive, risqué, but also humorous manner (Dunham 1983:41–48). In ritual proceedings, a shift to *mazone* dancing allows whoever is leading the service to rest; it permits a satisfied *lwa* to leave; and it reduces tension all around (Dunham 1983:52–53; see also Bahian *ere* arrival in chapter 7). When performed at the end of a Nago sequence, however, the *mazone* takes on the qualities of the warrior *nasyon.*[7] *Mazone* is also popular at Carnival time as a social processional dance.

Another important African-derived dance and music form apart from the sacred Vodou *nasyons* is *konbit* music and dance. This type of dance/music occurs in relation to a work project. A *konbit* (also *cuvé*) or work party often proceeds to a worksite while singing and dancing a step called, *charyio-pye* (*chairo-pie* in Dunham 1983:18, 55). Within this traditional communal work setting, performers use a conch shell as the call to gather, either for work or revolt; in colonial times the conch call was for religious ceremonies. Drums, rattles, and *vaksins* (lengths of bamboo that are blown as flute orchestras) are also used in *konbit* performance.

Intermittently during the work process, workers take breaks and perform satirical songs and dances. Their employers are then compelled to pay money or provide more food and drink because the songs and dances are so amusing, critical, or both. The *konbit* organization continues today as a small work party and as an increasingly important political base for parading crowds, which use percussion and improvised chants and song lyrics that ignite critical sociopolitical commentary (see Laguerre 1989 and McAlister 2002).

"Pure Mix" of Nations

Similar to Dunham's field investigations, Yarborough's research was based on living continuously in Haiti for more than forty years, from the 1940s to the 1980s. She had been a principal dancer in Dunham's company, as well as an accomplished ballet dancer. After making the island her home, she concentrated on the dances of Haitian Vodou ritual, but also on the varied social dances that exhibited the European and African mélange. She wrote of her practical experience of dancing the dances on the island and produced an excellent little book, *Haiti-Dance* (c. 1958), that categorizes and, most important, describes the dances as they were performed in the 1950s.

Yarborough had direct access to the Haitian social dances of the twentieth century when she described the dances that took place within private homes, public halls, urban nightclubs and hotels, and outdoors in the countryside. More traditional Haitian social dances are generally called *banbòchs,* which are gatherings for food, drink, dance, and music-making at the end of the week and during holidays. Many of the same dance forms are performed in the *peristil* or *tonnel,* the covered outdoor space (roofed or thatched, respectively) of a Vodou *ounfo* or temple. On weekends, Christmas, and New Year's Day, for example, Haitian, Dominican, and Cuban music is played in small instrumental ensembles, while revelers dance *merengs*—the Haitian national dance, *rumbas, boleros,* and other Caribbean and U.S. American popular social dances. The characteristic movement that occurs within Haitian social dance, especially in Carnival and *Mardi Gras* dances, is still called *grouyad.* And according to Fleurant, the *Congo minuet* is still danced in the mountain communities with its strict meter and African-derived nuances in torso division and hip isolation, as well as in instrumentation that includes the drums.[8]

The last dance form that I need to discuss in order to assess the dance movement vocabulary of Haiti in terms of selected ritual movement is *Rara,* an important rural, street processional form that continues today. *Rara* should not be confused with Rada in Haitian Vodou. *Rara* is a communal procession, led by a lead dancer (*la-lwa-di* or *majò jon),* and it travels from house to house, town to town, during Holy Week, and continues Kongo-Angola characteristics in dance performance. Dunham discussed *Rara* in terms of its religious connection to the Easter season and Holy Week and its clear involvement of huge crowds and mass dance abandonment.

Rara continues as a serious outdoor display, commemorating a theme of resurrection within an ambiance of diversion that heralds the sociopolitical

Chart 4. *Nasyons, Lwas,* and Haitian Dances

Nasyons	Lwas	Dances
Haitian Social Dances		
African		*Calenda, Chica*
European		*Contredanse*
Creole		*Affranchi, Calenda, Chica*
Haitian		*Mereng, Rara, Carnival*
		(Grouyad)
Caribbean		*Banbòchs*
		(rumba, reggae, etc.)
Haitian Vodou Dances		
Vodou Rada/Congo Rite:		
(Rada rite)		
Rada	Papa Legba	*Yanvalu, Mayí, Zépòl*
Rada	Loko	*Yanvalu, Mayí, Zépòl*
Rada	Aizan	*Yanvalu, Mayí, Zépò*
Rada	Dambala	*Yanvalu, Mayí, Zépòl*
Rada	Ayida Wèdo	*Yanvalu, Mayí, Zépòl*
Rada	Agwé	*Yanvalu, Mayí, Zépòl*
Mahí		*Mayí*
Rada	Azaka, Kuzen Zaka	*Zépòl*
Rada	Marasa	
Rada	Sobo, Bede	*Yanvalu, Mayí, Zépòl*
Rada	Agasu	*Yanvalu, Mayí, Zépòl*
Rada	Agawo	*Yanvalu, Mayí, Zépòl*
Rada	Ezili	*Yanvalu, Mayí, Zépòl*
Rada	Belekou Yenou	*Yanvalu, Mayí, Zépòl*
Rada	Sen Jak Majè	*Mayí, Zépòl*
Rada	Langaj, Zila Moyo	*Twa rigol*
Nago (Yoruba)	Ogou Feray	*Nago, Gran cou, Cho*
Nago	Ogou Badagri	*Nago, Gran cou, Cho*
Ibo	Legba Ibo	*Ibo*
Ibo	Ibo Mariani	*Ibo*
		Mazone
Rada		*Vodou*
Rada	Simbi	
(Congo Rite)		
Congo		*Juba*
Congo	Simbi	*Congo*
Congo	Marinette	*Congo*
Congo	Ezili	*Congo, Fran, Ronn, Payet*
Gédé	Baron Sanmdi	*Banda*
Gédé		*Zarenyen*
Vodou Petwo/Congo Rite		
(Petwo Rite)		
Petwo	Ti Jean Petwo	*Petwo*

Chart 4, cont.

Petwo	Ezili Jeruge	*Petwo*
Petwo	Ezili Danto	*Petwo*
Petwo	Ogou Petwo	*Petwo, Kita, Boumba*
(Congo Rite)		
Congo		*Juba*
Congo	Simbi	*Congo*
Congo	Marinette	*Congo*
Congo	Ezili	*Congo, Fran, Ronn, Payet*
Gédé	Baron Sanmdi	*Banda*
Gédé		*Zarenyen*

voices of the rural poor (see McAlister 2002; cf. Honorat 1955:130–31). It contrasts sharply with contemporary social dances of Haitian origin like *kompas*, of Caribbean origins like reggae and rumba, and of U.S. origin like hip-hop, all of which reside in Haiti today.

I see commonalities in the abundant dance materials that I have just reviewed. First there is a leader and group construct: *oungans, manbos, oungenikons* and their Vodou communities; *majordomos*, Kings and Queens of Carnival bands; and *la-lwa-di* and *majò jon* in *Rara* processions. Also in the *banbòchs*, there are leaders, *met-la-dans*. Thus, leader and chorus, call and response, statement and answer become a major organizing principle beyond musical structure in Haitian dance performance.

Often a common dance step is performed despite secular or sacred settings. Group dances that proceed from small ensembles to large mass dancing regularly use the *charyio-pye* step and Kongo-Angola hip circling, shifting the religious function of Lent to a social function of dance abandonment in Carnival dances. Also, the religious function of *Rara* bands shifts between its mass Catholic processions to social gatherings that are potentially sociopolitical community events. Lastly, the historical *affranchi* dances use the common walking/gliding step to transpose European form with African content.

The settings of Vodou and social life are shared. The close relationship between Vodou and other segments of social life is underscored by the use of the outdoor ceremonial dance space for social *banbòchs* as well as for summoning the *lwas*. *Rara* especially demonstrates the pervasiveness of Vodou within its Catholic theme, as do Carnival and *konbits*. Vodou is a common thread that binds Haitian life together, consciously and unconsciously.

In summary, Haitian dance history has highlighted several sources of dance movement vocabulary: African *nasyons, affranchis,* Carnival and *Rara* dance parading, and *banbòch* dances, all of which were used within a develop-ing Haitian liturgical performance. Dance materials from these forms influ-enced and solidified Haiti's ritual performance practice.[9]

Cuba's Nation Dance Diversity

In looking at Cuba's dance history, I find a rich, vibrant, and complex array. There are few other places in the Americas where the African nation traditions are so fully elaborated as in dance traditions of twenty-first-century Cuba. From the late fifteenth to the mid-nineteenth century, Cuban dance percolated with tremendously varied ingredients until it solidified culturally. It is the presence and maintenance of distinct, but related, cultural traditions in the form of African nations, with the almost constant reinforcement of fresh cultural seg-ments, that generates Cuba's ample dance history.[10] With Haiti's shores closed to enslaved Africans at the beginning of the nineteenth century and with the development of sugar production and refinement throughout the nineteenth century in Cuba, colonial exploiters had fewer but more active markets for their trade (Pérez 1988; Knight 1978). These conditions in the Americas were added to shifting developments in the Bight of Benin during the same time period (Matory 1994). On the continent, Yoruba kingdoms were defeated, and Yoruba peoples were sold into captivity in greater numbers than before. By the end of the nineteenth century, many different ethnic groups from both Europe and Africa had replaced Cuba's native populations, and most of these nations left their mark in terms of dance style and music-making traditions.

The Vanquished Nations

Incredible as it may seem, we have descriptions of native dance in Cuba from the texts of the European contact period (Las FAR 1971; Fernandez de Oviedo 1850 in Las FAR; Hernandez 1980). The conquistadors wrote about massive group dances that were performed in their presence. These chroniclers de-scribed indigenous dances as group forms that demanded easy steps for hun-dreds, if not thousands, of dancers to perform in unison. The unison move-ments, however, were performed in intricate spatial configurations. Dance formations were performed to secure good relations between native peoples and their spiritual world. Women and men (or one gender only) produced line, circle, and zigzag patterns, and often the performers danced in procession, holding hands or with locked elbows. The early chroniclers called these indigenous Cuban dance forms *areítos,* meaning indigenous dance and song.[11]

National Influence of Spain and French Haiti

European dance forms came to Cuba with Spaniards from southern Spain and with French colonists who had previously settled on the neighboring island of Saint Domingue (Linares 1989 [1974]:18–31; León 1984:95–118; Hernandez 1980:12–20; Carbonero and Lamerán 1982:23–27; Alén 1992:5–27; Daniel 1995:30–33, 37–38). The first Spaniards came in the fifteenth century, and the French came in significant numbers just prior to and at the time of the Haitian Revolution at the end of the eighteenth century. Due to these colonial invasions, two distinct styles of European dance culture were brought to the island: Spanish *zapateo* and French *contredanse.* These made immeasurable contributions to Cuban social dance formation, but the European dance/music forms also had an impact on African liturgical formation.

Over time, the Spanish language influenced ritual as well as social performance. Spanish literary forms accompanied the dance in a manner that began in Spain and has influenced the literary production of the Caribbean, Europe, and the Central and South American continent for the last five hundred years. Spanish lyrics in songs and chants were based on a ten-syllable line within a ten-line stanza, called the *décima.* Their structure evolved into a very descriptive stanza that repeated a two-line or couplet refrain. Spaniards also brought several types of guitar-like string instruments—the *bandurria, el tiple,* and *las bandolas*—to complete the sound background for the early music/dance on the island (for instrumentation, see León 1984 and Alén 1992).

The *décima* songs, as sung poetry, accompanied rhythmic foot stamping, *zapateo* or *zapateado,* which became a signature of southern Andalucian dancing, where *flamenco* was forming also as a significant Spanish dance (Phillips 1987:48–49). Spanish colonists and small farm owners continued the elaborate rhythms of *zapateo* dance in Cuba. They further developed the form when Caribbean sandals replaced Spanish shoes, and they called the dance *chancletas.* Later the dance forms of the rural farm workers were more generally called *guajiro* and were closely identified with the development of a ballad singing tradition.

The emphasis on the Spanish language, the *décima*-like stanza with answering couplet verse, and *zapateo* movement continued on the island as European contributions to what was to become Cuban culture, which also influenced African nation liturgical dance. For example, within the Yoruba ritual dance for Yemayá, a clear foot-stamping pattern occurs, and it is called *zapateo de Yemayá*. Ochún's dance in Cuba also is taught as a continuous "*zapateo* step," since it has a heel hit before each step at the beginning of an alternating pattern (see dance step examples in chapter 8).

In addition to the *zapateo*, the Spaniards brought dance formations from the European courts. These were exemplified most in the *contredanse*, but also in *cuadrillos, minuets,* and the typical small dance suite forms of the sixteenth- and seventeenth-century courts (e.g., *allemande, courante sarabande, bourrée, minuet, gavotte, passepied, gavotte, pavane, gigue*). Many of these became parlor or salon dances in Cuba and displayed the same configurations and general rhythms of the European courts. *Contradanza francesa,* the name in Spanish, relied on binary or two-part form (aa, bb) in the music, where each of two contrasting sections was repeated.[12]

Generally, men and women danced in lines and exchanged places and partners in intricate floor patterns. Couples touched hands and fingers occasionally as they promenaded and crossed the dance space in rhythmic time to ensemble wind and string instruments. Spanish dancing characteristically utilized an elongated, uplifted upper body above the moving (running or jumping) feet. Extended arm movements that encircled the upper body in circular patterns accompanied the lifted chest. This upper body stance and the characteristic interest in rhythmic foot patterns also combined some hip emphases. This was characteristically different from other European nation dances, which had a solid torso for upright body orientation.

African continuities came to Cuba from two European sources: Spain and Haiti (Alén 1987; León 1984). Within Spanish culture (through Andalucians, Canarios, Castellanos, Asturianos, Gallegos, Catalanes, etc.; an amalgam of regions and classes), African cultural elements entered Cuba early. The invasion of Spain by al Moravids and al Mohads, Islamized Africans of Berber and Arab stock, commonly called Moors, had provided the presence of North African culture within a developing Spanish culture from 711 to 1492. As a result of such tremendous African presence in Spain, some free Spanish-speaking Africans, known as *Ladinos* in literature, but Afro-Spaniards nevertheless, came in the first waves of European contact to the Americas. And with them we can presume came some African orientation to the body, namely, hip movement and rhythmic interest. The first African blood and culture did not come to Cuba with the slave trade, but with the early Spanish explorers.

In addition, with the independence of enslaved Africans in Haiti, many frightened French colonists escaped to Cuba, Puerto Rico, French Caribbean territories (Martinique, Guadeloupe, and Dominica), the southern United States (especially Louisiana), or back to France. Those French colonials who came to Cuba brought the same European court dances that the Spaniards had brought earlier. In addition they brought their plantation families and, in effect, were responsible for transporting a Haitian Creole dance form, a combination of French and African dance that had formed in Haiti among their plantation black families. As a result, Europeans facilitated the arrival of new African-derived dance forms.

In terms of European contributions, however, the most important influences on Cuban dance/music were from its Spanish heritage, which gave emerging Cuban liturgies their language and the two-line couplet refrain. The Spanish *coro* or answering refrain later reinforced the African call-and-response form in ritual performance settings.

Multiple African *Naciones* Practices

The group of dances I mentioned above that came with African Haitians as they journeyed for refuge was called *tumba francesa* in Cuba. Enslaved Africans from Haitian plantations, including the "black wives" and their offspring of French owners, had been constructing an emerging Haitian culture from the late fifteenth century to late eighteenth century. Their dances were different from the dances of enslaved Africans in Cuba at the time of their contact in the late eighteenth and early nineteenth centuries. First, their dances were accompanied in Creole French, and not in Spanish. Second, these dances were different from African forms that were already present in Cuba because they appeared like European courtly forms, although with definite African elements (Alén 1987; León 1984:21–23; Daniel 1995:37–38).

In contrast to the European *contredanse,* which was performed by both the Spanish and the French, and very much like the *affranchis* form in Haiti, the dances of new African Haitian refugees were performed to drums instead of the string and woodwind accompaniment of other court-like forms (see video, Daniel 1992a). Their versions of *contredanse, quadrilles, minuets,* and *cotillions* resulted in formidable displays. There were set spatial configurations, highly organized rhythms, and distinctive improvisational elements in drumming and in the dancing bodies, often with hip movements that coincided with the hip interest of their Spanish *zapateo* performance.

Tumba francesa performers viewed their dance as "French-Haitian," an identifying product of Haiti, now residing in Cuba. Cubans considered it a genre of "African" dance that was performed by the African-derived peoples brought from Haiti. In reality, *tumba francesa* included a mélange of African dance concepts folded into performance, including the prominent recognition of Kings and Queens, processional dance, virtuoso displays, and public flirtation (Alén 1987). These elements and characteristics were integrated into African imitations of Creole French practices and African imitations of Creole French imitations of French court practices. These dances continued in Cuba as a distinct tradition from the late 1700s to the present! Their continuity is a result of *cabildo* organization, which I will elaborate upon shortly, and its connection to the Catholic Church.

African Haitian refugees also brought *Rara* processions, which became Gagá in Cuba with prominent kings and queens, virtuoso dance leaders, and connections to the church calendar. The leader often used a whistle and twirled a baton and, in a seemingly nontrance state, was able to draw a sharp knife across delicate parts of his body. Without breaking the skin, he performed other incredible feats. At the end of Holy week and almost constant processional dancing, an effigy of Judas was beaten and burned. The rest of Easter Sunday was spent in dress clothes, eating and celebrating resurrection in both the Catholic and the Vodú (Spanish spelling of Vodou) world, as well as confirming African Kings and Queens of the town and community associations.

The ordeals that the *Gagá* leader must overcome while dancing include preventing his tongue from being cut, his neck from being sliced, and his back from being perforated with glass fragments. When these episodes occurred (at frequent intervals), the focus was on a solo performer. These were not behaviors associated with the Roman Catholic Church, but they are similar to behaviors of spiritual protection that worshipers gain when their divinities are incorporated within their bodies. Thus *Gagá* also contains a Vodú dance presence throughout the Christian Holy Week. The time of year and the involvement of a Judas figure and its destruction mark the Catholic presence within *Gagá* bands.

Other African influences in Cuba outnumbered the impact of *tumba francesa* or *Gagá*. With the need for an increased labor force in the production and refining of sugar, Africans from the coasts of West and West Central Africa were forced into slavery in staggering numbers and taken to Cuba as well as to other Caribbean ports. Many African ethnic groups were transported to Cuba from the sixteenth century until the late 1800s.

West-Central Africa—in other words sites near the mouth of the Zaire River and from Luanda, Benguela and the adjacent regions—is still the dominant regional supplier of slaves in the eighteenth and nineteenth centuries. . . . This large region south of the equator supplied 40 per cent of the slaves entering the Atlantic slave trade. However, while West-Central Africa was far more important than any of the three individual West African regions examined here [Bight of Benin, Bight of Biafra, and the Gold Coast], the size of the three regions together is comparable to the West-Central African slave provenance zone as a whole. (Eltis and Richardson 1997:17)

It is likely that departures from the Bight of Benin exceeded 10,000 per year over a period of 125 years from 1687 to 1811. . . . The two peaks in the traffic from this region came at the very beginning—1687–1711—and near the end—1787–1811—of these 125 years. (Eltis and Richardson 1997:18)

To be sure, all the regions of Africa sent slaves to almost all the regions of the Americas, but people tended to flow in one dominant channel. (Morgan 1997:125)

With the weakening of previously powerful African nations on the continent, the rise of labor demands, and the continuity of slavery in the Americas, certain African nations came through an American cultural sieve. As a result of massive forced migration and cohabitation, four nations of African American culture emerged in Cuba. Cuba is unique in conserving a fourth African culture in its religious and artistic repertoire. In addition to its Fon-derived Arará, its Cuban Yoruba cultures from West Africa, and its Kongo-Angola culture from West Central Africa, it also retained culture from around the Calabar River, Carabalí culture from the Bight of Biafa in West Africa (Ortiz 1951 [1985]; León 1984; Cabrera 1970 [1958], 1983 [1954], 1986 [1979]; Lachatánere 1961; Knight 1970; Lopez Valdés 1986, 1988; Pérez 1995).

Kongo-Angola beliefs, practices, and influence from West Central Africa arrived first in Cuba and in great numbers during the contact period. This type of African culture dominated central and eastern Cuba; it became secondary over time in western Cuba. Arará beliefs, practices, and influence from the Fon people of the Bight of Benin were limited to the northwest of Cuba. Carabalí beliefs, practices, and influence from the borders of the Calabar River (now in Cameroon and Nigeria) were confined in the northwest of Cuba as well. Yoruba influence from the Bight of Benin became primary in northwestern Cuba and secondary in eastern Cuba. These patterns developed due to several socio-politico-economic conditions: particular ports of entry and colonial shipping patterns; smallpox epidemics; international politics; domestic tensions toward increasing sugar, tobacco, and coffee production; legal abolition of slavery in 1866; presence of indentured Chinese workers; and the Ten Years'

War with Spain (Knight 1970:121–78). By far, however, the European recruit-
ment of specific African skills had the most long-lasting and significant effects
(see Harris 2001; Inikori 2001; Dodson 2001). All factors had an influence on
the organization of African populations in Cuban regional sectors.

All African nations had deep cultural roots in and around the ports of
Matanzas and Havana provinces in northwest Cuba. Cubans generally considered Matanzas the "soul" of African culture in Cuba (and Havana as the
administrative international capital) because it held major resource roots for
each of the four African nations. Since the end of the twentieth century, with
intermarriages, improved transportation, and domestic migration (especially
after the Cuban Revolution in 1959), each African nation has had an influence throughout Cuba, and they all have points of interconnection. What
is important to sacred ritual performance and the development of Cuban
liturgical orders is the fact that ethnic nation amalgams resulted in religious
distinctions that generated distinct practices in Cuba with some differences
from their African core cultures on the continent (cf. Ajayi 1998).

Despite overwhelming colonial power and restrictions, permission for
Africans to congregate and to practice African rituals was granted in Cuba
for calculated economic reasons; namely, to maximize sugar and tobacco
production (Ortiz 1940; Deschamps Chapeaux 1971; Moreno Fraginals 1977
[1984]). Full production could not be guaranteed in the midst of rebellions
and insurrections, which were thought to be imminent with large numbers
of enslaved peoples and few white colonials in authority, particularly after
the success of the Haitian Revolution. Spanish Catholic organization became
an operating model that served to structure and secure new African nation
organization.

In Spain, religious brotherhoods and mutual aid societies had included
both black membership and totally black organizations since the fifteenth
century (Brandon 1993:70). These religious brotherhoods, called *cabildos* or
cofradías, were originally Catholic groups of mutual aid, like lodges. In Cuba,
there were African nation groups that solidified as *cabildos,* African American
religious organizations with identifiable music and dance orientations (Brandon 1993; Alén 1987; León 1984; Cabrera 1986 [1979], 1970 [1958]).

While notions of African impotency during enslavement would include
the idea that culture and history were destroyed, Cuban *cabildo* organization
proves this was not the case. On the one hand, plantation owners tried to
strip enslaved Africans of identity, cohesion, and dignity. On the other hand,
thinking of being placed in jeopardy among huge numbers of Africans, white

colonists hoped to continue age-old grievances and ethnic conflicts from Africa—the divide-and-conquer rule—by permitting the organization of distinct African nations into *cabildo* associations. Within such organizations, Africans were permitted to meet with regularity, to use African languages in chants and songs, and to practice distinctive dance/music. They wore particular colors as insignia of separate African nationhood, designated Kings and Queens and a hierarchical leadership, and practiced religious rituals that were native to their homelands on the continent. *Cabildo* organization thereby maintained ethnic oppositions that existed in continental Africa, while it also guarded distinct African cultures (Moreno Fraginals 1977 [1984]; Serviat 1980; Deschamps Chapeaux 1971).[13]

For example, several French Haitian (*tumba francesa*) organizations took hold and continue in the present as *cabildos* in eastern enclaves of the island, while Arará, Iyesá, and Abakuá *cabildos* are still active in Matanzas. In the twenty-first century, most *cabildos* operate as religious and cultural centers, providing specific African perspectives and approaches to community life. Members maintain philosophical views that are based in particular religious practices and serve community needs through music and dance performance associated with ritual and cultural (tourist) displays.

Cabildos were legally allowed to operate until the early nineteenth century with the previously mentioned colonial concerns in mind. With persistent development of African as opposed to Catholic cultural behavior, however, laws were passed to shape African *cabildo* practices in terms of Spanish Catholic understandings. Fortunately, in the interim (between the fifteenth and nineteenth centuries), several African languages (KiKongo, Fon, Yoruba, Carabalí), ritual practices, and belief systems were institutionalized (Brandon 1993; cf. Desmangles 1992:38–47 for a similar pattern in Haitian Vodou development). Even after the *cabildos* were restricted in public activities, many African ethnic groups were able to wedge their influence within the four distinct nations. Yoruba, Lucumí, Eyo, Egbado, Ilesha, Ewe-Fon, Efik, Ibo, Ibibio, Loango, Bavili, Kongo, Mayombe, Ndongo, Gangas, and other ethnic and linguistic groups contributed to the crystallization of the four styles of African music and dance in Cuba (Alén 1987:1; Sosa 1984; Cabrera 1970 [1958]; Ortiz 1950, 1951 [1985]).

Early examples of the many differing African nations that were transported forcefully to the Americas can best be found in Cuban performances of *Dia de los reyes,* in parading *parrandas* (storytelling parades at Christmas and New Year's), and carnivals (parading and festivities around Lent). Annual celebrations and other festive saints' day processions from the Catholic Church facilitated a slow process of continuity and interchange, what Fernando Ortiz termed "transculturation." This indicated that Spanish and African cultures meshed at certain points and to varying degrees and eventually formed a new Cuban culture (Ortiz 1951 [1985]; Brandon 1993:70–74; Klein 1986:100). The chance to perform and display memories and customs of African nationhood was exceedingly important to the new "Cubans." Today, for example, they still possess whole liturgies and many ritual procedures that were associated with *cabildo* practices and underscored in *cabildo* parading.

Dia de los reyes, the Day of the (Three) Kings (or Twelfth Night), was and still is a Catholic celebration with a black Magus or King Balthazar/Melchior. On January 6 (Epiphany of the Christian calendar), the Roman Catholic Church and Spanish civil authorities encouraged a collective praying through the streets with music, dance, and masking. This was a substitute for the earlier celebration of Corpus Christi in May, which was deemed too serious an ecclesiastic event to permit black participation in the festivities (León 1984:35–37). On the *Dia de los reyes,* Africans and African Americans participated in processional displays that were presented to governing captains, their entourages, and church officials in return for Christmas gifts, usually clothing, that the African population had received a few days earlier. Each *cabildo* performed its special songs and dances as representations of their nation or ethnic group, but also in playful imitation of European customs and behaviors. Performers were dressed in costumes that included peacock feathers, tutus, high silk hats, face paints, and sailors' uniforms, as well as in raffia or grass skirts and decorated face masks and headdresses (see now-famous drawings in Emery 1972 [1985]:31 and Ortiz 1951 [1985]:286, 440, 447).

This celebration was the most festive occasion of colonial time for enslaved peoples, as they were essentially free for the day. Clear documentation for Cuba augments what we know occurred in Haiti. In the midst of the imitations, African Kings and Queens marched in elaborate processions, and those who were selected to lead each *cabildo* nation danced to their separate nations' drums. Often they continued their festivities in their own quarters, sharing in African commonalities and meshing many ethnic traditions, as well as restaging parts of their histories in *parranda* events. The enslaved joined free blacks and celebrated to the extent that they could in practicing the drumming, songs, and dances of their ancestries. Even when *cabildos* were restricted to their *cabildo* quarters or allowed to perform only at the outer reaches of the city, the dance/music traditions became public emblems of the associated personal identities within codified beliefs of African nations in the Americas (Ortiz 1951 [1985]; León 1984; Alén 1987).

Each African *cabildo* in Cuba had a repository of sacred dance/music and performance style. While colonists emphasized their differences and although visually they appeared as separate parading nations, continuous cultural contact resulted in intra-African syncretism. For example, the Cuban ethnologist Fernando Ortiz reported both the similarities and sharing that occurred between Catholicism and specifically Yoruba religious thought, and also that which occurred among the major nations or *cabildos* within Cuban culture (1951 [1985]:381–87; cf. Barnet 1961; Feijo 1986).

George Brandon, a sociologist from the United States and a specialist in the history of Yoruba belief in the Americas, spelled out the dynamic process of historical interaction among folk Catholic and African religious practices as well (1993). Brandon's study points to continuous interactions among different Yoruba nations in Cuba, between Yoruba and other African nations, and later among these African nations and both rural folk Catholics and Kardecian spiritists (followers of Allan Kardec, a French spiritist). Brandon's investigations demonstrate the opportunities for African syncretism over centuries, while Ortiz's investigations emphasize the Catholic syncretism that also took place. Brandon's data indicate a continuum from ritual practices among enslaved Africans to developed practices among enslaved and free Africans, as well as among European Americans.

Cabildo activities consistently included dance, singing, and drumming and simultaneously connected African and emerging African American identities. Religious and ritual performance differences among the four African nations in Cuba and between these and the French Haitian *tumba francesa* are great. Each is marked with special instrumentation and a characteristic dance style among many different dances within each dance/music tradition (Ortiz 1951 [1985]; Carbonero 1980; León 1984:7–32; Alén 1992:5–24; Daniel 1989:60–97, 1995:33–37).

For example, the Yoruba use several drum types, but most often two: three *batá* drums or three *Iyesa* drums, double-headed and cylindrical drums, respectively. Among the Arará *cabildos,* the drum battery basic unit is five elongated drums instead of three, with their specific nation rhythms and a distinctive *agogó* or gong pattern. The Kongo-Angola nations feature the barrel-shaped *congas* for both their ritual and social drumming, and the Carabalí nations use very small hand-held, specialized drums to call their *íremes* or nation divinities.

While the nations have surely changed from their sources over the five centuries of African presence in Cuba, these four are considered "African," and secondarily "Cuban" by many Cubans, since they are a result of original African creativity that continues to a great degree. Other Cubans and non-Cubans commonly refer to these as "Afro-Cuban" traditions, because of the Cuban influences that have shaped them since leaving Africa. Each presents distinctive movement material for the formation and continuity of African liturgies in the Americas.

KONGO-ANGOLA NACIÓN The largest numbers of enslaved Africans in the Cuban slave trade were among the Kongo-Angola nations of West Central Africa (Eltis and Richardson 1997; Janzen and MacGaffey 1974; MacGaffey 1986; Thompson and Cornet 1981; Thompson 1983).[14] While Kongo-Angola culture is, at first examination, the least elaborated, least public, and therefore the least visible among the African nations in Cuba, in fact it is one of the most pervasive cultures (e.g., *los muertos* of the Yoruba practice can often be Kongo-Angola spirits). In many sectors, Kongo-Angola nation is considered the most powerful in Cuba.

Kongo-Angola culture in Cuba does not rely on visual decoration or extraordinary artifacts; it does not necessitate ornate symbols or huge numbers of material items for much of its practice. Its belief system has remained attached to nature, the earth and its orientation to the sun, moon, and stars. It focuses on humans in a natural or unelaborated state, and in balanced relationships as well. The practices, therefore, while powerful in terms of belief and efficacy, could be part of everyday activity. The division between the sacred and the ordinary does not have boundaries in common within their understandings; ritual behaviors can easily look like ordinary social events. In fact, Kongo-Angola culture underlies much of culture in the African Americas (see Lopez Valdés 1988; Alan and Wilcken 1998; Bilby and Fu-Kiau 1983; Crowell 2002).

In terms of dance and music performance, Kongo-Angola peoples are responsible for *congas/tumbadores,* barrel-shaped drums, and their music patterns often form the rhythmic base for long-lasting indoor and outdoor community social dance in Cuba and elsewhere in the Americas. Kongo-Angola dance was the means for and product of one of the most basic African and African American social gatherings, particularly in colonial times. Its name, *conga* or *comparsa* (interchangeable in Cuba, meaning a community procession with music and dance), was used in the procession dances of *cabildo* organizations.

The idea of processional dance is intriguing upon examination. Each performer performed individualistically, and yet all performers were, in effect, creating a unified whole, a dancing line, a chain of interconnectedness in a multiethnic, social community.[15] The *congas* and *comparsas* of Cuba maintained African distinctiveness in parading nations, but they also referenced specific Kongo-Angola culture.

Other specific contributions include another type of dance structure and particular movement material. Very often in Kongo-Angola dance in Cuba, as was the case in Haitian Congo dances, a dancing couple encircles each other and displays hip circling and a sudden execution of significant gestures. The timing of the dancers' gestures usually coincides with rhythmic accents from the accompanying drums. For example, in *yuca,* one of Cuba's Kongo-Angola dances, male and female partners almost never touch, but they alternately advance toward one another, often with the hip-circling step, and then, spontaneously, they push both abdomens forward and quickly spin away from one another. A pelvic thrust, a navel bumping, or a throwing gesture toward the dancing partner's abdomen initiates a retreat pattern. Kongo-Angola dance culture also characteristically includes sensuous hip circling, slow or fast. Even when dancers eliminate the abdomen or pelvic thrust, they still concentrate on playful flirtation; for example, in *makuta,* both male and female performers accentuate the hips in sensuous display.

Early Kongo-Angola dance in Haiti had similar characteristics. In fact, Moreau de St. Méry's descriptions of *calenda* and *chica* find several historical descendents in Cuba. The historical and contemporary Haitian *congo* and *grouyad* steps share the same emphases. Also in Bahia and across Brazil, the *samba* has similar obvious Kongo-Angola legacies. Moreover, Kongo-Angola influence and consequences are found elsewhere in Caribbean and Latin American niches beyond Haiti, Cuba, and Bahia.[16]

Kongo-Angola culture is also responsible for a Cuban martial art/dance form, *juego de maní* or peanut game, also called *juego de maní con grasa* (peanut with grease game) or *bambosa* because of its smooth and slippery qualities (Ortiz 1951 [1985]:396–429). In colonial Cuba, *juego de maní* involved a solo dancer who danced within a circle of opponents. His opponents tried to strike blows as he executed various jumps and "evasive steps." Accompanying musicians were expected to synchronize drumming accents with movement accents in the performance. This form was popular in Matanzas and Las Villas provinces and featured circling, competitive male dancing, which later affected dances of Cuban creation, such as *rumba columbia* (Daniel 1995). The Cuban martial art form risked particular danger, since the dancer sometimes had leather wrist covers (muñequeras) that were decorated with nails and other sorts of metal (Ortiz 1951 [1985]:398). Originally, Cuban women also danced juego de maní. This particular Cuban form was outlawed in the 1930s, although it was still apparently performed until the time of Ortiz's publication (see also León 1984:71–73).[17]

Kongo-Angola dance is tremendously impressive, although not very ostentatious. In general, Kongo-Angola dance contains highly percussive, often sensuous, but generally sharp, angular, and nonlyrical movement material. The dancers' backs are usually bent forward or exceedingly low, despite the fact of powerful jumping and multiple isolations of body parts. It is quite dynamic, even explosive in character. The movements have a huge range of complexity from the independence of torso and limbs in simultaneous activity to the total isolation of the hips, initiating a wide range of gyrating circles and swings from side to side (e.g., velele in Kongo-Angola dances [Fu-Kiau 1993: personal communication; Casquelourds 1993: personal communication; cf. Mufwene 1993]).

Palo or Palo Monte, the Kongo-Angola-derived religion of Cuba, relies on some of these dance materials to assist spiritual communication of worshipers.[18] Palo is a complex belief system with a group of divinities or nkisis and their dances and rhythms (Cabrera 1986 [1979]; Bolívar 1994, 1996). The names of the Kongo-Angola nkisis are divided between Spanish and Bantu languages, supporting the early arrival of this nation amalgam and the interpenetration of and later transfer to the Spanish language. For example, the main nkisis in Palo are Lucero, Sarabanda, Pata Llaga, Tiembla Tierra, Brazo Fuerte, Ensasi or Siete Rayos, Ndoqui (or Centella Ndoqui), Madre de Agua, and Shola Anguenmue, most of whom are sung and danced to in a specific order. The dances have only a few variations in the steps or movement vocabulary.

The dancing that accompanies each nkisi's acknowledgment has common foot patterns with slightly different hand, arm, and head gestures. The most common traveling or locomotor movements are running and hopping foot patterns that support loose, fast, and alternating full-arm raises, from thighs to chest, with palms facing upward. The overarching feel and pattern for Palo dancing includes a crunched or very flexed body performing hopping or running steps, periodic jumping, and gestures that reference slicing or tying something invisible in front of the body. Short forearm slicing movements alternate from right to left, or both hands make tying and knotting movements, so as to tie a string around a small package swiftly and tightly. Facial expressions sustain defiant frowns, and at times blubbering shakes of the head and face, side-to-side, accent the dancers' fast-paced rhythmic repetition. While Kongo-Angola dance contribution to African American liturgical rituals is minimal relative to other nation dances, it is spirit-raising and definitely exhilarating for performers and exciting for observers.

Religious practice has combined such that Cubans often refer to the Kongo-Angola divinities in Yoruba terms. For example, the Kongo-Angola divinity named Sarabanda is worshipped, danced to, sung about, and drummed to but is referred to on occasion as Ogún in ordinary conversation.

Overall, there is great sociability in the dances and music within Kongo-Angola nation, and distinctions between male and female behaviors are strict. For example, a male chorus is quite prominent in Palo ceremonies, whereas in other nation practices, women are often in the leadership, and both males and females participate about equally in choruses. In the ceremonies that I have attended, several males constantly competed for leading a series of animated songs in a structured order, while most of the congregation danced in unison or as male/female partners in one of the dance steps described above.

ARARÁ NACIÓN Arará in Cuba originates with the peoples within and near the old Allada Kingdom of Benin and with the contemporary towns of Allada, Abomey, and Ouidah. The people in the region are mainly Fon, but their ancient and current neighbors, such as the Adja, Ewe, and Yoruba, also contribute to the large Arará tradition in Cuba. In fact, with the notable exception of Yorubas and the limited Carabalí groups, most West African nations became known as Ararás in Cuba.[19]

The Cuban drums of Arará nation are formed like many cylindrical drums from the Benin region (as opposed to the Kongo-Angola barrel-shaped drums) and are accompanied by a metal gong/bell or *oggán* (Vineuza 1988). The drums are played with sticks rather than with the hands, and, in Cuba, drummers stand as they play, with the drums often leaning on a bench in front of them. Like many African musics, this nation's music contains dense rhythms, which are danced within a common style. Dancers focus most often on the first two of three beats, and in so doing, they establish a counter-rhythm to the drum battery. This slow and accented triple meter distinguishes Arará dance from that of other nations.

Arará dances are distinctive also because they emphasize shoulder movements more than other body parts. Like the *zépòl* of Haiti and the characteristic ritual dancing I saw in recent times around Cotonou and Abomey, the shoulders are constantly pushing backward or raising and lowering above all other complex body-part movements. No matter where the floor pattern directs the dancer or how high or low the body is carried—the dancer can be bent over or more upright—the shoulders keep pulsing precisely. This is exceedingly strenuous for the performer and powerful to witness. It also makes the tradition highly visible and recognizable.

In western Cuba within Arará ceremonies, the liturgy unfolds a series of salutations for the *fodunes* or *vodunes,* the Arará divinities: Jurajó, Kututó, Dalluá, Gebioso, Argüe, Fodún Mase (or Masen), Ajuanjún, Afrekete (or Ferequete), and Ojún Degara, among other divinities. These are quickly translated into syncretized Yoruba names by informants, but with different characteristics in the dance patterns. For example, Gebioso, the Arará divinity of fire and thunder (from the Fon Hebioso, divinity of thunder), is danced upright with shoulders pressing backward constantly. In Cuba, the Yoruba Changó is sometimes called Gebioso, but Arará Gebioso dances unlike Yoruba Gebioso—with very distinct hand and arm movements that circle wrists and alternately fling out and pull in the lower arm in front of the torso.

The pattern for Afrequete, the Arará divinity of ocean water (like Yoruba Yemayá), is danced with an explicit accent on the second of a three-beat walking pattern. Her skirt swings to alternate sides and accents the second beat on each hip. This occurs simultaneously with the shoulders rhythmically pulsing backward. Then there is the dance for Fodún Mase, the Arará river water divinity (like Yoruba Ochún), which uses the same accented two-step Arará foot pattern while clapping out the typical rhythm. She lowers her body to a sitting pose near the ground and rises up, both in four slow counts, and then dances upright, traveling forward to complete a repeated pattern.

The most important Arará *fodún,* not simply to the Arará nation but to the Yoruba and Kongo-Angola nations as well, is Sagpana, or St. Lazarus from the Catholic Church, as he became popularly known throughout Cuba (also Sonponna, Sankanan, Ntotonsaba, Nsooba, and, in Bahia, Omolu). This is a favored divinity of smallpox and disease, who, in effect, washes ritual community members and assures health and well-being. He is a good example of how, regardless of which name he is called by, his presence is understood in each of the African nation traditions. His Arará movements are brushing or wiping strokes of the hand on the chest. His shoulders are constantly pumping, and he affects a limp as he walks on two of three beats.

What ultimately results from listening to and observing an Arará ceremony is an understanding of a structural order that clearly echoes Yoruba worship. In fact, a Cuban specialist in Arará music, María Elena Vinueza, states that Yoruba divinities have been "substituted" for ancient Fon divinities because the Arará divinities *"no tienen 'caballos'"* (1988:56); that is, no one receives the divinities any more (literally, "there are no more horses").[20] This was not my experience in 1987 and 1997, when I witnessed several *fodún* manifestations in Matanzas. Still, I agree that participants quickly explained Arará divinities within ordinary conversation in Yoruba terms. Songs, prayers, and dances for each *fodún* continue in the ritual setting with precision in a set of special songs and dances for each *fodún* until the liturgical order is completed.

Additionally, there are dances from Haitian Vodou in eastern Cuba that are related to Cuban Arará because of their shared Fon and Yoruba heritage and their early mixture in the colonial and enslavement period. The French Creole-speaking Africans who came to Cuba at the end of the eighteenth century with *tumba francesa* also brought the worship of Vodú; see James, Millet, and Alarcón 1992). Vodú in Cuba and its dance performances differ from Cuban Arará beliefs and Arará dance; it is a transposed version of Haitian Vodou.

Vodú ceremonies in Cuba take place over a series of days and nights, with much of the ceremony taking place outside. A display of feats is customary and seems to occur more often than in the Haitian case. One Vodou service that I witnessed in Camagüey, near the center of the island, began with sung prayers in a small house apart from the main house; it was like a large altar room in Haiti. Then the ceremony continued with an afternoon of dancing and singing in a patio-like space outdoors in front of the drums. The dancing and drumming were interrupted with a display of specific feats. Separately, two performers picked up a table with their teeth and several worshipers danced with machetes and passed them over their tongues and necks. One dancing worshiper lay in shattered glass as people stepped, and even jumped, on his back and later on his stomach; the glass never perforated his skin. After more singing and dancing, there was a transformation, and a divinity crawled on the ground like a snake, a Dambala symbol, and everyone went inside to be fed the blessed foods and to receive advice.

The Vodú ceremony in Cuba, like the Beninois rituals I witnessed, was concerned with the virtuoso display of believers' commitment, which divine association or manifestation of divinity permits. The dance behavior seemed to be generalized to shoulder and foot movement. In Cuban Vodú, there were undulations like in Haitian *yanvalu,* but not as much pronounced shoulder movement as in Haitian *zépòl* or as in Cuban Arará.

The second Haitian immigration to Cuba was a periodic and seasonal influx of Haitian immigrants, often temporary, but sometimes permanent. Haitian immigration began after the formal abolition of Cuban slavery in 1886 and continued with waves of Haitian and other Caribbean workers for the Cuban sugarcane industry in the early twentieth century (1920–25). Both temporary and permanent workers replenished Haitian beliefs and customs in Cuba and continued the core of Vodú that the early African Haitians had brought to their new environment. Hence, the dances of Haiti—Vodou and *affranchi,* as well as *meringue*—are also performed in Cuba. Additionally, the *Rara* music/dance organizations of Haiti became *Gagá* in Cuba. Cuban *Gagá* expresses Catholic Church influence during Holy Week and is also tied to Vodú. Thus, Haitian forms continue among Haitian descendents and more contemporary Haitian residents of Cuba.

Despite its many related forms, the Arará tradition of music and dance promoted its nation style within the Cuban ritual dance category. It provided very rhythmic stylistic elements to the Cuban dance vocabulary, as it echoed its roots in both Benin and Haiti.

CARABALÍ NACIÓN A very distinct African nation in Cuba is from the Calabar River region and is associated with secret societies in what are now Cameroon and Nigeria. The nation became known in Cuba as Carabalí, Abakuá, or Ñáñigo, a formidable, male secret society, as well as a dance/music tradition (Cabrera 1970 [1958]). There are secret societies among the Efik and Ejagham in Nigeria and among the Banyang in Cameroon, and also throughout the Calabar River area (Blier 1980; Thompson 1983:227–69). They all contain masked dance forms, but "Abakuá," as the society is most popularly known in Cuba, is the only surviving mask tradition in Cuba. Enslaved Africans replicated and maintained dance and drumming patterns, as well as songs and chants, in the languages of the Calabar region.

Abakuá dancing reenacts stories of mysterious beings, called *íremes, Ñáñigos,* or *diablitos* (little devils), who communicate through postures, gestures, movement motifs, and the intangible expressiveness of masks. The masks command awe because of their tall, cone-shaped heads and the lack of noses and mouths. The dancing masks are spiritual entities that affirm secret society attitudes and values through a special ritual language and through rigid rules of performance. The *íremes* dance in the *plante* or society meeting place. They are elongated beings, short and tall, who sporadically lunge and recover, vibrate their bodies so that bells hung at their waists ring and shake, and then gracefully step high to travel across the space. They dance to the sound of a male chorus that sings, alternating in unison and three-part harmony.

It is a unique experience to see an Abakuá performance: two to twenty males dancing calmly and mysteriously, not fiercely. Visitors are permitted to observe only parts of the ceremony at certain times of the ritual calendar, usually once per year, and this is generally reserved for male visitors. I saw them first in a Matanzas *plante* where I was admitted briefly and only in close proximity to the front door while several *íremes* were dancing in a distant courtyard. Even with this glimpse, as a dancer I found their gestures and movement sequences fascinating. There was excitement as they danced across the dusty courtyard; participants crowded near them but gave them respectful distance to dance their unusual gestures. Years later, I was privileged to visit a *plante* during the annual open event in which special female participants are included. I observed another ritual display with a female anthropologist colleague. Despite the intoxication of most of the participants and the lack of translation of the ritual language spoken to the *íremes,* I found that the dancing *íremes* generated special affection from ritual participants.

The characteristic movements are smooth and sustained lunging stances that alternate with standing positions, which require the performer to be high on the toes, all muscles pulled up and tight, and with all energy contained. Both the pointed, cone-shaped head of the mask and the tiny drum (*enkríkamo*), which invokes the dancing divinities, further identify Abakuá distinctiveness. While the performers lunge to one side, they make gestures with short, hand-held dance sticks or batons. Often and most characteristically, they kneel on one knee and make long sweeping gestures along the entire body or body part (leg, arm, or chest of the dancer), as if to cleanse the body. These movements are preceded and followed by vibrations of the hips, the whole body, or sometimes simply a vibratory hand gesture. The dance movements in sum create an aura of "the strange," "the out-of-this-world," a quiet and calm, nonhuman presence. The dance/music of Abakuá can be incredibly beautiful and mysterious, whether in genuine ceremonial performance or on stage in the theater.

Abakuá men must be strong and moral; they understand the society as a religious community. The society has strict precepts of mutual aid, which makes radical social action possible when necessary. Each male must be an honorable family protector and a responsible community member. Membership is not given quickly or easily. Men must earn their eligibility through service to the community. When social injustice occurs, it is the secret society that resolves situations. Abakuá members are known to punish offenders and establish justice. Their behavior is strong and severe and is accompanied by absolute allegiance to the society.

Although it is not generally discussed, women and families can dance portions of the secret society music/dance tradition, and a few women hold important ceremonial roles within the male organization (Matanzeros 1996, 1997, 1998: personal communication). In separate formations, but without the masked spirit dancing of íremes, women dance and sing their complementary Carabalí patterns, called Bríkamo, lunging intermittently within the traveling rhythmic dance pattern and brushing their bodies with sweeping, cleansing gestures. The Carabalí nation, in sum, presents very distinctive movement material and another structured spiritual legacy as its contributions to African liturgies in the Americas.

YORUBA NACIÓN The latest Africans to arrive in Cuba in massive numbers were the Yorubas; they came because of civil wars among neighboring Yorubas as well as attacks from the Fon and Fulani over time (Brandon 1993:55–59). Many came from what are now Nigeria and Benin up through the last decades of the nineteenth century. Yorubas had entered the Americas earlier, but in smaller numbers. Their dance/music tradition is familiar to most observers of Cuban culture, and their dance culture is often thought to be the only remaining African culture in Cuba—because of its ornate visibility.

Yoruba dance/music is recognizable because of its impressive visual symbols and its diverse array of divinities, who enter the bodies of worshipers and dance sweetly or fiercely. Many specialists have focused on Yoruba culture and have published on their elaborate altars, necklaces, and shrines, as well as on their ceremonial practice (Ortiz 1951 [1985]; Thompson 1974, 1983; Omari 1984; Murphy 1988; Daniel 1989; Drewal, Pemberton, and Abiodun 1989; Bolívar 1990; Mason 1992; Brandon 1993; Canizares 1999; Lindsay 1996; Vega 2000; Murphy and Sanford 2001). The dance/music comprises a continuum of varied, codified movement sequences and identifying gestures that represent differing divine personalities. The divinities dance as chartering characters of behavior, archetypes that guard the many domains of human social life. In very general terms and in comparison with the other three nations of African music/dance traditions of Cuba, Yoruba movements are lyrical and often make the dancer seem to undulate vertically and repeatedly from the pelvic area up through the chest, shoulders, neck, and head.

Yoruba dance/music tradition is a group of specific dances that personify the *orichas* in movement. They abstract activities and the characteristics of the *orichas* and pantomime episodes from their lives, defining what are called *caminos* or paths, which vary the qualities of a divinity and his/her dance.[21] The instruments, songs, and gestures articulate rhythmic invocations to the divinities, who are also referred to in everyday conversation as Catholic saints (cf. Canizares 1999; Bolívar 1990; Sandoval 1989; Murphy 1988, 1994; Bascom 1950; Herskovits 1941).[22] Again, before describing the dances singularly, I emphasize that these are broad generalizations of a large repertoire of dances. The movement sequences visually clarify who the performance is created for or offered to. When *orichas* appear as a result of the rhythmic invocations and dances of worshipers, they dance the same codified gestures and signature movements that worshipers dance, but with more forceful energy.

We have already met up with the *oricha* named Elegba. He dances in red and black with a forked branch, a *garabato,* in one hand. His movements are generally in small, quick, and irregular patterns. He is perceived as a divine but mischievous child, or a wise, secretive elder, and so his body is low to the ground and his gestures shift and change abruptly. His floor pattern often traces the four cardinal directions or the crossroads. He runs and jumps, animating all possible space. He powerfully governs opportunities and chances; he opens doors and closes them. He is both the beginning and the end and is often painted red or white on one side of his body with the other side revealing his skin to mark his unity of oppositions. His different but related names, like Elegba and Elegbara, are for different paths or aspects of his life history. Elegba and Elegbara are for his opening dimension; his Echu or Exu name is his closing dimension; and Ena is his duality. All names signify his activating, energetic energy. He is Vital Force with any of his names and stimulates movement throughout his environment.

When Ogún dances, he uses a diagonal pattern as he strikes with his machete. Ogún is a divine warrior whose protection is as fierce as the strength of iron. His foot pattern clears a given space, thrusting to both sides and constantly moving through and around. His arm gestures alternately slice, cut, or chop the forested area of his habitat or a perceived opponent. His movements are so strong that he shakes fiercely and vibrates forcefully with each accumulating gesture.

Ochosi is a third warrior *oricha.* He is a warrior/hunter who has a bow and arrow and is responsible for forest animals and also for the distant future. In his dance, he takes his arrow from the quiver, places it in the bow, and calculates important dimensions of the impending shot. His body reacts in a jerking undulation from the force at the release of the arrow, the achievement of the chase, the accomplishment of all tedious and time-consuming preparation. His dance demonstrates the hunt, his search for a particular destination. His presence focuses long-range decisions.

Ochún dances as the divine river, fresh water that flows happily and bubbly, yet carefully and meaningfully, over waterfalls and around embedded rocks. Her movements are sensuous and flowing, like her source in nature, but also female-body-centered, as womankind in her most beautiful and alluring state in the human body, ready for social excitation and procreation. Crystal clear in direction and point of view, Ochún dances in golden yellow and giggles over the sounds of the drums.

Changó is another type of *oricha;* he is a king, and in that sense, a divine warrior too. He is powerful and fierce, but his domain is not the forested area as Ogún or Ochosi. His sphere is higher communication, music, and intellect, and he dresses in red and white. His dance involves a characteristic kick that accompanies an arm gesture, which symbolizes his extraordinary potency. With this gesture and kick, he brings the energy of lightning and thunder from the sky above into his genitals for the ultimate protection of the nation. As he fights for the survival of the nation, he is the only dancing *oricha* who leaps. Many divinities use forceful runs and powerful turns; Ogún and Elegba can hop and jump; but it is Changó's dance that has leaps, tumbling, and kicks.

As Yemayá dances, she converts duple to triple rhythm so that the viewer senses the repetitious and soothing quality of the sea, divine creative source of life. Her dance traces the movement of waves, of whirlpools, and of oars. Her force is as powerful as the ocean, saltwater, and the sea. She is the omnipotent mother, maternal power—caring, nurturing, and incredibly protective.

Obatalá's dance symbolizes his position as the most powerful *oricha,* divine father of all the *orichas* and judge of humankind. He is cool, elegant, and stately. He does not move swiftly but walks and dances bent over, in the determined and mindful manner of the eldest of elders. When he dances as his younger form, he gallops carrying a white fly whisk. His dance symbolizes peace, balance, and justice, as do his white clothes.

Oyá is the female divine warrior, the *oricha* with a continuum of air energy. She can dance with gentle charm as a breeze or with fire and force as a tornado or hurricane. She is wind all-powerful, totally unpredictable, and incomparably forceful. She wears every color simultaneously, and she appears at times and in places of extreme change—in the marketplace, at the end of the year, in Carnival. She fears nothing, not even death, so it is she who gallops everywhere, including the cemetery, where she guards the "living dead." Her dance is provocative and unpredictable. She dashes and gallops across space with the horse step, *caballo,* carrying a dark-colored fly whisk, often while screaming.

Babaluayé's dance is performed while stooped over, trembling and positioned in an array of grotesque shapes. He behaves with the erratic movements of someone who is sick. Babaluayé is the divinity of smallpox and other diseases, and he takes on the sickness and disease of the community as a leper or a smallpox victim. In time, he reaches for health as his dance cleanses the body, the mind, and, ultimately, the ritual community.

The Yoruba dances are numerous, and each has several contrasting sections, but those just described are the most characteristic. As I have noted, the Yoruba nations had strong influence on other African nations, not only in nineteenth-century Cuba but also earlier in Haiti; Yoruba Ogou was present in Haitian Rada rites as early as the 1790s. I have also pointed out Yoruba structural influence when describing Cuban Palo that follows a similar order to invoke and praise each divinity until s/he arrives. It is often through Yoruba divinities that other African divinities are explained and understood. Intra-African syncretism accounts for some of the threads of commonality that they all contain. Some Yoruba influence, however, is the result of the Yoruba hegemony that occurred in the nineteenth century and later in the post-emancipation era. Additionally, throughout the twentieth century, scholars have sometimes reified Yoruba culture above other African ethnic groups (see Matory 2001b; chapter 1).

Discrete Mix in Cuba

African dance liturgies of Cuba demonstrate a syncretism or parallel integration of divinities, called *nkisis* among Kongo-Angola worshiper, *fodunes* or *vodunes* among Arará worshipers, *íremes* among the Carabalí, *orichas* among Cuban Yoruba worshipers, and *luas* (Vodú *lwas* in Spanish) among descendents of French-Haitian Vodouists in Cuba. Taking the Kongo-Angola nation mix first, Cuban descendents have gradually substituted Spanish names for some of the *nkisis,* as well as submerged Kongo-Angola legacies within the more recent Yoruba influence. In the dance practice, a few dances are performed for several Kongo-Angola *nkisis,* and similar gestures relate to other African *cabildo* dance traditions. For the Arará nation, the examples of interaction and intra-African syncretism occurred in terms of Fon heritage that was mixed with Yoruba heritage in Cuba, just as it did historically in Benin and Nigeria. For the many Yoruba nations, one chartering *cabildo* emerged. For the Carabalí nation also, what materials survived in Cuba did so as a distinct *cabildo*.

Thus, Cuban dance history yields a huge variety of dance movement materials. The indelible remnants of Spanish *zapateo* surface in secular circumstances and also infiltrate African liturgical dance as the *zapateo* for Yemayá and in Ochún's basic step (as I will discuss further in the next chapter). French influence from Haiti provided one type of *cabildo* in the east and also brought Haitian Vodú, Gagá, and Tumba Francesa to the Cuban movement vocabulary. The largest contribution of varied movements, however, came directly from the evolution of African nation dances and their stylistic preferences. Cuba's dance history emphasized the major annual religious event, *Dia de los reyes,* which in turn provided regular time and space for nation identification and display of different African customs. Differences among nations were acknowledged, yet ritual structures were held in common, and the more flamboyant Yoruba names were often used as an alternative to other nation names of divinities.

Cabildo organization facilitates an understanding of the wealth of movement material in Cuba. Stylistically different African dance/music traditions continued as separate religious traditions and social markers for African nations in the Americas. They served also as matrix movement material for the development of "Cuban" dance and music forms. For example, *son, rumba, mambo,* and *salsa* developed over time, and currently hip-hop and *timba* in popular dance culture and *danza contemporánea* in concert dance culture have emerged as well. These all find their roots most fundamentally in the Spanish, French-Haitian, and African nation movement matrix just described.[23]

Chart 5. Cuban *Naciones* and Their Dances

Naciones	Dances
Native American	*Areítos*
Spain	*Contradanza*
	Zapateos
	Guajiro
Haiti	*Contredanse*
	Tumba Francesa
	Vodú ritual dances
	Gagá

Chart 5, cont.

African

Kongo-Angola

Yuca
Makuta
Conga (Comparsa)
Juego de maní
Palo ritual dances
  Lucero
  Sarabanda
  Pata Llaga
  Tiembla Tierra
  Brazo Fuerte
  Ensasi (Siete Rayos)
  Ndoqui (Centella Ndoqui)
  Madre de Agua
  Shola Anguenmue, etc.

Arará

Arará ritual dances
  Jurajó
  Kutotó
  Dalluá
  Gebioso
  Argüe
  Mase (Masen)
  Ajuanjun
  Afrequete (Frerequete)
  Ojún Degara, etc.
  Sagpana

Carabalí

Abakuá
Bríkamo

Yoruba

Oricha ritual dances
  Elegba
  Ogún
  Ochosi
  Yemayá
  Obatalá
  Babaluayé
  Changó
  Ochún
  Oyá
  Elegba, Exú

Cuba

Son
Rumba
Danzón
Chachachá
Mambo, etc.
Danza contemporánea
Timba
Hip-hop cubano

Bahian Nation Dances

Brazilian dance history has fewer references than other sites of dance performance. Brazilian dance researchers Marilia de Andrade and Katia Canton have collected, reviewed, and evaluated the literature to date and report only a few reliable studies, and these deal mainly with ballet productions and ballet training from the late nineteenth century and in the twentieth century (1996:114–22). They found that both the circulation of publications and critical collegial exchange had serious problems, in terms of developing the field of Brazilian dance research. Brazilians are addressing these issues currently.

My experiences in visiting Bahia and navigating the university system as well as visiting community sites of education and performance have yielded understanding of Bahian Afro-Brazilian dance vocabulary and an overview of Brazilian forms. For example, Raimundo Bispo dos Santos, affectionately known by his *capoeira* title Mestre King, the first Afro-Brazilian graduate of the University of Bahia's Dance Department and a major stylist and teacher, has codified his perspective over years of teaching and teacher-training in Bahia. One of his students, Rosangela Sylvestre, has been writing a book on her version of Mestre King's technique and how to portray Afro-Brazilian dance best on the concert stage. Linda Yudin, a dancer and researcher from the United States who collaborates with another of Mestre King's students, Luiz Badaró, gave a public presentation at the American Anthropological Association meetings on the most influential dancers in the *Afro-contemporaneo* genre, including the other important disciple, Augusto Omolu (1996). I have gained other insights as I studied Bahian ritual dance forms and when I taught Dunham technique in Bahia during a university workshop. From time to time, I have also had informative exchange and critique with Brazilian dancers who work in the States.

The Missing Indigenous Dance

I see a pattern in Bahian dance development similar to the one that emerged elsewhere in the African Americas. Despite limited sources (that I have been able to find and those recounted and evaluated by de Andrade and Canton), I find a similarity within indigenous, European, and African contributions to a Brazilian dance typology that I have given for Haitian and Cuban dance typologies; I also see the differentiation of three African amalgam nations with their dance/music traditions. The unique issue for Brazil, however, is that it still has numerous native peoples, unlike Haiti or Cuba, and their documented dance history is so far not readily accessible. What we know is that even with the advance of industrialization, technology, and globalization, the dance culture of Brazil's heterogeneous indigenous population survives; they, like all humans, dance. Their forms are sometimes called *caboclo,* meaning "Afro-indigenous" and "from or of native Brazilians." The literature, on the other hand, makes it appear as if the numerous native groups were decimated along with those of Haiti and Cuba. De Andrade and Canton cite only one work for native Brazilian dances: Felicitas's *Danças do Brasil* (1983, in de Andrade and Canton 1996).

European Dance Practices

European folk and court forms emerged with the arrival of the Portuguese, and Africans arrived with the Portuguese in the early seventeenth century (Freyre 1946; Harding 2000). Portuguese colonists were under the same overwhelming influence of the French court system during the sixteenth and seventeenth centuries as were the Spaniards. Accordingly, they brought an assortment of both folk and court forms, most of which were echoed in the popular *contredanse,* or in Portuguese, *contradança* of Brazil. The dances were interspersed within Roman Catholic plays and other colonial diversions that, according to de Andrade and Canton, sometimes included references to native forms (1996).

The Catholic influence on dance practices grew particularly by the nineteenth century to not simply include but also to emphasize *Carnaval* displays just before the Lenten season. Public displays of festive excess and social inversion (where the poor and the powerful shifted positions for a day) were common, and an accompaniment of lavish and ornate dance parading grew (Crowley 1984).

African *Nação* Formation

With the effects of the Atlantic slave trade, differing African populations came into the social mix and began to manage the danced dialogue of cultures as well. The recreation of European lay Catholic brother- and sisterhoods in the Americas, called *irmandades* in Brazil, provided time and space not only for Portuguese settlers but also for African nations to present their distinctiveness and to influence one another. The African *irmandade* organizations, like the *konbits* and *Rara* bands of Haiti and the *cabildos* and *Gagá* bands of Cuba, served their respective societies in terms of mutual aid within the Afro-Brazilian population (Reis 1977).

In Bahia, these organizations also preserved African notions of *nação*, even the notion of dual and multiple *nações*. For this reason, *irmandades* were important in the retention of African values and the continuity of African and religious practices. Historian Rachel Harding makes the resulting intra-African syncretism clear when she outlines the interconnections and changes among the three amalgam groups and their influence on Candomblé formation in Bahia. She states:

> Candomblé is a Bantu term used to describe a religious form with strong West African structural components. Bantu-speaking people constituted the first large-scale source of enslaved labor in Bahia; their importation began in the early seventeenth century. In many regions of Brazil, Central Africans constituted a majority (or at least a large proportion) of slaves until the end of the colonial era. . . . West Africans of the Aja-Fon-Ewe ethnic and language groups (collectively known as Jejes in Bahia) were the most numerous immediate predecessors to Yorubas in the province; most were imported between the 1770s and the first decades of the nineteenth century. Documents on Afro-Brazilian religion in Brazil between the late eighteenth century and 1830 evidence a strong Jeje influence and a marked presence of Jejes among African spiritual leaders. . . . [The year] 1807, . . . was the same year in which the term "Candomblé" first appeared in written documents as a reference to Afro-Bahian religion. . . . In either case, mention of the Dahomean term for deity or spirit suggests that Jeje influence on the Afro-Bahian religious landscape was not insignificant. . . . In the 1890s [Nina] Rodrigues identified major ritual elements of Candomblé in Bahia to be of distinctly Yoruba origin. (2000:45–49)

European dance forms arrived and took dominant positions in the dance practices, although anthropologist Sheila Walker has found Kongo-Angola forms from Maranhão in the north to Rio Grande do Sul in the south (2003: personal communication). Discrete African ritual dance styles, predicated on Fon, called *Jêje* in Brazil, Yoruba, and Kongo/Angola amalgams, continued in American ritual contexts.

Brazilian Dance Formation

Even without a wealth of literature to prove how traditions were carried forth, many native, European, and African dance/music traditions continued, as well as surfaced, in new "Brazilian" forms. In both the nineteenth and twentieth centuries, social dance forms appeared that were primarily influenced by the experience of Europeans and Africans in the Americas. De Andrade and Canton (1996) report that those dance forms attributed to Brazilian origins are led by *samba,* the national dance, with others that have varied in popularity, depending on historical period or region (e.g. *maracatú, congada, quilombo*). National development of other forms includes a variant of *capoeira,* identified as *capoeira regional,* and a fad dance of the 1980s called *lambada,* which was added to the major Latin popular dance types. Probably the most informative and accessible analysis of Brazilian dance forms is Barbara Browning's analysis of *samba* (1995). Through her examination of dance and society, readers gain a clear understanding of the contributions of Europeans, Africans, and Brazilians to Brazil's dance history.

Chart 6. Bahian *Nações* and Their Dances

Nações	Dances
Numerous indigenous	*Caboclo*
Portugal	*Contradança*
	Carnaval
African	
Angola	Candomblé Angola ritual dances
	Capoeira Angola
	Maculele
	Congada
	Maracatú
Jêje	Candomblé Jêje ritual dances
Nago/Ketu	Candomblé *Orixá* ritual dances
	Exu (Elegbara, Ena)
	Ogun
	Oxossi
	Ossein
	Omolu
	Xangó
	Oxumare
	Yansan or Oya
	Yemanja
	Oxun
	Oba
	Eua
	Nana
	Oxalá (Oxalufan, Oxaguian)
Brazil	*Samba*
	Umbanda ritual dances
	Capoeira Regional
	Lambada
	Many other popular dances

Three Sites, One Pattern

The African amalgams of my discussion for Haiti and Cuba are prominent as well for Bahia. The Fon, Yoruba, and Kongo-Angola nations exist in all three sites with varying degrees of emphasis on a given amalgam. Each ritual tradition retains the nation designation that was recognized over centuries *by and through* the remembrance of its particular dance and music structures. In presenting three case studies, I have concentrated on two amalgams only: Fon-based *nasyons* in Haiti and Yoruba-based *naciones* or *nações* (Cuban Yoruba and Bahian Nago/Ketu). These particular nations assist in the description and analysis of those practices that led to the development of African American liturgical orders.

FIVE

Praise Dance and Liturgical Orders

God planted a rice field one year. It was a rice field that was equal to His station and circumstances. It began to ripen and God began to look forward to the day of reaping. One day a message came to God saying, "God the pintards [guinea fowl] are eating up all of your rice. If you don't do something about it, there won't be any rice to reap."

So God called the Angel Michael . . . , as well as Gabriel and Peter, who all took their guns to kill the pintards, but they all returned with a shamed face because of the compelling sweetness in the songs and rhythms of the pintards.

So God took the gun and went down to His rice fields Himself. The pintards saw Him coming and left the rice and flew up into the tree again. They saw it was God Himself, so they sang a new song and put on a double rhythm and then they doubled it again. God aimed the gun but before He knew it He was dancing and because of the song, He didn't care whether he saved any rice or not. So He said, "I can't kill these pintards—they are too happy and joyful to be killed. But I do want my rice fields so I know what I will do. There is the world that I have made and so far it is sad and nobody is happy there and nothing goes right. I'll send these pintards down there to make music and laughter so the world can forget its troubles."

And that is what He did. He called Shango, the god of thunder and lightning and he made a shaft of lightning and the pintards slid down it and landed in Guinea. So that is why music and dancing came from Guinea—God sent it there first.

—Zora Neale Hurston

Everywhere I study, the dance is just that joyful; there is little distinction between ritual and diversion. Dancing and music-making are the presents that my Diaspora companions have given and shared with me. These can be received as tokens of the blessed understanding that we were meant to enjoy. These can also be received as the treasures that they are, filled with thick layers of information. From *yanvalu* and the dance for Ochún to *salsa* and hip-hop culture with break dancing, dancing allows humans to transcend into altered spaces and altered time. In these three cases, the transcendence is into praise performance. It is the formulas and orders of praise performance that I am after, as I now fill in some of the gaps from my previous discussions of personal experiences and dance histories. Praise performance has required structure and specific elements.

Evolved Liturgical Orders

The liturgical orders that we see as African American ceremonies today do not completely replicate religious orders in Nigeria, Benin, or the Kongo-Angola region. They closely resemble continental ritual activity; participants relay that they imitate cultural memories from various parts of Africa and share basic philosophical and religious tenets. Haitian Vodou, Cuban Yoruba, and Bahian Candomblé are, however, evolved liturgies that are based on a combined legacy organization and differentiated African religious orientations. In American environments, their main purpose is still to maintain spiritual knowledge for the well-being of the ritual family—to find balance within both the human social and suprahuman spiritual worlds through transformative practices.

In order to acknowledge many nations and many knowledgeable ancestors, different African-derived ritual officials were compelled to develop inclusive practices. Their origin cultures were honorably acknowledged in public most often within composite ritual orders, as well as in separated serial rites. African American liturgies resulted from African blueprints; they are evolved liturgies with compelling influences and selected preferences (cf. origin culture studies in Ajayi 1998; Drewal and Drewal 1983; Drewal, Pemberton, and Abiodun 1989; Abiodun, Drewal, and Pemberton 1991; Galembo et al. 1993; Christophe and Oberlander 1996; and Thompson and Cornet 1981). What follows are generalized liturgies for the Americas.

A Haitian Ceremòni

The Haitian culture that resulted from both African/African and European/ African encounters for more than three hundred years (1501–1804) became isolated with independence. The Roman Catholic Church distanced itself from the newly independent nation at the outset and did not resume relations for fifty-six years (from 1804 to 1860) (Desmangles 1992:42–43). During Haiti's political and religious isolation, Vodou liturgical orders developed that used specific elements from Haiti's history and Haiti's dance history. Liturgies were organized as "rites" or divisions within Vodou *dans, fets,* or *ceremònis* that were Rada/Congo or Rada/Petwo.

Rada rites are usually enacted first, followed by some Congo salutations or formal greetings, and ending ideally with the Gédé *nasyon.* In effect, the salutations honor and acknowledge the *lwas* of all *nasyons.* Additionally, there are separate nation rites where everything concerns one *nasyon* (as in the Kongo rites of Sucrie Danasch described in the next chapter), but often even these have a section for the acknowledgment of other nations. In addition among all *nasyons* there are funereal rites of separation for the dead, *ley mo,* as well as annual and even longer cyclic rites for the varied processes of either incorporating dead ancestors as new *lwas* or raising the statuses of the *lwas* (e.g., three-year, seven-year, and twenty-to-thirty-year rites, as in Karen Kramer's film, *To Serve the Gods,* 1981).

All Haitian liturgies follow an order of spoken prayer, offerings, animal sacrifice, and music and dance in the presence of the *lwas,* who arrive and dance also. After much music-making and dancing, the *lwas* retire to complete the praise and recognition of all *lwa nasyons* (see chart 7). Food is the last element of most services; it is a reciprocal "present" that worshipers first give to the *lwas* as sacred animal and plant offerings and which they later receive as blessed food from the *lwas* for the children of the *lwas.*

In Vodou belief, art, nature, and the human body are united in the invocation of divine spirits. Dancing worshipers draw the artistic representation of the *lwas* on or at the foot of the *potomitan.* Abstract and representational designs are drawn on the ground by letting cornmeal or flour flow through the fingers of skilled *oungans* and/or *manbos.* These visual art representations are followed by the aural representations of the *lwas,* the set drum rhythms that announce each characteristic *nasyon* with its chants and songs. The music initiates a third and kinesthetic representation, the specific dance movements that summon the *lwas.* Then, a fourth representation, prayer as poetic and powerful literature, called *Priyé Guinen* (African prayer), is recited by the *pre savann* and the congregation, relying on Catholic prayers and psalms but ending with "ancient *Vodu"/langaj* from Benin, Yoruba, and Congo ritual prose (Deren 1953:208; Laguerre 1980).

Art, then, is the Haitian vehicle that connects the spiraling realms of existence. Visual art, music, poetry, and dance reach for and reference nature in the universe through the dancing body. Art and nature are joined within the body, in addition to the body's carrying [the dance] function. The combination permits the body to gather sensual data beyond intensified repetitive movement and hypnotic musical responses. A preponderance of aesthetic behavior has the potential to influence a change in the axis of spiraling energy, from the human plane of existence to the ancestor or cosmic planes of existence.

Services are constructed so that the living community can access the spirit world and receive spiritual time, counsel, and nourishment (see Price-Mars 1983; Métraux 1972 [1959]; Deren 1953; Desmangles 1992). Dancing worshipers give themselves to ceremonial manifestation of the *lwas*. Adults and children are prepared over time for an altered state of consciousness through repeated attendance at Vodou services, as well as through exacting apprenticeship within initiation procedures. The procedures train the body, the "horse," to receive *lwa* energy. As Haitian Vodou worshipers say, the procedures prepare their bodies to "gallop" first with an "empty saddle," then to receive a *lwa* "rider," and finally to obey her/his commands.

It is possible for anyone to feel or display *lwa* energy—that is, to manifest spiritual entity. Haitian Vodou is really a "democratic" religion in this regard, since it allows any person—male or female, adult or child, initiated or even uninitiated—to receive spiritual energies and display manifestation (Courlander 1973; Daniel 1980). I should emphasize, however, that uninitiated persons are not encouraged to display or give themselves fully to divine manifestation. Requisite training that prepares the body for the powerful unfolding of spiritual energy is considered crucial. Deliberate and incremental stages of learning are preferred to the *bozal* or "wild" access of spiritual energy, although this type of "mounting" or altered state of consciousness occurs sometimes nevertheless. The deliberate, apprenticed initiation permits the *lwas* to dance and commune comfortably with the living community.

The dancing body then references a cosmic order that welcomes many *nasyons* in one ceremony. First the Rada rite acknowledges Papa Legba, Papa Dambala, Metres Ayida Wèdo, Agwé, and Kuzen Zaka. This *lwa nasyon* uses the colors blue and white, since these colors are said to refer to the cool, peaceful protection that the "African" *lwas* give; they keep the service lively but steady in powerful performance style. The ambiance of the ritual setting, filled with visual art, instrumental and vocal music, and dancing, is exciting but also formal and cool. When the Nago *nasyon* is danced and sung, the ambiance becomes thick and has less predictability. The Haitian Ogou color is red, which heats the space, the worshipping dancers, and the *lwas*. The Congo *nasyon* uses red also. Here the gaiety and sociability of the *lwa* dances suspend the accumulated tension with a leveling-off period of play, still thick in musical, danced, and social texture. The next family, the Petwo *nasyon,* is fire, red, ferocious, and fierce. Demands and requests from these *lwas* are imperative; these *lwas* are the most impatient in character and aggressive in dance style. And the final *nasyon* to appear, the Gédé family, marks death and simultaneously rebirth with the colors black and white and sometimes purple.

Haitian ceremonies use two styles of drumming and two different sets of drums. For Rada rites, they use stick drumming on cylindrical drums. The sharp and shrill tones of the Rada rites are retired when the Congo/Petwo *nasyons* begin. These are rounded barrel-shaped drums that are played with the hands. Skin on skin—human skin on animal skin—makes a muted and rounded sound—that of the Congo and Petwo rites. Rhythms set up a specific dance pattern for each *nasyon,* but their alternate *kasé* pattern really pushes the dancer toward the altered state of manifestation, of *espri* (the spirit) or *nam* (the soul) in *lwa* form.

In dancing the *nasyon* dances, there is always a *feint* at the musical *kasé.* The *feint* stretches and opens the entire body in the style of the dance, providing an opportunity for the *lwas* to enter. For example, the *feint* in *yanvalu* retains the undulation quality of the dance within its opening of the body. The dancer rises from the lowered, tight, and closed position of the main step and lifts the knee across the body to extend the leg fully in front of the body. As soon as it reaches its farthest point, the leg lowers and the foot touches the floor. The body follows in sequential undulation downward: toe, ball of toe, heel, leg, hips, chest and arms, neck and head. The leg comes back to its original side, whereupon the other knee brings the same undulating lift pattern to the opposite side.

With each alternating extension, a smacking pulse from the drums marks the landing of the extended foot and heightens the shift from the small, tight undulation in *yanvalu* pattern to the big, open undulation of the *kasé* pattern. The same principle operates in *mayi.* The *kasé* is quick and abrupt, taking its style from the quick, rhythmic, bouncy pattern of the main step. Also, the *mayí kasé* maintains a vertical stance in opposition to a bent or forward tilted back pattern in the main step. For *mayí kasé*, each foot alternates a quick punch step into the ground in the manner of planting a seed, which also characterizes this agricultural dance.

The drummers determine the alternation of the main pattern and the *kasé* pattern of each dance. They watch to support and "grow" a manifestation. The *ogan* or gong pattern helps to mesmerize the dancers and to keep all dancers and musicians in sync. The *oungenikon* calls out the lyrics and the worshipping community of initiates, called *ouncis*, answers in short repeated phrases. Haitian lyrics are often harsh and cryptic (see Brown 1989 for a fine study of interpreting the words in terms of history and religious culture; see also chapter 6).

An *oungan* or *manbo* directs the service and assists the desires and requirements of each *lwa* as s/he arrives. Initiates and senior ritual members dance in a circle around the *potomitan* or in front of the drums; others in the congregation and guests dance at the periphery. Dancers and musicians usually play throughout the night and into the wee hours of the morning. It takes time to recognize each *nasyon* and its family of spirit divinities.

Chart 7. Generic Structure of a *Ceremòni*

1. Libations	To drums, *potomitan,* doors, and altar rooms for all ritual community and all guests
2. Salutation points	*Laplas'* and *podwapos'* sword salutation to drums, *potomitan,* cardinal directions, all ritual personnel, and the elders
3. *Nasyons* order	Rada singing and dancing
4. Priyé Guinen	Catholic prayers, *langaj* (Fon, Yoruba, and Kikongo prayers, sometimes heard at beginning of ceremony)
5. Continued *Nasyon* order	Finish Rada singing and dancing; Gédé singing and dancing; sometimes also Congo/Petwo singing and dancing; finally Gédé singing and dancing; *lwas* arrive and dance with the community
6. Socializing	People drinking and eating; *lwas dancing,* giving advice and counsel
7. *Lwa* departure	
8. Retiring of drums	Departure of guests

A Cuban Wemilere

Similar to Haitian culture, Cuban culture resulted from African/African and European/African encounters. In Cuba these interactions lasted nearly four hundred years (from 1506 until 1886). As massive numbers of enslaved Africans secured a forceful influence on the emerging Cuban culture, they also provided huge resources of African continuity for the Americas. Europeans also influenced the formation and development of African American liturgies, even as powerful elites who wanted to separate themselves from anything African (except as labor or potential profit).

For example, in the 1870s Frenchman Hippolyte Rivail introduced a Christian practice, called Spiritism or *Espiritismo,* which was influential in Europe, North and South America, and the Caribbean (Brandon 1993:85–90). Writing under the pseudonym of Allan Kardec, Rivail proposed "scientific" or progressive religious ideology within ritualistic meetings in which mediums would receive messages from the spirits of dead people. *Espiritismo* was based on statements and references from the Holy Bible; it became the rage in the Caribbean and South America. Since *Espiritismo* accommodated the worshiper's ability to be incorporated by spirits of the dead, it quickly meshed with ideas and practices that were familiar among Africans and African Americans. Although *Espiritismo* did not present significant dance/music formation, it influenced African American religious practice. Within Cuban Yoruba practices (and as a consequence in Puerto Rico, e.g., LaRuffa 1971), services for *los muertos* occasionally feature a *mesa blanca* or "white table" ceremony, which follows Kardecian principles and practices and is now found within the standard liturgical structure for some worshipers (cf. Brandon 1993 and Vega 2000).

For Cuban Yoruba specifically, the liturgical orders have particular names in Spanish and in Yoruba; uninitiated participants and the lay public use the terms interchangeably and often imprecisely. Generally, a *wemilere* is a sung and danced liturgy with drumming on consecrated or "baptized" drums. A *wemilere* includes a *toque* at its beginning that is a separate musical offering (drumming only) and is played in front of an altar. The word *toque* can also be used colloquially to mean a ceremony on drums that have not been consecrated, but the term *bembé* is most often used in that case. *Bembés* are often given at night after sundown, whereas *wemileres* and *toques* are more often given in Cuba before sunset. In each type of ceremony, the *orichas* are invoked and praised in the same general order (see chart 8).

Most of the major *orichas* within the amalgam of Yoruba nations, who in

Benin and Nigeria would ideally and most often be affiliated with a particular territory and its specified group of related families, are greeted together with great respect in one Cuban ceremony. After the formal reception of all significant *orichas,* the focus of the *wemilere* is on one *oricha,* the one to whom the ceremony is dedicated, with a series of special songs and rhythms, called a *tratao.* If other *orichas* arrive besides the one for whom the ceremony is dedicated, they are treated to their series of songs and dances, their *trataos.* All Cuban *wemileres, toques,* or *bembés* begin and end with drumming, singing, and dancing or only drumming for Elegba. The closing signal with a bucket, as I described in chapter 1, might be construed as an ending, but in reality only the formal part of the *wemilere* is over. After the upturned bucket closes the music/dance, worshipers eat the foods that have been cooked in honor of the *orichas.* Blessed food that is shared by all participants and observers is the appropriate and satisfying ending of a *wemilere, toque,* or *bembé.*

In Cuba, the lead drummer *(olubatá)* coordinates the voices of the *batá* drum battery. This drum battery contains *fundamento,* the sacred blessing elements for drums. Usually the *Oru seco* or *Oru de batá* begins the *wemilere* with its *toque* of twenty-four to twenty-six rhythms (Amira and Cornelius 1992:22–23). This is a contained rite that is performed for members of the religious family only, although special guests are occasionally invited. The rhythms are then played a second time as the *wemilere* proceeds to its public dimension, this time with singing and dancing (*Oru de Eya Aranla* or *Oru de cantos*). This section of the ceremony is for initiated and uninitiated members of the ritual community and their guests and takes place in a large room, often adjacent to a patio or open courtyard *(ibánbalo),* between the hours of midday and sunset. After dark, the same rhythms and dances can be performed in a party atmosphere, a *bembé* or *rumbón* for the *orichas;* however, the baptized *batá* drums are not usually played after dark. The drums that do play are called *aberícula,* since they are not baptized or prepared for the most sacred rituals.

The dancing is initiated by the prescribed order of chants and their specific rhythms. The *akpwon* (leader of the songs), who can be male or female, sings memorized verses of literally thousands of chants (Mason 1992). The singing community, the ritual family, or the congregation answers her/him. The *babaloricha* or *iyaloricha,* the male or female healer and leader of ceremonies, conducts the necessary rites and sings and dances; the diviner or *babalawo* usually does not dance but officiates and attends various stages of the ritual before and after the *wemilere.* The diviner is the only official who can use the entire knowledge and practice within the divining system; he divines through special

Chart 8. Generic Structure of a *Wemilere*

1. *Orú seco* /Toque	Private liturgical order on baptized drums, played without dancing or singing, in front of a decorated altar with offerings from initiated and ritual family
2. *Orú de cantos* /Toque	Liturgical order of drum rhythms played with singing and dancing for ritual family and guests
	a. Libations and salutation to Elegba to open service
	b. Salutation to all *orichas* in a set order of dance/music
	c. Chants and dancing for the dedicated *oricha*
	d. Advice and counsel from the *orichas*
	e. Closing to Elegba and retiring of drums
	f. Sharing the dedicated foods with all present
3. *Bembé*	Liturgical order of drums, played on *aberícula* drums or *chekeres*
	a. Salutation to Elegba to open service; libations
	b. Salutation to all *orichas* in a set order
	c. Chants and dancing for the dedicated *oricha*
	d. Advice and counsel from the *orichas*
	e. Closing to Elegba and retiring of drums
	f. Sharing the dedicated foods with all present

chains, seeds, stones, and sixteen cowries. Leaders of families or temples can use a cowry or coconut shell system for divining. And in Cuba, laypersons who participate but are not initiated, called *aberícula,* join ritual officials and dance enthusiastically to nonbaptized drums, also called *aberícula.*

A Bahian Xirê

In terms of African beliefs, Bahians bonded similarly to their Candomblé religion as did Haitians and Cubans. Overall, their liturgies display the same *nação* differentiation of Fon, Yoruba, and Kongo-Angola amalgams that I have discussed earlier, but in Bahia there is much additional variety.[1] My personal experience over many years of trying to find "a" or "the" Bahian model structure has been to use the organization of ritual rites as they are performed but to know that there are many exceptions. For example, in the rituals that I have witnessed or within which I have participated, I have regularly been told that the ceremony is Nago/Ketu. Later within the same ceremony, people have identified Jêje (Fon) chants or Angola costumes. When I have questioned them, their responses have usually conveyed giving proper respect either to another branch of their African (genealogical) tree or to a particular friend of the *terreiro* who was present (Eunice 1994: personal communication; Pai

Carlinhos 2003: personal communication). Regardless of the extent of intra-African syncretism in Bahia, the divinities are called by separate names (unlike in Haiti, where they are all called *lwas*, but like in Cuba, where there are multiple names). Divinities are called *orixás* in the Nago/Ketu *nação*, *voduns* in the Jêje *nação*, and *nkisis* in the Angola *nação*.

Bahian commitment to the Nago/Ketu practices in the past is legendary. For example, in the post-emancipation era, continuity and revitalization efforts were grounded by sending some children or members of the priesthood to the continent of Africa for education (e.g., Bastide 1978:77, 147; Landes 1947 [1994]:22; Harding 2000:101–2). Today, the Bahian ideal is clear: *nações* should keep their distinctions. In practice, combinations and exceptions appear, due to competing values of respect for all elders, nations, and/or ancient knowledge.

In dance ceremonies, called *xirês* or *festas* (the Yoruba and Portuguese word, respectively, is used interchangeably), *terreiro* worshipers first make a greeting to the sacred centermost spot of the dance space, where offerings of dedication are buried. Then they dance in a counterclockwise direction around the hallowed ground in a Nago/Ketu *xirê* order (see chart 9). Visitors and guests of the temple can join the dancing of initiated worshipers on only two occasions: during the temple's annual celebration for its patron *orixá* or during infrequent funereal procedures, called an *axêxê* (a ceremony apart from an actual funeral that is meant to lift a dead ancestor to a higher status or level).

After much singing and dancing, the *orixás* arrive and then, are taken out of the dance space to be dressed appropriately. Bahian white skirts, blouses, and shirts are taken off, and the bodies of worshipers are adorned with the clothing of their *orixás*. Headscarves that have been unwrapped are placed under arms to bind chests; both female and male *orixás* have cloth wrapped around their bodies and tied according to gender: front for female *orixás* and back for male *orixás*. They are returned to the dance space in strapless cloth wraps over pants or pants with vests over bare chests for male *orixás*. For female *orixás*, elaborate crowns with long, elegant, strapless wide skirts with pantaloons decorate the human vessels who, accordingly, are now worthy of praise. The change in dress from white to all the colors of the *orixás* shifts the ambiance from cool to warm. The *orixás* dance, and the participants sing and clap in support.

Each dance performance contains special elements that define an *orixá*, as well as the general characteristics that are agreed upon and understood by the ritual community. The special elements reference different aspects of a divinity or several related divinities, Omolu and Babaluayé, Oxalufan and Oxaguian, or Yansan and Oya in the Nago/Ketu *nacão,* for example. These are *caminhas* or *tipos de* Omolu, Oxalá, and Yansan, representing different qualities within the personality of a given *orixá* or contrasting stages within the life cycle of each *orixá.* In the Yoruba *nación* of Cuba, these are regularly called *caminos* or paths of a given divinity.[2] Paths are depicted in performance as variations within the main dance in terms of sequences of rhythms, chants, and consequent movement material. These variations multiply the ways in which the *orixá* and his/her path are understood.

Just as in Haitian Vodou and Cuban Yoruba, Bahian worshipers give themselves ceremonially to cosmic divinities for the resultant spiritual experience and advice they receive later (see Walker 1972, 1980, 1990; Deren 1983; Bourguignon 1968; Gleason 1987; Drewal 1975; Thompson 1974, 1983, 1995). They do so by dancing but also by preparing their heads *(fazem a cabeça).* Worshipers prepare their *ori* (spiritual essence), which is inside their heads, in a variety of ways including baths and wraps, instruction and study, prayer and consecration rituals. Over time, when worshipers dance in ritual performance, their prepared *ori* accesses the spiritual or coronal plane of existence, and manifestation or incorporation is complete.

For the conclusion of the ceremony, the *orixás* are coaxed back to their preparation room and bid farewell. As these divinities leave the Bahian dancing body, some playful, childlike, coda divinities, called *eres,* may displace the *orixá.* They play boisterously for a short while, and then they also take their leave. When all divinities have returned to the *Orun* (where the *orixás* reside), the drumming and singing stop, and delicious, consecrated foods are shared and eaten with everyone.

Chart 9 indicates the structure for two types of Bahian ceremonies: *xirês* given on the annual day for a given divinity, and *xirês* given throughout the calendar year on the birthdays of initiates (meaning birthdays of initiation). The Brazilian drum battery of *atabaques* speaks through pitch and interplay of rhythms, encourages dancing among the initiates of the *terreiro,* and invokes the presence of the *orixás. Iyawos/filhos de santos* join their godparent priest-mentors in dancing specific dance motifs for each *orixá.*

As a result of what the *orixás* advise in a Yoruba dance music ceremony (Bahian *xirê* or Cuban *wemilere*), or more often as instructed through an Ifa reading, there may be *odus* (or *ebos*) to complete. These are short and condensed or long and involved ceremonial practices of offering and sacrifice. They secure the blessings of the *orixás* (or *orichas*) for particular individuals and thus assist well-being and spiritual growth. I supply the order of one *odu* ceremony for a Bahian initiate in celebration of his ritual birthday, giving acknowledgment to the *orixás* who most closely guide his life. It is also a good example of the contemporary intra-African syncretism I have reported, indicating Angola, Jêje, and other *nações* within Nago/Ketu practice (chart 10).

Chart 9. Generic Structure of a *Xirê*

1. *Pade Exu*	Generally private or semiprivate ceremony seven days before *xirê*; or sacrifices, prayers, chants, and offerings just before the *xirê*
2. *Xirê*	Libations and salutation to all *orixás* in set order with chants and dancing around the sacred center space for ritual community members; arrival of *orixás* and first exit;
	orixás return in regal attire and dance; community singing; second exit of *orixás*, retiring of drums, eating of consecrated foods, departure of some guests
3. *Eres* visitation	Visitations of *eres* among ritual members; departure of *eres*; departure of all guests

---

Chart 10. Generic Structure of an Initiate's *Odu* in a Nago/Keto *Terreiro*

Odu for Oxossi in Bahia

Preparations: Prepare foods; travel with foods in bowls in counterclockwise circle throughout a forested area, while singing chants; pour libations and place offerings in front of Oxossi's house; everyone enters and sits on an earthen floor; offerings are brought inside one by one.

Chanting: Chants for Elegbara, Exu (from Ketu and Angola), Ogun, Yemanja, Xangó, Voduns (from Jêje), and Oxossi are sung by initiates and guests.

Offerings: Corn and coconut, cooked black-eyed peas, dried shrimp and onions, white corn, roasted black-eyed peas, and fruits are presented with everyone kneeling on ground.

Arrival of Divinities and Spirit: Yemanja and Exu; Chapeu-de-couro (old woodsman spirit); everyone rises from the floor and greets the divinities and old spirits who are present.

Advice and Counsel Given

Departure of Divinities

Prayer/Song Closing

Comparative Praise Performances

In Haitian Vodou, Cuban Yoruba, and Bahian Candomblé, there is lots of variety; however, all three religions hold in common several performance requisites. All three use percussion instruments (drums, shakers, and gongs) and complex polyrhythms that identify several strong African amalgam nations. All three have call-and-response musical structure in which a singer leads a chorus, which usually answers in a two- to four-line refrain. All three exhibit vocal music in nineteenth-century African languages, such as ritual Fon, Yoruba, and KiKongo (and other Bantu-related languages), often interspersed with Haitian Creole, Spanish, or Portuguese. Additionally, body orientation in space is generally low, with loosely bent knees, feet firmly planted, and chest leaning slightly forward in a "ready for anything" posture.[3] In this position, the upper and lower torso can divide and move fluidly or percussively. The hips are not constrained or obstructed and can circle in either direction, flex forward and back, or swing side to side. Arm and leg gestures code different divinities as the dancing worshiper prepares for praise performance. Most often, the performer is imitating or suggesting natural elements (air, water, fire, lightning, etc.) and symbolically re-presenting the source of life and survival in life-giving and/or healing motions.

Having *nasyon, nación,* or *nacão* knowledge of the chants, drumming, and dances permits inclusion in the liturgy and secures ritual acknowledgment of specific ethnic groupings, referencing and glorifying some over others. Having embodied dance/music knowledge helps confirm the past and affirm the combined liturgical orders, with each site displaying local and regional variations.

The worshipers whom I study believe that through initiation, divination, routine prayerful celebration, and funereal requisites, a believer can grow in spiritual strength, maintain balance in the material world, and profit by the wisdom of cosmological and ancestor divinities. Rites of adoration and petition that emphasize elements of praise performance permit a transformation, an appearance, a manifestation, or a reincarnation of divine energy. As specific body movements are danced, and often as special foods and drinks are consumed, the essences of particularized energy (the divinities) arrive within the body of a participating believer in order to celebrate and advise the ritual congregation. As drums voice each divinity's particular set of rhythms, as certain chants are sung in ritual languages, as drawings are sketched on the ground or in the air, the divinities appear dancing. They establish, support, and/or rejuvenate spirituality in the ritual community.

Isn't this intriguingly similar to African American religious practice outside of the African religions? For example, don't the same fundamental beliefs reside in the Christian Church? Don't both Protestant and Catholic worshipers believe that through baptism and/or catechism (initiation rites), grace and destiny (preconceived divination), regular church attendance and prayer (routine prayerful celebration), and burial with blessings (funereal requisites) that a believer can grow in spiritual strength, maintain balance in the material world, and profit by the Holy Bible, Torah, or Koran and the dictates of the religious ministry (the wisdom of cosmological and ancestor divinities)? And don't many worshipers reveal or display their praise in performance rituals?

The liturgical structure of my three Diaspora cases is most often performed in appreciation, remembrance, and celebration of spiritual interconnectedness. It follows a familiar order found in many religious services: praise, invocation, devotion, divination, confirmation, sacrifice and/or offering segments, before a closing prayer.

Rites of adoration and petition in Haiti, Cuba, and Bahia, as in many religious systems, facilitate divine transformation in both short-lived and long-term experiences. As the body is filled with praiseful movement and special foods and drinks, the essence of holiness arrives within a worshipping believer's body. When several bodies come together with such an intention and are filled with belief and holiness, a congregation is affected. Instrumental and vocal music initiates, supports, and complements the body in the accruing of spirituality and understanding of religious ideology. The architectural shaping of the space in which spirituality is invoked is planned and efficaciously structured, just as in the African American *ounfos, casas,* and *terreiros* I have described. No less than spiritual awe or divine inspiration result, in both the situations I describe for Haitians, Cubans, and Bahians and the situations of worshipping Christians, Muslims, and Jews and other religious believers. Accordingly, I am hoping that previous evaluations of "Voodoo" and "Santería" will be reassessed, and that many researchers, and particularly interested laypersons, will be persuaded to use more accurate descriptions when discussing the African Diaspora religions. They should regard them less pejoratively and more objectively.

Still, Diaspora liturgical orders are not always neat packages. Their variants and differing versions are determined by the multiple reasons for contact with the spiritual domain: adoration, petition, birth, death, and so on. For

Chart 11. A Comparative Yoruba Liturgical Order

Cuba	Bahia
Elegba	Exu
Ogún	Ogun
Ochosi	Oxossi
Oricha Oko	Ossein
Inle	Omolu
Babaluayé	Oxumare
Obatalá	Xangó
Dadá	Yansan/Oya
Oggué	Yemanja
Agayú	Oxun
Ibedys	Oba
Changó	Ewa
Obba	Nana
Yeggua	Oxalá
Oyá/Yansán	
Yemayá	
Ochún	
Orunla/Ifa	
Elegba	

example, a Yoruba drumming-only ceremony differs slightly from a dance and drumming ceremony. In chart 11 I cite the general orders for a dance and drumming ceremony in two Yoruba sites for comparison.

All of the charts I have presented summarize only the most frequently performed, public ceremonial structures of Haitian, Cuban, and Bahian liturgical orders as I have witnessed them.[4] I have compared these orders and examined them with dance and music specialists in the three sites of this study. What I have tried to indicate are three ways in which "the pintards' joyous singing and beating of their wings" clustered and gelled (Hurston 1938:273–75).

It is through repeated codified movement motifs in combination with visual art, instrumental music, human singing, colors, specific prayer-filled words, and ultimately through belief that divinities are incorporated. Ecstasy and anxiety are experienced; equilibrium between the spiritual worlds and the human world is eventually established. Inside all of these events and elements, powerful moral principles are projected, such as respect for elders, reciprocity, humility, and generosity. African belief vibrates and lives on in the Diaspora.

SIX

Informal Learning with Haitian *Lwas*

What has impressed me most over the years in my direct contact with Diaspora religions is the transition of trivial things and events into important information, from seemingly inconsequential events to pertinent material. I have observed this with worshipers in Haiti, Cuba, and Brazil, but also in myself. My instructions from my Cuban *madrina's madrina,* my godmother's godmother—to burn four white candles each night on a table with nine pineapples, to talk to the universe about my desires, to deposit fruits in a forested area after nine days—seemed so disjointed and unrelated at first. On reflection, those procedures introduced me to a way of living, a process, that has caused me to be forever keenly attentive to life, its cycle, its natural pace, its separate beauties, and its full wonder. Those procedures and other similar procedures underscored my attention and realization repeatedly and echoed the larger purpose of the dance ceremonies in Haitian Vodou, Cuban Yoruba, and Bahian Candomblé.

The dance ceremonies provide a space and time for personal integration, for the experience of relief (from tension or stress) via an expressive means, and for a sense of balance with regard to other living things in the natural universe. The dancing body within the ceremonies is paramount in this process. It accelerates or heightens the mind/body connection. Still, it was hard for my skeptical and investigative self to allow my intuitive self to lead in Haiti.

Manbo Ceremony with Ezili

I am always ready to record the mind/body connection in dance performance within most ritual occasions. This time, it was in the summer of 1991 and my first opportunity, in a long time, to revisit old Haitian friends and remembered sites.

So much had happened to me during my fifteen-year absence from Haiti; I had gone to the university and had been trained beyond dance and music in social science analyses (namely, British social anthropology). Additionally, there were numerous and severe political changes by 1991, such that I considered myself a true newcomer, even though I had visited often between 1969 and 1976. On Haitian soil again, I heard about the unique celebrations that were about to occur at Bois Cayman. President Aristide, the Catholic priest who had championed the causes of the Haitian workers in his political election, had declared a national celebration of Haitian Vodou at the site of its legendary and historic origins. That site marked not only the beginnings of Haitian Vodou but also where Vodou was inextricably intertwined with the Haitian Revolution.

My trip was filled with feelings of nostalgia. I was now residing at the famous Hotel Oloffson, a Haitian and international hangout. I watched the international, long-term residents and thought of my friends from previous trips. I observed the Haitian local bourgeoisie mix with the new tourists and remembered characters I had met while dancing years ago.

Each night, the tourists watched the same six dancers and three drummers perform the Vodou dances. They danced a variety of Vodou nation dances and folk dances (e.g., *Rara, affranchi*). Each time, the audience waited for the dance *banda,* the ultimate Vodou expression of death, and thereby of life also. The tourists seemed to view the dance as total exotica. The men gathered in groups to jeer and laugh when the dancer came out in her skin-tight white unitard with a tall black hat and a cigar. They whistled and cried out when she tipped her hat and spread her legs wide and executed explicit *grouyad* circles that ended with a pelvic thrust. They seemed not to care or understand that this dance performance was about keeping life vital and that it was not simply about the female body and sex. I, too, was interested in the expressive body, but more so in the performance quality and style of the dancer, as well as the selection of the programmed nation dances. That year I filmed the national theater style in addition to the hotel style in Port-au-Prince, but I looked forward to the ritual style and the deeper body/mind connection that I assumed I would see at Bois Cayman.

Fortuitously for my research, I was invited to a meet a *manbo* in Port-au-Prince before the bicentennial. Madame Joli was charming, in speech and personality, but also in her delightful cross-cultural joking. She was also a resident of Brooklyn who was visiting her mother's *ounfo*. (Both she and her mother were *manbos*.) I told her of my interest in Vodou and my impending trip to Bois Cayman but asked about the possibility of a filmed interview with her, and then added her mother as a possibility also. I had my video camera and was prepared whenever it was convenient. I also requested a "reading" or consultation.[1]

As *manbo* Joli took me on a tour of the first level of a three-story home after our consultation, it became obvious that preparations were being made for a *ceremòni*. Many men were in the large indoor rectangular space, which served as a *peristil* or ritual space with the *potomitan* at the center. They were laughing and talking casually but also working at small tasks in arranging the room. They carried the drums in and placed them at the front end of the room in a corner. One of them began to "dress" a table with scarves, candles, and sweets of some sort in another area.

Madame Joli told me that a few initiated members of her mother's congregation were being "raised," elevated to a higher level in the priesthood, and that as a supporter of one of them, she would participate in the *ceremòni*. And then she asked if I would like to stay for the *ceremòni;* she even volunteered that I could film if I stayed in one place and did not interrupt the flow of events.

It was too good to be true! I usually took care to develop a relationship, even if limited, before I dared to request permission to film any sort of religious event. Out of habit, since my first uncomfortable experience, I would go early on the day of a ceremony to make the acquaintance of other ritual members who might not have heard of my permission to film, and to be available to explain my reasons for wanting to do so. Madame Joli warmly explained that some members of the ritual family would be filming also, so it would not be an additional intrusion.

I decided to take advantage of her offer to stay, even though I had made no preparations in terms of food, gifts, or transportation back to the hotel. I had walked about three or four miles in from the main road and followed my hotel-worker friend, Jera, through winding dusty paths, behind and in between many impoverished dwellings, to this one large house. We had left the hotel after lunch in a bright hot sun. I had been thinking that I would be out for about two, three, possibly four hours, but the invitation afforded me ten more hours of ritual observation.

The *ceremòni* was wonderful, despite the later discomforts of walking through the mud and risky waters (see video, Daniel 1997b). The actual *ceremòni* began with libations, drumming, and ritual greetings to the drums, the drummers, the *potomitan,* and the cardinal directions that were made by the officiating *oungan* and his female assistant, who carried the candle to light the paths of the *lwa.*[2] The sword bearer, or *laplas,* with his two female assistants, followed with ritual salutations at each of the same places and additionally in front of all *oungans* and *manbos* who were present. The *oungan,* the *laplas,* and their assistants danced *yanvalu* with deep knee bends that brought their upper bodies down low and parallel to the ground. Their backs showed the familiar rippling, undulating movement that was dynamically hypnotizing, smooth, steady, and relaxed. Their movements were "knowing," effortless, truly secure and familiar in their bodies and among the congregation. Some worshipers around the room, transformed into a *peristil* or indoor dance ceremony space, answered the projected undulations with subtle ones—just in their upper bodies—as they sat or stood.

After almost an hour of singing and drumming, the *manbos* entered with their sponsors and danced around the *potomitan.* Their movements were subdued; their heads were bowed under large straw hats with many straw strings hanging in front of their faces. This first counterclockwise procession was solemn. Drummers played forcefully, and other worshipers (men, women, and children) who had arrived and filled the seats around all four walls sang with vigor. The *manbos* exited as a chain of bent heads in multicolored dresses, each with a large shoulder bag slung over one shoulder, one of the symbols of Kuzen Zaka, the *lwa* of agriculture and the comforter of the struggling Haitian agricultural workers.

During the second entrance and circling of the same group, I could see parts of the faces of the *manbos.* The backs of the *manbos* and the male and female sponsors were more erect now, and the *manbos'* hats were placed straight across their heads. I could see the stoic, black faces of thirty-five- to fifty-year-old women, six in all. Their processional movement was in time, rhythmically, but it was also muted or withdrawn, not moving with full-out energy. The drums played on, and the congregation sang repeatedly. During the intervals between the *manbo* entrances, a trio of adolescent girls led the dancing in front of the drums. They were noticeably affected by the camera and had fits of laughter, covering their faces often, and starting and stopping over and over. My camera was the only one filming now, since the family relative had elected to stop early when his floodlights kept blowing the circuits. Even though there was not much light except from two lightbulbs at either end of the long room, I preferred the absence of the floodlights and relished in my one camera at a corner end of the ritual space.

All of a sudden, the officiating *oungan* came over and asked me for money, an offering he said. I gave him all the change I had left in my pockets, which was not much, like a good tip for restaurant service, but not a respectable gift for the *ceremòni*. He came back a few minutes later, complaining, and I explained that I had not planned to attend the *ceremòni* and had, in fact, given my last dollars to my hostess for my consultation. At that point, Jera and our hostess pulled him aside and apparently substantiated my explanations.

I turned my attention back to the *ceremòni* and the dance. The young girls' dance movements proceeded from *yanvalu* to *zépòl* and *mayí,* but they were not spectacular dancers and did not inspire many others to dance with them consistently. They were not concentrating on the movements fully. They were merely performing ritual movements. They did keep the ceremony going, however, especially at those times when the officiating *oungan* was busy with other procedures. I began to notice the singing: "That hurts us. Pray, oh pray. The *lwas* are people. It's in the yard that this happens . . . that hurts us . . ." (translation by Joanne Violin and Sara Quessa).[3]

The words were strange, but they reminded me that Haitian *lwas* were magnificent protectors, human-like with talents, preferences, and strengths, as well as grievances, upsets, and faults. The ritual community could hurt them, and they could retaliate with less attention and imbalance in earthly lives—in the "yard" of their *ounfo* dwelling. What was needed was prayer, ritual attention to the spirits, both proper ritual and social behavior, for all to be well.

The drummers stopped a while, after the second procession and exit of *manbos,* and I presumed there would be a break, since about two hours had passed without a rest period. Instead, the focus of the ritual shifted from the *potomitan* to the table that was being "dressed" earlier. The table, now an altar, was midway in the long room, on the right side, and was marked by the canopy of scarves that were above it. The canopy seemed to be attached to the ceiling decorations of cut paper.

I heard only praying. The *pre savann* led the prayers and everyone joined in after a while. The prayers were a soft mumble that rose to a higher pitch periodically when worshipers answered en masse. After the Lord's Prayer and other notable prayers, they recited:

St. Philomin, Jesus in the sky. You ask us to come to pray at the feet of Mary, Blessed Mary. Bless the Mother of Jesus. Dambala . . . [more names of Vodou *lwas*]. We are calling Dambala. He's our Angel. We're calling Dambala. He's coming from the hand of God. He is one of the Saints. (Translation by Quessa and Violin)

They resumed singing:

Legba aloe. Legba, Legba aloe.

Oh Legba, I'm leaving. Legba, Legba we're going. (Translation by Violin and Quessa)

And somewhat later, they chanted:

Let the gossipers talk, my friend. When they arrive, they'll be sorry. You'll tell them to say my name. That's what they heard when they were talking behind my back. (Translation by Quessa and Violin)

I wondered about their invocations later while studying the translations. I understood Dambala and Papa Legba, but again I noticed the human behaviors referred to in the lyrics and wondered why their invocations to the *lwas* included rectifying gossip. The *lwas* were often happy, but sometimes they were upset, as in this chant, and they gave instructions to believers for their comfort as well as for the comfort of dancing worshipers.

I scanned the altar with my telescopic lens and saw statues, flowers, candles, and cakes, as most of the worshipers recited their prayers. Others suspended the sense of ritual or prayer and talked not so softly at the door or went outside for cigarettes. Finally there was a break in the drumming and singing for everyone. Apparently, a portion of the *ceremòni* was completed, and there was time for the initiates to ready themselves for what was to follow. Cokes and other soft drinks were passed around to all.

It was hot and humid, and worshipers were fatigued by the crowded surroundings. I, too, was feeling the weight of the camera and the tension in my muscles from standing or sitting in a constrained position for long periods.

Suddenly I was aware of the dark blue scarf on the altar and realized that my *manbo* hostess was moving it from its place among other colored scarves. She brought it to me and told me to treat it well and pray to Ezili on Tuesdays (for happiness in love matters). I have ever since treated it well, keeping it in a special place on my altar-bedecked dresser with other treasured items. Unfortunately, I can't judge its effectiveness, since I remember only as I am writing this that I did not always pray to Ezili on Tuesdays.

There was more singing, drumming, and especially more dancing after the prayers in Latin and Kreyol. Several enthusiastic worshipers on the periphery shouted and urged the others on. Everyone looked like they were enjoying themselves, either singing or dancing and apparently gossiping some of the time. A voice that seemed to come from the scarf called out over all the celebratory chaos. I looked around, but no one else seemed to notice the voice. I looked back at the scarf and received a greeting from Ezili.

I heard Ezili's voice in my ears: *"Bon swa, pitite mwen!"*

I answered, "Ayi bobo, ma gwanme mwen. Koma uye?"

"M' pa pi mal! Tend bien, Manbo yo antre, Manbo yo fe yon lot antre se toasiem nan ki fe yo diferan. Gade pwen tete chapo yo. Yo leve yo pou you decouvri figui yo. Manbo yo ap montre yon bagaye aswe an. Gade, apre sa ma pale ave ou."

"Good evening my dear," Ezili began after my astonished greeting, *"I'm not feeling too bad. Watch carefully as the* manbos *come in. They will make another entrance,* la troisième—*the third, which will be very different. Look for the edges of their straw hats. They will be pressed upward with no strings or fronds to hide their faces. These* manbos *will show you something special tonight. Look, and then I talk again"* (translation by Quessa and Violin).

There was no special salutation or body movement when I recognized Ezili's presence. There was no *viré* or ritual turning to publicly acknowledge her presence. My answer out loud, *"Ayi bobo,"* was the only empirical proof that let me or anyone know that she had addressed me from a dark blue scarf over the solitary space of the altar, and what she said was true.

The *manbos'* third entrance was noticeable for their upright and active posture. They sang loudly, and I noticed that the congregation was standing all around them across the entire space, accompanying them at the windows and at the front door near the drums. The *manbos* were not muted beings now. They were energized worshipers with the sacred rattle or *asson* in full view in their right hands.

"Sa se yon vre ceremoni," Ezili continued. *"This is a real fet. Look at how they take the* asson; *look at how they manage it. This is the time to make sure the*

new ones know it well and to make sure that they know all that the asson can do. Watch it through your camera. These are ancient moves, repeated over and over from parent to child, teacher to student, sponsor to client. The asson dancing like that tries to control the lwas, but we know its secrets and we can outsmart it sometimes. It depends on what has happened in the family—for me to disregard what the asson says in its sacred movements. Sometimes the family needs more talking to; sometimes they need our warning; sometimes they need to do more or do better. So we jump ahead of the wise asson, and the oungan or the manbo can't catch us quickly. Then, he or she must follow us. See how they manage it?"

My *manbo* hostess was in front of me; she told me to come to the center of the room and step up on the ledge of the *potomitan* so that I could see and film better. I thought this would be sacrilegious, but I followed her instructions and stepped up high above all participants and looked down both sides of the entire room. No one seemed to have any awareness of me or where I was; they were too busy praising the *lwas*.

The congregation had been singing and dancing for a total of about six hours, but it didn't seem to matter. Some worshipers were singing and dancing full-out in front of the drums. Others were packed around the *potomitan* singing, kibitzing, and dancing. It sounded like so much fun, and people were so enthusiastic as they sang that it surprised me at first to discover the lyric translations:

Kote ya mete lwa yo? Yo di konsa yap dechouke oungan yo. Kote yap mete lwa yo? Yo di konsa yap dechouke oungan yo. Ki lwa sa yo? Se lwa manman mwe? Se lwa papa mwen? Yo di konsa yap dechouke oungan yo. Kote yap mete lwa yo?

Where are they going to put the *lwas*? They say they'll take out the *oungan*. Where are they going to put the *lwas*? They say they will destroy the *oungan*. Whose *lwas* are those? My mother's *lwas*? My father's *lwas*? They say they'll take out the *oungan*. And so where are they going to put the *lwas*? (Translation by Violin and Quessa)

Nan peyi sa oungan rayi oungan, nan payi sa manbo rayi manbo. Nan peyi sa oungan rayi oungan, nan payi sa manbo rayi manbo. Ki mele mwen avèk yo? Nan peyi sa oungan rayi oungan, nan payi sa manbo rayi manbo. Ki mele mwen avèk yo? Se nan racin yo ban swen pwouin. Si pwouin an gate, ma jouin yon lot. Ki mele mwen avèk yo?

In this country, *oungan* hates *oungan* and *manbo* hates *manbo*. In this country, *oungan* hates *oungan* and *manbo* hates *manbo*. Who cares about them?

In this country, *manbo* hates *manbo* and *oungan* hates *oungan*. Who cares about them?/I don't care. It's in the roots that I got my degree [my power]. If the power is ruined, I'll find another one. Who cares about them?/Who gives a damn? [No one can destroy my power from my African roots.] (Translation by Quessa and Violin; also Desmangles)

The gregarious congregation was professing their utmost reliance on the African *lwas*, but right then a transition was taking place. New *manbos* were being raised up with new identities and new powers. The ambiguous moments of ritual raised questions that could be answered only at the end. Regardless of the so-called answers, the community was following the regulations of its temple, the oral tradition of their forefathers and foremothers.

A huge number of participants were crowded at the far end of the room where the elders had been sitting all night. The elders had been watching the *manbos* display *asson* rites and salutations; they were mindful of and attentive to the erudite communication among the wise and knowledgeable *oungans* and *manbos* of the community. They solemnly watched the mirrored and then dialoguing movements between the *assons* of the senior and junior *manbos*, which looked like a mysterious dance of gestures in the air.

Each new *manbo* seemed to be paired with either her supporter or another *oungan* or *manbo* in order to display her knowledge of the ritual movements to the learned community.[4] Most of this group watched attentively as the old and newly elevated priestesses dialogued in symbolic gestures, which were punctuated with ritual turns and curtseys, in reality—a long and extensive examination. There was absolute seriousness; both senior and junior *manbos* concentrated on the movements; both unconsciously attended to body/mind connections.

As I scanned the initiated group, I also saw the joyous faces of those who were dancing vigorously and sensuously to the rhythms of the distant drums, even if in one spot. Some of these dancers were in direct eye contact with other dancing worshipers, but others were reveling in themselves, dancing and singing by themselves in the midst of hundreds of dancing worshipers, deep into their own thoughts. Most were waiting their turn, their test of danced dialogue with their elders.

"You see, my child, this is the old African way. Everyone in the family learns certain things together and at certain times. The *konesanz* (knowledge) is kept clear and straight in each family. Each family learns together; each family knows the important actions; each family is clear about the way to talk with the ancestors and the *lwas*. And the Africans always had a way of straightening everything out if anyone forgot. When an elder made a mistake in the ceremony, no one says [sic] too much. They wait until he die and then his replacement fix everything. That way, everyone gives respect. It's our way to keep the rules straight. If the *lwas* are strong, if we are fed well and often, we can help. We can use the *konesanz* as we tell our horses.[5] Remember Tuesdays and talk to me out loud. Now watch the *asson* lessons. They have the *konesanz*."

I was mindful that again I was in conversation with Ezili, her voice coming from the dark satin scarf that had hung over the altar. No one else seemed to hear what I was hearing. I was mindful also that no one had asked me to stop filming this esoteric medley of movements. I looked for the officiating *oungan* who had asked for money before. He was part of the observing elders at the far end of the room, neglecting me entirely. If these ritual gestures assisted the manner in which *oungans* and *manbos* directed the ceremonies in honor of the *lwas,* why wasn't this part of the service more secretive, I asked my *manbo* hostess? She answered the same as other ritual leaders had in countless ceremonies of Haiti. She assured me that much of what happens in public ceremonies is not hidden or secret.

The dance ceremonies, in particular, encouraged participation from all worshipers and their neighbors. This was an important part of Haitian life, and Haitians were not ashamed in front of others, nor did they reject those who were not initiated. Ultimately, they were a family. In fact, she added, outsiders and nonbelievers could have all the ingredients and instructions and still would not be able to make things function properly. Even with all the material, only those with sufficient *konesanz* could fashion an efficacious communication with the *lwas* and the worshipping community. She was not worried about my camera or what my students might see; it was only one layer of *konesanz.*

What was noticeable to me also, particularly after fourteen hours with my generous hosts, was that no one had obviously, or in an overt manner, received the *lwas.* Only a few times did I see dancers begin to express the *debatment* before a *lwa* begins to "ride her/his horse." Only once, at the peak of strenuous dancing, powerful singing, and punctuating drum calls amid complex rhythms, did I see the telling movements of a *lwa* entering the premises noticeably, in the body of one of the young adolescent dancers. I realized that it was one of the playful dancers who had been moving in the repeated steps of old and who eventually came into that concentrated state of mind/body connection. Quickly and firmly, that dancer was seated and calmed down;

she did not continue the manifestation. Apparently for this service or perhaps only for the part of the *ceremòni* that I witnessed, the reincorporation of the social community, this *ounfo* community with its newly installed *asson* carriers, was the most important accomplishment for the evening.[6] It is also possible that each of the newly installed *manbos* was already manifesting; the *lwas* can remain for hours and for days at a time.

Many worshipers left early during the night's festivities; there were no more children and young adults at the windows and doors outside. I left the crowded dance ceremony at four o'clock in the morning just after a rainstorm, having thanked my hostess and her mother profusely, and walked cautiously behind Jera in the predawn darkness and in the after-the-rain-fresh air. My consultation had taken a little over two hours, and the ritual event had taken about eight hours and was still going on as we left. The storm that had come during the *ceremòni,* virtually unnoticed, had brought forceful rain, and the paths we had crossed earlier were unrecognizable. The main road would be impenetrable for cars until dawn, at least, and there would be no taxis at that time of night. I would have to walk through the swift and sometimes deep water runoff (carrying everything from soil to sewage) as I followed my friend out toward the port area and then up again to the hotel.

My thoughts focused on my experience with and my greeting from Ezili that evening, on the position of dance in Haitian Vodou, and on my fatigued neck and arm muscles from ten hours of filming. My thoughts about dancing for the *lwas* changed somewhat and my thoughts about trance and "possession" changed also. That night I was reminded, as I had been in other intense ritual displays, that although dancing and music-making certainly surrounded important ritual events, neither was the sine qua non of Haitian Vodou. As I had observed years earlier at a popular pilgrimage site, Saut d'eau, drumming, chanting, and dancing were not always necessary for powerful spiritual communication between the spirit and human worlds.

At Saut d'eau, with only the praying of thousands of worshipers (that is, without drumming and dancing), the *lwas* came through a large tree and through the waterfalls. Music and dance were significant elements of Vodou practice, but like other significant elements, such as *asson* gestures or evaluation by elders, they were equivalent parts of an even larger whole.

Ceremonial behavior did not always have to include manifesting the *lwas,* as many documentaries on Vodou would have people believe. Several reciprocal and requisite behaviors should be accomplished before invocations take place. Praising and honoring the ancestor spirits are considered offerings that should be prepared and completed in ceremonial rites before a *ceremòni,* *fet,* or *dans* that would call the Haitian *lwas.* All rites or particular sequences of ritual ceremonies should be performed before invocations are made; the space, the people, the animals, and the plants should be readied, all of which takes time. While *lwa* presence is treasured and the goal of most *ceremònis,* it is not proper to call them at just any time. They are always remembered in prayer, blessings, and sung or danced offerings. At particular identified ceremonies, they are invoked, invited, and brought forth in human bodies within prepared spaces. Sometimes, however, they do as they please and arrive at their own discretion, especially the Gédé family.

That night I was reminded of the core of Haitian belief and its emphasis and concentration on the *fanmi,* not just the extended ritual family, but also the spiritual family of *lwas.* That was most important in Vodou, and in reaffirming that, I released some of my single-mindedness on the unique qualities and elements of Vodou. Music and dance, which facilitated manifestation of the ancestors and divinities, were needed and important, and they operated for efficient and particular communication, but they were not the only requisites of fine form and deep content in Vodou. Many elements of ritual belief were needed for transformation and transmission; these needed to be in combination. Haitian worshipers took great care with each and every element of Vodou.

I tempered my own interests in dance and music to the reality of Haitian Vodou practice. I found dance and music vital to the *ceremòni* but not "everything" for its newly raised *manbos* at the center. With powerful dance performance, however, spiritual lessons could be mastered.

Celebrations for the 200th Birthday of Vodou

A few days later, I was at Bois Cayman with a group of five U.S. Americans among hundreds of people who had come for the significant birthday celebration of Vodou, two hundred years after the events that sparked the Haitian Revolution (1791).[7] The activities were in full swing upon our arrival late in the day on the eve of the event.

Everything was almost like I had imagined it over the years. A clearing in the grove contained a tremendously wide and aged tree at the center, and I could see the shadows of a mountainous ridge in the distance as we drove in. Tables were set up like stalls in a huge ring, marking the periphery with foods for families to eat and for others to buy. Some tables were stacked with T-shirts and others with cassettes, but what was most commercial was a small, but invasive, film crew (from Switzerland or Sweden).

Much as I would now love to see what was filmed, it was annoying then to have the constant movement of cameramen, poles with microphones, and incessant blasts of light as the celebratory proceedings went on. It was particularly intrusive as the night went on and the dancing became more intense. I kept seeing a swarm of white men rushing in to the central space of activity and attention. They turned floodlights onto the bodies of black folks, who were busy praising their *lwas*. I was upset; I had a philosophical difference with the methods of some photographers, videographers, and filmmakers. I was traveling with other photographers and filmmakers (and one other female, a psychologist), so my upset was mainly confined to philosophical discussions.[8]

Because of the differently colored dress of several groups and the obviously different songs and rhythms they were playing simultaneously, it seemed as if the *nasyons* were organized in certain areas of the huge grounds around the main tree. Since some were in a vivid dark blue, some in blue prints, some in yellow prints, others in red, and still others in multicolors, I presumed they represented factions and the colors of the Rada, Nago, Mahí, Ibo, Congo, and Petwo *nasyons*. Each area had a full complement of drums, drummers, and *oungenikons* or song leaders. As I passed around the periphery by myself, I tried to listen to the rhythmic distinctions of each area, but it was hard to hear clearly with so many drums simultaneously playing very different rhythms. Also, it was hard to see what was happening all through the night, as the crowds moved in swiftly with any crescendo of excitement in a particular area. I left relatively early, in frustration that I could not see, hear, or understand much, but content that the Haitian Vodouists seemed to be so happy in their celebration. They were busy singing, drumming, and dancing; they were exuberant with the official and public recognition of their religion by the Haitian state and, with so many foreign visitors in attendance, apparently by many others in the world.

The next morning, I could see and hear more than before. I was able to film a bit of the activities around the immense central tree. I saw the elaborate *veves* (drawings that bring the *lwas* to ceremonies) drawn exquisitely with cornmeal or flour at the base of the tree. Some of the drawings were from the night before, fading and worn, but now others were being freshly drawn with prayer accompaniment. Many *oungans* and *manbos* were present. One *oungan* was sitting on the ground as he drew; others lighted candles and closed their eyes in prayer beneath the leafy branches that gave a gentle breeze in the early morning sun.

I could see the remnants of the previous night's activities, bare tables and scarce paraphernalia to sell. A little to the side of the tree in the opening, it looked, by the dress colors of different groups, like several of the separated *nasyons* joined together to sing. They made a wide circle near the tree, almost all women, with a male *oungenikon* and a few drummers. When the chorus of a song began, the singers became noticeably exuberant. Every singer belted out the familiar refrain and there were smiles on many of their faces.

Peyi a pa pou blanc. Gonaivo, yo rele Desalin o. Gonaivo, yo rele Desalin o. Predikatè kampe an lè!

The country is not for the whites. Gonaive people, they call to Dessalines. Gonaive people, call to Dessalines. The preachers are standing on air! (Translation by Violin and Quessa; also Desmangles)

I thought to myself: This was a celebration of a black republic, of continuous African nationhood, and the celebration of Vodou. How did Vodouists view the European film crew and other white tourists on the sacred historical grounds? (I thought later: What were those singers thinking, as it turned out, a few nights before the first coup against Aristide?) And then the crowds and film crew descended, and I decided to leave and let the Haitians celebrate Vodou with one less foreigner.

The next day, I decided to go for my own pilgrimage to the Citadel at Cap-Haïtien. La Citadelle is truly an eighth wonder of the world, although only recognized as such since 1982 (when it was placed on the UNESCO World Heritage list). Haiti has often been relegated to the lowest rung of the global economic ladder, but La Citadelle is a fort that sits at the top of its high mountain on the north coast. Its view permits accurate naval information as to any navigation headed for the island from any direction except south, and it could easily forecast the actions of any group coming by land from the south. For Henri Christophe, the Haitian king, and his subjects who built it after the Revolution, it was a fortress of protection. Its fame and its wonder are in how and where it was built, solely by manual labor and sweat in such a forbidding mountainous zone.

Workers apparently had to carry each stone for its tall walls and dungeons, in addition to several cannons with a full supply of cannon balls. During the years of construction, many workers had accidents or were killed while attempting to reach the high altitude with limited technology. Haitians say that the blood of workers was used to wedge the countless stones within the fort's monumental construction.

The space is historical as a result, for both Haitians and others, and for some, spiritual as well. Thoughts of this construction and this location are common themes that I have heard on my four trips as they were discussed along the route to the top, and especially on the path after the journey's end. Visitors recalled the walk of thousands of workers on the sharp inclines as they gripped the rocky edges. Grim images formed to haunt the dirt path during the steep and narrow ordeal to the top and back. La Citadelle has become not only a memorial, perhaps a shrine, to the dead Africans who built it and fought for Haiti's independence, but also an inspiration for the living who still struggle for freedom and triumph.

At the base, on my return, I was taken to a Vodou *ounfo*. The *oungan,* a heavy man of average height, listened to my guide's explanations concerning my interest in Vodou and agreed to open his altar room for a look inside. As he opened the first locked door, I saw the symbols of the *lwas,* many *govis* (jars with the *gwo bonanjs* of family members), stones, staffs, and other implements. As he showed me various items, I told him the words for the Cuban *oricha* equivalents. When he opened the next altar room door, he began to tremble. He went limp and his *lwa* appeared with a loud voice, in stark contrast to his whispering tones before. There was no apparent reason for the mounting of the *oungan* that followed.

He seemed like Kuzen (Zaka) as he began dancing and singing under a tree opposite the temple rooms he had just unlocked. Two men came out of a nearby dwelling, probably because of his loud voice, and questioned him and then us. They reentered their doorway and returned with drums and began a *ceremòni.* I was totally prepared for it to be a fake for commercial purposes—near the base of La Citadelle. What followed began to convince me that I was at an impromptu Vodou *ceremòni,* eventually with fifteen men, who seemed to come from nowhere, but who actually came from the nearby houses. Two females joined us, one older woman who danced, and a very young child. The *oungan* sang:

Se pa Bondye. Se pa Bondye. Lavi wè sa mwen fè pou lwa yo.

It's not God. It's not God. Life sees that I do for the *lwas*. (Translation by Desmangles)

Two other men started to dance and became the most responsible for dance performance. Their dance appeared like a *mazone* or a *banda* with the long-legged men prancing in irregular designs and with occasional pelvic thrusts.[9] They danced around on the earthen floor in front of the *oungan's* row of locked doors. Their knees were active and much of the movement was made with kicks, jumps, and quick-paced steps in deep knee flexion. On occasions, the two men came close to one another, facing one another, and competed with each other in sensual hip circles (*grouyad),* then, laughing, separated and continued their individual dances apart from one another.

Four or five other men danced with them, mainly alternating between a spirited quick dance, followed by a slower dance. These men mostly danced a step, step, step, and kick pattern from side to side (1, 2, 3, kick right; 1, 2, 3, kick left) and then positioned themselves around the drummers. They sang and assisted the *lwa,* who directed the activities.

As a result of the continuous drumming, singing, and intermittent dancing, the participating crowd of Haitians swelled to about fifty. Curiously, as people greeted the *oungan cum* Kuzen, he became yet another *lwa* entity. He went inside his temple room and returned in a bright yellow and blue blouse with a blue head-wrap. He was now she, an Ezili with rosewater to share with everyone. She passed it around and let participants wipe it soothingly at the base of their necks and across their faces. She sang and danced noticeably more slowly and more gracefully than the *lwa* before. She remained for the rest of the little *fet.*[10] She sang:

Rele Ezili. Rele Ezili. Ezili kite mòn la. Li pote dlo.

Call Ezili. Call Ezili. Ezili left the mountain. She brought water. (Translation by Violin and Quessa)

Only one of two females danced, an older woman with gray hair. She was very energetic and moved gracefully. I was filming her when my guide took my camera and encouraged me to dance with her as he filmed the whole group and me. I took advantage of the moment and his offer and enjoyed mirroring her Vodou movements, even though it was not the classic *yanvalu* that I knew. She did not dance it bent over or in a low position, but upright, proudly and elegantly.

DANCING WISDOM

After two hours of singing and dancing in a slightly different style than I knew from ceremonies around Port-au-Prince, I was convinced that it was a genuine *ceremòni*. I realized that the *lwa* had organized and directed a pleasant party for about fifty or sixty people, perhaps ultimately a celebration of the beginnings of Vodou at another site of ancestral history, the base of La Citadelle. I was delighted with this ceremony because it explicitly showed how the Haitian spirit world is connected to the social world, beyond problems or upset. This was not about sickness either. In this instance, the *lwas* had come to greet a stranger and to fraternize with members of the community family. This was a perfect example of the goodness, blessings, and appreciation that positive relations with the *lwas* (*orichas* and *orixás*) can bring. It counters the Vodou stereotypes in which the *lwas* come only when there is something "wrong," when "mean-spiritedness" is around. It counters a one-dimensional understanding of a complex worldview and a maligned belief system.

The *lwas* gave us blessings and sprinkled us with perfumed water and gave rum to the six drummers who alternated during the spontaneous *ceremòni*. The familiar bottle of innumerable "things" was passed around to the important personages, such as the lead drummer, the lead singer, and my guide. They were singing earnestly, just as they had in the beginning, as I informed the guide that I was leaving.

> Rele Ezili. Rele Ezili. Ezili kit mòn la. Li pote dlo. Sa nap pote? Na pote pou timoun la ki vini? Ezili kite mòn la. Li pote dlo.

> Call Ezili. Call Ezili. Ezili left the mountain. She brought water. What shall we give? What shall we give to the little child that came? Ezili left the mountain. She brought water. (Translation by Quessa and Violin; also Desmangles)

I gave my offering for the *oungan* and his temple, and wished them well. I scurried from the dance space to join my little group. They had just returned from their hike up to La Citadelle and had started to watch the little impromptu *ceremòni* and had begun taking pictures. I was afraid that there were too many outsiders present, and I also feared what my photographer friends might generate with the three of them running up in people's faces or lying down on the ground in front of the drums in order to get a shot of the bottle as it was being passed. For me, photographers can be very disruptive, and I anticipated problems if we stayed!

Later that night at Bois Cayman, we heard repeated loud, overlapping drumming, as each *nasyon* sounded out its songs and rhythms simultaneously around the immense, central tree. We witnessed an even larger community of Vodouists the second night, still singing, drumming, and dancing at the foot of the ancient tree with packed crowds of participants and onlookers.

> Yo kampe an lè! Yo pa kampe an lè anyen—predikatè, politisyen, edikatè e tout oratrè! Yo pa kampe an lè anyen! Peyi a pa pou blan. Moun Gonaive, rele Dessalin. . . . Yo kampe an lè! Yo kampe an lè anyen!

> They are standing on air! They are standing on nothing—the preachers, the politicians, the educators, and all the orators! They are standing on nothing! The country is not for the whites. Gonaive people, call to Dessalines. . . . They are standing on air! They are standing on nothing. (Translations by Violin and Quessa.)

The Haitian spirit is indomitable! Centuries of militaries, politicians, and religious missionaries have not yet succeeded in conquering Vodou!

Congo Rites at Sucrie Danasch

Right after the celebrations at Bois Cayman, there was another intriguing event. My small group of photographers and filmmakers had made arrangements to go to a Congo ceremony that I had heard about years ago, an ancestor and water service that was performed annually in Sucrie Danasch, a small village near Gonaive. All relatives of Congo families try to congregate there every July for a special ancestor *ceremòni*. The leader of our team met with the village elders upon arrival and had to renegotiate the official permission we had been given earlier to photograph and film. Our entrance into the village and into the *peristil* at the first prayers with our cameras clicking had angered the elders and head *oungan*. Eventually we were given permission to film outside of the *peristil*, where most of the annual ritual would take place.

As the prayers were recited, and with no drumming or singing, the sounds of arriving *lwas* began to pierce and then thunder the air as many, many worshipers received their divinities—too many to count, perhaps hundreds. For the familiar, it was still absolutely fascinating to see each local family group of about twenty-five to fifty Congo descendents exit,[11] group after group, into a courtyard; for the unfamiliar, it was perhaps unsettling. Each family leader carried a sacrificed goat around his/her neck, and bright red blood stained his/her white shirt at the shoulders. Each worshiper also bore the red—red colorings on their white head-wraps and white dresses or pants—as they too addressed the sacrifice made for them by touching their heads to the head of the goat. The entire dusty village, a conglomeration of family compounds or *lakous,* was filled with white white and red red!

The ritual community flowed out of the small building and went to the cardinal points at the edges of the village. There were probably more than a thousand people who followed the ritual leaders in processional dance, many manifesting their ancestor *lwas,*[12] all coifed with a uniformly wrapped headdress. I watched a sea of white-clothed people stream in the distance as thousands of worshipers followed the officials to varied locations in the village. At one site, around a rather scrawny but leafy tree, a bull sacrifice was made. The bull was mounted by each of the reigning *oungans* and *manbos,* prayed over, sprayed with rum (*kleren*), and swiftly killed as an offering. I wondered how that bull, even with all his meat, could possibly feed the *lwas* and the thousands of participants.

I focused on the dancing at the foot of another prominent, but not so large, tree. Trees were often the sites of ritual. First they served as the living *potomitan* for outdoor events, and then they were repositories or resting places where the *lwas* congregated (Desmangles 2002: personal communication). Three drummers and an *agogo* player had their backs to the trunk of the tree, and about a hundred dancers inched their way forward toward the drummers in rhythmic unity. Their step was flat-footed and barely lifted, scraping or dragging one foot after the other in an irregular accent. Their arms hung loosely at their sides, and their heads flopped aimlessly, as if an inner impulse deep within their abdomens carried all their body parts decidedly forward. A lead dancer occasionally faced the group and set it in a particular direction, and then he, too, joined the forward-rocking dance.

During the three or four hours of the first dancing segment, the performers used one step primarily. It was an uneven sliding of each planted foot, causing a heavy accented (ONE, two) pattern. The body was tilted very low, and the arms extended forward and back as the feet stepped their pattern. All women and men who danced used this step to the cardinal directions. Near the end of this dance ritual segment, however, I noticed another step. A couple, a man and a woman, danced a foot pattern that replicated the cardinal directions (right step forward, left step center or in place, right step to the left, left foot step in the center, right step to the right, left step in center, right step in center, left step in center). It appeared to be significant since it was the only change of step that afternoon, but it was danced to a very short song.

Soft undulating bodies, crowded together shoulder to shoulder, pressed toward the drumming with occasional erratic slinging of the arms and head. It was hypnotizing to see, but also, probably for each dancer, it was compelling and powerful to dance the same gestures in the midst of so many other dancers as they all transformed embodied feelings into actions.

For me there was no more beautiful picture than their believing, invested, totally dedicated, black faces over a sea of white-clothed and white head-wrapped bodies, all dancing. All hunched over and mashed together, moving in small but decided steps, accenting only the left side, and few if any gestures or striking, independent movements, propelled by the incessant rhythms of human hands on animal skins only—no stick drumming, outbursts, or cries, totally committed, totally involved. The mind/body connection was struggling toward visibility. Dust blew into my camera frame as the dancers stopped at the *kasés* and stood upright, swooning for just a moment before starting their pattern again in a new direction. They danced even when the rain began, and for hours, anywhere one looked, there was a sea of white—pulsing, rocking in place, or traveling. Congo dancing was mesmerizing for dancers and onlookers alike, and the persistent dance finished the morning section of the ritual.

While dancers danced and *oungans* and *manbos* led prayers all around the village, other worshipers were cooking the sacrificed animals, including the bull and goats from the morning, and preparing a sumptuous feast for the evening. It would take some time to prepare meals for the thousands of participants.

As the day wore on, many worshipers and guests were encouraged to walk to the river on the other side of a field of grain, beyond the village compounds. The walk was in bright afternoon sun for about a mile beyond the village. This was the first time that I could make out some of the visitors who were in attendance, as opposed to the local participants. Haitians were carrying microphones and tape recorders, recording their experience, recording their own religious music and dancing, recording their future memories.

We walked through the field to a tree-lined river. It was cool in the shade of the trees, and the crowd spread out along the banks of the river. Only our photographer waded across the narrow span and perched in a low branch of a tree on the opposite side of the river. Talking seemed to be the only activity; there was no music or dancing for quite a while. I wondered why we were all perched at the riverbanks and when something else was going to happen. After perhaps almost an hour, commotions started—near me and also farther down the bank.

Simbi en dlo (Simbi is in the water).
Simbi en dlo (Simbi is in the water).

The familiar cries of the *lwas* seemed to ricochet from place to place along the river; people were shouting; there was loud splashing. Participants shifted from side to side with a few and then many worshipers, raising their hands above their heads, skipping toward the bank, lowering their bodies, and sliding down into the river water. Hundreds of flinging bodies fell into the water, splashed around excitedly, greeted others in the water, and made their presence known to relatives on the banks. Some had eyes that were stretched wide open with looks of apprehension; others looked quite calm, normal, sensing the cool water against their bodies. I wondered at the time if these were *lwas* or *ley mo;* I was told that these were Congo *lwas* who had come to the present.

It was as if everyone had been waiting for this. The Congo *nasyon* in white knew it was important to be there, and the visiting relatives in other colors had come to participate in or witness the annual ritual. They knew that they were supposed to return to Sucrie Danasch territory. They knew that they must be there among their relatives. They knew when someone entered the water that they too must enter or reach their hands out for the water presence of their ancestors. It was inside their bodies, within their memories, something instinctual, compelling, and satisfying.

Even in the water, the movements were contagious. Each worshiper proceeded to dance his or her contribution to the whole. A woman in a yellow dress just in front of me jumped up in the air, arms reaching high, and twisted her upper body from side to side. People nearby pulled away and in so doing made a path for her to reach the bank. She dropped down to sit with her legs stretched out in front of her. Still twisting at the waist, she gradually scooted herself to the edge of the bank and then fell forward. In a second, she was up and jumping in the shallow water. She was swishing, splashing, and falling backward. After only a few seconds of floating, she was swishing and splashing again. She was like many others; perhaps a third of the congregation was now in the water, conversing loudly with each other, splash dancing or standing, vibrating, while praying.

Gradually, the communication on the banks was more important than the splashing water. Gradually, the bathed bodies cupped water in their hands and took it to the shores. There, the out-stretched hands of relatives were waiting. Good-natured greetings came from their mouths, but their hands spoke, requesting the precious water from the drenched *lwas*. Within fifteen minutes, the entire community was quiet in prayerful murmurs that were exchanged between those in the water and those on the banks. The drenched Congos took handfuls of water and spread them all over the faces, necks, and hands of their relatives. Some others placed water on top of their relatives' heads and let it drain across their faces.

> Sa' m ouè nan dlo, mwen paka pale. Mwen wè trop bagay; mwen pakab pale. Sa' m ouè nan dlo, mwen paka pale. Mwen wè trop bagay; mwen pakab pale.

> What I see in the water, I can't talk about. I've seen so much; I can't talk about it. What I see in the water, I can't talk about. I've seen so much; I can't talk about it. (Translation by Desmangles; also Quessa and Violin)

I watched the exchanges for some time. Some manifesting ancestors came very close to the banks and addressed members of the ritual community separately. They held family members' hands, patted their shoulders and backs, and poured river water over them. Often they lingered with a particular member, talking privately, and then with embraces and parting kisses, they said good-bye, only to receive another family member.

> O male. O male.
> Oh, I'm leaving. I'm leaving.
> (Translation by Violin and Quessa)

Some families came out of the water, and I noticed that drums and drummers were seated a short distance from the water's edge. Drumming started, away from the bank toward the grain field. Several dancers in front of the drums were still wearing their white dresses from the morning, but now they were not reddened with blood, but washed white from the water ritual. They danced individually and not in the huge, packed groups of the morning, drying their clothes and seemingly not aware of their wetness. This was the mind/body connection I had waited to film.

One worshiper was dressed in military fatigues, carrying a sword and fully spiritually involved. He would dance to the rhythms and then at the *kasé*, he would lean on his sword to steady his swerving body, drop his head, and close his eyes. As the rhythms resumed, he too returned to his repeated, if somewhat imprecise, foot pattern. Another worshiper continued to dance even when the drummers stopped. Utterly oblivious to everyone, she danced to, for, or as her Congo ancestors. She was spirited, energetic, but loose and sporadic in her repeated foot pattern.

After another few hours of dispersed dancing and private family consultations, I noticed families walking back to the village center. The men were some of the last to leave the riverbank area. I realized later while reviewing my videotapes that these men were famous Haitian musicians who had been recording all the ritual songs that were sung. Some of the men were from popular music groups, such as Boukman Eksperyans, and others were music professors from prestigious universities, including Harvard University and Wellesley College. I remembered seeing them during the day when they were close to the drummers with their microphones.

Back at the village, there was a great deal of activity in all directions. I followed the drummers to a clearing with an old tree with few leaves. The officiating *oungans* from the morning rituals were there, pouring libations and offering rum drinks to a few. After the libations, many worshipers paraded around the tree, now a *potomitan,* in a counterclockwise fashion, singing strongly. I recorded their song, which curiously referred to the snake, a Rada symbol.

Met Agwé ap tounin koulèv, O Met Agwé. O Met Agwé, apre ou tounin koulèv, ou a mache a tè. Agwé, ou tounin koulèv. Agwé, apre ou tounin koulèv, ou a mache a tè.

Master Agwé can turn into a snake, Oh Master Agwé. O Master Agwé, after you turn into a snake, you'll return to the ground. Agwé, you turn into a snake. Agwé, after you turn into a snake, you return to the ground. (Translation by Quessa and Violin)

Since it was repeated again and again, I think it was the respectful acknowledgment of the Rada *nasyon* at the close of the multiple activities for the Congo *nasyon,* an indication of the continuing intra-African syncretism that still exists in Haiti, this time Congo/Rada. It was evidence for the understanding of Vodou as a combination of Rada, Congo, and Petwo rites and the Haitian ritual acknowledgment of *nasyons.* A Rada *nasyon* song was sung around the *potomitan* to conclude the day's activities of a Congo celebration.

What went through my head, hauntingly, was the other song that had been sung over and over after crowds had entered the water:

Sa' m ouè nan dlo, mwen paka pale.
What I see in the water, I can't talk about.

The drummers and the *agogo* player came to a simultaneous halt at the end of the song, and then everything stopped. Worshipers began to drift off in many directions.

Elsewhere in the village, some people were bathing and changing clothes; others were cooking and cleaning; most were happily visiting with family and friends. My little group gathered, after being dispersed most of the day, and briefly exchanged impressions and feelings about what we had witnessed from our varying vantage points. We had witnessed only one day, one part of a Congo rite that was to last several days, but there was so much to think about.[13]

In contrast to other rites, I found this day's events quite different in quality, even though structurally it was part of a familiar set of Vodou ceremonies. There were no elaborate costumes, no flags, little sense of ornate procedures, and no outrageously incredible dance movements—not even the promotion of spectacular voices or extraordinary drumming. Every element of the ritual was simple and direct; yet the whole was powerful, impressive, and indelible on my mind's eye.

Community members had worn clean, white street clothing with uniformly wrapped head-wraps (women and some men). The officiating *oungans* and *manbos* had led the community to the cardinal points of the village for prayers and libations, prepared the sacrificial bull, led the congregation to the dance space, then to the riverbank, and back around a *potomitan,* and then ended that phase of the *ceremòni.* Few mysterious gestures of the *asson* occurred; only those at the beginning with the entire community marching to the four cardinal points of the village and those over the selected bull and over the sea of worshipers.

The power of repetitious ceremonial performance created a huge layering of sensory stimulation for eight or nine hours. There were countless manifestations, and these lasted as long as we were there! The proper and appropriate steps were taken in order to complete spiritual communication with Congo *lwas;* respect for the ancestors was stated in explicit behavior. Ancient Congo cultures were honored implicitly and modeled for future generations. I thought of Kongo-Angola rituals elsewhere and remembered this song:

> Ye ye mbongi (ye).
> Ye ye mbongi (ye).
> Ahhh ah, Ye ye mbongi (ye).
>
> Ye ye ye Yeee mbongi (ye).
> Ahhh ah, mbongi (ye).
> Ye ye ye Yeee mbongi (ye).
> Ahhh ah, mbongi (ye).

Mbongi (ye), mbongi (ye),
Mbongi (ye) ka bulutina yu mbongi (ye).
Mbongi (ye), mbongi (ye),
Mbongi (ye) ka bulutina yu mbongi (ye).

Why do you leave the *mbongi,* the gathering place of the community, the village, and the family? Kongo people who go away forget their culture. Always think back to your culture, to your village, to the *mbongi* gathering place, where all major issues are discussed and all decisions are made. Although you've left, run away, or stayed away a long time ago, we are worried about you. (BaKongo chant, Malonga Casquelourds 1993: personal communication)[14]

Unlike the *manbo ceremòni* of Port-au-Prince, this one was about manifestations. Spiritual contact with the other realms of existence was imperative, and literally hundreds occurred. So many people bridged the boundary of rational understanding; hundreds of worshipers embodied their *lwas.* It was incredible for me, even as accustomed to manifestations as I had become by then.

SEVEN

Informal Learning
with Bahian *Orixás*

Each morning I walked along the shore in Itapua, never quite believing what I saw was real. Long miles of beachfront and the insistent crashing of the waves seemed like they should be shared with crowds of people, but instead I found myself alone in this astonishing natural beauty. Most Bahians were working as I walked briskly for at least an hour every morning. Another reason that I rarely saw anyone on this gorgeous stretch of ocean was because it was July, their winter, and despite the wondrous sun, Brazilians did not frequent the beaches in "winter" very often. So, for two glorious months I had the sun, the beach, and the ocean each morning almost all to myself as my daily wakening ritual. I was, as Bahians often told me, the offshore breeze, the air, and the wind, Oyá, also called Yansan. Epa-hayeeeiiiiiii!

Yansan on the Beach and at Oxun's Xirê

Yansan stretched out her vast arms and legs across the beach, like a huge luxurious yawn, more sound than fury. She watched the fishermen first, as they

188

paraded their large handwoven nets to the water's edge. They entered into the crystal-clear shallows and, in coordinated bent postures against the dawning light, lodged and set their porous sea cloths, their netted traps. And then she whisked and stroked the faces of the Bahianas, who were ambling slowly and seductively toward the opposite edge of the beach, not the shoreline but the walled line. They were setting their culinary traps with multicolored oils and peppers. They decorated their stalls with the flavors and scents of *acarajé* and *vatapá*. They acknowledged Yansan with the multicolors of their foods, especially with thick *dendé*, red palm oil. They also recognized her publicly with wide lengths of lace, which shaded their wares and danced in the breezes throughout the day. Yansan is mute, you know, but she let her thoughts be known in nature's gestures and within the inner voices of the mind.

The wind could be abrupt, irregular, gusting at times as workers attended the afternoon clients: the expatriate and international beachcombers. After midday the beach was slightly populated; a few hardy tourists would sunbathe, read, or jog on the beach. The Brazilian population on the beach was mainly a group of entrepreneurs. Under *barracas* (open-air, thatched-roof beach stands), they sold beer, *caipirinhas* (drinks made with *cachaça*—Brazilian white rum—lime, and lots of sugar), and freshly fried fish with plantains. The most distinctive Brazilian addition to any plate of food was *farinha*, a white cassava meal that was piled high at the side of the entrée.

The youngest entrepreneurs were the nine- to fourteen-year-old boys who ran between towels on the sand and the *barraca*, carrying messages from clients to the bosses, the *barraca* owners, and carrying drinks and food from the bosses to the clients at their towels on the sand. The boys lived in lofts or shelves beneath the thatched roofs of the *barracas*, literally chained in at night until daybreak and the spreading of Yansan's breezy arms. Yes, the boys "belonged" to the *barracas*. They worked until they were old enough or bored enough to look for more lucrative enterprises. They often stole wares that might assist their new ventures. Usually, the new ventures were selling shirts or jewelry on the beaches for a meager commission from a new boss. Some of them landed jobs in elite and middle-class households as servants who took care of the dogs or who worked as helpers for a main housekeeper. Their lives were set, predetermined: they worked excruciatingly hard for exceedingly long hours every day of their lives, except during Carnival perhaps, when everyone was supposedly "free." (Many people must continue working during Carnival, selling their wares and serving the wealthy free.)

The other beach entrepreneurs were the "bosses" who were trying to eke out a living for themselves and their (usually large) families. Constantly in debt for the expenses of operating a food and drink booth, they worked for desired profits that rarely came when or in the amount they needed. Yansan blew a few chances toward them but mostly gave them lessons in endurance as they struggled against the winds to make ends meet and to keep standing at the water's edge.

"I am very worried about Paulo," said Yansan through the breeze. *"He is getting too street-smart and finding fault in working at the barraca. He's only ten, and if he leaves now, he will eventually roam the city streets at night with a displaced rat pack of children. He needs to stay with Manuel, at least for a few more years. He has his work with Manuel, serving drinks and running errands, and his parents keep in contact and still let him visit. He has a beautiful relationship with the terreiro, with his Pai Silvio, but still he worries me.*

"Paulo is studying the songs (cançoes) and learning all about the orixás as he makes your beaded necklaces (contas). As he strings them for you, he rehearses the weekly verses that he has been given by Silvio. Your need for the necklaces furthers learning for the two of you. I know you think you are getting them for your teaching—so that you can explain a few things to your students. But the necklaces are for you.

"You are almost like Paulo, a youngster compared to Mãe Menininha who had about seventy-five of her ninety years in the religion. He is teaching you as he sings for you and as he chooses among the colors of the beads. When you spend time with him, he is learning as he teaches."

"As we all do," I said aloud.

"Children of the terreiro often teach adults of the world.

"But in order to spend time at the terreiro after working on the beach, Paolo has to stay among a few unsavory characters sometimes. He is prey for these lechers, and I am worried about him. I cannot always decide for him, and I have comforted too many dying children.

"Right now, you are a good thing for him. Go to the ceremony with him, with Narcis and Manuel. It will be good for you to see more than the 'cathedral terreiros,' as you call them—Casa Branca, Gantois, and Axé Opô Afonjá. With Paulo, Narcis, and Manuel, you can see how the less fortunate worship and what they learn through their belief. You can learn from them as you learn about them."

"Epa-hey, Yansan, I will go."

And with my words, she soared high above the beach and floated gently across the sea, the sand, and the *barracas,* and around all of us. I kept thinking about what she said.

It was true that of my five visits to Brazil (1980, 1985, 1991, 1994, and 2002), four were rather formal. Most often, I visited the ritual communities with an influential group of elite Brazilians, from movie stars to psychologists and from anthropologists to television personalities. Most of these person- ages, however, were committed to the ritual practices, with patient and pious actions that expressed, if not proved, their commitment. On my last visit and in addition to Itapua, I lived for the major part of my stay on *terreiro* grounds in Itaparica, the big island in the bay, and mainly among modest, faithful worshipers.

Bahian Candomblé, as I had witnessed it in the large and well-known temples, was so different from the familial Vodou services and crowded, semi- public Cuban Yoruba ceremonies that I knew. Bahian ritual seemed more rigid and orthodox. While many ceremonies were larger than those I attended in Haiti or Cuba, the sense of community involvement was different in Bahia. Bahian ceremonies at the large *terreiros* appealed most to my theatrical per- formance background, as you will hear about shortly.

Probably, the continued direct contact with Benin and Nigeria through Bahian returnees (those who returned first to Africa and then came back to the Americas) after the slave trade ended and the influential contact of elite Yorubas helped to maintain Yoruba custom and traditions in Bahia (see Ma- tory 1999:88–92). Also, these historic ties established a contemporary spatial and psychological hierarchy beyond that of ranked religious specialists. Ritual practices at the large *terreiros* developed definite borders between those who can dance and receive divinities and those who can witness and sing; from a dancer's perspective, this translates as between performers and spectators. Yoruba authority was established as the Nago/Ketu *nação,* which was expressed in limited participatory style within *xirês* or dance ceremonies. I looked for- ward to the practices of a small *terreiro* elsewhere in Bahia, among my friends from the *barraca.*

> Oya couro ilye o geregere; Oya couro la o garagara
> Ygbiy sala courou le o; Geregere ya camurelo.
>
> The wind that walks over the earth lives, lives.
> Wind that reigns over life, which lives and is born.
> Crowned child of Oxalá on Earth,
> The child that will live and live,
> Mother of the Dead that will come.
> (Translated song for Yansan as the breeze, by Pai Carlinhos and
> Augusto Soledade)[1]

We arranged to meet at the *barraca* after washing away the salt and sand of yet another long day at the beach. It was a pleasure to see how each person dressed in special attire, regardless of how meager their resources for clothes were. There were three men and two boys (Narcis, Manuel, a Spaniard I did not know, and Paulo and Saulo, Paulo's friend), and two women (Eunice and a Spanish woman). The men were dressed in sharply pressed pants and freshly washed shirts in bright colors: turquoise and prints. Even the white shirts had bluing to make them whiter. The Brazilians were so handsome and changed. By day and over weeks—in fact, during the three years that I had known them—Manuel, Paulo, and Narcis wore clean but bedraggled shorts or jeans and were bare-chested and barefoot against the heat. The Spaniard was totally new to me, but he was "pressed" and looked very nice in his summer slacks and white, white shirt. Everyone was oiled and manicured with bronzed faces, coiffed hair, cool outfits, and beaded necklaces. Their smiles were the same—full and uninhibited as always—and their greeting kisses on both sides of my face allowed their bathed freshness to perfume the night air.

The women were almost strangers to me, and at first I wondered how I was perceived among my "Brazilian buddies." Were these male Brazilians collecting all of their foreign female friends to take to a ceremony? I thought I had made "special" friendships and that was why, after many months of their knowing my activities within Candomblé *terreiros,* they had invited me to see their own rituals. I remembered, and had to admit in that moment, that I was like other foreign visitors passing through Bahia, a nice but privileged traveler who happened to admire and spend both money and time on their religious rituals.

Apparently, Narcis and Manuel had met the other two women earlier in the day and had invited them in the excitement of the day's preparations. Eunice was a Brazilian regular at their *barracas,* an unusual Brazilian customer who worked as a social worker in a nearby district. She was one of the rare Brazilians who frequented the beach on occasion in the winter. That morning she had joined Paulo while he was singing songs and chants for me. Amazingly to me (because I would never expect someone to sing ritual songs as if in a challenge event on the beach), she countered Paulo's Candomblé songs with answering songs, which I recorded.[2] And she did this for about two hours. Afterward, she retired farther down the beach to her towel and beer. The other woman was a blond Spaniard who accompanied the Spanish man and who had heard us talking earlier. After I had left, she told the Bahians that she wanted to see and hear a Brazilian ritual also.

We took four thirty- to forty-minute bus rides and walked about half a mile on dirt roads before climbing down a very steep incline and seeing the house where the ceremony would take place. We crossed a makeshift bridge of wooden slats and passed through palm leaves and other fronds at the entrance to the *barracão,* the dance ceremony room. It was small, about ten by ten feet, with three doors, including the front door that we had entered through. The second door appeared to lead to a kitchen, and the third led to the back rooms where the *orixás* were dressed upon arrival and where other rituals were performed.

I was introduced to the *iyalorixá* as soon as we entered, and she told me of the prior arrangement with Narcis that I could videotape all that transpired. It seemed that Narcis's wife was expected to embody the divinity that night, and he (or she) wanted to have Oxun's presence on tape.

At the *terreiros* that I had visited previously, women who regularly embodied the *orixás* never talked about their *orixá;* in fact, to question someone who regularly received the *orixás* about the experience was considered quite bad mannered. Since the *xirê* was at the *terreiro* to which Narcis and his wife belonged and since at least one of them was intrigued with the idea of seeing this *orixá* on tape, all important parties had agreed. I could stand in the very back of the room and record whatever might transpire.

The *iyalorixá* looked straight into my eyes, listened to my Portuñol (Spanish/Portuguese) greetings and explanations, and watched me closely as I listened to her Portuguese. With my ritual kissing of her hand, she left the room to prepare the countless things that she and her family had to finish before the ceremony began.

Soon the room began to rumble with conversation as more people arrived and as everyone greeted each other with ritual gestures and kisses. The room divided quickly by gender. Women were on the left facing the drums, which straddled a corner, and men were on the right. The *xirê* began with drumming and without singing. Then suddenly, with a call from the *iyalorixá,* other personnel began to sing: her assistant, the *iyakekere, ekedis* who assist the *orixás* when they arrive, and *iyawos* (initiates). About six ritual kin, all females, danced a circle in a counterclockwise direction with minimal movement beyond a rhythmic traveling step.

The dances I witnessed that night were performed in a rather tight space. The room was crowded within a short period of time with about fifty or sixty people. Only the important ritual kin danced, and a singer, who happened to be an *ogan,* sang while everyone else sang the responses to the songs as they stood in their gendered spaces. Among the ritual performers, each dancer was doing her/his own version of each dance; I rarely saw uniformity during the four or five hours that we participated. For example, the *iyalorixá* danced on the first and strongest beat of the musical measure; she stepped on a counterclockwise circular path with some chest rotations to the right and then left sides, on beats one and two and then three and four, respectively. Another dancer danced her four steps in counterclockwise circular patterns also but did not make the chest twists that the *iyalorixá* accomplished as a result of her pattern. Their arms differed as well. The *iyalorixá* had arms bent at the elbow, pulling gently back every two beats. The other dancer marked the four beats of the measure with four separate gestures and directions of the lower arms. Visually, it looked as if the dancers did not share the same musical phrasing, or the same sense of rhythm, although they performed a similar dance pattern.

From the viewpoint of a trained dancer or of a general observer, this individuality seemed more characteristic of Bahian Yoruba than Cuban Yoruba or Haitian Vodou, and, in a sense, it contradicted other rigid elements of Bahian practice. I remembered this irregular individualized dancing when it occurred at the other *terreiros,* but to a lesser extent than at this small-scale service. (In Cuba and Haiti, you almost always see uniform rhythm, even though there is stylistic variation among individual dancers. And most dancing worshipers keep the same beat.) It was hard for me to select one particular dancer in order to film a "requisite" or "typical" style of Bahia. Usually this is not a problem, but my filming eye made this Bahian difference very clear, and did so quickly.

All ritual dancers had similar, serious facial expressions, despite their rhythmically varied dancing. I figured that there would be moments of self-consciousness; so, early on, I periodically turned the camera off. Their fixed, introverted expressions continued. Since it was rare for filming permission to be granted, I filmed substantial parts of each section of the ritual. I kept my position at the extreme back wall in a corner, directly opposite the drummers' corner, and I alternated filming with singing and minimal group dance movement—swaying.

I was not the only one to document the occasion. Later and often, I noticed other members of the congregation who used flash cameras as the dancers passed by. I presumed these community members must be important since they were seated next to the drums. The ceremonial space was packed. The men's side was particularly dense with forty or so men. I could not film certain parts of the women's side either, because a few tall women were in front of me, making it difficult to see.

Gradually men took on significant roles. One took over from the *iyalorixá;* he was an important *ogan*, an administrator for the *terreiro* who does not generally manifest divinities and who often sings the songs or plays the drums that push the ceremony forward. (Roles are fluid in small *terreiros—ogans* acting as *alebês* or drummers, for example.) Another male eventually danced in the circle with the female initiates and priestesses. Several members were late and came into the dance circle to ritually greet the elder *iyalorixás* and *ekedis,* who were dancing around three objects in the center of the floor: a statue, a bowl with either liquid or powder, and a square tablet. The latecomers touched the drums and greeted other ritual functionaries with bows and kisses. They touched the ceremonial sacred center of the *terreiro,* touched their foreheads, the back of their necks, and again their foreheads. Narcis's wife was late also and took off her headscarf to ritually greet the main *iyalorixá,* the *ogan,* the drums, and the central objects. The *iyalorixá* retied her head-wrap and then placed her in the circle to dance with the others. They danced for almost an hour with a few breaks for the start of new songs.

At one point, my attention was drawn to the left as a woman bent over and let out a loud cry. An *ekedi* from the dance circle came to her and, after a few minutes, guided her into the dancing file of circling dancers for only a few circle turns, and then led her out of the room. A few moments later, a young woman who had been dancing also bent over in *jika* vibrations. She was escorted out as well. Then Narcis's wife became animated while dancing; she hesitated slightly in the dance circle, closed her eyes, and shuddered abruptly. Swiftly and calmly, her head-wrap was removed, while others continued to dance. Then the *iyalorixá* took her out of the circle and through the third door at the back of the room. There was a short pause in the drumming, but the drumming and singing started again.

The dancing of the inner ritual circle and the singing and very modified movement in the surrounding gendered spaces escalated in volume and a bit in speed. (Both men and women in the congregation area stood the entire time, so they did move rhythmically [swaying] to the familiar drum rhythms.) Anticipation gripped the room; mine was intense, but I noticed several others, dancers especially, looking over their shoulders occasionally for something or someone. When the door reopened, Oxun entered the dance space in the body of Narcis's wife. She was beautifully and elegantly dressed, levels beyond anyone else in the room. She sparkled with golden-threaded cloth and bright,

bright yellow in her gown and on her crown. She glistened all over behind a panoply of hanging golden threads in front of her face. She shimmered with delicate vibrations. It appeared that everyone was happy and excited to see her loveliness.

She was demure, with her head constantly lowered. She carried a huge bouquet of fresh flowers in a gold plastic sheath and held a jeweled mirror. She did not dance with any more vigor than anyone else, which was noticeable in comparison to Cuban and Haitian female divinity performance. She was gentle and soft, unadulterated femininity. She danced with the others, both males and females, for about half an hour more. Then the *xirê* was interrupted with the arrival of another *orixá*.

Yansan had taken a young man in the front row of male participants. The *xirê* continued with welcoming songs to her, but s(he)[3] was not taken out of the room. His shoes and white T-shirt were taken off, and then she was wrapped with a white headscarf and a long length of multicolored fabric from her armpits to her ankles. Yansan danced facing the male sector of the room; she was turned to face the congregation, not the drums. Her cries were more like piercing yelps than shattering screams, and her shoulders vibrated between her waving arms and fluid, shifting hip movements. Yansan's dance was faster than the fastest Oxun rhythms so far, and more agitated.

Oxun was still on my side of the room, the women's side of the room, during the arrival and first songs of Oya. She was escorted out by *ekedis* in a sweet, seemingly happy and enthusiastic manner. Attention went to Yansan with another series of songs. She danced several dances, but then, and I am not clear how this occurred, she was moved aside and eventually out of the space. Probably, she was persuaded to leave, since the *xirê* was for Oxun. Worshipers did not seem as prepared for Yansan, even though as co-wives of Xangó, Oxun and Yansan can both come in the same *xirê*. The terreiro gave Yansan respect and then assisted her departure.

At that moment, I was more concerned with my film, which suddenly ended as I had finished off two, two-hour batteries. I had noticed the one electric lightbulb that lit the room earlier, and I now looked for an outlet to plug in the camera. Apparently, it was on the far side of the room, where I felt I could not go without disturbing the entire *xirê*. So I put the camera in its pack as quickly as possible and simply rejoined the congregation as an observing participant. My attention, and everyone else's, focused on the loud and strenuous songs for Oxun coming from alternating male lead singers and a mixed group of male and female dancers in the center of the space. Suddenly the third door reopened and Oxun reentered in her sparkling glory. This time she danced more vigorously and directly toward the female side of the room. I gasped and wished for the batteries that might have recorded her stunning and sensuous reentry. She lowered her entire body to the floor and everyone showered her with perfumed rice. The whole room shifted from hot humidity to fresh and sweet interlude. The smell and effect of Oxun reigned.

Worshipers poked me, motioning for me to film this part, this climax of Oxun's dance, while she was bathing. They did not comprehend my dilemma at first but tried to assist me. What I couldn't translate into Portuguese was how often mechanical failures (of cameras and recorders) took place at the climax of a ceremony or in the presence of the *orixás!* I was used to these events, despite backup supplies and preparations, and I tried not to treat them as disappointments or disasters, but as potential lessons in sentience and sensibilities.

For me, it was time for full concentration, concentration on my senses in terms of what was going on in front of me. I examined Oxun's full splendor. I looked at Oxun in the waterfall of showered perfumed rice, softly giggling, smiling serenely. I looked into the wondrous eyes of believers, who crowded all around her. They registered her presence and reached for her longingly.

I also looked for Yansan and wondered why she had entered what was apparently a specific ceremony for Oxun. Perhaps the *xirê* was an extravagant *odu* ceremony, given as part of an offering to Oxun. Oxun was obviously expected: her clothing was elaborate; her flowers were abundant; her ritual objects were immaculate. Yansan was quickly and improvisationally dressed; her clothing was a sparse substitute for her usual grandiose and colorful apparel; her ritual objects were missing, but her demands were answered in simple, unadorned behaviors. Of course, in the Oracle stories (*orikis, irikis,* or *patakines*), both are the wives of Xangó, as one colleague reminded me, giving them something in common and perhaps a reason for their dual participation.

This small ceremony had simplicity and improvisation, and as always at least one lesson. The lesson I learned that night from Bahia's proper ritual behavior, from a small-scale and less ornate Candomblé community than I had previously known, and from dance performance analysis, was about competing wishes, competing desires, or competing goals. Both divinities were present; both required ritual salutation and obeisance; both needed community attention. Instead of tension, conflict, or a battle in the center space of two deserving and powerful forces, instead of oppositional stances and responding oppositions for the congregation, the two spiritual entities were honored respectfully.

First, the occasion was Oxun's *xirê*, so she received center stage facing the drums, while Yansan was turned away from the drums toward the supporting congregation to receive her songs of praise. Yansan was encouraged to dance her dance and then to leave the ceremony altogether, so that the full climax of congregational devotion was literally showered on Oxun.

The win-win potential of all conflicts was meted out slowly in measured thought and ritual action. All ritual obligations were attended to and completed, and all worshipers watched and witnessed the delicate and important lessons. The lessons of negotiation, respect, equality, and reconciliation were danced and sung in shifting ritual sequences. No one lost, but not everyone could be "first"; still, everyone was acknowledged.

Paulo looked over from his space in the front line of men. He had witnessed an example of the teachings of the *orixás* that had been quickly applied to the *orixás* themselves. I wondered how much of the (social, political, economic, emotional) lesson he understood. His apprehensive expression disappeared, and a smile broke out across his face, as he turned to look at me and then threw fragrances and adored his beautiful Oxun.

> Ora ye ye u-u!
> Oyeyeu o lore o, o yeyeu o lo reo
> Oyeyeu o lore o, o yeyeu o lo reo.
>
> Daughter of Beauty,
> Indulgent/excessive daughter,
> Daughter of beautiful water,
> Beautiful daughter
> Come to me.
> (Song for Oxun while she is bathing, when worshipers throw rice and rosewater; translated by Pai Carlinhos and Augusto Soledade)

Oxalá at Casa Branca

Since my time with Eunice at the small Candomblé *xirê*, I looked forward to the days she spent on the beach. She was curious about me and I about her, and we laughed and talked woman-talk comfortably. One day I was supposed to meet a woman from the United States who had brought a group of U.S. Americans to experience Brazilian rituals. I took Eunice with me to the four-star hotel in town to meet her and her group.

The American turned out to be a soft-spoken African American woman from Brooklyn, Oseye. She was not the novice tourist leader I had anticipated, but a learned Yoruba ritual specialist who regularly brought students and adherents of the religion to Oxalá's water ceremony, *aguas de Oxalá* at Casa Branca. She did not bring them for consecration or initiation, but mainly for the experience of Yoruba religion among a majority black population. She wanted them to feel a majority situation among African religious communities, as opposed to their understanding and experience within Brooklyn's minority ritual population.

As we spoke in the lobby, it became apparent that Oseye was rushing off to a ceremony. She invited Eunice and me to the *aguas de Oxalá* and even let us borrow white blouses for the occasion. It did seem strange for a person from the United States to give us clothes to wear a few minutes after meeting us. I had experienced similar or parallel gestures among other Caribbean and Latin American people during my trips, but rarely from anyone from the United States within such a short period of time. We dashed off with Oseye. For Eunice, it promised to be a first visit to a well-known *terreiro,* and her chance to see my responses before inviting me to her Caboclo ceremonies. For me, it promised a possible new version of Candomblé, a measure of excitement, but mostly a grand opportunity to have my questions answered about the same ceremony from a Brazilian as well as a U.S. African American perspective.

The ceremony had not begun when we entered the historic *terreiro,* "mother" to the two other large-scale temples. There were hundreds of ritual kin passing through or outside the room reserved for visitors. Oseye was taken into the intimate spaces along with other initiated travelers in her group. Eunice and I sat quietly in anticipation but also talked from time to time with other Brazilians and foreigners among the visitors. It turned out that a colleague of mine from the University of California at Berkeley was there, and just as we had established minimal contact, the solemn ceremony began. Women were given small, empty clay jugs, while men were given quite large pitchers; some were clay, but most looked like porcelain or painted aluminum. We formed a very long line and understood that no talking was permitted from now on.

For hours we walked down and up fifty or more stairs; I believe we climbed and descended sixteen times each way. First, when we walked downstairs, we collected water in our jugs, and then we carried the water upstairs on our heads. Upstairs, a huge container had to be filled, and it took probably sixty to a hundred people several hours to complete the task. We worked all night long, up and down several flights of stairs in silent darkness, with the exception of the star-filled sky and moonlight.

I was aware of how steadily and slowly I had to walk so as not to spill the topped-off jug. I had to transfer my weight from foot to foot in a conscious and smooth gait. And I had to climb steps, narrow steps, in the dark. When my arm tired of balancing the water-filled jug and I switched to the other side, I immediately felt I had made an error and changed back. In the moonlight on the stairs, I could see only the person in front of me plus a few people walking nearby in the opposite direction, but I could feel unspoken rules and the solemn calm of deliberate group action.

It was mesmerizing, calming, taking me to heightened sensitivity. I had started thinking with intellectual curiosity, but with each journey down and up the stairs, the experience became more than walking up and down. The quiet, steady ensemble movement deepened first awareness and then concentration. The ritual generated seriousness and also a physical, kinesthetic connection among the file of worshipers and witnesses.

> Orixá ure saul laxé, Orixá ure oberi o ma.
> Orixá ure saul laxé, Orixá ure oberi o ma.

> Blessed Orixá, Blessed with your powerful life force.
> Blessed Orixá, Carry me.
> (Translated by Pai Carlinhos and Augusto Soledade)

When all the water had been transported upstairs, a big ceremonial room was opened for all to enter. Oxalá's altar was at the apex, and a line of greeters automatically formed. Everyone present walked forward individually and made a ritual salutation, either the male or female version of the *dobale,* toward the altar, with the ritual community of Casa Branca looking on. Two of the foreign visitors were Catholic nuns, and I wondered what they would do at their turn to greet Oxalá. They walked forward and simply bowed their heads ever so slightly and then returned to places on the periphery of the room.

I wondered also about my own salutation gestures: should I simply bow my head respectfully as an uninitiated North American, or should I make the ritual greeting that my Cuban godmother had taught me for my guiding *orixá?* I remembered also Ezili's tale of mistakes and corrections:

> But all the old ones, the ones with the *konesanz,* they saw it [the mistake] ... [and] when that old one dies ... they "fix" the mistake. That way, everyone gives respect.

I lingered on her notion of "respect." I knew that whatever mistake I might make would be rectified and also received in accordance with my intentions.

I think it was the first time that I made the ritual *dobale* publicly. I watched line after line of gesturing participants, and I noticed the Brooklyn Americans too. I wanted to be recognized as different from the nuns and other foreigners who had simply bowed their heads in respect at their turn to salute Oxalá. I walked toward the raised shrine of all-encompassing white and lowered my entire body to the floor. I kissed the ground with the sacred power and blessing buried there. Then I turned onto my right hip and raised my upper body to rest on my right elbow and pulled my left hand to my left hip. Directly after that set of gesturing movements, I did the same movements on my left side, looking to the right. With those three sequences completed, I stood up and retreated toward the periphery as other greeters took my place. Afterward, but only for a few seconds, I wondered what my Berkeley colleague thought of my ritual allegiance made public. I saw her again when the dancing started; she came over to dance with Eunice and me. I knew she knew me as a dance teacher as well as an anthropologist. Unfortunately, we never talked after the dancing; in fact, I have not ever seen her again to talk about our shared experience.

The drumming and singing started. I picked out a few elder female dancers to follow, thinking that there would be an order of dances and I did not have my familiar Brazilian contacts to guide me in whispers or gestures. Nevertheless, I noticed that they began with the very difficult dance for Oxalá. The dance space was very large, and all of us had ample room to comfortably execute all the steps of all the *orixás*. I was expecting to follow a *xirê* order with all of the *orixás'* dances, but as we traveled in a counterclockwise direction, the only dance we performed was the beautiful but strenuous dance for Oxalá.

> Orixá ure, Osaguian, Ajaguna Baba o,
> Ajaguna elemoxo Babaloro Ogun. Ajagouna Baba o.
>
> Oh Father Ajaguna, Defender, Protector, Father of many
> concerns, Ajaguna, Warrior Father.
> (Translated by Pai Carlinhos and Augusto Soledade)

We were bent over for what seemed to be many hours, although in reality it was probably about two hours. Regardless, it was a very long time for this type of dance, and I took the challenge early to continue dancing until the ceremony was over, no matter how painful my back might become. My eyes followed two older ladies who seemed to have zest and definitiveness in their movements. They kept to the rhythm precisely, and I could imitate accordingly, releasing my Cuban style of dance and accessing their Brazilian style. The nuns and several others did not dance but stayed to observe from the periphery. I danced with the ritual family: the *ekedis, ebomis,* and I assumed other *iawos,* but also with non-initiates like my Berkeley colleague, Eunice, and the Brooklynites (only some of whom were initiates). I found out later that this was one of the few occasions when all present are permitted to dance in the circle of praise.[4]

There were moments of rest when the drummers stopped as they alternated positions. On these infrequent breaks, I stood slowly and stretched carefully. Eunice was the first in our little group to go to the sideline. I used her exit as a means of rest when I came past her again and stopped to ask her if she was all right. Upon hearing she was only tired, not sick, I felt my commitment resurge, and I joined the dances again, having benefited from a bit of rest. I saw my Berkeley colleague in ritual imitation and noticed her large, exaggerated movements and strong sense of energy. I gradually lowered my posture, but not as low as my models' postures, and I began to compute their every nuance. They did not use all the energy that my colleague or I had been using. They were relaxed, but exceedingly active. I tried to replicate their posture, steps, dynamics, and expression and knew all along that I, too, was displaying too much energy or force in the movements.

Ample energy was needed at first to approximate each unfamiliar movement, but with repetition, it was not needed. I got closer to the feel of the dance, if not the look of it, with less force and more relaxation. I knew I would never get the look of the dance until I lowered myself closer to the floor, and this I figured would come with the fatigue I was beginning to experience. At the time, I was presuming that the dances for Oxalá would end soon, and that other dances would be included in the celebration and would also ease my overused muscles. With rest by means of another dance, I was sure that by the ceremony's end, I would "know" Oxalá's dance and be able to perform it in fair facsimile. But other dances did not accompany this ceremony. In fact, Oxalá's dance usually ends a Bahian ceremony (see comparative Cuban and Bahian Yoruba orders in chart 11 of chapter 5).

My back was truly hurting. I looked at my two dancing elders and kept going. They appeared to be about sixty or sixty-five years old, which meant they were probably seventy or eighty. I felt that my forty-five-year-old dancing body should be able to maintain their level of stamina, and I continued. I danced with dedication to our ritual journey in the moonlight, dedication to Oxalá's demand for water jugs on our heads, and dedication to all I knew about Yoruba faith at that time. I focused on rhythmic endurance that night, following my two ladies in their incredible and constant motion. I never thought or realized until the end, as my last lady was literally pulled from the room (the last dancer of the hundred or so dancing worshipers) that I had been foolishly competing with Oxalá himself. This lady was no lady, but the relentless sage. I discovered this when others were trying to lead him away from the dance; they did not touch him but with great respect tried to coax him away when the familiar muffled, groaning sounds of an *orixá* came from his mouth. He had kept her body in a very lowered position and at the same pace for hours. I could not win.

What Oxalá gave me in return for my devoted concentration and hours of dance-work was surprising—a body free of pain and aches, unusually strong and flexible for the next few days. I had presumed I would be aching for days afterward, but incredibly, this did not happen. Perhaps my routine of walking on the beach each morning had built sufficient conditioning such that my back and entire skeleton were in good alignment and gave exceptional muscular strength. Still, Oxalá blessed me with euphoria of both body and mind as a wonderful prize for staying with the demanding dance for as long as I did. I felt the *axé* of the entire night's activities, including the water rites and the dancing. The exquisite evening ritual reconfirmed *axé*, the transcendence of excruciating pain, infirmity, tension, or stress in the mental commitment of doing the ritual movements exactly like the knowing elders had modeled.

Passing beyond ordeals, the physical challenge to the presumed mental and emotional reward is a common path in most rituals. In this one, I felt a surging growth or development, a keen awareness of inner fortitude. I recognized the mind/body connection that comes with acute awareness of the human body while in movement. It was splendid and revealing. My dance effort and my back were my supreme offerings to Oxalá at Casa Branca that August night, in the company of incredible dancing *orixás*.

> Fururu mo ure ailala Baba kem em Elegibo
> Yle Ifa me jua Baba a Giborele
> Mojuba o orum a e maor ala use.
> Fururu mo ure ailala Baba kem em Elegibo
> Yle Ifa me jug Baba a Giborele

Mojuba o orum a e maor ala use.
E, E, E,
Maor Baba Pele o e maor ala use.

Bright light, Bless me. Walk with me to Elegibo.
Ifa asks that you return home.
Father, the house, the people who abandoned you ask for
    forgiveness.
Heaven and Earth bring life over the Ala, the white cloth.
(Translated by Pai Carlinhos and Augusto Soledade)

EIGHT

Formal Learning
with Cuban *Orichas*

"*I,* *Changó, want good ceremonies, and that means excellent participation.*
That also means I have to help the dancers and musicians, so they can
learn quickly and allow the ceremonies to flow. You know the chants direct
my drums and the dancers too, and sometimes both the drummers and the dancers
have to sing as they play their parts too. So musicians and dancers need to learn the
lyrics of the chants and then concentrate on their rhythms and dance steps."

"This is no easy feat to accomplish—for either dancer or musician! For
this feat of rendering the music/dance ceremonies smooth, I turn to you,
Changó, and the Cuban Yoruba liturgy. Your chapter is for the dance or music specialist who wants a concise example of what goes on in a *wemilere* or
bembé in Cuba. You have space to provide a sample order and indicate how
the chants, drumming, and movement patterns fit together. Simultaneously,
this will give nonperformers an appreciation of the interconnectedness of
performance elements. Your chapter can serve as a guide for apprenticing
dancers in terms of which rhythms are generally played and which dance
steps should be performed when a particular *oricha* is invoked. Your chapter

can replicate only a few set orders, called 'roads' (*trataos*) of chants and dances, since these vary depending on regional practice and the knowledge of a given lead singer (*akpwon*).[1] Additionally for drummers, I hope you will present the structure of the music."

"*But no batá rhythms will be spelled out here.*"

"I want you to give me the skeletal organization of a typical public ceremony (see Ortiz 1951 [1985], Friedman 1982, and Amira and Cornelius 1992 for sample rhythmic transcriptions). My motivation for writing out familiar orders with detailed dance and music information comes from repeated requests of my students, but also from several practitioners outside of Cuba and from many dancing Cubanophiles. I think your report can bring together information that has been scattered and compartmentalized so that what might have been learned over a period of years, in childhood and young adulthood in Cuba, can be more easily studied and practiced by reading these remarks. Many good dancers know the steps but need the appropriate chants with their accompanying dance step noted. Often also, dancers are not taught about the precise names of drums rhythms that are used. With the following charts, dance students can access the lyrics of chants, use these to learn the name and character of the drum rhythms, and feel secure in performing the appropriate movement sequences. The skeletal information here should also help students to understand ritual structure and reinforce actual participation and formal 'body learning.'"

Chango: Integration of Voice, Drum, and Body

"*Mi vida, los cantos son esenciales para el progreso ritual. Siguen un orden litúrgico, pero en un orden rítmico también. Primero, se cantan con yakotá que es muy suave y despacio. Entonces, tenemos un ñongo, que tu sabes es un poquito más rápido, hasta el momento del chachaolokofún, que es él ritmo más rápido, exaltado y sensual. Al fin, como en mi tratao, el mío termina con la meta, el más fuerte y macho de todos.*"

Translation: "*My dear, the chants are pivotal for ritual progression. They follow a liturgical order, but also a rhythmic order. They are sung to a slow rhythm, usually yakotá, followed by a medium-paced rhythm, ñongo, a fast rhythm, chachaolokofún, and then the fastest, most prominent and exciting rhythm for that particular oricha. At the end, like in my tratao, mine ends with la meta, you know, the strongest and most fierce of all rhythms*" (see chart 12, first section).

"*This rhythmic structure is followed for each oricha* (for each segment of the liturgical order), *creating a dynamic series of crescendos and decrescendos in terms of speed, texture, and dramatic tension. In fact, the order is a succession of greetings to all the orichas and after these are completed, the excitement of the community supports the focus of the ceremony toward the dedicated oricha. Then it is fine to have hours of songs and drum dancing! Of course, you have to begin and end with Elegba.*"[2]

Generic Musical Structure

"*Each oricha has his/her own order of chants, but all of them follow this sequence. And I have my list here. My list of chants shows the general organization of the Oru de cantos. I give tratao examples for several orichas, but not for all of them because there are too many. When you transpose these, you must put the drum rhythms with the dance step for each chant in my tratao example, but with a strong warning that there are many ways in which the Cuban religious communities sing and dance for the orichas.*"[3]

"*I have created names for a few dance steps, in contrast to the many names that are recognized for the rhythms. But you can identify the dance steps by my descriptive names. Each set of chants, rhythms, and dance movements forms a tratao for a particular oricha. Each tratao relates to a story within its lyrics; it gives references to a particular part of an oricha's life history. It is also a rhythmic whole, containing a full building up or climax from slow to fastest tempo. Tratao chants in a particular order can be substituted by other chants, but the rhythms and dance steps remain the same*" (see Chant, Drum, and Dance Composites in Chart 12).

Chart 12. Generic Structure of Drum Rhythm Sequences (called a "road" or *"tratao"* for each *oricha*)

1. *Yakotá*
   Slow tempo rhythm with numerous chants

2. *Ñongo*
   Medium tempo rhythm with numerous chants

3. *Chachaolokofún*
   Fast rhythm with numerous chants

4. Fastest rhythm of a given *oricha*
   with differing names, often the *rezo* (prayer) for the *oricha*
   is sung on top, slowly, *contra tiempo*

Chant, Drum, and Dance Composites[4]

AN ELEGUA *TRATAO*

Chant	Drum Rhythm	Main Dance Step
1. BARA SUAYO (REZO)	LA LUBANCHE	WALK 1,2,1,2,3 or CABALLO (horse step): RLR, LRL, RLR, LRL 312,312,312,312
2. I BARA AGO	LA TOKPA	TOUCH,BACK,STEP,STEP R L R
3. ECHUO ELEGBARA-E	LA TOKPA	TOUCH BACK STEP
4. TEREMINA	Rumba Ochosi/Oggue	CROSSING STEP: a)R cross front, b)L, c)R side, d)L, e)Rcross front, f)L, g)R center; repeat always R
5. KIRINYA	ÑONGO	CABALLO
6. OCHIMINI E A	IYESA or CHACHAOLOKOFÚN	IYESA STEP: Side R, R place, Side L, L place; JUMP & KICK STEP: KICK RRRR, KICK LLLL
7. SOSA SOKERE	LLESA or CHACHA	JUMP & KICK STEP; IYESA; or CABALLO

AN OGÚN *TRATAO*

Chant	Drum Rhythm	Main Dance Step
1. MARIWO YEYEYE	OGUN/KOBU	DIAGONAL STEP—Rcross forward, Lback, Rplace, Hold; Lcross forward, Rback, Lplace, Hold
2. IBARIBA CHEKECHEKE	Rumba Ochosi/Oggue	PIVOTING STEP: R to L diagonal, L toe step, R to R diagonal, L toe step; On beat 4, R hand throws to right diagonal
3. OGUNDERE ARERE	OGUN WADO	DIAGONAL STEP
4. ONILE	ÑONGO/CHACHA	DIAGONAL STEP
5. OGUN BABALA	(BATÁ or GUIRO)	CHOPPING STEP CHOP RRRR, CHOP LLLL
6. AMALA OGUN	ÑONGO/CHACHA	CABALLO OR DIAGONAL
7. E AFEREYO	ÑONGO/CHACHA	DIAGONAL/CABALLO
8. KOMARERE	ÑONGO/CHACHA	DIAGONAL STEP
9. OGUN ELESE	ÑONGO	DIAGONAL/CABALLO
10. SARA Y KOKO	CHACHA	DIAGONAL STEP

AN OCHOSI *TRATAO*

Chant	Drum Rhythm	Main Dance Step
1. YAKUO	AGUERE (6 PARTS)	a) IYESA b) CROSSING STEP c) IYESA d) SHOOTING ARROW STEP: pivoting feet with Ochosi arms/fingers to R, to L, touch back of right shoulder with R hand, R arm shoots arrow; e) IYESA on 1&2, SHOOTING ARROW on 3&4 f) Kick 2R, Kick 2L with arms alternating R, L and shooting with each kick; then Kick and shoot on every beat
2. SIRE SIRE	Rumba Ochosi/Oggue	DIAGONAL or 1,2,1,2,3 on R, L, RLR, L, R, LRL
3. YAMBELEKE	OGGUE	DIAGONAL OR 1,2,1,2,3
4. IWARA ODDEFA	OGGUE	DIAGONAL OR 1,2,1,2,3
5. AWARE EKUN FOYA	OGGUE	DIAGONAL OR 1,2,1,2,3

A BABALUAYÉ *TRATAO*

Chant	Drum	Main Dance Step
1. AGADA GODO (REZO)	IBA IBA OGGEDE MA	LOW CRAMPED WALKS, ALTERNATING SHOULDERS TO KNEE-1,2,1,2,3
2. BABA E, BABA SOROSO	IBA IBA OGGEDE MA	LOW CRAMPED WALKS
3. TOWE TOWE	ARARÁ/YEWA	WALK RL HOLD, RL HOLD (with constant shoulder pulses)
4. ASOKARA KARA SUNAWEA	ARARÁ/YEWA	WALK RL HOLD, RL HOLD

AN OBATALÁ *TRATAO*

Chant	Drum Rhythm	Main Dance Step
1. BABA ALA YEO (REZO)	EGGUADO	VERY SLOW WALKS: RL, RL
2. FEE EKWA O	EGGUADO	SLOW WALKS: RL, RLR, LR, LRL
3. ERIBODE	ÑONGO	UPRIGHT ADVANCING STEP: 1,2,1,2,3
4. OBATALA ELONA	ÑONGO	UPRIGHT ADVANCING
5. TOTO ITO	CHACHA/AYEMBELEKO	UPRIGHT (with arms folded on chest); IYESA
6. WA E WA E LO MIO	IYESA	IYESA

A CHANGÓ *TRATAO*

Chant	Drum	Main Dance Step
1. IYA MASE	OPOLAYO/SERABASE/IYA MA	TOUCH BACK STEP
2. EWAYO	OPOLAYO/SERABASE	TOUCH BACK STEP
3. MOFORI NANA	SERABASE/IYA MA	WALK SIDE RL, LR; WALK FRONT RL, LR; WALK BACK RL, LR
4. MALAMALA	OPOLAYO/SERABASE/IYA MA	LRR, LRR, LRR, L; ALTERNATE R
5. ALA MALA	AGAYU #4	FRONT RL, BACK RL, SIDE RL, SIDE LR
6. MALA MALALUO	ÑONGO	CABALLO
7. MOFORI BORERE	CHACHAOLOKOFÚN	CHANGO STEP: R HIT/KICK, RLR, ALTERNATE
8. KABO E	CHACHAOLOKOFÚN	CHANGO STEP/CABALLO
9. OBA IBO (REZO)	META/ALUYA	CHANGO STEP

AN OYA *TRATAO*

Chant	Drum Rhythm	Main Dance Step
1. YE OYA WIMI (REZO)	OYA BIKU	OYA FOOT PATTERN: FRONT BACK CHACHACHA R FRONT, L BACK, RLR TO R-SIDE; LFRONT, R BACK, LRL TO L-SIDE
2. OYADE	YAKOTA/JUESO/OBA	OYA FOOT PATTERN
3. OYADEO	TRANSITION	CABALLO
4. LONGOITO	ÑONGO	FRONT BACK CHACHACHA
5. EEAAH	ÑONGO	FRONT BACK CHACHACHA
6. KORO UNLE O	ÑONGO	FRONT BACK CHACHACHA
7. OLELE	ÑONGO	FRONT BACK CHACHACHA
8. OYA GAGA	ÑONGO	FRONT BACK CHACHACHA
9. OYA WIMA	ÑONGO	FRONT BACK CHACHACHA
10. OYANSAN A SERE	ÑONGO	FRONT BACK CHACHACHA
11. OYA OYA O	CHACHAOLOKOFÚN	CABALLO
12. OYANKO EMI	CHACHAOLOKOFÚN	CABALLO
13. YE OYA WIMI (REZO)	TUITUI	TUITUI R,L,R, LFOOT POINT SIDE 2 3 4, & DA 1 L,R,L, RFOOT POINT SIDE 2 3 4, & DA 1

A YEMAYÁ *TRATAO*

Chant	Drum Rhythm	Main Dance Step
1. ASESU	YAKOTÁ	LOW, SLOW RL, RL IN 3'S SLIDE R BACK, SLIDE R FORWARD, SLIDE L BACK, SLIDE L FORWARD
2. SOKUTANI WO	YAKOTÁ/SOKUTANI WO	LOW 3'S
3. BARAGO YEMAYA	YAKOTÁ	LOW 3'S
4. ODDA ASESU	YAKOTÁ	LOW 3'S
5. OKOTA	YAKOTÁ	LOW 3'S
6. OMOLODE	ZAPATEO	ZAPATEO STEP #1: R HEEL, R FORWARD, R BACK L HEEL, L FORWARD, L BACK
7. EMI ODE	ZAPATEO	ZAPATEO
8. OLUBA CHIKINI	ZAPATEO	ZAPATEO
9. ALA MODANSE	ZAPATEO	ZAPATEO #2 OR CLAVE: R, L, RLR; L, R, LRL
———		
10. LARIOKE	ÑONGO	CABALLO, ZAPATEO #1
11. KAI KAI KAI	ÑONGO	CABALLO, ZAPATEO #1
12. WARO MIO	CHACHAOLOKUFÚN	ZAPATEO #1, CABALLO
13. AGOLONAE	ARO	TURNING, SPINNING
14. OKUO YALE ARO	ARO	SPINNING/CHANGO META
(REZO)		KICKING STEP, throwing skirt

AN OCHÚN *TRATAO*

Chant	Drum Rhythm	Main Dance Step
1. IYA MILE (REZO)	CHENCHEKURURU	WALKING, CABALLO
2. YEYE MORO IGI	YAKOTÁ	TOUCH BACK STEP
3. ALADEYE	IBALOKE	TOUCH BACK STEP
4. OMA OMA	IBALOKE	TOUCH BACK STEP
5. YEYE BIO	YAKOTÁ	TOUCH BACK STEP
6. OLU WERE	YAKOTÁ	TOUCH BACK STEP
7. IMBE IMBE	IYESA	IYESA, CABALLO
8. ORE ORE	IYESA	IYESA, CABALLO
9. ALA UNBANCHE	IYESA	IYESA
10. IDE WERE WERE	DADA/WOLENCHE	ZAPATEO #1
11. ALA IYEYE	DADA/WOLENCHE	DIP, TURN, ZAPATEO #1 R&L
12. GBOGBOSUN	DADA/WOLENCHE	BOUNCE STEP: RL, LR, RL, LR with skirt alternating side to side at hip
13. YEYE YEYEO	ÑONGO	ZAPATEO #1, IYESA
14. EYURE AMALA	TRANSITION	CABALLO
15. YAN YAN IROKO	CHACHAOLOKUFÚN	CABALLO, ZAPATEO/IYESA

Another Elegua Tratao to end

Orúnmila's Patakines

"There are thousands of stories about the lives and interrelationships of the orichas, and they come from the teachings of Orúnmila, guardian of the Ifa Oracle. Worshipers become acquainted with different oricha energies through the life stories or patakines (orikis or irikis) of the orichas. It's good to know some of these as you dance."

"Worshipers learn as they dance how to balance, confront, and manage different sorts of *oricha* energy. They can then see, feel, or sense *oricha* energy among humans, and comport themselves accordingly. The interactions among the *orichas* display the comforts, concerns, tendencies, and temptations of social life. These reassure the individual of her/his own normalcy and provide opportunities to select and choose certain behaviors in real life."

"The patakines place a moral code around the ritual community. You can record some of these while I prepare the chants. I will return."

"At their cores, the stories often parallel biblical parables, Greek and Roman mythologies, East Indian epic legends, and Native American visionary quests. Here are two examples."

For Oyá, Changó, and Yemayá

One of Oyá's stories shows how she developed her physical and mental abilities. She loved and tricked Changó! At that time, Changó was living with Yemayá, and Yemayá was taking care of the young Oyá. Oyá pretended to be a boy in order to be alone with Changó. Changó took her hunting, and she was a spectacular student, learning fast and enjoying time and attention in Changó's presence. Changó admired his young colleague and thought he was teaching "him" how to ride horses, how to hunt, how to maneuver and strategize. He was proud of his protégé's success.

Then one day, Oyá revealed that she was a woman. After his brief shock, Changó was amazed and enamored. He was stunned that a woman could keep up with him on his horse, riding skillfully and fast. He realized also that she now knew all his secrets of hunting and she knew no fear. She was awesome, and he had to have her as his wife. So they became lovers. When Yemayá discovered them, she put them out of her house. Later, after years of intimacy, trust, and caring, Changó asked Oyá to bring his fire to him, and in so doing, Oyá learned the miracle of fire. This made Oyá as powerful as Changó, ultimately his equal. Perhaps she became superior, especially because Changó knew fear, and Oyá remained fearless.

For Ochún and Ogún

Ochún was so beautiful that the people of Ogún's village implored her to help them bring Ogún out of the mountains and forested regions. No one had been successful in calling him to the village, and they needed him for protection. Ochún went into the forested area and began to sing. Ogún noticed her voice and peeked through the leaves to see who was singing so sweetly. Ochún saw him but didn't let him know. She continued to sing and to wander farther and farther into the woods. When she came to a lake, she began to undress, knowing that Ogún would see her eventually. She took off her earrings, her necklaces, and all of her bracelets and then slowly unwound the cloths that were draped around her beautiful body. She then took honey, *omi,* and smoothed it over all her body, still singing and laughing as she felt Ogún's presence. It was too much of an attraction and temptation for Ogún. Even though he had been living with Oyá deep in the forest at that time, he followed the song and

Ochún's sensuous display, and the two became devoted lovers. Ochún then escorted Ogún back to the people of the village, where he was happy to help them, having been so satisfied with Ochún.

Chant Lyrics for the Orichas

"Por fin. Estoy aquí con las palabras de los cantos en la manera en que cantamos en Cuba. Yo escribí algunas para los principales y los preferidos. I included the prayer, el rezo, for each oricha at the end of each tratao, and sometimes I put in the call from the akpwon (a) with the answer of the coro *(c). Most of these are the* coro's *parts, however. Enjoy."*

CHANTS FOR ELEGUA[5]

A(kpwón)&C(oro):
REZO: BARA SUAYO OMON YALA GUANA MAMA
  KENYAIRAWO E (2X)
OBARA SUAYO EKE ESHU ODARA
OMON YALA GUANA MAMA KENYAIRAWO E

A&C: I BARA AGO MOYUBA (2X)
  OMODDE KO NI KO SIBARA AGO
  AGO MOYUBA ELEGBA ECHULONA

A&C: ECHUO ELEGBARA E (2X)
  ELEGBARA MOFORIBANLE
  ELEGBARA AGO

A&C: ICHONCHO ABE (2X)
  ODDARA COLORILEYO
  ICHONCHO ABE ODDARA
  OLORILEYO BABA EMI
  ICHONCHO ABE

C: AGO AGO (2X), AGO ILE AGO

C: TEREMINA MINA TERE (2X)

A: KIRINYA, KIRINYA AGO KIRINYA

C: KIRINYA, KIRINYA AGO KIRINYA

A&C: OCHINIMI EA, ALA DONICHE, OCHINIMI

A&C: ADO ACHUREO (2X)
  BARA LAYIKI ADDO ACHUREO

A&C: AGO ELEGBA ABUKENKE (2X)
A: ABUKENKE ABUKENKE
    ELEGBA MASANKIO

C: ABUKENKE ABUKENKE

A&C: ELEGBA, ELEGBA, A SOKERE KEYE MEYE ELEGBA,
    ELEGBA, A LA GWANA KILAMBOCHE

C: SOSA SOKERE

A&C: ELEGBA AGO, ELEGBA AGO ANYAN (2X)
    A LAROYE MASANKIO ELEGBA AGO ANYAN

CHANTS FOR OGÚN

REZO: MARIWO YEYEYE MARIWO YEYEYE OGUN
    ALA WEDE (2X)
ENI MOWONIWO ENI MOWONIWO OGUN ALA WEDE

IBARIBA CHEKECHEKE

A&C: OGUNDERE ARERE
    ILE BOGBO LOKUA
    OGUN WANILE OKE WALONA
    ILE BOGBO LOKUA E

A&C: ONILE ONILE (2X)
    ARERE MARIWO
    OGUN BAMBALA CHECHE

A&C: AMALA OGUN ARERE AMALA E A

A&C: E AFERE YO

A&C: OGUN ELESE ARIWO (2X)
    BABA ELEGBA OYA
    OGUN ELESE ARIWO

A&C: SARA Y KOKO OGUNDE

A&C: KWAO KWAO KWAO
    AREDE KWAO KWAO

CHANTS FOR OCHOSI

A: YAKU MAKARERE ABATA
C: ERO SIBABA KARERE

A&C: BABA OCHOSI, AYI LODA ALA MADE

A: SIRE SIRE
C: ODE MATA ORE ORE

A: WOLE WOLE
C: ODE MATA ORE ORE

A&C: YAMBELEKE IWORO
ODE MATA AGOLONA

A: ODE MATA
C: IWARA ODEFA

A: AWALERE KOFOYA ODEDE
C: AWALERE KOFOYA

CHANTS FOR BABALUAYÉ

REZO: A: ABERIKUTU AWA LERISO (2X)
ORE BABA, BABALUAYE AWA LERISO, ORE BABA
C: A BERIKUTU AWA LERISO (2X)
ORE BABA, BABALUAYE AWA LERISO, ORE BABA

A: BARIBA OGUEDEMA
C: MOLE YANSA AMOLEYA
A: ENI BAGUE, BAGUE, BAGUE
C: MOLE YANSA AMOLEYA

A&C: ABERIKUTU AWA LERISO (2X)
ORE BABA, BABLUAYE AWA LERISO ORE BABA
A&C: BABA E BABA SOROSO (2X)
BABALUAYE IYAMBO MODE BABA SIRE SIRE

A: SIRERE SIRERE MOBA
C: BABA SIRE SIRE

A: TOWE TOWE MARUFINA MAWE
MARUFINA MAWE MARUFINA MAWEA
C: TOWE TOWE MARUFINA MAWE

A: ASOKARA KARA SUNAWEA
SUNAWEA ASOJAWO SUNAWEA
C: ASOKARA KARA SUNAWEA

A: SOYI BOIBO BORA A FIMAYE SOKERE A
C: SOYI BOIBO BORA
A: AFIMAYE SOKEREA
C: SOYI BOIBO BORA

CHANTS FOR OBATALÁ

REZO: BABA ALA YEO (2X)
BABA KUE URO
OCHA MIBIO LA YEYEO
OKUNYO BABA

A&C: AKETE OBA OBA SENIYE (2X)
BALA YOKODARA,
OBANLA ESE, OBANLA ESE
BABA FUMILAYE

A&C: BABA FURURU EREREO
OCAN YENYE LERIWO
ELERIFA OBA SI WASABO
ERIBO RERE OBA SI WAO
ENU AYE AWA LORO
EMI AYA LORO ELESIOCAN

A: BABA ELESIO CAN BABA ELESIO CAN
C: EMI AWA LORO ELESIOCAN

A&C: ODUAREMUO BI IYO
ODUAREMUO BELONA
ALA AGOGO EMISE ELEYO
AREMU CUELAYE

A: ODUDU CUELAYE
BABA MI CHOKOTO AREMU CUELAYE
C: BABA MI CHOKOTO AREMU CUELAYE

A&C: FE E EKWA O

A&C: ERIBODE ERIBODE

A: OBATALA BERONA
C: BABA BERONA ENIBODE

A: TOTO ITO
C: A YEMEBELEKO

A&C: WA E WA E LO MIO

CHANTS FOR CHANGÓ

A&C: IYA MASE LOBI CHANGO (2X)
BOBO ARAYE ONI KEULE
IYA MASE LOBI CHANGO
BOBO ARAYE ONI KUELE

A&C: E WAYO
ALADO ALUFINYA EWA O

A&C: MOFORI ANYA, MOFORI SOLE (2X)
    MOFORI SOLE AKUKUA ARO
    ALA ALADO FEYESUO

A&C: MALA MALA MALALUO (4X)
    OBI NISA FU CHANGO
    MALA MALA MALALUO

A&C: MOFORI BORERE
    MOFORI BORERE O, CHANGO TOPAN DOLAE

A&C: KABO E KABO E KABO E KABIOSILE O

A&C: EMI ALADO KO YUEWOLE (2X)
    TITI LAYE CHANGO BAOSO

A&C: REZO: OBA IBO SI AREO (2X)
    ERUA MALA IPO ERA OWO
    OBA KOSO ACHERE

CHANTS FOR OYÁ

REZO: YE OYA WIMI ORO E (2X)
O YANSAN ARO WESA E O
A WIMA YOYO EKE OLA

A&C: KORO UNLE O KARA KARA (2X)
    OROBINI AYEUN KORO UNLEO
    KARA KARA LAUMBO KOLEYA

A&C: OYADE IBA RIBA CHE KE CHE (2X)
    AGO ILE AGO LOYA
    OYAN SILE O LO OYADE

A&C: AYI LODA YA OKUO
    TOWO MODE EYO AYABA (2X)

A&C: OYADE MARIWO
    OMESAN LORO YOKORO (2X)

A&C: OYADE O AINA OYADE

A&C: LONGO LOYA LONGO LOYA
    LONGOITO MI LOYA

A&C: EH AH EH AH
    OYANKALA AYILODA MARERE O

A&C: MARERE O

A&C: JEREMI OYA
    OLOYA LOKWA A KARA KOLORO

KALA KALA WO OMIO
KALA LAWO OLELE
OYA OYANKALA OYANKALA
KALA OLELE

A: OWIMI OWIMI
C: OLELE
A: OYA MESAN ONIYI
C: OLELE
A: OYA MESAN A MEMO
C: OLELE

A: KALA KALA WO ONI
    KALA LAWO OLELE
C: OYANKALA ONIKALA LAWO
    OYAKALA ONI KARA OLELE

A&C: OYADE MARIWO
       OMESAN LORO YOKORO (2X)

A&C: OYADE O AINA OYADE

A&C: LONGO LOYA LONGO LOYA
       LONGOITO MI LOYA

A&C: BEMBE OYA OYA LA FINDA E

A&C: MAMA LOYAE ADIE ADIE OYA (2X)

A&C: OYA GAGA CHANGO KWERE LAYE O, OYA GAGA (2X)
       OGODO MI CHOKOTO, OMO SESE AWA
       OYA GAGA CHANGO KWERE LAYE

A&C: OYA WIMA WIMA, YANSAN WIMA WIMA
       CHOKOTO KWENKWE ALA KWEMI OYA

CHANTS FOR YEMAYÁ

A&C: YEMAYA ASESU, ASESU YEMAYA
       YEMAYA OLODO, OLODO YEMAYA

A&C: SOKUTANI WO AWA ASESU
       EWIMA SERE ERO MIDE

A&C: BARAGO AGO YEMAYA, BARAGO AGO OROMI

A: ODDA ASESU
C: OMI YEMAYA
A: ODDA ACHADA
C: OMI YEMAYA
    AKOTA KWELE O AWA SESU

A&C: WERE WERE ACHO EWE
     WERE WERE ACHO EWE

A&C: OMOLODDE OMO TITIYO
     E YO LADE

A&C: ILUBA CHIQUINI ILUBA (2X)
     ERAN KWIKWO KOLE YAN YANO
     ONI OLO OMI ODDE

A: CHIQUI CHIQUINI
C: ALA MODANSE

A&C: EMI ODDE, OMO ODDE
     OMO ODDE, EMI ODDE
     KA CHU MAMA IYA KWELE YO

A&C: LADIOKE, LADIOKE

A&C: OKE OKE LADIOKE

A&C: KAI KAI KAI YEMAYA OLODO
     KAI KAI KAI ASESU OLODO

A&C: WARO MIO WARO YEO

REZO: OKUO YALE YA LU MAO YALE OMI ALE
      YAWA MIO (2X)
AGOLONA AYE YALE YALE YA LU MAO YALE OMI
      ALE YAWA MIO

CHANTS FOR OCHÚN

REZO: IYA MILE ODDO (2X)
IBOBO ACHE ISEMI SARAMA WOE
IYA MILE ODDO
KOWANIE, KOWANIE..MOYUBA..
IYA MILE ODDO

A&C: YEYE MORO IGI (2X)
     SEKURE A LA I DO IGI
     YEYE MORO ONI ABE
     ONI ABE

A&C: ALADE YE ALADE YE MORO

A&C: OMA OMA OKE OKE

A&C: YEYE BIO BIO SUO (2X)
     TANIMAKWA UPO EKWE O

A: OHURO WERE WERE WERE OHURO
   AQUETE FOMO LOROUN
C: OHURO WERE WERE WERE OHURO

A&C: IDE WERE WERE ITA OSUO IDE WERE WERE
   IDE WERE WERE ITA OSUO IDE WERE WERE ITA IYA
   OCHA KINIWA ITA OSUN
   CHEKE CHEKE ITA IYA
   IDE WERE WERE

A: ALA IYEYE WALERE A
   EYA WANLERE
C: ALA IYEYE WALERE A

A: A IYA KATANA
C: BOGBOSUN
A: SORO CARUKU YEYE
C: EYURE EYURE EYURE
A: SORO CARUKU YEYE
C: AMALA AMALA AMALA
A: SORO CARUKU YEYEO
C: OMODDE OMODDE OMODDE
A: SORO BANBILO
C: YAN YAN IROKO YAN YAN

A&C: IMBE IMBE MAYEYE
   IMBE IMBE LOROKE

A&C: ORE ORE
   IRE OCHUN MO DE IO ORE

A&C: OMI OMI YEYE
   OMI YEYE MASARAWAO

A&C: ALA MISERE MISERE (2X)
A: ALA UNBANCHE MACHE
   OCHI MILODO
C: ALA UNBANCHE MACHE
A&C: CHINIWA IYA LODE
   CHINIWA IYA LODE YA LODE

CHANTS FOR OSAIN
A&C: EWE ADADARA MADAO
   OSAIN ADADARA MADA
   EWE ADADARA MADAO
   OSAIN ADADARA MADA

EWE DAMIWO ODA MAWO
ADADARA MADA

A&C: EWE MASIBOROYU
EWE MASIBORORO
EWE MASIBOROYU
EWE MASIBORORO
BAMBIOKEYO
MASIBOROYU
MASIBORORO

A&C: BAMULA MOFIYE
BAMULA BAMBALOROKE

A: CURU CURU BETE
C: MARIBO SAIN MARIBODE MARIBO

"And now mi cielo, now that I have given so much to the dancers and musi-cians—and to you—tell me how you use these fantastic rhythms, these mysterious colors, these ancient chants, and these ever-present movements. Now, you must give me something."

"Certainly, Changó. I give you two detailed movement descriptions. The first is choreographed movement based on the nations that I have seen in Haiti, Cuba, and Bahia; the second is the movement journey of Afro-Cuban dance outside of Cuba, at least what I know of it. For you, Changó, I describe dancing divinity."

Opening the Sacred: Dancing Divinity

"As you know, Changó, worshipping Africans in the Diaspora have made philosophy indelible and cosmology visible by means of the intricate and elaborate interrelationship between sound and gesture, music and dance. Through articulated rhythms played on instruments and articulated melodies and harmonies of human vocal ensembles, understandings of the universe have been remembered. Through articulated, rhythmic, purposeful human movement or dance behavior, the divinities have come to help believers become divine themselves.

"Each of the three ritual communities that I have experienced over the years found ways to interject ritual beliefs and behaviors into everyday events. Worshipers thought that if they lived in a manner of thanksgiving and accep-tance, if they honored their ancestors and cosmic divinities with food, drink, song, drumming, dancing, and merriment, that a balance would be struck. Their blessed and prayed-over offerings would be received, and other blessings—health, goodness, and peace—would emerge in the lives of worshipers. So at each meal, before each bottle of rum or wine was opened, before a tree was cut, each morning, each night, and dutifully on holy days, they gave offerings.

"In my Haitian example in chapter 1, I watched for hours as the *oungan* washed and blessed every little object in the room before the ceremony started. In my Cuban example, I watched many affected dancers delay the onset of Oyá's manifestation, almost painfully, so that ritual responsibilities would be completed before ritual requests were made. In my Bahian example, I had to finish an elaborate set of chores and procedures before my communication with the spiritual world could go forward. Opening the way for the sacred involved many actions; opening the way for the sacred involved many dances.

"In following the advice of Elegba/Elegbara, the Vital Force that opens and closes, I open this section on this side of the gate in the United States with comparative analyses. My stories of African American ritual performances offer understanding of how structures within Diaspora liturgies revolve around and depend on dance/music performance. The religious practice remains heavily dance-dependent and dance-initiated."

Structural Analysis of a Choreographic Synthesis

"Several years ago, I set out to create a dance performance that would honor multiple religious communities. I wanted to show respect for several major, yet differing, belief systems that were being brought into a common ritual setting. I wanted to craft a choreography that honored and respected an African mélange in the Americas.

"The choreography was initiated by a request from an ecumenical group that had planned a pilgrimage from Massachusetts to Johannesburg, South Africa. The pilgrimage would take one year, from May 1998 to May 1999. Its objective was to symbolically erase racism from global society, to ritually cleanse the planet of the lingering aftermath of slavery and colonialism. 'The Interfaith Pilgrimage of the Middle Passage' reversed the historical slave trade routes. One group started in the United States and traveled across the Caribbean, and then to North, West, and Central Africa and finally to South Africa. Another group began in Europe and traveled across the Mediterranean Sea to North, West and eventually to South Africa. I was asked to perform after the first full day of walking from Leverett to Northampton, Massachusetts, with a "danced tribute to the African past." The danced ritual would take place in the main chapel of a large Presbyterian church and in front of the pulpit and choir pews.

"Because of the multiple religious perspectives of the participants (Protestant, Catholic, Buddhist, Jewish, Yoruba, Kongo, perhaps even Muslim and Shinto), I planned a dance presentation within a composite African religious structure. I began with a brief contextual explanation that was necessary for cross-cultural religious understanding. This addressed the concerns of the majority audience—Christians and Jews who probably needed to have clarity on African concepts of 'God' and 'religion.' Upon reflection afterward, I found that my choreography within the presentation pointed out some of the difficulties of inclusion and equality among several strong African belief systems as they first encountered one another in the Americas.

"Changó, it was an exercise in syncretism, and now I see that its analysis offers insights into early African religious syncretism in the Diaspora."

Discussion of Choreography

(Outline of the choreography "On Beginning Again")

1. Introduction, Cross-cultural Understanding
2. Drumming for Elegba/Elegbara
3. Yoruba Prayer for the Supreme Being in Yoruba and in English
4. Haitian Drumming with the *Vévé* Flag Dance
5. Batá Drumming for Oddudua
6. Chants, Drumming, and Dancing for Obatalá, Ochún, and Yemayá
7. Kongo Drumming for the Spirits
8. Ending for Elegba/Exu
9. Communal Response

"The title of the dance presentation was 'On Beginning Again,' which characterized the pilgrimage's peaceful objective but also was in honor of the Buddhists who would be present. Buddhists believe that every day each individual literally 'starts again.' Worshipers and those who commit themselves to a higher consciousness recommit daily to principles and behaviors that bring ultimate good. In this way also, African belief systems assume errors in the past but concentrate on reconciliation today for the future. Each person has continuous opportunity to grow spiritually and socially by respecting the past through offerings and remembrances, but not dwelling altogether on the past. As the title suggested, starting each day anew, in repeated commitment to principles that honor life, and building a formidable spiritual foundation were important ideals in the belief systems I referenced.

"The choreography began with the sounding of the Cuban Yoruba *batá* drums alone in order to signal the spiritual and human interchange that was being encouraged. A Yoruba prayer was read next for the Supreme Being, the Absolute Almighty, and the Ultimate Reality, recited in both Yoruba and English."

A YORUBA PRAYER FOR THE ALMIGHTY

OLUDUMARE, OLOFI, ORULA, ORUNMILA, ODDUDUA
OLORUN, OLOKUN
Mojiloni mowogun merinaye
Igun Kini, Igun Kegi, Igun Keta, Igun Kerin
Olojo oni bogbo iregba
Togba wanile aye
Ire fun awon egun
Bogbo ire funwa
Aché, Aché, Aché.

Translation:

Oludumare (other names for the Supreme Entity, Ultimate Reality, Almighty Being, and the Oldest of the Old),
Oludumare, Ultimate reality that binds us all (no matter what we call Her/Him/ It),
Owner of this day,
The one who sees all things from the four directions into the world—
The air, the fire, the earth, and the water—
The source of all life!
All blessings to the world.
Blessings to the ancestors.
Blessings to the human village, all human vessels.
Power, spirit, powerful spirit forever!
May humanity be renewed (out of this pilgrimage).
(Translation by BABALAWO FAGBEMI)

"The power and sanctity of prayer, the word or *nommo* (according to Dogon philosopher Ogotemmeli in Griaule 1965 [1948]), means to give, share, and send forth life/spirit force. Received in the mind and heart of the worshiper/speaker, the prayer was put into intellectual activity within the minds and hearts of listening others, as a topic or focus for consideration. Its two languages encouraged the listener to attend sharply for her/his individual connection and understanding. The main function of the prayer was to initiate contact with divinity, to invoke or communicate with, and in so doing to revere, a Supreme Life Force, whatever he or she might be called. In this choreography, it was the African American worshiper who invoked and praised the many Yoruba names for the Ultimate Understanding, God: Oludumare, Oddudua, Olofi, Ochanla, and Olorún.

"Another function of the prayer in ecumenical performance was to assault the stereotype of African belief systems as simple, polytheistic systems, and to affirm the insufficiencies of linguistic translation, particularly for words such as 'God' or 'gods and goddesses.' I wanted to bring an ecumenical audience toward an African Diaspora perspective. For example, I used the terms 'divinities' and 'spiritual forces' in place of 'gods' and 'goddesses,' so that the concept of 'God,' 'Supreme Creator' or as I used in the choreography, 'Divinity,' would remain as it actually does—at the core of African Diaspora religious belief. Audience members discovered many names for spiritual forces or divinities, as I suspect readers of this study will within the three religions under examination. These are often aspects of a singular concept of Divinity.

"'Divinity,' as you know, Changó, and for my friends, associates, and cultural contacts in ritual communities, signifies an immediate whole of spiritual force or vital power. For members of my spiritual communities, a universe that is composed of interacting but distinct life realms, cosmic forces, and divinities does not contradict one with a Supreme Being or Omnipotent Creator.

"Many people have reference frames of 'God' or 'gods' that are underpinned with value judgments. Their understanding of 'goddesses' and 'gods' in African worship becomes a polar opposite to the strong belief in 'One God Almighty.' Conversely, many worshipping Africans in the Diaspora would want others to know that they do believe in a Supreme Being, Gwan Met, Oludumare, and so on.[6]

"In the prayer, the belief in an order amid the chaos of life (ongoing events and all things in the Universe) was voiced publicly in bold assertiveness. The prayer was also a response to the original drumming at the beginning of the presentation (the drum solo for Elegbara or Elegba), the primal force of meeting and communion, the guardian and opener of the gates, pathways and roads.

"The previous drumming was solemn; worshipers would call it 'dry.' It was a rhythmic invocation of the drums alone—without singing—in order to stimulate all channels of spiritual communication. In the answering prayer, the human voice doubled the previously sounded invocation of the drums and stated its respect and requests. The spoken prayer underscored the intent and reaffirmed the objectives of the performance practice, which were to initiate spiritual communication between the human world and the spiritual world.

"Next, Haitian religious culture was placed contiguous with Cuban religious culture. The lighting softened from the bright lights for the prayer in order to focus on the deep voice of a solo *maman,* the lead Haitian Vodou drum. The *maman* sounded a long and intense roll, only to stop abruptly with a slap, and then sang out a hypnotic invocation."

> (a) Dambala-O, Dambala Wèdo
> Dambala, Dambala nou veni (2 x)
> (Katherine Dunham and Ruth Beckford, both provided this chant from Haiti, 1930s and 1940s: personal communication)

> *Translation:*
> Dambala-O (praise name of *lwa*),
> Dambala of Ouidah (Dambala's place of origin in Benin) Dambala, Dambala, We've come to you.
> Dambala, Dambala, We've come to you.
> (Translation by the author)

> (b) Bo swe, Dambala Wèdo; koma ou ye?
> Bo swe Ayida Wèdo, koma ou ye?
> Dambala Wèdo repon mwe la.
> Ayida Wèdo repon mwe la.
> Bo swe, Dambala Wèdo, koma ou ye?
> (Joan Burroughs provided this chant from Brooklyn, 1990s: personal communication)

> *Translation:*
> Good evening, Dambala Weydo. How are you?
> Good evening, Ayida Wèdo (praise name of *lwa*).
> How are you?
> Answer me Dambala Wèdo.
> Answer me Ayida Wèdo.
> Good evening, Dambala. How are you?
> (Translation by the author)

"A Haitian *dwapo* (flag) with an exquisite *vévé* glistened in the low light with silver sequins and multicolored glass beads. The sequined flag was across the back of a female dancer and seemed to be rippling very slowly across the floor in the dim light. She was dressed in a long white skirt, a sleeved white blouse, and a plain white headscarf. She bent low while dancing, almost squat-ting as her back miraculously undulated to the repeated drumming pattern of invocation. *Yanvalu*, the dance itself, was an invocation, and the dancer varied her small, demure steps by stretching and undulating her arms horizontally and parallel to the floor or by placing her cupped hands over her kneecaps to intensify the undulation of her back.

"The dancer's chest touched her thighs and knees as she undulated close to the floor. She traveled across the space between the altar and the congre-gation, forward and backward in the repetitive rhythm of her feet with her head also rolling back and forward as a consequence of the undulations of her torso. From time to time, she would dance backward in small circles; then she danced to each cardinal point of the room.

"Suddenly both the drummer and the dancer shifted to a more open and expansive pattern. The dancer stood vertically on her toes and then lifted one knee high to her chest. That leg began to extend from her knee to her toe as it reached diagonally across her body and literally pulled the rest of her body in one big slow-motion stretch as it fell to the floor and the rest of her body followed sequentially downward. The dancer immediately pulled herself up and stepped to the other side. With a noticeable inhalation, she raised her other knee to her chest to extend forward and repeat the same big slow-mo-tion stretch to the diagonal across her body again. With the third repetition and in complete surprise, since the viewer presumed a symmetrical pattern had been established, she began to stretch her arms high above her head and to walk with big knee-high steps. She changed directions constantly and quickened her pace to cause a walking pattern with a vertical undulation of her torso that accompanied each high step. The walking pattern was a huge exaggeration of inhalations and exhalations, forcing the entire body to open or stretch to its fullest with the flag now appearing high in the air above her head. The dancer undulated across the space as a consequence of her legs reaching out and her pelvic contractions.

"Changó, I used the undulation within the *yanvalu* dance pattern, which was the typical movement of a Haitian worshiper's body, but it was also move-ment of the social body, the ritual community in ritual practice. The move-ment of the upper body emphasized the breath as the performer inhaled and the chest lifted accordingly. With exhalation, the upper torso reached outward and then gave in, with the head following closely behind. The movement in repetition went beyond mere inhalation and exhalation to communicate the sense of reaching out and giving in, or yearning and accepting.

"Most often in Vodou understanding, *yanvalu* simultaneously presents and represents the danced expression of Papa Dambala or Metres Ayida Wèdo of the Rada rites in soft, sustained, or smooth, sequential motion. The motion is like that of a crawling snake or the ebbing and flowing of ocean waves. The movement, by extension, is like the undulating, ongoing pattern of daily existence.

"In choreographic terms, Changó, I wanted the *yanvalu* dancing in combination with the previous sensory stimuli of drumming and prayer to build aesthetic interest. Viewers were then bombarded with even more aesthetic stimuli. This time, it was rhythmic drum patterns, dramatic recitation, sparkling colors of the sequined flag, dynamic improvisation in the drums, audible breathing of the performing dancer, and undulating and expansive dance movement—all added special effect.

"Dancing the flag in ritual supplication signaled the *obesanz* to ancient African rites with improvised dancing to *yanvalu* drumming. In Haitian ritual practice, the *dwapos* are danced at the beginning of a ceremony. So in this choreography, the danced flag followed immediately after the initial prayers, as a beginning offering to a contemporary ritual dance from the Vodou liturgy.

"I made the dance movements follow a Vodou structure, highlighting different *nasyons*. Already this Rada *yanvalu* dance had been inserted among Yoruba drumming and prayers. It referenced respect for Vodou, one of the oldest consolidations of African spiritual practice in the African Americas. I could not, however, place it at the very beginning, even though it was the first danced segment. The majority population in performance and in the congregation did not have ethnic or cultural ties to Vodou practice, so the very opening was in deference to the majority ecumenical leanings of the larger group and the Yoruba leanings of performers. For those who knew history, however, the first section of dancing publicly recognized the historical importance of Vodou religious practice. For others, Haitian ritual dance was a separate and distinct dance and music within the choreographic whole, but a unique display for everyone to remember.

"For Haitian worshipers, the flag announced Ezili. She was, in fact, the heart that was sequined as a *vévé* on the flag's center. Ezili is love eternal, symbolized by ebbing and flowing of movement, but constant, consistently present. The heart on the *veve* flag in this performance signified a dimension of the divinity that is the nurturer of Haitian life, the beat of life-giving breath (see Denbow 1999), a solitary mother whose care, concern, or love simply are, unconditionally. Ezili's heart also initiated a danced metaphor of sensuality and sensory consciousness. The human body itself, in desire of spiritual contact, articulated Ezili's flirtatious excitation and seduction.

"In dancing for Ezili, the worshiper accepts the precepts of Haitian belief, the rules of social life in religious culture, and commits herself/himself in reverence to the Divine by lowering both the head and the heart and repeating the undulating pattern of life. At the same time in ritual practice, s/he implores the spiritual connection of humans and divinity by means of rhythmic repetition, symbolic gesture, and dynamic emotional and physical intensity. With that approximated in an ecumenical performance, the female dancer exited while dancing.

"*Batá* ritual drumming came next, echoing a dispersed Yoruba land in Cuba's Havana style."

"*Que bueno, chica!*"

"Lights came up fully on three two-headed drums that spelled out the mathematical, as well as artistic, creativity of one of the most complex drum traditions from the African continent. This percussion section, without words, sung melody, or dance, was taken from the drummed liturgy of Cuban Yoruba. The drummed section was a musical indication of how each aspect of the Supreme Being, Ultimate Reality, or Divinity could be acknowledged as divinity, divine spirit, cosmic essence, one tremendous dimension, called *oricha*. In performance, the experiential librarians of Yoruba practice drummed mathematical wisdom to the present.

"Musicians were responsible for sounding out and developing rhythmic and tonal formulas exponentially, which spoke to and of Oddudua, the Ultimate Father. The librarians-turned-performers relied on the incredible journey of the drums and gave reverence to several drum liturgies that survived the Middle Passage.

"The three musicians represented many other musicians; they were all professional descendents of Yoruba men, dedicated to you, Changó, who brought this particular drum tradition to Cuba (Michael Spiro: personal communication; Victor Sterling-Duprey: personal communication; cf. Amira and Cornelius 1992:9–12). Even today, Cubans tell of two *batá* musicians who found each other and, through their separate but dependent skills, made the first *batá* drums in the Americas. Their original set of *batá* drums facilitated the production of sixteen more sets over the next thirty years. The cooperative, interdependent work of these two drummers is an example of how the old ways still operate in modern times, as they pass on knowledge that is based in the wisdom of the past.

"My musicians announced the depth, range, and qualities of the Supreme Spiritual Entity through their performance for and of Oddudua. Their drumming spoke numbers sounded in rhythms, rhythms manipulated in perfect and imperfect equations among the six heads of the drums. Six heads of drums, six hands, and three brains created rhythmic beauty and displayed abundant intelligence.

"The regular practice of combined drumming, chanting, and dancing followed next; this combination ultimately occurs in most African American ritual, whether Vodou or the Yoruba-based religions of Cuba and Bahia. The musical and danced complex of Cuban Yoruba belief suggests core understandings about the universe—you know, Changó, those that yield a philosophical expression in words regarding notions of Divinity.

"Aché, mi amor."

"Most often, in learning how to perform the dance sequences, the chants, or the rhythms, worshipers become acquainted with many specified dimensions of Divinity. The first-level dimensions of Divinity are supraspiritual essences, called alternately (and, at times, in seeming contradiction) Olofi or God, Oddudua or Supreme Spirit, Oludumare or Holy Father, God of Creation, Ochanla or God of all Divinities, or Olorún, God Almighty, Creator of the Universe, and Olokun, Holy Force in the Deepest Part of the Ocean.

"Again as you know, Changó, but for others who do not, the dancing worshipers relate more frequently with a second level of Divinity. These include a single aspect within the many dimensions of Divinity, called a *lwa*, an *oricha*, an *orixá* or divinities. Performing worshipers relate to focused aspects or separate divinities as, perhaps, dimensions of a celestial orange, an orange in sections that are mostly equal, but different. Worshipers look to the divinities as guardians of specific domains of life, or protectors within sectors or spheres of the universe. They address the divinities as protectors or guardians, much like apprentices and advisees look toward a protective specialist or mentor, much like I address you, Changó. Worshipers come to understand their protective forces as knowledgeable dancers, as powerful performers who are able to create, protect, destroy, but who have vulnerabilities as well.

"Worshipers also relate to the divinities as *aché* or vital essence, life force, or as *espri*—powerful divine energy. Worshipers believe as well that as *lwas, orichas* and *orixas,* humankind crystallizes into divinity. Powerful energy, vital life force, is shared within each living thing, including plants and animals from the horizontal plane of existence and including divinities and Divinity.

"In deepening my practice after my first Haitian, Cuban, and Brazilian experiences and in learning the dance patterns, I have come to understand that the dances reference a cosmic plane of existence with powerful knowledge, which in turn assumes other planes of existence and knowledge. I had to learn not simply the dance patterns but, importantly, the chants, the resultant rhythms, and the chartering histories of the *lwas, orichas,* and *orixás* before I could truly grasp the significance of dance in Cuban, Brazilian, or Haitian belief. (Actually, this is life's process, Changó.) The music and dance forms are expressive patterns that connect to and are able to connect all spheres of life and knowledge.

"As I proposed earlier, the spheres of existence can be thought of as the locus of existence in human, animal, and plant form, the arena of ancient life and its sustaining knowledge (that of the living dead), and the plane of multiple aspects of the Divine. The three realms of existence produce a worldview of power and knowledge in the universe, and when two of the planes converge, spiritual communication is in its optimum range. For example, the plane of humans, animals, and plants converges with the plane of the cosmic divinities and produces the presence of divinity—*aché* or *axê.* Or the plane of humans, animals, and plants converges with the plane of the ancient elders, the living dead, and produces crystallized *bonanj—lwas* within the human body. In these examples, a dancing worshiper is transformed into a divinity.

"The goal of my choreography and of religious dance performance among these kinds of worshipers is not simply individual empowerment, although that is a major effect, but also it is the convergence of life planes. That convergence, which occurs in dance ritual performance, is also for the enrichment of the social body or worshipping community."

"*Aché, mi vida.*"

"In performance, the resultant rhythms of three *batá* drums show how music attempts the convergence of several planes of existence. Vibrations of animals and plants that have been blessed with prayers and perfumed waters enter human bodies and minds to stimulate cycling energy and more vibrations. Bodies and minds reverberate and give access to the perceived weight, deliberateness, and mighty power of Oludumare (God), Olofi (God, the Eternal Father), and Ochanla (God, the Holiest Spirit, the oldest of all *orichas*). Spiritual power, authority, and honor are recognized with respectful distance, calm, and quiet, but also with repetitive codified movement that eventually increases in intensity."

"Aché, aché."

"As the listener becomes more fluent in the language of the *batá* and its chants, and as the drumming, chanting, and dancing worshiper discovers his/her individual bridge to the overarching principles of belief, a distinct human connection to the spiritual sphere is made possible, and convergence results in transformations."

"Aché, aché, aché."

In this performance, the combined dance and music was for Obatalá (the father of all the divinities, the judge of all things), Ochún (guardian of love, river water, female wisdom, and knowing interpreter of Ifa divining practice), and Yemayá (mother of all the divinities, ocean water, nurturer, and caregiver). For Obatalá, the dancer was in all white as she had been for Haitian Ezili, but this time she danced more upright, although flexed at the knee joints, with attention to gentle hand gestures. She slowly pressed her wrists down and pulled them up, twice on each side in front of her body. She walked as if in a procession from one side of the church to the other and then back. Then she traveled out from a center spot to eight different points, dividing the space in eight parts with a common center. These points were walked in deliberate steps, with tranquil demeanor, poise, and calm. It was a simple dance, filled with the elegance and stateliness of Obatalá.

"In dancing for Obatalá within the pilgrimage choreography, the gestures of the hands and the slow weighted footsteps suggested the calm and peace that Obatalá is understood to embody as well as transmit. His pace is slow, metered, forceful, and majestic, and therefore the choreography included a solid, bent, walking sequence in eight specific directions, marking his number as well as the multiple planes of his/her domain, as father of all the *orichas*. He is also the anthropomorphic She, a male *oricha* syncretized as a female saint, *La Virgen de las Mercedes,* who judges all disputes. The peace of his simple danced movements suggested resolution.

"In ritual practice there are beautiful chants and only a few dance patterns for Obatalá. Often the apprentices and children of Ochún dance for Obatalá, in recognition of her as his wife and for her associated knowledge. The choreography included this connection by placing two sections of the liturgical order together in an abbreviated form, one for Obatalá and one for Ochún. I made the Ochún section contrast visually and dynamically with the Obatalá section. Ochún's movements were light-hearted, bubbly, and sensuous, contrasting her worldlier domain of love with Obatalá's more reserved spiritual domain of peace. Still, her dance was spiritual, filled with the splendor of female beauty, intelligence, and powerful shrewdness.

"For Ochún, the lights changed to amber shades and the church interior was soft and warm. The gold in the sanctuary above sparkled in the yellow light, as did the gold in the fabrics that decorated the pulpit behind the drummers. The dancer wrapped a yellow scarf around her white head-wrap and put on gold earrings, bracelets, and rings as she danced. When she finished adding to her costume, she moved about the space with a little rhythmic accent from her heel just before she stepped to each side. She was laughing, and her demeanor had changed entirely in contrast with the serious and calm representation of Obatalá. She was now vivacious and lively, animated and gregarious, and eventually exited playfully.

"The lights then changed again to soft but darkened blue, marking a new rhythm in the drumming and a new quality of movement. The dancer entered the same space with all yellow removed from sight; in its place were a blue headscarf, a multi-toned blue overskirt, and shell necklaces and bracelets. These were the signs of Yemayá, divine sea or ocean, the source of all life, and in human form, formidable mother. The dancer drew figure eights in the air with her skirts swirling on each side of her hips, in the floor pattern as she traveled around the dance space, and also in her upper torso, which seemed to allow her chest to lift high and lower in a three-dimensional plane. The space was filled with circling patterns of billowing blue skirts. They often covered the dancer as they made waves throughout the space, revolving as she traveled on a counterclockwise circular pattern until she too exited.

"The ending of the combined drum, chant, and dance section was a danced dedication to Yemayá. Her dance provided two acknowledgments: a recognition of the mother, as we had already performed for the father of the *orichas,* and a recognition of another type of water, ocean saltwater in contrast with sweet river water of Ochún's dance earlier. Yemayá's dance gathered force as she transformed her mothering image into one of bold waves that swirled and thrashed as the powerful sea, and ended this Yoruba section.

"The last drumming inserted recognition of the interpenetrating Kongo-Angola cultures that have permeated so many Diaspora religions."

"*Que bueno!*"

"In my pilgrimage choreography, Kongo-Angola culture was contiguous with Cuban and Haitian cultures. The switch from *batás* to conga drums, like the switch from Haitian *yanvalu* drumming to Cuban *batá* rhythms earlier, marked another acknowledgment, a distinctiveness within sameness, among African American religions. West Central African rhythms needed guaranteed acknowledgment within the choreography, as they need in the American context of both ritual and social performance. Conga drums, however, are more familiar as secular or social drums, and in the choreography they sounded out the depths of African philosophies and the ambiguities of European and European American interpretation, that is, the blurred boundary between what is considered "sacred" or ritual and what is considered "secular" or social. In their distinctive way, the congas suggested the potential spirituality within each ambiance. In the pilgrimage choreography, the high speed, triple-pitched, virtuoso display of the conga drums exemplified power within ambiguity, in that what was heard was incredibly joyful, but simultaneously profoundly serious. In fact, few things are deemed playful by worshipping dancers and musicians.

"It was important to close the choreography, now a true dance offering, in proper order with a closing to Elegba or Exu. Again there was a switch back to *batá* drums and chanting. The Cuban Yoruba chants invoked the guardian of spiritual communication to tie a bow on the music/dance present as offering. This type of ending also reconciled the ethnic and cultural allegiances of the majority within the performing personnel. The performance specialists were predominantly from the Cuban Yoruba nation, making it appropriate to create the ending in Cuban Yoruba terms, but these were also consonant with other Vodou and Kongo-Angola concepts of closure.

"Overall, the choreography worked as a commencement for interaction among the diverse religious perspectives of pilgrims. As the performance ended, a relevant addition was spontaneously realized. Pilgrims and supporters of the pilgrimage flooded the performance space in front of the drums. Along with the solo dancer, the public offered its dancing as reciprocity for receiving the dedicated mélange. The ecumenical gathering responded to the spirituality it had witnessed within dancing and music-making bodies. The community placed a communal *coda* onto my dance presentation."

"*Qué aché!*"

"The pilgrimage choreography served as one example of the many ways in which African religious ritual could have meshed and formed within the Americas. It reminded me of a particular ceremony for the divinities that took place in California in 1989. It was unusually small, with only about eight to ten people, including three musicians. The worshipers came mainly from the

United States but also from Mexico, Brazil, and Cuba. The unique element in the ceremony was that there were Portuguese speakers, Spanish speakers, and English speakers, but only one Yoruba—or ritual language—speaker. Things did not go as planned and the person who understood ritual language best manifested an invoked *oricha*. No one remaining could determine what the *oricha* wanted or how to progress with the ceremony because no one knew ritual language."

"*¿Qué cosa es ésta?*"

"The California ritual members drifted into the dance steps that they all could remember, dances of remembrance. They tried to acknowledge the divinities of each Portuguese, Spanish, and English speaker who was present.

"At the time, I reflected on history and what it must have been like for multiple African ethnic nations to create appropriate religious rituals in the midst of so many allegiances and languages. Through this upsetting experience, I sensed how disturbing days of remembrance and how stressful rituals of recognition could be. There was resolution, however, because of common understandings—as in the Elegba/Exu closing rhythms, gestures, and song.

"Of course, it's important to remember also that not all interactions were smooth. In the end, however, alliances were made and necessary distinctions were acknowledged. The resulting ritual communities continued.

"Now, Changó, let me trace another choreography, the choreographed journey of Cuban dance/music outside of Cuba, my second gift to you."

Case Studies in Teaching Cuban Dance

"In teaching the dances of Haitian Vodou, Cuban Yoruba, and to a lesser extent Bahian Candomblé, I have become more aware of the nuances within performance than when I was taking classes as a student. I compare learning from teaching to the intuitive, informal embodied learning of performance; realizations abound. In learning formally, however, from direct instructions and linear thinking, I have felt my own culture: a comfort zone in writing, reading, and analyzing. There is much to be gained from both modes of education; body learning and mind learning complement each other."

Stanford University Cuban Dance Project (1990)

"Since 1987, I have been trying to reinforce the body learning I had accomplished in dancing and singing the African American liturgies with more formal modes of learning and understanding. I have worked to bring Cuban specialists to the United States by writing grants and trying to generate interest in Afro-Caribbean performance through my own teaching contacts, at first at the University of California, Berkeley, Peralta Community College District, and Mills College, and later at Smith College and the Five College Dance Department as well as throughout the country.

"At Stanford University, I found equal interest in bringing Cuban dance to college students and strong support in Susan Cashion, chair of the dance division. Stanford had an established and successful summer workshop in Latin American dance forms, and we thought a project to bring three members of the Conjunto Folklórico Nacional (National Folkloric Company of Cuba) would be exciting within that established program. During the late 1980s, however, it was difficult to get a Cuban project discussed in the United States, to say nothing of funded. Additionally, and especially with Folklórico Nacional's administration at the time and the political climate in Cuba, it was difficult to make our vision work. In the summer of 1988, I returned from Cuba with news that Danza Nacional, the National Modern Dance Company, was interested, if Folklórico was not. The Danza Nacional administrators followed through with eager and professional interest. By the fall of 1989, Cashion and I were seriously involved in planning a session for summer 1990 on the Stanford campus, even though I was leaving the area for a new position in Massachusetts. As a result, Stanford personnel carried out the administrative nuts and bolts of the project, but the basic educational paradigm was developed from the collaborative and creative discussions between Cashion and me. We came up with what I now call the 'Masters' Model.'

"Early on, we had sketched out a curriculum for the ten-day intensive study. It offered beginning/intermediate and intermediate/advanced levels of Cuban folkloric dance—dances of Cuban Yoruba, Arará, and Palo traditions, *rumba,* and popular dance (*son, danzón, mambo,* etc.), as well as an introduction to the specialized development of modern dance, called *danza cubana.* We were able to span the entire dance heritage of Cuba within the specialty of the teachers who were invited: dancers Manolo Vazquez Robaina and Margarita Vilela Criegh, and musician Regino Jimenez Saez.[7] We also had a class

238

in chants or music each morning to augment and reinforce the dancing and drumming lessons later in the day.

"The model of the curriculum was a variant of the one I had experienced in Cuba as a member of Folklórico Nacional and one with specific new developments that I thought would fit both the Cuban teachers' mode of teaching and the receptivity of non-native students. I added two classes to the Cuban curriculum, a class in Cuban dance for musicians and a class in Cuban music for dancers, which proved to be important for amateurs and professionals. Cashion added an overview lecture in Cuban music and another in Cuban dance taught by U.S. American specialists (Michael Spiro and me, respectively) to ground participants in the basic understanding of each tradition or form that the Cuban teachers would present. At the end of each day, we added a full group meeting—students and teachers, beginners and advanced performers—to discuss and clarify the dance/music experience of the day.

"This was a historic exchange, the first that we were aware of since the Cuban Revolution in 1959, in which Cuban artists taught classes in the United States. Students came from Oregon, Washington, Massachusetts, Virginia, and California. Most of the professional dance teachers and drummers in the Bay Area attended or visited, as did the Cuban music community. Moreover, it had sparked the interest in Cuba and its dance/music culture that many U.S. Americans had. This was the first wave of dance workshops and music exchanges that were to happen over the next decade. Dance teachers with this first Cuban workshop in the United States continued their studies and started teaching Cuban forms elsewhere across the United States and Canada. Some also went to Tijuana, Mexico, where Cuban dance teachers were invited to teach by a few Cubano-philes (ultimately the beginning of a California organization that took U.S. students to Cuba over the next few years)."

Colorado Dance Festival (1993, 1994)

"Two years later, I was bombarded with telephone calls and questions about Cuban music/dance and about Cuban artists who might be invited to the Colorado Dance Festival. The founder and director, Marda Kirn, was totally committed to bringing Los Muñequitos to perform and teach in the dance workshops of her program the following year. She and I developed another model for learning Cuban Yoruba and *rumba* dances. She invited me to prepare students through a week of daily classes for another week of intensive study with the Cuban masters from Los Muñequitos. During the process of this curriculum, other dance/music artists, including professional dancers from Urban Bush Women, took classes with me and then with the Cuban masters. These and other professional dancers at the festival had little trouble completing or accomplishing the movements, but they had to work at accessing the subtle and differentiated styles. When they were in class, they frequently reported their appreciation for this type of cross-cultural introduction to the new material.

"In later discussions with Jawole Willa Jo Zollar, artistic director of Urban Bush Women, we both noted the advantages of accessing appropriate style from this 'Cross-Cultural Model' of learning. As a member of U.S. American culture and as a dance specialist, I could present the same Cuban material that the Cuban specialists would, but I could make associations and movement bridges from dance material with which these students were very familiar. With a cross-cultural perspective and significant practice first, students were successful with the intensified and detailed lessons of the masters later. With the Cross-Cultural Model, learning seemed swift and precise for both professional artists and dance students.

"The following year, 1994, when it was not possible to bring back the Cuban masters, the administrators of the Colorado Dance Festival allowed me to augment my class syllabus. They facilitated the integration of music into the dance course. For students, the model gave comfortable access to the material while emphasizing a practice based on the chants and specific rhythms from the ritual setting."[8]

Afro-Cubanismo at Banff (1994, 1996)

"Immediately following the Colorado Dance Festival in 1994 and then again in 1996, there was another organized program of instruction in Cuban music and dance in Canada at its National Performing Arts Centre in Banff. The program was initiated by ethnomusicologist Andrew Sloss with musical organization directed by Michael Spiro and dance organization directed by me. The entire project was funded through the University of Vancouver and Banff Centre for the Arts with generous patrons from the Latin music world. It was offered within Banff's programming of Canada's unique and daring Afro-Cubanismo music festival, which additionally sought to unite Cuban master musicians and dancers with international performers and students.

"The curricula for the 1994 and 1996 sessions of *Afro-Cubanismo* were identical. Although there were differences in personnel and administrative procedures, both dance programs were based on the Masters' Model at Stanford, including history overview lectures and Music for Dancers and Dance for Musicians within many specialized dance and music offerings. The dance studio classes stressed clear and precise style among traditions and emphasized Cuban Yoruba. Classes in chants were offered consistently, and a spectacular performance series was offered to students and the public as a result of the presence of world-class Cuban artists, including flautist Richard Egües; pianist and conductor Chucho Valdés and his group, *Irakere;* dancers Eduardo Rivera, Alfredo O'Farril, Librada Quesada, Sylvina Fabars; musical ensembles Los Muñequitos and Afro-Cuba; as well as other featured percussionists including Changuito, Regino Jimenez, Fermin Nani, Jose Pilar; and singers Amelia Pedroso and Mayra Valdés.

"Dance students profited from the Masters' Model most when they had had a previous introduction to the Cuban materials. This model facilitated detailed study—the organized singing of whole *trataos* and the flow of ritually consecutive dances, for example. With masters leading the classes in each domain, the full range of performance possibilities could be experienced and encouraged in classroom performance. Lead singers had a chorus of learned singers; specialized drummers could follow and lead dance instruction in requisite orders and rhythms; and dance teachers and special students turned into exquisite performers. Teachers and professional artists left the Afro-Cubanismo sessions and the Masters' Model more learned and more committed to practice in the nation styles as a result of their exciting, formal learning experiences.

"The second Cross-Cultural Model that was developed at Colorado worked best for all types of students, but its advantage was that it ensured a more comfortable learning experience for beginning students. Certainly, beginners to the forms needed more clarification of basic steps, more time spent in making these familiar to the body, and additional help in clarifying mistakes than they received within the Masters' Model. Students in the Cross-Cultural Model could practice a series of related steps, identify nation-differentiated styles (Yoruba, Arará, Kongo-Angola, and Carabalí), and more carefully digest an overall Cuban style, not only through new dance experiences but also through familiar comparisons. Students left the Cross-Cultural Model as secure performers in Cuban style, ready for the distinctions of Cuban forms."

FolkCuba Especial (1999)

"While my former projects facilitated the visits of Cuban dance and music artists as cultural ambassadors to the United States, I also hoped to augment the experiences of U.S. American students to see and explore their own under-standings of Cuban music/dance within its site of origin. I was concerned with opportunities to learn Cuban performance style and the fact that students were so hungry for the Cuban Yoruba dances in particular. Then there were only a few Cubans who were teaching: Xiomara Rodrigues in New York City, Juanita Baró in Miami, Judith Justíz in San Francisco and Roberto Burrell in Oakland. (Juan Barroso in Oakland and Neri Torres in Miami came later; and Elena Garcia had stopped dancing in Miami at that time.) In the dance field, there had been sparse migration of knowledgeable dancers as compared with drummers and singers until the early 1990s.[9] In any case, I began to look for ways to take students to Cuba and to collaborate with Cuban colleagues.

"In the summer of 1998 I brought a group of a dozen specialists to Folklórico Nacional for intensive study. I worked with my friend and colleague Lourdes Tamayo, a soloist with the national company and a dance educator in Havana. During my years of traveling back and forth to Cuba, she and I had dreamed of ways in which to improve dance curricula for Cuban dance forms. *FolkCuba Especial* became our dream curriculum for one undergraduate student, six dance teachers, two musicians, and three anthropologists from California, Oregon, Washington, New York, New Jersey, Texas, Massachusetts, and Brazil. It was a wonderfully cooperative and supportive group, despite the constraints within the program. The result, however, was a developed version of the Stanford/Banff Masters' Model of teaching Cuban dance with deeper immersion into Cuban culture and perfection of performance style. Thus, in addition to the main daily dance classes from 10 A.M. to noon and 2 to 4 P.M., as well as the 9 to 10 A.M. daily class in chants and music, there were daily lectures in Cuban culture: contemporary music with a radio music personality, a newspaper journalist on contemporary political issues, *oricha* iconography with a costume design historian, music panorama of Cuban music complexes, and visual artists, Haitian Cuban performers, and so on.

"It was an ambitious program for the two of us to attempt without the financial backing of an institution. Participants paid for all classes and services through the Folklórico administration. Lecturers were treated to lunch or din-ner and a very modest honorarium by the two organizers. The Cuban admin-istration did not fully support the new dimension in our program, the lectures, nor did it always provide live accompaniment for dance classes, which was its responsibility. Cuban musicians, however, donated much of their time and expertise as a result. Students were exceedingly generous as were the Cuban teachers, who valued the keen talents and concentrated efforts that group members demonstrated. The dance teachers went back to their communities (Mexican, Filipino, African American, Brazilian, European American) with clarity and professionalism in Cuban performance and with added cultural content with which to give context to questions asked of them about Cuba or about ideal Cuban performance.

"While the program barely paid for itself, relationships were set in motion. Most importantly, the formal learning within the curriculum and its Cuban context made a difference in quality of performance. Performers knew more; and performance at the end of the course was enriched accordingly."

Cuba J-Term, Smith College (2002)

"In an effort to build on the benefits of FolkCuba Especial, I investigated the possibility of taking students to Cuba through Smith College's international study program. In the process, Smith's Spanish Department was also investigating a language and dance program in Spain, and the dean of international studies put both departments together. After much deliberation, a joint project of Spanish language and Cuban dance was approved as an intensive undergraduate course with the generous support of the Smith College administration. Students were particularly happy to have a program in Cuba for credit. In January 2002, Patricia Gonzalez of the Spanish and Portuguese Department and I took twenty-one young women to Cuba for intense study of Spanish language and Afro-Cuban culture.

"Again the program was revised, but a Cross-Cultural Model was employed. The biggest differences between the two study groups (*FolkCuba Especial* and Smith J-term) were the language component and the undergraduate/graduate level of participants. The language classes took half of the allotted classroom time and, for credit, had to be taken at the University of Havana from 9:00 until 12:30 daily. The undergraduate level in the J-term student group was in stark contrast to the skilled, professional level of the 1998 Especial group. From 3:00 until 6:00, however, students took dance or theater classes with specialists in mainly Yoruba culture. With reduced time, little practice in Arará, Carabalí, or Palo was possible; there was significant time given, however, for popular dance as an alternative to the intensity of Yoruba training.

"Dancing for three hours a day for three weeks really deepens skill level. Even the least prepared students were able to demonstrate good Cuban style on our return. The dance portion of both programs developed into a body learning experience since students imitated movements and movement qualities repeatedly and relied on the body's muscle memory, strength, and conditioning to replicate dance stylistic distinctions. The group performances were quite lovely. The Cuban community audience who watched them were publicly and privately impressed."

Formal Learning Discussion

"On three occasions, despite complicated organizational issues and even more difficult funding, I was able to invite Cuban dance specialists to visit and teach in my classes at Smith College and in the Five College Dance Department. I brought Los Muñequitos to Mt. Holyoke College, the Five College Dance Department, and the Latin community of western Massachusetts in 1993. After this tour ended, Ana Perez of Los Muñequitos came as guest artist to teach in a few of my classes as well. Lourdes Tamayo of Folklórico Nacional joined us and taught for two weeks and again in 1996. Also, I was able to facilitate the appearance of the entire company, Folklórico Nacional, at the University of Massachusetts, Amherst, at the Fine Arts Center in 1996. In the summer of 2000, I worked again with Los Muñequitos and with the Jacob's Pillow Summer Dance Festival. I prepared press packages and gave preconcert talks to interested dance specialists, and also to a curious U.S. American public.

"My work has been personally gratifying, Changó, even considering the huge political obstacles and financial hindrances that have to be negotiated before, during, and after anything happens between Cuba and the United States. It has allowed me to examine the ways in which eager learners learn.

"It seems that students are hungry, in fact greedy, for the Cuban Yoruba dance/music forms. For sure, beginning students enter and accomplish the movements comfortably and successfully when there is some cross-cultural comparative manner of introducing the material. This is also a secure entrance for intermediate and advanced dancers. Once basic muscular coordination and locomotor patterns are set, more detailed and complex instruction is possible from specialists. Body language, of course, works exceedingly well in dance courses. Students of dance are usually positioned in their bodies and readily sensitized to receive and yield learning.

"Regardless of level, I have observed a contagious element in the Cuban Yoruba dances that has captivated most students. I believe it is the combined or thick texture of the dance practice and its performance: its necessary vocal musical cues, the satisfaction in the two-line responsorial chorus, the hypnotic drum rhythms, the accessible body movements for most everyone, the story-revealing connections of music and dance to philosophy and/or history, the resultant physical sense of well-being, and its spiritual effect—even in popular dance. All of this texture is absorbed by the body and mind jointly, the stimulated and sensitized body and mind, and gives the student a wonderful performing independence, and simultaneously a sense of community. Dancing divinity is most stirring and contagious. Formal learning makes all of this clear and apparent.

"There, Changó, my presents for you—two choreographic movements—an analysis of my choreographed African nations dance and a geographical score of Cuban dance as it has spread between Cuba and the United States—and requisite reciprocity. *Cabiosile-o.*"

"*Aché, mi vida; aché.*"

NINE

The Dancing Body and Embodied Wisdom

For images of the past and recollected knowledge of the past . . .
are conveyed and sustained by (more or less ritual) performances. . . .
Commemorative ceremonies prove to be commemorative only in so far as
they are performative; performativity cannot be thought without
a concept of habit; and habit cannot be thought
without a notion of bodily automatisms.

—Paul Connerton

I n trying to relay "what—what the dance does—does" (what dance means),
I am eventually coerced to access the multiple channels of sensory per-
ception that I have felt when I have repeatedly performed these sacred
dance offerings. Since dance behavior comprises such perceptions, I am using these in addition to my observations of emotive body states that other
worshipping performers have presented. Also I am assessing the comments of
other performers. I search for words in English that correspond closely to what
participants say about their access before being transformed, their knowledge
of the performance practice, or, later as a result of transformation, their con-

sequences and their sensibilities. My words are not always their words, but when I have told my friends about what I have written and how I am writing in English, they say that they recognize the performance, the divinities, and what they have told me in different ways. I am trying to translate what the body discovers and knows through dancing, and trying not to make my friends and mentors objects, but still subjects.

In this chapter also, I am privileging Cuba. While I have explained my focus on three sites and my correspondingly different entrance and access to cultural data, I have also tried to balance my reporting of the data in each chapter with obviously emphasized chapters for the three sites. In concluding this book, I now emphasize, more than before, my extensive and profound relationship to Cuba and both Cuban dance and Cuban religious behaviors.

Embodied Knowledge of Oyá

In the beginning of Oyá's dance performance, you see balance if you look carefully.[1] The drums play a slow *jueso* (*oyade*) rhythm, and she projects balance: right and left, high and low, forward and backward. All directions are covered, all dimensions, all spheres of existence are acknowledged equally. She makes a foot pattern that alternates evenly and constantly, an elaborate foot pattern that marks the cardinal directions as well: (Right) forward, (Left) back, (RLR) right side one two three, (L) forward, (R) back, (LRL) left side one two three, and so on. Her foot pattern as the gentle breeze does not exude femininity. It is more like that of several male divinities, emphasizing the warrior-like strength of womankind; in fact this first step is a variant of Ogún's forceful foot pattern (R) forward, (L) back, (R) side; L forward, (R) back, (L) side; and so forth.

I often think of John Mason's descriptions of Oyá in his literal English translations of the Yoruba chants that invoke the presence of the divinities within Yoruba cosmology (1992). He says that Oyá is a mighty power that has potential to clean, destroy, or change. From dancing, performers say Oyá is forceful, takes space, and draws out woman's fierce and militant qualities. We know (from chapters 1 and 4) that she is air, all types of air, and she is accordingly dynamic, changing constantly. Her arms wave majestically and authoritatively with the *íruke* or dark-haired fly whisk above her head. From analysis, we observe her balance, and it disarms us; we await change.

CHANT FOR OYÁ

Oyá de, iba ri iba; (a)'se ke (a)'se.
Ago ile; ago lona. Oyá de ire O, Oyá de.

The Tearer arrives. Homage finds homage; authority hails authority. Make way in the house; make way on the road. The Tearer comes
with goodness; the Tearer comes. (Mason 1992:327)

The chant, the rhythm, the gestures, and the hundreds of *patakines* concerning Oyá describe her as tornado energy. Her cosmic power is also referenced in animal form as the quiet, massive, overwhelmingly fierce buffalo.
Judith Gleason has given meteorological analysis of wind patterns that govern
West Africa, and the fierce atmospheric conditions that have become associated with the force of Oyá and the Niger River in Yorubaland, Oyá's original
shrine and worship site (Gleason 1987). Oyá is associated with the Niger River
and with two rivers that flow in opposite directions, thus aligning her and her
devotees or godchildren with places and times of dynamic change, whether
in revolution, the marketplace, the carnival and masking, or simply with the
last breath of all life. She is a female warrior in the midst of change; she also
fights for change (Mason 1992:336; see Oya in chapter 8).

These references to disquieting fierceness anticipate the next series of
songs that are performed for Oyá to a different set of rhythms, generically
called *ñongo*. With this faster pace, Oyá is summoned with increased tension.
The songs for the second stage of an Oyá dance/music offering speak of

one who turns in another direction is perplexing. . . . Please come, I will be
happy . . . [when you] gush into the house. Oyá is strong and capable . . .
the tearer continually speaks, continually speaks. (Mason 1992:321–26)

In the dance patterns, Oyá begins to lope and gallop like the massive
buffalo that she is aligned with.

The one who turns things and changes them,
The woman who you make way for when she turns,
Massive structure that sits on the ground;
The woman who wears short pants
[is ready to fight].
Who can capture the head of Oyá?
Oyá, the quick-eyed, we salute you. (Mason 1985:70)

Her danced body rhythms play a three against two pattern (in which
the same time length is divided into threes and divided into twos and played

together among drum voicings). The pattern encourages dynamic mathematics—both in the drumming and dance practices, a demonstration of skill, craft, intelligence, and inventiveness (Friedman 1982; Perez 1987: personal communication; Burrell 1995: personal communication). The dancer can alternate, starting with the cool, gentle dance of the breeze and a balanced sense of timing in fours (4/4 even meter) and then picking up speed with the texture change of the *caballo* or horse step, which emphasizes a sense of three (3/4 meter; see Oyá *tratao* in chapter 8). Singer, chorus, and drummers transit from the slow *jueso* rhythm that marks the cardinal points to *ñongo* rhythm, which quickens the pace and intensifies the dancing.

When I dance for Oyá, it is this alternation that is most useful in acquiring the energy that is necessary to produce and display Oyá's pace, timing, velocity, and power. I alternate often in order to place myself firmly into the rocking, smooth horse pattern that begins her cantering gallop. With the next rhythmic pattern, the *chacha* or *chachaolokofún* of the *batá* drums,[2] and with appropriately irregular and agitating chants, I can perform within a heightened movement expression at an even swifter pace, using *caballo* to push the canter into a speeding, flying gallop. While the pattern repeats and while I listen for exacting rhythmic cues, I scan through my body, making sure that all of me is aware and present, earnestly at work in presenting and representing the movements of Oyá.

Repetition is critical. It is necessary to build and intensify each body part's involvement. It is through repetition that dancing worshipers harness and display all the energy possible in a given set of movements. At first the pattern is consciously discernable, but with maximum repetition, the dancing worshiper is fully confident, engrossed in the muscular movement, articulating every nuance in every part of the body. The mind is submerged in the dancing and the music, discerning mysteries. Both the body and the mind transcend.

Then there is a complete shift in the air; Oyá is a screaming buffalo. There is a change to Oyá's most aggressive movement pattern, the *tuitui* rhythm, which is distinct from all previous rhythms. It is as if you cannot dance any harder or more correctly; you have to yield from repetition to creativity or burst in trying. You have felt Oyá, the buffalo-warrior imminent.

Oyá's dance is full of independent womanpower, but also fierce fighting power for the community. She starts the *tuitui* and does not usually alternate with any other dance steps. The *tuitui* pattern consists of three huge, percussive torso undulations that alternate side to side. Literally on top of this, the arms, which have been carrying the *íruke,* finish the pattern by slashing downward from high in the air to at least hip height, alternately on each side. It is as if Oyá has accrued all the physical power possible and now directs mental power on top of the displayed physical strength. She is purposeful, strategic, and mighty.

Oyá engages the full physical and mentally strategic force of mature women. She is still the revolutionary activist, who is impatient for anything other than meaningful action, but she goes beyond the issues to cures and resolutions. She is careful in her swift assuredness.

Oyá is the guardian of the cemetery in Cuba and is feared or avoided at times because she associates with the awesome Eguns. Her proximity to death and the living dead is explained beyond the chants and the dance within *patakines*. Worshipping performers are told of her devotion to nine stillborn children and how she stays near the cemetery to protect them. At other times, she whirls, spins, and churns the air like tornadoes, hurricanes, and cyclones. Her spinning force connotes that she has little fear of others, of death, or even of fear itself; she is female all powerful. She is the female warrior who gallops and swirls across space and through time.

In all of the *oricha* dance performances, transformations take place. First, dancing worshipers are transformed into the divinity through imposed recognition of complementary relationships. Believers recognize and acknowledge relationships between animals, plants, and themselves on the horizontal plane of existence. They construct, experience, and deepen their relationship to vocal sentiment, instrumental sound, and human movement. They become increasingly aware of all the senses—taste, smell, touch, seeing, hearing—and in acutely recognizing these, they gain familiarity with their personal relationship to the senses as channels of awareness and learning. They submit themselves fully to sensory stimuli.

Dancing worshipers acknowledge the relationship between the principles of cooperation and reciprocity and the dancing *oricha* in the present. For example, in order to prepare worshipers for Oyá's appearance and consequent advice, humans are bathed in or dusted with particular leaves and herbs, perhaps lavender water, sugar water, or rain water with *bari'a* (*Cordia gerascanthus*) or *caimitillo* (*Chrysophylum oliviforme*) (Cabrera 1983 [1954]:335, 349). Plants are cooked with emphasis on Oyá's preference for eggplant, sweet potatoes, and especially black-eyed peas. Animals—goats, hens, pigeons, and guinea hens, for example—are dedicated to her and her community of godchildren. The animals are later eaten as nourishing medicinal food from the *oricha* to humans in a reciprocal relationship with the *orichas*.

In order for a transformation to occur from invisible to visible energy, the entire family of ancestors, the living dead on the sagittal plane of existence, is praised and acknowledged. The ancestors are accorded recognition within a plant-animal-human connection with offerings of foods, flowers, and liquids, particularly water. These are symbolic affirmations of social cohesion among family members in the present by restating the locus of interpersonal relations and invoking the requisite behavior that is proper for reciprocity to succeed. In other words, the present community is reminded of its common heritage and its elders. Community members are encouraged to perform respectful behaviors in order that reciprocity and balance between the ancestral and human worlds continue. Specific behaviors permit the ancestors of the sagittal plane to communicate with humans on the horizontal plane. Dancing worshipers reaffirm their interconnections with all life when animals and plants are transformed into nourishment—that is, food for the dancing divinities, food for the ritual community, and food for the participant-observing public.

Humans, plants, and animals, transformed as music and dance, are utilized jointly to effect other transformations. Transformed plants, as wooden drums and beaded shakers, create a solitary, demanding resultant call. Wood, bamboo, and gourds join with metal gongs and combine again with solo and group voices to collectively implore social and spiritual communication. Transformed animals as drum heads that give impulse to instrumental sound, and transformed animals as blood that expresses the utmost sincerity and seriousness of the endeavor, are employed in concert with the lead singer and the chorus to initiate and access spiritual transformations. Thus, abstract rhythm, melody, and gesture are transformed into visual and audible mathematical configurations, *los orichas,* the dancing divinities.

Once all ceremonial elements combine, the notion of time itself is transformed. Specific time becomes nonspecific and relative. In these situations, there are only four times that are relevant. Time is calculated as before and after sunrise or before and after sunset (Perez 1987: personal communication; de Santana Rodrigué 1991: personal communication). After the dancing divinities appear, another transformation presents itself. The divinities are transformed into advisers, godmothers and godfathers, therapists who bathe people with herbal waters and body sweat, who greet them, dance with them, eat with them, and then sit down and talk to them with counsel for problems and everyday situations.

Sometimes the counsel they give is symbolic. Behavior speaks as Oyá joins the human community. She demands cognitive action, for example, by forcefully hugging an uninitiated participant for a noticeable period of time and then specifically dancing with her/him. In so doing, she gives her wish for incorporation, silently but physically in danced movement. Or she might take the hands of quarreling neighbors and forcibly shake them together. No one speaks, but the advice is heard in physical movement and discernable behavior. The principles of incorporation, respect, generosity, and sharing are made evident in danced movement. Oyá imposes chores, at first glance seemingly trivial and unrelated obligations, but which ideally are understood over time to provide individual tranquility, careful and loving relationships between plants and animals, and peaceful respect within the group. The ritual community, the social body, experiences social balance and wisdom.

Oyá in the contemporary world is found in poignant words and burning assertions of female strength and wisdom. These provide contemporary charters for strength, modern models of vivacious power, and ancient charters for the worshipping performer to aggregate or call on Oyá energy. When I asked my friends in the religion when they felt Oyá in today's world, they likened her presence to times of struggle and tenacity and also to the human will that it takes to continue to live and go forward. They insisted that she reminded them to remember the preciousness of life and the precariousness of death. Neither they, nor I, would be upset by her erratic, jerking, undulating unabashedly asymmetrical and rhythmically sophisticated *tuitui* movements that speak to and defend that preciousness.

When *oricha* dance movements are performed, they provide for historical catharsis, contemporary release, and meaningful social action. These are dances of human resilience. In the moment of performance, the nonverbal messages—both displayed visually and experienced physically—of persistence, deliberation, dedication, reliability, resourceful resilience, and, ultimately, calm, strength, and endurance are all taught, learned over time, and transferred beyond the dance/music event to other arenas of social life. Transformed as Oyá, for example, the worshipping dancer soars through space and time on the coronal plane of existence. S/he reestablishes those maintenance patterns that have repeatedly confronted and resisted the magnetized dehumanizing elements within contemporary situations.

The dances express the collective memory and understanding of the cosmos, as they relate to wholeness in the present. The dance performances teach balance, discipline, and humanity in a silent lecture within a loud, multicolored and multisensory experience. The social body experiences the remembered patterns that constitute a balance of each interfacing realm of knowledge and integrates those experiences into daily routine and critical situations.

Experiential Librarians

It could be argued by worshipers that writing down the varied dance practices, praise songs, percussive rhythms, and ritual understandings from certain Diaspora religious systems is ultimately a doomed affair. Some community spiritual leaders suggest that the power of the expressions and force of the beliefs will be diminished, destroyed, or converted as they are disseminated among outsiders, strangers, and unincorporated others. Religious community leaders often think that the outsiders' pattern of behavior (historically that of missionaries, travelers, military personnel, anthropologists, journalists, politicians, and profit-seeking others) has resulted in exploitation or destruction, and only occasionally in respectful understanding. Even when the intent to explain or understand rather than to exploit was consciously sincere, the element of power relations between ritual practitioners and ritual observers has generally been ignored. Thoughtful analyses, but also misconceptions about African American religions, have resulted.

Several interpretations of belief and dance ritual in the Diaspora have been analyzed during academic conferences and on video documentaries, but rarely does this happen with the concurrent critical evaluation of community specialists. Further, both natives and non-natives often re-present religious dance traditions, representing African nations in the process, but, again, often without community discussion, consensus, or approval. Such patterns (one-sided views, potential misrepresentation, and exploitation) have tended to publicly silence the expert voices from community specialists; several important perspectives have gone further "underground" from their out-of-sight beginnings in African ritual communities of the Americas.

Subsequently, secrecy itself is embedded in African religious culture across the Diaspora. Among the Yoruba, for example, there is no exact word for "religion"; its closest concept is found in their word *awo* (secret), and the high priest of the Yoruba religion, the *babalawo,* is thereby "guardian of secrets." In Haiti, the *konesanz* resides in "mysteries," the *mistès* or the *lwas* themselves, and is guarded by levels of understanding among *manbos* and *oungans* who have completed *canzo* and *pri je* ceremonies. Haitian secrecy is slightly different, however.

Remember, there was no problem for me to film the entire *manbo* ceremony, including the sacred dialogue of the *asson*. Haitian Vodouists have fewer reasons than Cuban *iyalorichas* and *babalorichas* or Bahian *iyalorixás* and *babalorixás* to hide ritual behavior, because they are and have been part of the majority within a black nation for centuries; they are, in effect, owners of the land. Unfortunately, Vodouists' beliefs and actions have also been condemned as barbaric by powerful compatriots who own even more of the land. The upper-class few control the land's resources and often identify more with European philosophies and ideologies than with those of Africa. As a result, *oungans* and *manbos* also revert to secrecy at times. It is difficult, therefore, to disregard the force of secrecy in firmly held beliefs.

Worshipers believe that power resides in the knowledge of certain practices. Such power has been protected first by secrecy within intimate ritual families until persons were sufficiently prepared or learned to receive power-filled information. Then beliefs and practices were kept from the often devastating actions of ignorant officials, whether colonial overseers of old or contemporary mainstream lawmakers, dilettantes, and wannabes.

Biases and rejections due to Africanity are not limited to European-derived peoples. Similar behaviors of African Americans have disrupted knowledge system legacies. African Americans have shunned African religions and African ways of being as well. In the United States, in fact, some researchers believe that there is more African knowledge among some southern, rural white folk (recognized or unrecognized) than among African Americans in general (e.g., Phillips 1991:225–39). Some African Americans are ignorant of current, revisionist history that has been documented over the past few decades (e.g., Walker 2001; Gilroy 1993; Brandon 1993; Mazrui 1993; Hilliard 1990; Bernal 1987; ben Jochannan 1991). These elders and youngsters have not always studied African religions or African philosophy with the enthusiasm and excitement with which they have devoured the literature, philosophy, and scientific output of other cultures (see also Mosley 1995).

Additionally, there is a growing group of young "global individualists" in the African Diaspora who are so subsumed by desires for material improvement and financial success in the international, mainstream world that they replace religion and philosophy with pragmatic, political, and economic ideologies. Other young people in the African Diaspora neglect religion, philosophy, and politics altogether. They are constantly preparing for an impending violent attack within the subculture of poverty (since, very often, these young people have been denied the politico-economic mobility of the global individualists) and are socialized without much concern for economic or spiritual commitment.

As a result, many African American spiritual perspectives and practices have been neglected, ridiculed, or diluted in African communities of Haiti, Cuba, and Brazil, as well as in the United States. The philosophical underpinnings of African religions have been minimized. First, the Roman Catholic Church has tolerated the connection between Christian saints and African divinities. The Church often counts the (sometimes nominal) declaration of faith from Vodouists, *iyalorichas* and *babalorichas,* and *iyalorixás* and *babalorixás* as Catholics, without taking seriously the totality of worshipers' beliefs and their predominant practices.

Protestant Christianity does the same in its own way. In the teaching of Protestant Christianity, African traditional religions remain as examples of superstition, witchcraft, and polytheistic and/or satanic worship. In the circum-Caribbean, Protestant beliefs still have much Africanity within their practices, for example, shouting and music-making, calls and responsorial singing while manifesting very similar behaviors, and belief in multidimensional divinities (God, the Father, the Son, and the Holy Ghost). Many African American Protestants conceive of and often ridicule African belief systems as marginal or superstitious, as do some Haitians, Cubans, and Afro-Bahians, rather than examine the reverent and complex world of spirituality that I have tried to indicate from my studies.

Even some professed worshipers within Haitian Vodou, Cuban Yoruba, and Bahian Candomblé have employed a superficial emphasis on the material attributes of African ritual practice. For example, in Haiti people told me stories of *oungans* and *manbos* who were initiating others before completing their own major confirmation of spiritual knowledge (see Dunham 1983: ix–xiv; 1995: personal communication). In Cuba, these types of practitioners seem to be concerned more often with the collection of beaded necklaces, the procuring of protective emblems, or the power and authority of their roles. They relish in the public attention of the dances and the music. In Bahia, I heard stories about trips to Nigeria where some worshipers who believed they had undergone initiation had received merely commemorative symbols and had not been initiated in accordance to prescribed ritual. Behavioral changes are expected as a result of initiation and dedication to a particular religion; clear shifts in previous patterns of social behavior and deliberate reassessments of philosophical and theoretical estimations are usually observed and often expected.

Some practitioners, however, do not demonstrate such changed behaviors. More specific to the ritual practice in Cuba, a dissonance of practice and philosophy is emerging surrounding Ifa initiation. More Cubans are wearing the bracelet or outer sign of Ifa initiation in my observations. Those who study Ifa, *babalawos,* have historically been men in Cuban practice, and their studies have been notoriously long and intense (although a few are recognized as potential "keepers of Ifa" or *babalawos* at birth). Now not only have women been initiated in a three-day ceremony, but also a great number of males.

What is disquieting is the economic dimension of Cuban social reality that influences this solemn ritual practice. As an observer of Cuban ritual and social life for over eighteen years, I see an unusual rise in Ifa initiation (at least around Havana). Not only are more Cubans displaying Ifa initiation, but also so are more foreign visitors. Cuban ethnologist Rogelio Martinez-Fure calls this "instant Ifa *gineterismo*"—the prostitution of culture for immediate profit (2002: personal communication). It is a fact of social life that touring strangers are eager to receive whatever tie to the "backstage of culture" or "spiritual journey" that they can access (MacCannell 1976; Graburn 1989). In Cuba, a growing number of knowledgeable *babalawos* are willing and able to initiate almost anyone to this most sacred body of philosophical texts.[3] Tourists, therefore, scramble to connect with spiritual culture, with exotic religious orientations, with learned ancient knowledge, but hardly with the appropriate commitment that has been expected historically. The learning process of spiritual commitment, especially Ifa knowledge, is a lifelong dedication to its understanding.

Most of my research data, however, indicate that complex philosophies and reverent religiosity are revealed in African American ritual practices, and it is the musicians and dancers who house and protect libraries of codified knowledge. They are the experiential librarians who are used in order to reference ancient knowledge for contemporary use. Further, the experiential librarians help to uncover many kinds of knowledge when they activate belief systems in sacred performance.

With the exception of works by a few scholars— Hurston (1938), Dunham (1946, 1947, 1969), Ortiz (1950, 1951 [1985]), Deren (1983 [1953]), Honorat (1955), Paul (1962), and Courlander (1973), for example—the early academic literature on African American religions does not contain much analysis or discussion about the dance/music practices within these religious systems. In the works of Ruth Landes (1947 [1994]), Alfred Métraux (1972 [1959]), William Bascom (1950, 1951, 1969 [1991]), Pierre Verger (1957), and Roger Bastide (1978), for example, performance analysis is limited to the function of dance and music as a means to a trance or altered state of consciousness (see Walker 1972, 1991; Deren 1983; Bourguignon 1976; Drewal, 1975; Gleason 1987; Thompson 1971, 1983, 1995). With the details of a revisionist historical perspective spelled out earlier, in addition to the mapping of liturgical orders, dance/music phenomena take their place among the significant resources of religious understanding. With the inclusion of knowledge from chants, religious stories, drumming structures, and body movements, the experiential librarians, the musicians and dancers, relinquish and share levels of transposed knowledge. Dancers and musicians reveal dynamic body scores for individual identity, community solidarity, and spiritual well-being.

The Body Politic: Ochún and Changó

Performance analysis points out the power of the dancing human body and how it is exalted during ritual practice. Not only in Haitian Vodou, Cuban Yoruba, and Bahian Candomblé, but also as a universal human expression, the dance indicates the body politic (see Hanna 1979:128–78; Cowan 1990:3–27, 188–234; Sklar 1991, 1994; Novack 1990:194–213; and Nettleford 1985 for the dancing body; and, more generally, Bourdieu 1984). Using the dance of Ochún as one possible performance out of the series of divinity performances discussed earlier, I concentrate now on how *oricha* dances represent the body politic. In the dance of Ochún, the human body is artful, ingenious, shrewd, wise, prudent, judicious, crafty, and sometimes unscrupulous, thus very politic. The female body with its individual power is explored in addition to being implored within sacred Yoruba performance.

Ochún's dance is first of all an invocation for the spiritual energy of the universe that is dedicated to womankind, but woman in her special domain as female—total female. By this statement, I am differentiating one of three major facets or aspects of womankind: (1) female, woman, lover; (2) mother, nurturer, caretaker; and (3) warrior, champion, activist. In Cuban Yoruba and Bahian Candomblé religious thought, Ochún represents woman as the essence of young and vibrant female energy; Yemayá represents woman as the essence of mothering energy; and Oyá represents woman as the essence of female warrior or activist energy.[4]

All three *oricha* dances—Ochún, Yemayá, and Oyá—are about dynamic female energy that is found in oceans and rivers and in the air, woman energy. Each one is the name of a dance but also the name of the associated divinity who is called to the contemporary ritual or social setting by means of ritual drumming, chanting, and dancing. The dance of each *oricha* specifically signals the predominance of one aspect of female energy, although woman essence flows comfortably among concepts of "the sexual," "the nurturer," and "the fighter" in Yoruba concepts.[5]

In a Cuban Yoruba performance, as well as in a Bahian Candomblé performance, Ochún focuses on the sensual, soft, seductive, and simultaneously strong energy of woman. The movements of Ochún's dance encourage community attention to the female body itself.[6] Ochún first travels in her *zapateo* step as steadfastly as the river, alternating her body weight between her right and left foot, and, as a result, acquires her alluring quality. As the singer praises her profusely in musical rhythms, her hands move outstretched horizontally, either to the sides or above her head, and sometimes she extends her skirt wide. As the songs progress, she travels in many directions in front of the altar. At the signal of *Ala iyeye walere a,* she sinks down in the river, turns and ascends, and then alternates her first step from side to side, never once leaving the basic *zapateo* step, her river water constancy. Another change comes when she is fully engaged above the water and swishes her skirts at *gbogbosun* (or *mokosun*). Here Ochún pulls her petticoats and skirts across and around her body to land on her right hip and then alternates to the left hip. While her feet engage the "bounce step" (RL, LR, RL, LR), her upper body tilts to the opposite side of the arms on the hip and alternates. At *gbogbosun,* Ochún is filled with rhythm in multiple body parts; her shoulders, neck, and head rebound softly.

Gradually there is a transition to a slightly faster rhythm and more intensified movement pattern. Sometimes her pattern involves backing up to collect water and then throwing it over one shoulder; with other *trataos,* she performs her version of the *caballo* step, sensuous and flowing.

Yeye, Yeye-o! Her laughter comes softly at first, giggling above the drums intermittently. She looks in the mirror, smoothes her face with invisible creams and honey, and proceeds to put on her jewelry: earrings, rings, and many bracelets. Her laughter shifts in character, and as she is fully dressed and apparent, her physical and mentally shrewd self are also. She boldly dances her *caballo* or her *iyesa* at yet a faster pace, which involves the same body parts in a stronger and more explicit articulation of the female body. She dips into the water (or honey) and spreads it all over her face, shoulders, rib cage, abdomen, and hips. She is the epitome of sensation incorporated. *Yeye, yeye-o;* she shudders softly, her head and eyes lowered in bliss.

As worshipers imitate and perform her dance sequences repeatedly, they deepen into her spiritual essence with matching energy. Ochún's dance becomes not only an invocation for the essence of vibrant female energy but also a public display for the admiration and adoration of the female gender and female body form. Within the gestures of Ochún, the viewer sees the Yoruba concepts of beauty, grace, and femininity "read" as other qualities. Within the dance sequences and movements, Ochún's beauty is openness, independence, alertness, or mental strength, and an empowered sense of self.

Worshipping performers tell us that this dance, this *oricha,* is not only about "the feminine" or female sensuality, which are obvious references in the dance as well, but about sexuality in Ochún's life history, her accumulated wisdom and recognized weaknesses. *"Ella no es solo feminina, pero fuerte y orgullosa"* (She is not just feminine, but strong and proud) says one dancing worshiper (Tamayo 1997: personal communication). *"Ella es fuerte, fuerte, fuerte"* (She is strong, strong, strong) say others (Perez 1987, 2001: personal communication; Alfonso 1999: personal communication). She is not perfect or flawless but strong and reliable, and she is a genius in the African (and now feminist) sense of female body energy.

For believers, Ochún's dance references the female form as splendor among all physical forms. Ochún touches her own face, waist, and hips as she dances; she bathes and smoothes over her own feminine curves. She projects an acute sensitivity, so as to secure sensual stimulation in others, and she ultimately seeks to guarantee sexual satisfaction and procreation. She is vivacious, sane, and healthy, the female type that is needed to secure community survival, the part of every female that is happy within herself. A worshiper's dancing body visually displays such qualities of human strength, represents physical ability and force, and, in its female depiction as Ochún, embodies woman in her healthiest and most fertile physical condition.

The dance for Ochún is also a call for self-empowerment, the mental aspect of the totally healthy body. The dance transcends both feminine qualities and the female physical body to Ochún's other natural symbol, river water: cool, clear, sweet (as opposed to salt) running water. Ochún dances ostentatiously with rings, earrings, bracelets, and trinkets of brass and gold with which she adorns herself. They are also the glistening elements of a stream, a bubbling brook, or softly gurgling water. River water, however, has many qualities—not all bright and bubbly. Rivers are also deep, heavy, dark waters with strong currents that can carry a huge barge swiftly downstream or swallow a great transport entirely. So also does Ochún have deeper faculties beyond the physical.

Believers tell of Ochún's mental shrewdness, her keen analysis, her acute thinking. Her *patakines* reinforce understanding of her extreme intelligence and, when necessary, her cunning ways. Women, and men who have her as their guiding divinity, engage and request this aspect of her essence. Through their praise dancing and ardent bodily prayers, they petition for her qualities of meticulous clear thinking and resolution—thorough thinking that has reasoned a problem with all its possible resolutions. In daily life, worshipers reach for solutions that maximize Ochún's win-win approach, her impressive satisfaction of self while satisfying others. For the believing community, Ochún's dance is a charter for ways of behaving and ways of thinking. It encompasses female body power, self-power, real person power, individual power, and authority over self.

African and Cuban Yoruba minds selected the image and reinforced the understanding of Ochún. Through her, they memorialized the divine essence of woman and female form. In social life, believers in Ochún's power and in her danced messages are prepared with a model for healthy physical bodies and strong, mental endurance. Through her dance performance, believing performers are fortified mentally and physically. Thus, in practicing the drumming, chanting, and dancing for Ochún, Cuban Yoruba and Bahian Candomblé worshipers display, nurture, and maintain the body as deep water politics. Through their dance performances, they visually declare and nonverbally repeat (as believers have done for centuries) that the female body is powerful, strong, and quite remarkable.

CHANT FOR OCHÚN

Osun se're; (a)'kete 'mi owo;
Osun se're; (a)'kete 'mi owo
Omi dara o dara oge o
Osun se're; 'kete 'mi owo. . . .

Ase, ase, o se 'mi l'odo
Ala mba se maa se; se maa se
Ko se 'mi l'odo
Yeye ase, o se 'mi l'odo

A: Yeye we mi l'ere;
C: Ala yeye ma l'ere a!
A: Osa ki ni'wa;
C: Ko'wo'sun
A: Iy ka 'tanna;
C: Kowosun
A: A ri'ba lo mayo;
C: Ko'wo'sun
A: Osun ido'le alaawa'na;
C: Ko'wo'sun
(Mason 1992: 352–53)

Spring that makes blessings;
Resting place of the water of honor.
Spring that makes blessings;
Resting place of the water of honor.
Beautiful water, you are beautiful and ostentatious;
Spring that makes blessings;
Big Calabash for carrying the Water of Honor.

So be it, so be it, she causes the water in the river.
Imagine if she caused it not to be; caused it not to be;
Did not cause the water in the river.
Mother, so be it, you cause the water in the river.

Leader: Mother cleanse me to have profit;
Chorus: Imagine Mother that I will have profit ah!
Leader: Selected one, saluted for character,
Chorus: Teach respect, Osun.
Leader: Mother count the candles;
Chorus: Teach respect Osun.
Leader: We see homage used always for an important person.
Chorus: Teach respect Osun.
Leader: Osun, messenger from earth, the one who finds the way.
Chorus: Teach respect Osun (Mason 1992:352–53)

Judith Hanna, an anthropologist who studies dance behavior, has stated that the dancing body connotes health, but also power as life's vital force (1979:128–31). Merely seeing the human body in normal activity displays how marvelous and artful the human body is. But while dancing, the human body underscores quantities of force and power that it has at its disposal. The dancing body is truly politic, wise, and ingenious. And since the community depends on healthy bodies for survival, what better symbol of health can there be than the dancing body—both female and male?

In the previous example, Ochún exemplifies what other dancing divinities also represent in routine ceremonial practice. If we examine Changó's dance, we can see the body politic of *oricha* performance again as it generates individual self-assurance for males or for male energy in an *oricha* performance.[7]

Changó's dance is one of the most dynamic of the *oricha* dances, and thereby one of the most noticeable and recognizable even to the casual observer (cf. an African version of Şango's dance patterns in Ajayi 1998:88–90). Most characteristically, he gestures with his arms reaching above the head, descending downward and inward toward the lower abdomen and groin area, motioning alternately right and left from diagonal high to low. These movements trace an energy flow to earth from the sky or heavens and into the *oricha* as he appears, materialized and dancing on earth. The movements of Changó also refer to stories about his life history, preferences, and character. Songs and chants tell of Changó's mighty strength; he is an essence of the warning and warming powers found in thunder, lightning, and fire. In the dance, he pulls energy from the skies toward his genitals, harnessing the force of lightning, thunder, and that of the entire communal focus on sexual and social power.

Changó arrives in proud and stately form, his first pattern—(R) touch, (R) back, (L) forward, (R) forward, (L) touch, (L) back, (R) forward, (L) forward—affords a regal bearing as he purveys his kingdom, his people, his domain of power. His gait quickens as the drummers proceed to the *ñongo* rhythm, and he relishes in the cantor and later gallop of his personalized *caballo* step. At one point, he washes, puts on his pants, shaves, brushes his hair, and eats his favorite *amalá* (an okra-based food offering), all within the dance. Then clean, nourished, and fortified, he tumbles and leaps, jumps and gallops.

Kabo-e, Kabo-e, Kabo-e, Kabiosile-o, his sung prayer above a racing *meta* rhythm, announces his royal power. He kicks solidly between an alternating three-step pattern—(R) kick, (R) step, (L) step, (R) step, (L) kick, (L) step, (R) step, (L) step—marking the thrusts pointedly but intermittently. Gradually, however, the kicks are more plentiful, and his arm movements flash, fly, and fling potent male energy such that it surrounds him and all in his domain. Finally he is a mass of sharp pulsing strikes. His kicks are matched by the resonating depth of the *iya,* a hoarse growl from the inner core of the drum as well as the inner core of the earth, as the thundering force of Changó penetrates.

Changó's gesture of the forceful kick again points to his strength, but this time in his warrior role. Changó is known as a fighter, giving instant regard or punishment, and carrying a double-edged hatchet that allows striking from either direction. He is the epitome of youthful masculinity with high, broad steps, leaps, and acrobatic tumbling. When he dances, he wears his favorite red and white colors. He is then ready to "attack" living.

Changó is total male energy: hard, brash, physically energetic, and mentally alert. His is the most beautiful male body. His mind is quick and intelligent. He is the wittiest, the most handsome, and the most persuasive. He is masculine energy at the height of its strength and physical force, the epitome of young male essence. He is male lover, provider, and protector. He, too, requires his dancing children to match his energy, and accordingly they repeat his forceful and solid movements. As both males and females pull their arms toward their genitals and as they kick into the air, they deepen into male essence and they gather force and power. They reveal to themselves, first, the range and degree of strong self that is within them. They match Changó's energy and, in the process, demonstrate male power, quick bold energy. They mimic or exude the confidence, individual assurance, and self-esteem that are part of most young males—their Changó dimension. Again, another *oricha* generates individual body power, physical health, and mental strength, again the body politic.

In Cuba, Changó is also the guardian of truth, procreation, and communication, whose cosmic force is experienced as powerfully as lightning, thunder, and fire. His performance establishes the association of Changó as a strong male *oricha* who can be a source of creation and destruction, and one who can protect his children. In his *patakines,* he has made mistakes in the past and he has learned from his brashness, impulsive sensuality, and egotism. He has accumulated wisdom, and he is confident but cautious, now weighing his decisions before his actions. He is also the guardian of music and thereby the master of communication. He can sweet-talk and talk sweet, and his colors adorn the rum-baptized *batá* drums.

His dance makes physical the collective thought of Cuban Yoruba minds on being male, on responsibilities of strength and power, and on the skill of effective communication. His dance embodies such information as articulate behavior codes, making life principles literally vibrate. His ritual performance and those of all the *orichas* fortify community members religiously and socially against life's adversities and challenges. They first secure individual power and dignity from a dancing body politic.

Miseducation in the Twenty-first Century

In the so-called western, hegemonic world (really European and Euro-American), performance is not encouraged within many educational systems today. Generally, only those students who demonstrate exceptional talent in the arts are supported, and these are guided toward conservatories. Since the time of Carter G. Woodson (1933), critics have cited "miseducation" as the reality of many systems of education (Freire 1970; Carnoy 1973; Page 1989; Kramer 1991; Atkinson 1993; Macedo 2000). Study of the arts is usually an addendum to "real" studies or "real" education, which are founded in sciences or in business. Cuba serves as an exception to this type of educational and philosophical hierarchy. In fact, Cuba serves also as a reminder of the African presence, manifested in religions that are based on embodied knowledge and both the conscious and unconscious cultural premises that have inspired its educational philosophy and educational policies.

Despite Cuba's mammoth and critical education problems (concerning adequate numbers of books, state-of-the-art technology, etc.), Cuban educational policy starts with the premise that performance and artistic endeavor are important to basic knowledge of the individual and are therefore important for the nation. The study of the arts and performance in Cuba is required of a well-educated individual and for a healthy social community. The Cuban education paradigm seeks out, encourages, and supports—in genuine action—the development of the artistic dimensions of each student. It does so to the extent that it can manage practically, but in principle for sure, from early childhood through university.

Cuban government-spurred education programs also advocate and encourage an artistically enlightened audience. Free public access to cultural presentations, frequent artist/public dialogues and critiques, and reserved cultural spaces (*casas de cultura*) ensure arts-educated, generally well-informed, and potentially arts-activist audiences. Governmental monopoly of television and radio programming generally supports public education; however, it also reduces the maximum effects of that policy when public education is limited and critical thinking is controlled through the content of the school curricula and the programming of television networks and radio stations. The results so far are an impressive arts-appreciative and arts-involved lay public.

The African presence deep within Cuban thought and pervasive in Cuban culture, which values and asserts embodied knowledge, has assisted the formation and development of Cuba's exceptional education system. Such norms as are found in Cuba make the argument for embodied knowledge almost unnecessary. If each nation in the world were relying on both the stored and referenced knowledge within the body itself and a liberal or specialized education, perhaps my argument for embodied knowledge could be dismissed. My study, however, is helpful in this era of miseducation and of preference for theoretical and scientific knowledge, what I call disembodied knowledge. I argue for careful examination of embodied knowledge, specifically what is found within the performances of the dancing African American religions, to determine better strategies for fully and genuinely educated social citizens.

Educating from the Body

Although all of the dance performances in Haitian Vodou, Cuban Yoruba, and Bahian Candomblé have an individual consequence within their varied repertoire of movements, the movements for each divinity simultaneously conform to a basic and recognizable pattern for the community, the social body. That pattern alerts worshipers and participants to knowledge beyond the individual; the dance/music performances become enduring lessons that help individuals to bond as communities. The physical body sums up quantities of information and displays them in the interactive education situation of ceremonial performance. Community members are in an open classroom with dance and music behavior, in addition to their references in philosophy and religion, history, physiology, psychology, mathematics, and botany. These sorts of "knowledges" are on display as community instruction for social cohesion and cosmic balance. Participants learn from observation, witnessing, modeling, and active participation.

As worshipers perform in repetitive ritual sequences, they sense and learn. And as they continue to perform in ceremonial repetition over time, in the process of music-making and dance performance, embodied knowledge is accumulated and constantly consulted. For example, community members are exposed to certain processes: chants in nineteenth-century ritual language; songs; unaccompanied drumming excerpts; formal introduction of flowers, plants, and herbs (including placement in the room, treatments like bathing or brushing of leaves, and drinking of herbal infusions); music and dance segments; body manipulations (codified hand shakes, turning salutations, bows and other gestures on the floor). Then some of them sustain (short or long) periods of isolation. When the silence of these is broken, they are often asked about their sensations, feelings, and attitudes. Personal assessments continue periodically; community members are subtly directed (reminded) to survey what the dancing body has communicated and what the participating body is indicating silently, then to give voice to the body's mute delivery. The inquiry on the body, the focus on quiet *and* bombarding sensations, and the assessment of discoveries result in an ongoing method of consulting, a dynamic, practical current-referencing.

Yemayá and the Dancing Body

The ideas of community and education for ritual participants are expressed most fully in Cuba within the sacred choreography of Yemayá—the caring force, the essence of nurturing, the source of existence, the salt sea waters, the oceans.[8] Yemayá's dance compels the community to make the shape of the circle, to then furrow down and spin up through a circling spiral, and to reach spiritually for everyone and everything by encompassing or surrounding all Yemayá energy in the circle, and allowing it to radiate outward.

Yemayá's dance is performed within a triplet field to a rhythm called *yakotá* (see chapter 8, Yemayá *tratao*). Each drum plays a set two-pitch pattern, but the resultant rhythm audibly produces a time sense of three repeating beats. In her chants, the three-beat rhythm starts on an emphasized beat one, continues on beat two, and, deceptively as it begins to close on three, begins again with the accent on one. The sound process of Yemayá's three beats suggests a movement figure that is not entirely closed; it shifts in a new dimension like a spiral when it returns to repeat its three beats, ever growing, ever encompassing. In this manner, the rhythm and the dance leave an open space. In dancing "the three," worshipping performers imprint in space, on the ground, and in the air, the indelible statement that life is ongoing, alternating between planes, binding beings together, embracing matter, and encompassing energy.

The focus of the soothing and gentle Yemayá transits to her more powerful energy as she surfaces and waves splash on the shores with the call *Omolode*. When I dance for Yemayá, this part seems so big and radiating as I repeat her circling, now with head high and arms and shoulders pressing down. Yemayá dances her *zapateo #1* majestically, surveying all of the ocean and the circling bodies of her godchildren. She looks over all of her children, both the human and *oricha* children, to assure their safety. *Oluba chikini* is the chant signal for preparation; Yemayá's *zapateo #2* begins, and the *clave* of all Cuban music finds one of its origin roots: 1, 2/1, 2, 3// 1, 2/1, 2, 3//. Here Yemayá is woman, still fluid and resisting strict form—just like water; she is woman more so than mother or sea in this movement. She is sensual and exciting, vivacious, demanding and zealous. She swings her skirts, stretches the rhythms with syncopation, holds, and like the Haitian *feints* for Ezili (the codified irregular opening movements of the body in readiness to receive divinity), she is as alluring as ever "alluring" could be.

With the drum shift from *zapateo #2* to *aro*, her spinning begins. Yemayá starts turning around herself, at first as softly as the foam begins to rise at the shore's edge, but accelerating deliberately. When dancing the turns, there is no "spotting" like in ballet. I do remember getting slightly dizzy as I first danced her dance full-out. Later, it was easy to just keep turning, spinning, and circling. I remember one night as I danced Yemayá's *aro* that my drummers and students applauded, and their applause brought me to a stop. I only remember circling as if I could go on forever. Yemayá herself doesn't just circle; she spins and circles while waving her skirts in ripples and spinning them high and low—just as the whirlpool deepens, so do her rotations while circling.

Suddenly there is the smack of the *iya* and Yemayá is kicking—aligning her energy with Changó but simultaneously swishing and throwing her skirts outward in time with each smack. *Waro mio waro yeo; waro mio waro yeo, o mi Yemayá!* She ebbs and flows as she kicks and pulls, and then her shoulders are shuddering rapidly, vibrating intensively; she is backing away and drawing downward into the ocean again.

YEMAYÁ'S PRAYER
Okuo yale ya lu mao
Yale omi ale yawa mio.
Okuo yale ya lu mao
Yale omi ale yawa mio.
Agolona aye yale
Yale ya lu mao
Yale omi ale yawa mio.

Cycle of Rebirth, Reincarnation, and Resilience

Yemayá is socially defined as circling bodies in a circular space, the circle of the community. In singing, the community uses the praise song of this round, full mother in order to symbolically embrace living, life, and all existence.

Worshipping performers listen intently to her drummed rhythms, audibly recognized in her repetitive three-beat pattern. For the most part, she is identified with a circle, but the circle projected into space as a spiral.

She is the mother of all, all humans and all divinities. She includes all and she is mindful of all in the community. She teaches worshipers to accept different kinds of energy, as she accepts all of her children and takes care of them individually, irrespective of their different needs, preferences, and behaviors. She is the community's stalwart guardian, and the communal dimension of her performance reiterates the mother within the Yoruba woman principle. Her lesson is community, but she also reinforces the fact that through ceremonial repetition the community learns a social and spiritual lesson.

Yemayá's circle radiates energy both inward and outward, inward around and among those of her faith and her nation, but also outward to uninitiated members as well as to guests. The ceremony then is a source of spiritual energy, an energy that at its best teaches our interconnectedness as communities and as humans on the planet.

The ritual consequence of Yemayá's circling is the reiterated life cycle of Yoruba thought, which is seen in the ongoing life of plants, animals, and humans who are born, grow, and live and then decay and die, only to be reborn.[9] Anyone can be reborn, transformed, and reincarnated in the living dead as ancestor entities and *lwas* of Haitian Vodou or in the dancing *orichas* or *orixás* in Cuban Yoruba or Bahian Candomblé. In these realms, the lesson is history and accumulating knowledge of all that has gone on in the plant, animal, and human dimension over time. This knowledge defies outdating since it is about more than survival. As I have tried to communicate, this kind of knowledge is resilient, ever-relevant inside the body for the dignity of the individual and for the decency within human social behavior.

Contagious Remedies within the Body

Throughout this study, I have not exactly addressed definitions of knowledge, but I have suggested the inclusion of body knowledge and spiritual knowledge within the definition. I am now addressing the categorization of sorts of knowledge and their ranking with regard to standards of worth (Scheffler 1965:5). My position is that physical/cognitive/emotional/spiritual knowledge—embodied through dance behavior—has been greatly belittled and often devalued. When we anthropologists have posited knowing what another, foreign culture/society knows by means of participant observation and analysis, we have been questioned about our conclusions and evaluations because we have often understood these within our own reference frames of belief (e.g., Clifford 1988; cf. Bourdieu 1984). Here I concur with Bennetta Jules-Rosette (1979, 1981 1984; echoing Delmos Jones, 1970) when she notes the difference between "participant observers" and "observing participants." Both are also talking about "native-ness," and this is also important. As an African American from the United States, I quickly sense the commonalities of Diaspora cultures. I am an "easy camper" in the terrains of Haiti, Cuba, and Bahia because of my cultural affinity with African Diaspora communities—regardless of class differences. I am native to much of what I experienced in the silence of performance because of simply growing up in Harlem and the Bronx amid healthy doses of the arts and being happily and eagerly expressive in body ways.

Since being trained as an anthropologist, I consider myself to be an observing participant. It was almost impossible to be the traditional or classic participant observer. As an observing participant, I have placed myself among the dancing worshipers and have participated within the ritual communities that have welcomed me. This welcome and ease of entry have not made me less able to critically analyze what is before me. On the contrary, I have been more sensitive to and more understanding of what is around me and what is going on in my mind and body.

I am offering my anthropology colleagues my experience as a dancer, since it has been just as fruitful a method of gathering data as my social science training has been, probably more. Dancing is a method of perceiving and understanding the human condition; it permits knowing another cultural value system, and this is what I have been practicing for the past few decades.[10] This method of investigation is often more accurate than receiving verbal information from informants. What you learn through dance is silent embodied knowledge; it goes beyond being informed by texts and written information. It is, in fact, the silence of this embodied knowledge—its implications, if you will—that assists you in believing that you know something without its being expressed verbally. This method of knowing through dancing—through the body—compounds and verifies all evidence of how the social order functions and ultimately yields greater credence to the presumption that you know something about other cultures.

In dancing, you are the primary tool of the research experiment/experience; you are the connector between the physical action and the mental activity; you access the consequences of the physical and mental to register an emotional state; and you are the resultant expression of the whole. In dancing or in the kinesthetic world, you rely on a simultaneous multisensory experience that is at once physical, cognitive, and emotional. It is, in fact, the consequence of learning that is not simply learning about something but knowing something—being able to support the fact, person, or subject, risking your own inculcated beliefs, and based on the physical/mental/emotional and often spiritual experience of dancing. In simpler terms, dancing as an investigative method emphasizes the pragmatic approach to knowledge.

As a dance teacher, I have understood this as bodily truth. Now as an anthropologist, I am documenting how, through the medium of dance and its multivocalic nature, a person can become aware of, learn, and eventually know the ideas, attitudes, values, and concerns of a given society (cf. Royce 1977; Hanna 1979). I have used the dances of the African American religious communities in Haiti, Cuba, and Bahia to demonstrate dance behavior as a fundamental form of embodied knowledge. I have traveled to these sites repeatedly to dance. Often I have not been permitted to film sacred dance rituals, and I have not taken many photographs; my notes have been minimal and mostly in the form of daily calendar logs. I have made some extensive journal entries, but I mostly manage word cues for subjects, discoveries, quotes, and questions. I have relied fully on my bodily experiences and their stores of knowledge. I have tested the discoveries from observing participation with more linear and cognitive participant observation, as well as with cultural analysis and interpretation based on library research. I have relied also on interviews, but mostly on living among ritual specialists who dance, sing, and drum abundantly.

As a result of my spiritual journeys and dance/music performance among many dancing worshipers, I have acquired more assuredness and calm, and over time I have also connected with a powerful sense of cultural integrity, in the same ways that I have witnessed some ritual performers grow. When performers gain an acute sense of individual and community awareness, they behave with social responsibility. The dance practices they exhibit are resilient movement sequences that are first used for personal growth and maturation. Personal knowledge is then expanded in repetitive, ceremonial activity toward understanding of the ritual community and its survival. Dancing and music-making worshipers make the principles that guide African American social life visible and audible.

When I think of the main reasons for dance performance in contemporary African American communities, there seems to be an even larger concern, which I call "social medicine." Dance in the African Diaspora is more social medicine than it is an indicator of roles, status, or even ethnicity. This has been proven again and again by the overwhelming response to African-derived dance and music that comes in intercultural and international performances. This consistent response makes clear the most important characteristic of African Diaspora dance: it is contagious, and with contact—whether in ritual settings, secular dance classes, or popular social events—it augments the sensitivities of both performers and observers, first as music and dance, then as healing medicine for life. Through this study I have shared Haitian, Cuban, and Bahian sacred performances because they continue to provide energizing excitement, amazing knowledge, and social medicine for and with community members.[11]

Sacred Performance as Social Medicine in the Twenty-first Century

Social medicine is that which is instrumental for a sense of community cohesiveness or nationhood, something that cures, and something that heals as Cuban Babaluayé or Bahian Omolu does for the entire community.

CHANT FOR BABALUAYÉ
Aberickutu awa leriso, ore Baba
Babaluayé awa leriso, ore Baba

"Espera niña. Before you end, I want you to recognize Ms. Katherine Dunham again! Era ella; it was she who knew this about African people and who put it in print long ago."

"How nice of you to come, Baba. I'm pleased you were listening at this point about social medicine, and I know you were thinking about that connection to Ms. Dunham. Ms. Dunham, one of two grandes dames of African American dance (of course, Pearl Primus is the other) and one of the first American dance anthropologists,[12] knew that Africans preserved their dances with consistency and determination. She was the one who publicly asserted that Africans who came to American shores 'seemed to know innately that their dances were sources of their survival'" (see American Dance Performances video, 1988).

"She always said the importance of Haitian dance was the way it kept communities together, the way folks shared and helped one another, despite differences *and hardship. Dancing is a cure, and you are right, a contagious one. It's ideally so for African peoples everywhere—it's deep, you know."*

"Yes, Baba, divinity is imitated and then incorporated within the dances of the divinities, and healing forces result from their presence in the ceremonies. Dancing divinity stimulates transition, transformation, and transcendence. Initiation and routine participation demand behaviors that affect the lives and lifestyles of believers."

"At the very least, godchildren should try to live in the spiritual life of aché."

"Today, the divinities are challenged and almost lost entirely in the competing images of television, the business world, the images on the streets, and the ogres of war. Children and young people rush for the derived needs of contemporary society—the new name-brand sneakers, the fashionable jeans, a spot on a commercial, the lottery, a chance to be a multimillionaire—and opt out for a job rather than finishing school. Conditions of poverty, poor education, racism, and mounting health hazards subvert children and young adults toward alternative lifestyles that often exclude religion or spiritual practice, especially African practices. International conflicts and historical tensions make contemporary life difficult, to say the least. When exposure to Vodou, Cuban Yoruba, or Candomblé is available, many are hesitant.

"When African religions grow, they do not necessarily grow within African American communities. There are several mushrooming communities of primarily European Americans who dance and sing the ritual liturgies and who engage the linked spiritual practices in Colombia and Puerto Rico, Uruguay and Argentina, as well as in South Miami and northern California. The contagious nature of African dance/music has infected them with commitment to praise performance.

"There are also some pockets of resilient culture, ritual communities that do socialize members with Vodou, Cuban Yoruba, and Candomblé, and other African perspectives. These small religious communities read the symbols in the dances and music as a metaphor for cultural resistance, cultural conservation, and culture change. They convert the present social contingencies into spiritual challenges. They rely on Fon, Yoruba, and Kongo-Angola philosophies and integrate these legacies into their contemporary spiritual lives through dance and music practices, through closer relationships with nature and the contemporary environment, and through strong family-like relations with others. These practitioners strive to inject the political, social, and economic realities of their lives with the moral codes and philosophical precepts of African religious practices. They too are infected with the contagious music and dance of Africa's dancing religions."

CHANT FOR BABALUAYÉ

Baba E, Baba Soroso
Baba E, Baba Soroso
Babaluayé iyan fomode, Baba sire, sire.

"*Aché.*"

"*Aché,* Baba. Modupé."

African religions in the Diaspora offer a path toward social responsibility, in addition to compelling spirituality. They use dance/music as a primary mode of access to involve individuals with their higher consciousness. While promising divine incorporation, or at least divine communication, they create heightened celebratory ceremonies that either propel worshipers into altered spiritual planes of existence or provide opportunities to witness incredible human/spiritual experiences. In either case, there is a humbling result in knowing that such power and vital force exist and can do what they do. At best, worshipers evolve over time; they grow in an individual assuredness about who they are and their place, both in the community and in the cosmos. At worst, things continue as they are. Worshipers' responsibility is expected first in the ritual community, next in the social community, and then throughout life (e.g., the Brazilian Candomblé *terreiros* in the fight against AIDS in Browning 1998).

Through spiritual quests that utilize music and dance and other artistic materials, worshipers pierce the political, the social, and the economic realms with spiritual energy. These worshipers sear a framework of Divinity or Supreme Sacredness onto their lives and thought. Their dancing bodies physically imprint their understanding of the divinities as parts of the Ulitmate Divinity. Worshipers believe their practice can transform potential spiritual energy into positive community membership and positive social behavior. Those who practice their faiths sing, dance, and drum for and about Supreme Saredness.

The *orichas, orixás,* and *lwas* facilitate the conservation of both ancient knowledge and ancient strategies, including the spiritual understanding of Divinity within daily life. Worshipers relinquish doubt in the face of spiritual resilience over centuries; they activate philosophy in subsequent daily behavior. Their beliefs and philosophies change centuries of understandings toward twenty-first-century undertakings: the reintegration of spirituality into the significance of human interaction and social behavior.

In Their Own Words and Those of the Yoruba Oracles

"Remember, though, worshipers dance, sing, and drum divinity in order to express divine presence within, between, and among all planes of existence."

"Yes, but who is whispering to me now?"

"It is I, Oxalá."

> *Orixá ure saul laxé, Orixá ure oberi o ma.*
> *Orixá ure saul laxé, Orixá ure oberi o ma.*
>
> (Blessed *Orixá*, blessed with your powerful life force.
> Blessed *Orixá*, carry me.)

"Oxalá, I know that whether in Haiti, Cuba, Bahia, or the United States, dancing worshipers continue to conserve the whole of Divinity. Ideals that have been charted in the dances, songs, rhythms, and stories of the *lwas, orichas,* and *orixás* do not remain on one plane of existence or within one type of knowledge but rather constantly encompass all interfacing realms of existence and attend to all types of knowledge. While the philosophies are clear and tremendously moral, they do not exclude human mistakes or spiritual misbehavior. Rather, in the reconciliation of moral conduct and both human and suprahuman behavior, Divinity within Haitian, Cuban, and Bahian worship communities is humane. The heritages of African nations are invoked and embodied in danced philosophies that seek for and rely upon the divinities within us all."

"Dancing the powerful axé of the orixás is ultimately a way of communicating just behavior, right consciousness, and wisdom. Our model of Supreme Divinity, which is in all the dances and inside all humans too, is equated with initiated humans who highly value life and the living essence in all things. I, the father/mother of all orixás, Oxalá, expect them to apprentice throughout their lives in the paths that are pointed out by Ifa and the orixás. I do not expect perfection; rather, the goal should be clear, and efforts to that goal should be thoughtful and continuous. Many of my children in the terreiros fuss and argue, and from time to time grievous mistakes have been made. Still, I trust those who respect what they learn in ritual celebration, what you call the embodied knowledge that is learned in dancing, singing, and drumming, and in the end most will fulfill their responsibilities."

"*Axé*, Oxalá and thank you for your words of support and wisdom. *Olorún modupé.*"

"*Axé, axé, axé.*"

In summarizing my study with Gracinha, one of my best friends in the religion, an *iyalorixá* and specialist in the anthropology of religion, I concluded with statements about social and contagious medicine. She gasped as I ended, and she responded with a story, as is the custom in ritual communities. She answered my detailed summary with an *oriki* (like a *patakine*) from the Ifa Oracles in Yoruba worship. It was one that most closely related to what she had just heard and what worshipping performers know bodily from dancing the dances and musics of African religions in the Americas. She told me that in the Axé Opô Afonjá *terreiro* of Bahia, she and her elders retell the story of Orúnmila, guardian of Ifa divining, and how he rectified a situation of change, of difference, of healing:

> Some sickness had occurred, and the people of Orun, the home of the Yoruba divinities, were concerned. Orúnmila said he would remedy the sickness with those who knew about leaves, and he called a meeting of all the *orixás*. Ossein heard about the meeting and, knowing that leaves were his expertise, was eager to go. When he arrived and presented himself, Orúnmila was impressed and asked him to return with his sons for a second meeting. Orúnmila told Ossein that he would choose between his own sons and those of Ossein and he would decide who would be given the responsibility of fixing the sickness among the people. Ossein brought his sons, and Orúnmila selected one of each of their sons to be placed underground for fourteen days. He said when the first of them returned after their fourteen days, he would continue the ritual. They buried Ossein's son, Remedio, and Orúnmila's son, Oferta, and left them underground deep in the forest.
>
> All the animals of the forest were curious as to how the two would make out, and after three days, Rabbit decided to take a look at both of them. He went to Oferta and offered to help by arranging with the ants to have some food delivered. Oferta was thankful for the help and requested a favor. If Rabbit saw Remedio, he was to ask how he was doing and to send Oferta's regards. Rabbit agreed and went to check on Remedio. Remedio thanked Rabbit also for his arrangement with the ants and sent word to Oferta that he, Remedio, was okay. They continued for ten more days and nights.
>
> On the thirteenth day when Rabbit visited Oferta, Oferta had another message for Remedio. He asked whether Remedio preferred to go first, or earlier than him, in order to rejoin Orúnmila and the other *orixás* on the fourteenth day. If Remedio wanted to go first, he, Oferta, would oblige, although Oferta preferred to go first himself. Rabbit took the message and

returned saying that Remedio preferred to wait. In fact, Remedio relayed that it might be a long time before he returned, but he would come eventually. Oferta thanked Rabbit and went to meet with Orúnmila and the other *orixás* on the fourteenth day.

When Oferta entered the meeting, everyone was happy to see him, and Orúnmila accordingly gave his own son, Oferta, permission to treat the people with various leaves (his offerings).

Years went by with no sign of Remedio, until one day a townsperson saw a stranger in the center of town and thinking that he looked familiar, asked if he was Remedio, the son of Ossein. When the stranger answered "Yes," he told everyone that Remedio had finally returned. When Orúnmila heard the news, he told the people the ritual was complete. First sickness is treated with Oferta, offerings, and then with Remedio, remedies or medicine (de Santana Rodrigué: personal communication).

My book, which for me verifies embodied knowledge and its importance as social medicine, was for Yoruba believers simply another version of an Ifa principle within the Oracle *orikis*. This *oriki* showed the ancient wisdom that is present in continuing practices and contemporary thinking within the religions of the African Diaspora. Society and its people are occasionally sick. Different things happen that are outside of the normal happy life—the healthy, balanced life—and when those events happen, the *oriki* suggests that first we make offerings and then partake of available remedies. For Haitian, Cuban, and Bahian worshipers, music and dance performance is the offering, and what they receive in return for their offering is embodied knowledge—the remedy for both ritual and social life.

Postscript

What I have disclosed here is simply a contrast to the stereotypes most nonritual members have of African religions in the Diaspora.[13] Perhaps the only secret I share is the silent or muted lessons of experiential librarians—that is, what is within the dance/music, the embodied knowledge potential of the dancing religions, which I give to all readers. This postscript is directed, however, to my grandchildren and the youngest generation of Diaspora scholars.

Our lives are often so busy that we don't take time to reflect. But every once in a while, we need to take time, to make space and time for reflection. It is wise to reflect on how we have managed our lives up to or until a particular moment. As we go through more of life, we find that it becomes necessary to consciously choose our next path. Life doesn't get much easier, but it does get clearer.

I say these things out of my own ricocheting along life's corridors and out of my reflections as I have wandered through the African Diaspora. I find that I have used what I have learned through dance performance, particularly those dances from African American religions. Within the dances, I have found strong female and male divinities to identify with, to exemplify, and to rely upon. They are my other sisters, mothers, and grandmothers and my other brothers, fathers, and grandfathers, who are always in my corner with support and blessings and who help when everything seems in utter despair. Also I have discovered that I don't have to remember them only in times of stress and upset. They provide me with daily spiritual vitamins and help me to grow in strong social consciousness. I want to remind you of them as you prepare for your reflection time, in anticipation of a new chapter, a new path, and a new door of your wonderful life.

I want you to remember Yemayá in Cuban or Yemanja in Bahian understanding. She loves and supports the growth and progress of all humankind. As this study concludes, in the dancing of Yemayá or Yemanja, worshipping dancers affirm themselves and their community. They make a circle as the ongoing, ever-present motion of life—ebbing and flowing, rocking smoothly and crashing boldly, rotating, revolving, encircling individuals and making a communal group. In dancing Yemayá or Yemanja, beginners learn confidence. Her steps are easy, almost universal, and perfection is gained quickly. Her dance then furrows down and spirals up as the believing performer gains confidence and reaches for more complex rhythms and expanded space. In dancing Yemayá or Yemanja, both males and females access the continuous, undulating configuration of life's ultimate journey. With confidence in the performance, the individual establishes confidence in the self. This is a key gift.

I hope you will remember Ochún or Oxun; her dance is more complex. As we have learned, she is beautiful and smart, happy and loving, strong and shrewd. She has multiple gestures over a steady rhythmic foot pattern. Her dance teaches dancing believers to assert their own strength and ingenuity as they learn to perfect her dance. They keep their feet constant in the pattern, no matter how wide, long, or narrow the space, no matter what other body parts are moving. Dancing Ochún or Oxun teaches us to be spontaneous and intelligently creative on top of a steady secure pattern.

I want you to always remember the female warrior, Oyá or Yansan, and to understand that she teaches courage in the face of disaster and strength and endurance until triumph is attained. She blows away the inconsistencies and separates out the superfluous materials. She drives to the core essences, the most relevant issues for us to attend to, those that determine how lives are lived before we pass over to another realm.

Also, you must remember Haiti's *lwas*. Papa Dambala comforts us in his *yanvalu* of unending endurance. As a righteous snake, he undulates and reincarnates toward life eternal. Papa teaches us patience galore. And the true salt of the earth, Kuzen Zaka, aids our kitchens and our hearts, teaching us generosity and humility; these are two important lessons for the contemporary world. You must remember Ogou (Ogún or Ogun) too. Ogou works constantly, and we are eternally protected as a result. He has battled over centuries and defended both life and the community. Try to remember these male *lwas* for their protection.

Through the life stories of the divinities, we discover their faults and dilemmas, and we learn from these weaknesses. More so, in keeping *lwa, oricha, orixá* dances and their identifying gestures alive, we maintain the library of embodied knowledge and hopefully exhibit the wisdom that it yields in our daily interactions. With genuine spirituality among many human beings, there is hope for the dream of compatibility and neighborliness throughout this world of differences. Ezili, Yemayá, or Yemanja gives unconditional love for each and every human being as beautiful and whole creatures of the universe. Ezili (Freda), Ochún, or Oxun guides as a sensuous lover; she gives security in physical abilities and mental talents. Ezili (Danto), Oyá, or Yansan separates the ordinary from the extraordinary, blasts her fiery percolating energy, and fights to protect her godchildren; she gives us courage to be who we are in the face of seemingly overwhelming odds. Likewise, Ogou, Ogún, or Ogun infuses determination and tenacity into our gait, our pace of living. Kuzen guides our tempers and selfish tendencies and generates our human kindness within exchanges. Lastly, Papa Dambala leads us around the obstacles of challenge in peaceful and accepting demeanors and sets our path along the rainbow.

All divinities of *espri, aché,* or *axé* reside in humans in varying degrees of manifested energy; all push forward our individuality and independence; all demonstrate in their weaknesses and in their strengths our need for social exchange, solidarity, acknowledgment, and love. They can all function as charters for citizenship. In dancing their patterns, we flesh out our dignity and deepen in decency. We can act cooperatively and define a sense of social connectedness with others beyond the ritual community. The values within African religions of the Diaspora result in good individual citizenship and clear social responsibility. Their *lwa, oricha,* and *orixá* dances are social medicine, providing health and well-being, and potential aid and activism.

These dancing *lwas, orichas,* and *orixás* have become my models, and there are many more. These have guided me in gentle and human ways toward being the best that I can be, even though I have not always been successful. They have given me love and especially peace. My wish is to give them to you in performance for many years to come, to celebrate your Oxun beauty and intelligence, your Oyá strength and power, your Ogou protection, your Kuzen generosity, your Dambala humanitarianism, and especially your Ezili, Yemayá, and Yemanja love. Each morning as you look in the mirror, I challenge you to call upon your ancestors for remembrance and acknowledgment, and to use these dances and their concepts to keep you healthy and strong, truly beautiful community citizens.

NOTES

1. Deciphering Diaspora Dances:
Their Origin Nations and Belief Systems

1. I have used the names of my main community contacts and mentors when I have had their permission. I have used pseudonyms when I felt I might put someone in a difficult position by revealing what s/he had told me. My closest associates have shared personal evaluations of contemporary practices and are subject to community pressures, some of which I might not be aware. I have, however, used the proper names of publicly recognized authorities who have assisted my research and who would be difficult to render anonymous.

2. See the orthographic note at the beginning of the book. In chapter 3, I discuss the impact of Kongo-Angola and other African cultures in detail.

3. Throughout this study, I use the term "Cuban Yoruba" for the African American religion of Yoruba descent in Cuba. Cuban Yoruba religion is derived from the many related Yoruba peoples who historically populated what are now the Republic of Benin and Nigeria. While it is tempting to use the alternative names that are common in the literature on African religions in the Americas, *Santería* or *Lucumí*, I chose the term that is used with regard to dance/music traditions, as well as an alternative to the word *Santería*. In Cuba, *Santería* means "the way of the Saints" and usually refers to the syncretism between Catholic saints and African divinities. That is not my major concern. Here I want to underscore a "nation" relationship between this religion and its dance and music practices in Cuba and its related religions, dance/music traditions, and nations within the Diaspora. My reasoning for using "Cuban Yoruba" will become even more clear in thorough discussions throughout chapters 1 and 2 and particularly in chapter 3.

4. I am careful to recount the number of years of practice and study that I gave and received until either the divinities or my godparents and mentors released me to teach

the dances. This is one of the paramount ways that appropriate respect and patience are evaluated in Cuba and the one in which many Cubanophile lovers of the dance fail.

5. I have found more of this particular practice in the Caribbean and Brazil than in niches of Yoruba practice in the United States, although I have not frequented as many U.S. dance/drum ceremonies as I have in the Caribbean and South America.

6. In Cuba the Yoruba term *iawo* includes those who are initiated and can manifest *orichas* and those who are closely tied to the ritual community but do not manifest *orichas*. The latter become special assistants to those who are manifesting within a ceremony.

7. In Cuba, the Yoruba terms *ekedi* and *ebomi,* meaning ritual assistant and fully initiated or senior priest/healer, respectively, are rarely used. Rather, those who have completed one year of specialized training after initiation are referred to as *santeras* or *santeros*.

8. See the orthography note at the beginning of this volume.

9. I use the term "Bahian Candomblé," an umbrella term, throughout this study, but I need to emphasize that I am concentrating on only one nation out of three that make up Candomblé and, again, that Candomblé is only one of Brazil's African religious orientations. "Candomblé," a Bantu word meaning "ritual dance or gathering," generally includes what Brazilians in Bahia call Nago/Ketu, Jêje, and Angola nations and generally focuses on religious rites of the *orixás*. The practice of Nago/Ketu nation, on which I concentrate, became synonymous with a set of religious customs and referenced a form of Yoruba practice in Brazil that traced its origins to the Kingdom of Ketu in present-day Benin and to the sacred lineages of Oshogbo in present-day Nigeria. Most recently in Brazil, the religion's name is contested in favor of "Orixá religion." In order to comparatively discuss and differentiate between two Yoruba *orixá* religions, one in Cuba and one in Brazil, I use "Candomblé" for the Brazilian example. This terminology does not reference the European and African syncretism that exists at first glance. Rather, it reminds us all of the intra-African syncretism that is at its core, as we examine each religion from a Diaspora perspective.

10. Sometimes an entire *terreiro* is referred to as *roça*.

11. The Haitian emphasis has been on sequins and tiny seed beads, which they reserve for their elaborately decorated flags in honor of the *lwas* (Wexler 1997; Polk 1997).

12. When I refer to "the Americas," I am obviously thinking in hemispheric terms, from Canada to Cuba to Chile and not just about the United States. While Cubans, Brazilians, and Haitians consider their identities in national terms first, they profess their hemisphere identity as well. They too are "Americans in the Americas." I also use the term "African Americas" to locate the religious communities of African origins that I examine in the Americas.

13. Certainly in terms of religious culture, Bahia shares closer affinity with Cuba and Haiti than with religious cultures in other South American countries, such as Argentina, Uruguay, Peru, or Bolivia, for example. Current research by and about Afro-Argentines, Afro-Paraguayans, Afro-Bolivians (see Rodriguez in Walker 2001:314–42; Molina and Lopez in Walker 2001:332–47), Afro-Uruguayans (Olivera Chirimini in Walker 2001:256–74), and Afro-Peruvians (see also video *Scattered Africa* by Walker 2002, University of California Extension Media) indicates that Brazil is not alone in retaining niches of African culture in South America. Brazilian Yoruba practice has migrated

south, as I saw recently on a trip to Uruguay and Argentina (2003). Still, Colombia and Venezuela are probably the closest to Brazil in terms of huge African cultural legacies within their South American cultures (e.g., within the contemporary maroon community of Palenque de San Basilio in Colombia and, according to Garcia 2001:284–90, Afro-Venezuelan culture throughout Venezuela). These examples of African cultural roots have been missed or neglected previously in the literature, but work is now being publicly presented; for example, Suzana Baca's Afro-Peruvian songs in recordings and Sheila Walker's insightful comparative Diaspora account (2001:1–44).

14. Unfortunately, I am unable to give an example for each amalgam nation that I distinguish. While I do give three cases (one Fon amalgam and two Yoruba amalgams), I do not give a full analysis of a Kongo-Angola amalgam. I do present a Congo ceremony in Haiti, however (see chapter 6 and Daniel 1997b [video recording]).

2. Body Knowledge at the Crossroads

1. I presented this perspective on a panel of a new organization that helped me forward the ideas within this volume. That organization of scholars was formed in 1999 to discuss and disseminate research from the perspective of the worldwide African Diaspora. The Association for the Study of the Worldwide African Diaspora or ASWAD is currently established in New York City, cosponsored by the Schomburg Center for Research in Black Culture and New York University. Michael Gomez from the History Department of N.Y.U. is the founder and first chairperson. I am indebted to his initiative and to those in that panel audience.

2. A new addition to the field does this in more detail for contemporary African-derived as well as European-derived dancing body parts. In Brenda Dixon Gottschild's latest book, *The Black Dancing Body* (2003), meaning in the dance of U.S. African Americans registers around the multivalent properties of "race."

3. There are many worshipers and participants within the African American religions who are not African American or African. My concern in this book, however, is not with them, but with the nation legacy of African American believers and the deep cultural and historical connections of African American experience in three separate countries within one geocultural area.

4. In Bahia, *familias de santo* are composed of individuals and not so automatically blood kin; in Cuba and especially in Haiti, blood kin is more the norm, with affective and adopted kin included.

5. Ethnobotanist Wade Davis has provided extensive comparative data on poisons in particular among other classifications of Haiti's natural landscape (1988:124–80), but his concern is not with indigenous or African contributions to plant knowledge and that relationship to religion. Lydia Cabrera, although not an ethnobotanist, documents the known classifications of flora on Cuba, as well as African and some indigenous knowledge of these in terms of liturgy and medicine. She relies on African and African American herbalists and healers in mid-twentieth-century Cuba.

6. Voeks does note European knowledge of plants for medicinal purposes. For example, *rue* or *Ruta graveolens* was known in the Greek and Roman era as a "panacea for all ailments" (1997:24). It is now used by Bahians within their lovely lace headscarves to ward off the "evil eye." Mainly, however, Europeans brought basil, garlic, and other food crops.

7. In talking about Haitian dance and the body, I have to add some reference to the pronounced movements of Ibo divinities in Haitian dance; these are integral to any examination of Haitian ritual dance, even though outside the Fon, Yoruba, and Congo discussions here. Ibo peoples come from what is now mainly southeastern Nigeria, and in terms of body-part isolation, they provide some of the most striking movement patterns in a series of Haitian ritual dances. According to Madame Lavinia (often during classes and in other conversations), Ibo movements emphasize the chest with reference to the fierce force of Ibo spirits and their ability to repel even bullets off their chests (Yarborough 1970, 1974, 1982: personal communication). Enslaved Ibos danced these powerful movements to call upon their Ibo ancestors and were often reputed to commit suicide rather than continue in an enslaved condition.

8. I am especially grateful for time and consideration from Haitian master dancer Louinis Louinis who assisted with the listing in Chart 1. His thoughts regarding the emphasized body parts within the dances and my Afrogenic analysis are combined here.

9. Although the Fon divining system, Fa, is not recognized overtly in Haiti, the understanding of destiny and forces that manage and predict the future are basic to Vodou belief (Desmangles 1992:110; also Herskovits 1975 [1937]:152; Bascom 1969 [1991]:3). Like my colleague Gerdès Fleurant, I prefer to be cautious and say that Haiti is relatively unexplored in regard to the divination aspect of its belief system. Fleurant has organized a research center in Haiti (Leocardi Alexander Kenskoff Center) in order to make scholarly examinations of Haitian culture, including Vodou, without the biases that have so denigrated and maligned it in the past. For information, contact him through the Music Department of Wellesley College in Massachusetts.

10. This spot refers to a venerated *orixá* who protects the sacred *axé* of the *terreiro;* his name should not be uttered.

11. The closest activity of this nature that I have seen was on film. Karen Kramer (1981) documented a ceremony that occurs only every twenty or thirty years to celebrate family beliefs in serving the revered ancestors and giving reciprocity for family blessings.

12. For example, in very basic musical analysis, a tonal center of a composition is considered the "1," and four and a half tones above this pitch is called a "fifth" or the number "5." In the sounding of the "1," however, the ear can also hear overtones of at least the "5" or fifth, in addition to other pitches (Christ et al. 1966; "musimatics" in Boatner manuscript, n.d.).

13. "Muscle memory" and the more problematic "blood memory" are terms that modern and contemporary choreographers have used to reference what the body remembers and knows; for example, Graham (1991) and Chipaumire (2000). It is akin to intuitive knowing but is learned physical activity, a deep intramuscular understanding.

3. Days of Remembrance

1. Much of my Cuban fieldwork since 1985 suggests that intra-African syncretism has infiltrated Cuban practices as well, despite declared separations; still, no overarching name for such integration has emerged.

2. In Cuba they say that *Lucumí* is a term that finds its roots among the Oyo Yorubas,

who would often repeat to their neighbors, "*oLucumí*," meaning "my dear friend" (Marinez-Furé, Lázaro Ros and Alfredo Ofarril, Cuba 1986: personal communications).

3. Several scholars have sought to define and describe the process and conditions under which African religious practices solidified and to what extent and how these beliefs shifted or remained after contact with other belief systems in the new environment. For Haiti and Vodou, Leslie Desmangles has used the term "symbiosis" to refer to the parallel formation of Vodou in the shadow of a folk Roman Catholicism (1992). For Cuba, Raul Canizares has used the term "dissimulation," focusing more on the conscious attempt to reconcile African belief and custom in the colonial environment (1999). Melville Herskovits, however, was first to analyze the differentiated processes of culture contact, and his term "syncretism" was first applied to religious interchange between African and European beliefs and the reinterpretations that were required to retain African belief in the midst of Roman Catholic hegemony (1941).

4. All research on the African Diaspora owes tremendous debt to Melville Herskovits and his wife, Frances, for their relentless efforts to document the cultural history of Africans in the Americas at a time when the challenge to their work was monumental. My critique here is meant to build upon what they and others have done in the past, not to tear them down. My particular issue is that their understandings of syncretism have proven to be a major first step in understanding African American religions. Still, an Afrogenic perspective on the research is needed to complete its full analysis, which I present here.

5. Since the 1980s, there has been a public rejection of syncretism with the Catholic saints in Bahia, and thereby more distant relations with the Roman Catholic Church. Still, some *terreiros* continue cordial relations with the Church.

6. In a series of terms, I place the French Creole term first, for Haitian Vodou. Then I place the Cuban term in Spanish with the Yoruba term next (which is used often in Cuba) for Cuban Yoruba religion. I place the Brazilian term next, in Portuguese for Bahian Candomblé, and if there is another language that is relevant, I place that at the very end.

4. Dances of Memory

1. "Creole" is a term that has different meanings according to the time period and nation involved. For most of the early colonial period it referred to Europeans who were born in the Americas: "Creole" meant "white." Later it referred also to Africans born in the Americas; that is, "Creole" could also mean "black." Most often it means exhibiting a mixture of both African and European heritages. For the island of Saint Domingue at that time, it referred to a person of European heritage who was born in the Americas.

2. Dance historian Lynne Emery reminds us that Caribbean dances also included the dances performed as exercise during the Middle Passage and the forced dance in preparation for (or on) the auction block of slavery (1972 [1985]:5–12, 154–66).

3. The Congo minuet that Moreau de St. Méry refers to appears to be the minuet of the French court as it was transformed in the Americas, probably with the influence of some African musicians and the presence of the dancing African body. These two influences did not go unnoticed by European colonials, who performed their own imitations of African imitations of the minuet by the late eighteenth century. It appears from

Moreau de St. Méry's descriptions that this is a likely explanation for the name "Congo minuet" and its differentiation from the "regular minuet" that began an evening dance or party.

4. *Calenda* should not be confused with *kalinda*, a stick-fighting, dance-like activity from Trinidad (Ahye 1978:114–18).

5. The names of surviving African nations of Haiti have varied in the literature and among Haitian Vodou communities because liturgies are structured according to the memory of individual ritual families, and more so according to the immediate interests at hand within a ceremony. Also, linguistic distortions and developments occur routinely among different language speakers in close contact. See Joan Burroughs for a U.S. version of Haitian nation dances (1995:177–80).

6. Ezili is a *lwa* who comes from the region of the Azili River, home to her in Haitian remembrance, as well as to Ochún and Oxun in Yoruba thought. Perhaps because both the Fon and Yoruba peoples shared her in the earliest amalgams of the Americas, she was included in the Haitian Rada (Fon) *nasyon* and not in the Haitian Nago (Yoruba) *nasyon* (Desmangles 1992:10, 141–44, 167; Laguerre 1980; Métraux 1972 [1959]; Mason 1985; Abiodun et al. 1991).

7. Gerdès Fleurant says that *mazone* also references Amazon female warriors (2002: personal communication); my dance informants have never discussed Amazonian warriors so far. He and I agree that this and other Haitian dances have not been fully researched or documented recently.

8. Gerdès Fleurant has reported contemporary performance of the minuet, along with the *carabien* (*carabinien* or *contredanse*) in the recesses of the northern mountains (2002: personal communication). Again, more research is needed for definitive answers.

9. The following chart is a skeletal sketch for a wide variety of Haitian Vodou ceremonies that summon vast numbers of *lwas* and their *nasyons*. Many thanks to Professor Fleurant for his assistance.

10. Some of the following material was originally presented in my dissertation (University of California, Berkeley, 1989). These data have been amplified by additional library research, more Cuban fieldwork, and ongoing investigation. Another version of this section appeared in "Cuban Dance: An Orchard of Creativity" in *Caribbean Dance from Abakuá to Zouk* (in Sloat 2002:23–55).

11. Similar dance performances occur today in areas that the native peoples of Cuba either came from or fled to at the time of European conquest. In Jamaica, the Dominican Republic, and parts of Mexico, similar dance forms are called *areítos, taquis, mitotes,* or *batocos.* Modern and historical descriptions of these dance forms approximate the descriptions the conquistadors gave of indigenous Cuban dance.

12. The contrasts added dynamics and popularity to the dance. Usually, the first repeating sections were considered tranquil and the second two were rather lively, or vice versa. Also, within each repeated section, contrasts between loud and soft (forte and pianissimo) were commonly played.

13. Afrogenic scholarship on colonial history in the Atlantic slave trade period concentrates on the varied specialization and quantity of African continuities that resulted from *cabildo* organization and other high densities of particular African ethnic groups. Certainly, colonizing forces sought out and profited from the economic, intellectual,

and artistic expertise of Africans beyond the sweat of free manual labor (contributors in Walker 2001).

14. The descriptions of dance/music practices that I summarize here are general. It is *very* important to keep in mind that each African practice has a wide range of different dances. What I present in the following discussion is a broad, sweeping comparison in terms of dance styles. What I emphasize are the differences between those that are most obvious as first visual impressions and those distinctions that constitute the most important characteristics within a given dance tradition.

15. I can only speculate as to why a Kongo name, *conga,* has been used for this celebration and for the familiar enthusiasm and vitality of international dancers when performing in a "conga line" elsewhere. It does point to a profound and pervasive Kongo-Angola influence throughout the Americas.

16. In Jamaica, for example, both a dance and a religion of Kongo-Angola origins are called *Cumina.* These exemplify a parallel development of Kongo-Angola dance and Kongo-Angola religion (Bilby and Fu-Kiau 1983).

17. In Brazil, the related and continuing martial art/dance connection is *capoeira* Angola (Rego 1968; Frigerio 1988; Thompson 1983; Almeida 1986; Dosser 1992; Lewis 1992). In Martinique, a similar form is called *damier* (1997, 1999 personal fieldwork observations; Gerstin 1999: personal communication) and in Dunham's reports and choreographies of the 1930s, *ladja* or *la'guia* (Clark and Wilkerson 1978; Aschenbrenner 1980).

18. I do not have intimate information about Kongo-Angola traditions as I do about other traditions in Cuba. I did film a Palo ritual in Cuba, but I found that the interrelationship between Kongo-Angola and Yoruba practices was harder to access as a female researcher. While women participate and are initiated into Kongo-Angola practices, their roles are far less frequent than those of males. Since I relied most heavily on my female friends and contacts during fieldwork, it was more difficult for me to penetrate Kongo-Angola beliefs and practices in Cuba.

I found the same situation in the United States. During my research at the Smithsonian in 1991–92 on Kongo-Angola influence, male practitioners were my only contacts, and they were reticent about my inquiries.

I did experience the syncretism of Angola and Nago/Ketu with some frequency in Bahia, but again I did not observe Angola traditions per se. On the other hand, I have outlined fully my experience of a Congo annual ceremony in Haiti (chapter 6).

19. The term *Arará* included Yorubas when the Yoruba populations were small in Cuba, but the two nations are generally separated.

20. "Hemos observado que en la actualidad las manifestaciones danzarias arará, en la mayoría de los eventos rituals festivos que se celebran en los centros arará, han sido sustituidas por elementos danzarios propios de las festividades de antecedente yoruba e incluso, los informantes señalan que ya las deidades arará 'no se montan' porque no tienen 'caballos,' con excepción del caso de San Lázaro" (Vinueza 1988:56).

21. The concept of Yoruba *caminos* relates to the Vodou concept of *fanmis* of families of *lwas.* Each provides slight variations within the major understanding of an *oricha* or *lwa.* In Bahia, the Yoruba path concept is called *caminhos.*

22. Among the lay population of Cuba and to a lesser extent in Bahia, usage of Catho-

lic saint names alternates evenly with Yoruba *oricha* names. This is a result of linguistic patterns, built up over centuries, that were heavily influenced by the hegemony of both Catholic and colonial influence.

23. For general Cuban dance history, see Daniel 2002a:23–55; for history of Cuban musical complexes, see Alén 1992; for Latin American popular dance history, see Roberts 1979:3–23; for Cuban musical influence in New York, see Figueroa 1994.

5. Praise Dance and Liturgical Orders

1. Other mixtures, which I do not treat here, Umbanda and *caboclo* belief systems, for example, developed other characteristic styles and traditions (e.g., Wafer 1991; Leacock and Leacock 1975).

2. In Haiti, the pathlike dimensions are discussed in terms of a family with slightly differing *lwas*. For example, Ogou Badagri and Ogou Feray distinguish dimensions of the Ogou *fanmi*.

3. Robert Farris Thompson has vividly described African stance as "a get-down" position (1974), and Brenda Dixon Gottschild restates all of Thompson's important African art elements as "the blues aesthetic" of American dance (1996). Also, for at least six decades, since Katherine Dunham's teaching in the 1930s and 1940s, dance teachers in African-derived communities have passed down this dance aesthetic (Ruth Beckford 2000: personal communication; Naima Gwen Lewis 2000: personal communication; Tish Williams 2003: personal communication; see Daniel 1997a).

4. See other "order" comparisons: For dance, see Ortiz 1950:297–350; Carbonero 1980:1–78; Carbonero and Lamerán 1982:21–81; Dailey n.d.:187–93; and Hernandez 1980:21–25. For Haitian religion, see Métraux 1972 [1959]; Deren 1953; Brown 1991, Laguerre 1980; Desmangles 1992; Fleurant 1996. For Cuban Yoruba religion, see Lucas 1948; Carnet 1973; Bascom 1950, 1960, 1969 [1991], 1972, 1980; Sandoval, 1975, 1989; Brown 1991; Brandon 1993; Canizares 1999. For Candomblé, see Bastide 1978; Verger 1957; de Azevedo Santos 1982; Ortiz 1989; Harding 2000; Ligiero 2001; de Santana Rodrigué 2001.

6. Informal Learning with Haitian *Lwas*

1. A "reading" is a consultation or meeting with a ritual specialist (an *oungan* or a *manbo*, an *iyaloricha* or a *babaloricha*, an *iyalorixá* or a *babalorixá*, or a *babalawo*) that focuses on attaining balance within the personal, community, and spiritual aspects of an individual's life. People seek out a ritual specialist when they want to understand something. Often individuals go for readings when they have problems. Worshipers also consult ritual specialists for goodwill and general well-being. For example, some worshipers go for consultations on their birthdays, at the beginning of the calendar year, and on the anniversary of their initiation day. In Haiti, ritual specialists read palms, leaves, and cards as part of their reading process.

2. Compare this order with other Haitian ritual orders, since orders vary tremendously (cf. Dunham 1969:122; Deren 1953:122–30, 250–51; Laguerre 1974; Fleurant 1996). Many researchers note the beginning of a ritual with the Catholic prayers led by the *pre savann*. Among my ritual experiences in Haiti and mainly around Port-au-Prince, this happened only sometimes. My most notable example at the beginning of the ceremony was at the Congo rite I describe in this chapter. Most of the Rada ceremonies I witnessed had

an "intermission" within the middle of the service, where Vodouists recited Catholic prayers and then returned to the Vodou dedication.

3. Translations were made from a video recording of the entire ceremony. I did not have special microphones for the singers, so these words are taken from larger song texts that were difficult to hear. I am indebted, therefore, to my two student dancers and Haitian Kreyol speakers, Joanne Violin and Sara Quessa, who wrestled with several Kreyol translations in this chapter. Their translations were checked for current Kreyol spelling by Leslie Desmangles, as were other words in other chapters. I am particularly grateful for Desmangles's help in preparing the final draft with last-minute checks. Of course, I assume responsibility for transcribing their work and analyzing the content.

4. Since worshipers calculate their age in terms of initiation into the religion rather than chronological age, in this ceremony the "older" *oungans* and *manbos* were often younger than the middle-aged, but "younger," *manbos*.

5. Worshipers often talk of the divinities "mounting" people and "riding" them. When Ezili speaks in this case, as the *lwas* often do, she is referring to instructions given through both the *lwa* presence and through pointed instructions they give for their human horses after reincorporation.

6. I have witnessed other services where there was no apparent appearance of the expected divinities. For example, one was a Bahian ceremony for Oxun in which a small group of practitioners sang songs and gave gifts in front of the altar, but the *orixás* were not obviously present.

7. On April 4, 2003, Vodou was fully recognized by presidential decree as an ancestral religion, an essential element of Haitian national identity (www.haitisupport.gn.apc. org). As a result, exclusion of and discrimination against Vodouists are no longer tolerated by the Haitian state, and all Vodou organizations and temple officials are empowered to register with the Ministry of Culture and Religious Affairs. Plans were made to celebrate in 2004 for the end of the Revolution in August 1804, but now they were celebrating the first declarative defeat over Creole plantation owners and the French by extension.

8. These photographers, filmmakers, and videographers as well—my new friends— were aggressively "in search of their shots." The moment, I guess, was ever so important for them. To participants and to me as observers of their methods, they sometimes seemed rude, insensitive, and potentially disruptive in a religious effort toward spiritual display. They were running here and there, placing themselves at the center of action, between/among, under/over the ritual actors and generally interrupting an extended family event. I believe that John Marshall and Tim Asche have provided fine visual images and fine "in search of the shot" models without the frenzied intrusive clicking of many photographers and videographers.

9. See chapter 4 for Haitian dance history.

10. In the Haitian case, it is a relatively common occurrence that one individual worshiper can manifest several *lwas* in the course of one ceremony.

11. This particular ceremony is known to encourage all consanguine Kongo-Angola relatives to return to this place on Haitian soil for annual ancestor rites. It is also possible that members of the extended families (adopted kin or visitors like my team) would attend the ceremony as well.

12. Perhaps since this was my first view of an entire Congo rite, I was impressed by

their soft and gentle, wise and wonderful performance style. They did not appear like other more demonstrative *lwas;* I thought to call them "ancestor *lwas*" as I began to write about them. I never heard them referred to as *nkisi* either, the term used for Kongo-Angola divinities in Cuba and Bahia (see chapter 4). The term for Congo divinities in Haiti remains *lwas* (Desmangles 2003: personal communication).

13. Excerpts from the Haitian Vodou ceremonies that I have just discussed in this chapter are available on video, *Public Vodun Ceremonies of Haiti* (Daniel 1997b, Insight Media Distributors, New York, 800-233-9910 or 212-721-6316, fax 212-799-5309).

14. The late Malonga Casquelourds was MuKongo from the Republic of the Congo and my colleague in examining Kongo-Angola dance and music practices. He gave me the chant years ago in class, and I have used it to begin most of my studio courses. This song lyric is distinctive in the present section on Haiti, since it comes from the African continent and is not a part of routine Haitian sung ceremony. For me, however, its sentiment was the core of the Haitian ceremony I had just witnessed.

7. Informal Learning with Bahian *Orixás*

1. I am indebted to both Pai Carlinhos, a *babalorixá* from Itaparica, Bahia, who translated the Brazilian versions of Yoruba chants into Portuguese, and to my Smith College Dance Department colleague Augusto Soledade, who then translated Portuguese into English. Both went beyond literal translations to render the full meaning of the chants. The three of us indulged in a fascinating translation process in which we discussed the basic tenets of African American religious practice, as well as the distinctions that have grown up around them.

2. The songs she sang were either from the related *Caboclo* or Candomblé de *Caboclo* or from Candomblé de Angola, here referred to as Angola *nação*. *Caboclo* refers to a syncretic form that focuses on indigenous as well as African beliefs and practices. In this practice, worshipers regularly receive native Indian spirits, which are called *caboclos,* as well as Yoruba and Angola divinities (see Wafer 1991).

3. Yansan is a female *orixá* and, like most of the *orixás,* both men and women may receive her in their bodies. When she arrives, the person who receives her is understood socially as suprahuman female, despite her/his gender. Gender is flexible and shifts according to the divinity in Bahia, just like in Haiti and Cuba.

4. For a complete analysis of the seminal import of this ceremony for Candomblé believers, see de Santana Rodrigué 2001.

8. Formal Learning with Cuban *Orichas*

1. I give special thanks to my mentor and friend, Ana Perez, and her son, Sandi Garcia, both musicians of extraordinary regard from Matanzas who, over the years, have patiently answered many rudimentary and complex questions about the chants for particular *orichas* and the order of the liturgy. I began my inquiries with Ana's mother, who quickly and intuitively made a deep connection with me, but who passed on within three months of our splendid and unusual first dialogue. While Ana and Sandi have helped me to understand what is laid out in this chapter in various forms, they are not responsible for any omissions or possible errors. Also, I received enormous inspiration and encouragement in aligning the chants with the dance steps from Benito Aldamas

in 1987 while in Cárdenas. Later I had very generous assistance from Ernesto El Gato Gatell, a recognized musician from Havana. These four have helped me to organize the following data. I have also had additional checks from Harold Muñiz, Victor Papo Sterling, Tobaji Stewart and Nadhiyr Velez in the United States.

2. Later in this chapter, I give the Spanish phonetic wording for several of the hundreds of Yoruba chants for each *oricha,* as they are performed generally in Cuba (some in Matanzas style, others in Havana style).

3. When considering the order in which the liturgical chants are sung, there is tremendous variation within Cuban Yoruba practice: between regions (e.g., between Havana and Matanzas), between families (e.g., between Chucho's "house" in Matanzas and Dolores's "house" in Matanzas), and even within families (e.g., among the Pedrosos, between uncle and niece who are both *akpwones*). The rule of respect reigns in ritual; that is, practitioners should follow the order and pronunciation of the *akpwon* who happens to be leading the song.

4. There are usually three or more sung chants for each rhythm. The dance steps do not always have codified names, as the drum rhythms generally do. Here Changó gives descriptive dance names according to the gestures, locomotor or traveling pattern, and the visual appearance of the movements. The indicated dance patterns are not meant to teach beginners how to perform but are for knowledgeable dancers who need confirmation of the whole performance practice for a given *oricha.*

5. Recently several Cuban traditional artists have supplied familiar and less-known chants and songs on CDs (see Lázaro Ros collection; the Cigar Box collection; CubaDisc; and www.descarga.com). The chants listed here were accumulated orally and then written out in phonetic Spanish sounds for the Yoruba that was heard; often that is the way Cubans teach the chants. I first started gathering chant lyrics in Cuba during *coro* classes with Lázaro, Cándido, Chucho, and Petit in Havana, in private studies with Ana Perez and Benito Aldamas in Matanzas, and then in courses: Cuban dance in Tijuana, FolkCuba in Cuba, Cuban Summer Workshop at Stanford University, AfroCubanismo in Canada—with both Havana and Matanzas specialists (Minini, Dolores Perez, Amalia Pedrosa, Regino Jimenez, Carnet and Viriál). In 2001, I studied with Ernesto El Gato Gatell in Havana. I have consulted with drummers Sandi Garcia of Matanzas, Tobaji Stewart of Oakland, and Nadhiyr Velez of New York City, as well as with dancer Ernest Barthelemy of Brooklyn regarding the drum rhythms and charts; I am grateful for their corrections and suggestions. I have also consulted John Mason's translations (1992) for Yoruba spelling, but for the most part, the chants are written in the manner in which Cubans would transfer the chant knowledge of the Cuban Yoruba religion today.

6. As an anthropologist (not as a linguist, although I dare to think linguists would agree), I am keenly aware of the misunderstanding that scholars have either initiated or perpetuated by using terms such as "goddesses" and "gods." In trying to explain African worship practices to African Americans, Europeans, and European Americans, these terms set up unnecessary red flags and inhibit cross-cultural understanding. As stated earlier, I prefer the terms "divinities," "spiritual essences," or "suprahuman beings," although I too have used the terms "deities" and "goddesses" in the past.

7. If we had wanted ballet, we could have had that too. See the range and thoroughness of Cuban dance training in Cashion 1980.

8. Unlike the first Colorado Festival classes, more than dance movement was empha-sized. I shared my teaching (salary and classes) with Michael Spiro so that the music complement was more securely in place and so that dance students could experience the total music/dance tradition within classes of Cuban Yoruba performance practice. In this session, Spiro developed a version of playing the three *batá* rhythms among trap drums by himself. Despite the extreme difference in timbre between trap drums and *batás,* this proved to be effective in providing precise rhythmic support to the dance class environment when three knowledgeable drummers were not available or afford-able.

9. This affected the quality of ritual performances as well. Until Cuban dancers and dance teachers arrived in great numbers in the United States, ritual congregations could not always perform the different dances of *wemileres* to perfection.

9. The Dancing Body and Embodied Wisdom

1. Some of the following data are published in a slightly different form in my chapter in Walker 2001:352–61. For visual examples of Oyá, see two performances by Folklórico de Oriente and Folklórico Nacional in the video *Cuban Dance Examples* (Insight Media, New York City).

2. *Chachaolokofún* rhythm in Yoruba *batá* drumming should not be confused with *chachachá* rhythm of popular Cuban dance. The three running steps (RLR) or cha-cha-cha in popular dance, however, do resonate with Oyá's three running steps to the side in her first basic foot pattern.

3. The ceremony for women is short—two nights and three days; it is inexpensive as ceremonies go—$150; and it is accessible because so many *babalawos* are willing to perform it. The most blatant evidence of this alarming practice for both women and men results in little or no improved behavior after initiation; that is, no change in the person or her/his relations can be noticed. For one person whom I knew personally, there was no change; he continued to be a drunkard, although a fantastic drummer. In fact, the day he announced his new status as a *babalawo* to me, he was hysterically drunk. Neighbors criticized him behind his back because he was still a "wheeler-dealer" after his *babalawo* initiation.

4. These Yoruba models have parallel *lwas* who embody woman as self-honoring lover—Ezili Freda, ferocious mother—Ezili Dantor, and her water form, called La Siren (see Brown 1991; Cosentino 1995; Deren 1983; Laguerre 1989).

5. Fon concepts of womanhood in Haiti echo especially in Brown's (1991) activities with Mama Lola and in Deren's (1983) revelations about Ezili.

6. See chapter 8, Ochún's *tratao.* See chapter 8, Changó's *tratao.*

7. This Yoruba model has shared models among Haitian *lwas* between Ogou, the ultimate warrior and protector, and Agwé, the most fitting husband and procreator (see Brown 1989:65–89; and Deren 1983:119–37).

8. In Haiti, it is possible to analyze the dance practice for Dambala in a similar way; see Fleurant 1996 and Burroughs 1995. See chapter 8, Changó's *tratao.*

9. Parallels can be made for life cycles in both Fon and Kongo-Angola thought (cf. Deren 1983:114–19 and Thompson and Cornet 1981, respectively).

10. I first formally presented these ideas in a class lecture, "Embodiment of the Word in Caribbean Ritual" (1990), in the Smith College Department of Anthropology, as an

invited guest of Frederique Marglin. This presentation became a paper at the American Anthropological Association meetings in December 1991: "Embodied Knowledge within the Sacred Choreographies of the Orishas." I have been discussing this with students and colleagues ever since.

11. Popular music/dance is social medicine, which is also often dismissed, and can also be highly ritualized dance. Hip-hop culture, for example, contains a variant of Africanity in its contemporary B-boy and B-girl dancing (male and female break dancing or "breaking"). Like the secular or popular dance *rumba,* hip-hop is also often called "free form" and "improvisational." Yet hip-hop dance culture has set rules, guidelines, and boundaries. Within the rules, spirituality counts. Sensing, modeling, and giving extraordinary "spirit" are adjudicated and acknowledged. That is what feeds the individual and creates the potential for social citizenry either within the hip-hop circle or within the wider community. The music and the dance are social healing for community members.

12. The three American founders of the subdiscipline of dance in anthropology were Gertrude Kurath, Katherine Dunham, and Pearl Primus. Several other pioneers carried the discipline forward: Joann Kealiinohomoku, Drid Williams, Adrienne Kaeppler, and Anya Royce (see Daniel 2004: 347–56).

13. This postscript was originally presented in another version for the Women of Color Leadership Network at the University of Massachusetts, Amherst, April 19, 2001, as a speech for women graduates, entitled "A Woman's Trilogy for Proper Social Citizenry." I suppose other divinities can be used, Elegba or Oxalá, for example. Those would initiate slightly different characteristics and stories; however, they would surround and display the same values and commitments.

BIBLIOGRAPHY

Abimbola, Wande, ed. 1975. Yoruba Oral Tradition; Selections from the papers presented at the Seminar on Yoruba Oral Traditions: Poetry in Music, Dance, and Drama. Ile-Ife, Nigeria: Department of African Languages and Literatures, University of Ife.

———, ed..1977. Ifá Divination Poetry, translated, edited and with an introduction by Wande Abimbola. New York: NOK Publishers.

Abiodun, Roland, Henry Drewal, and John Pemberton III. 1991. The Yoruba Artist: New Theoretical Perspectives on African Arts. Washington: Smithsonian Institution Press.

Adefunmi I, Oba Osejiman Adelabu. 1982. Olorisha: A Guide Book into Yoruba Religion. Oyotunji Village, S.C.: Great Benin Books.

Ahye, Molly. 1978. Golden Heritage: Dances: The Dance in Trinidad and Tobago. Petit Valley, Trinidad: Heritage Cultures.

———. 1983. Cradle of Caribbean Dance. Petit Valley, Trinidad: Heritage Cultures.

Ajayi, Omofolabo. 1983. Dance as communication Symbol of Orisa Religion. In Proceedings of 2nd World Congress of Orisa Tradition and Culture, Bahia, Brazil.

———. 1998. Yoruba Dance: The Semiotics of Movement and Body Attitude in a Nigerian Culture. Trenton, N.J.: Africa World Press.

Alan, Ray, and Lois Wilcken, eds. 1998. Island Sounds in the Global City: Caribbean Popular Music and Identity in New York. New York: New York Folklore Society, Institute for Studies in American Music, Brooklyn College.

Alén, Olavo. 1987. La música de las sociedades de Tumba Francesa. Havana: Casa de las Américas.

———. 1992. Géneros musicales de Cuba: De lo Afrocubano a la Salsa. San Juan: Editorial Cubanacán.

Almeida, Bira. 1986. Capoeira: A Brazilian Art Form. Richmond, Calif.: North Atlantic Books.

Alvarez, Lizette. 1997. A Once-Hidden Faith Leaps Out into the Open. New York Times, Metro Section, B1:3–4.

Amira, John, and Steven Cornelius. 1992. The Music of Santería; Traditional Rhythms of the Batá. Crown Point, IN: West Cliffs Media Co.

Appleby, David. 1983. The Music of Brazil. Austin: University of Texas Press.

Aschenbrenner, Joyce. 1980. Katherine Dunham: Reflections on the Social and Political Contexts of Afro-American Dance. New York: CORD.

Asombang, Raymond. 1999. Sacred Centers and Urbanization in West Central Africa. *In* Beyond Chiefdoms: Pathways to Complexity in Africa. Susan McIntosh, ed. Cambridge: Cambridge University Press.

Atkinson, Pansye. 1993. Brown vs. Topeka: An African American's View: Desegregation and Mis-education. Chicago: African American Images.

Averill, Gage. 1997. A Day for the Hunter, a Day for the Prey: Popular Music and Power in Haiti. Chicago: University of Chicago Press.

Babayemi, S. O. 1980. Egungun among the Oyo Yoruba. Ibadan.

Balandier, Georges. 1968. Daily Life in the Kingdom of the Kongo: From the Sixteen to Eighteenth Century. Helen Weaver, trans. New York: The World Publishing Co.

Barnes, Sandra T., ed. 1989. Africa's Ogun: Old World and New. Bloomington: Indiana University Press.

Barnet, Miguel. 1961. La religión de los Yorubas y sus dioses. *In* Actos de folklore. Havana: Instituto de Etnología y Folklore, enero.

Bascom, William. 1950. The Focus of Cuban Santería. Southwestern Journal of Anthropology 6 (Spring) (1):64–68.

———. 1951. Two Forms of Afro-Cuban Divination. *In* Acculturation in the Americas. Sol Tax, ed. Proceedings of the 29th International Congress of Americanists, 2:169–79.

———. 1960. Yoruba Concepts of Soul. *In* Selected Papers of the 5th International Congress of Anthropological and Ethnological Sciences. Anthony Wallace, ed. Philadelphia: University of Pennsylvania Press. 401–10.

———. 1991 (1969). Ifa Divination. Communication between Gods and Men in West Africa. Bloomington: Indiana University Press.

———. 1972. Shango in the New World. Occasional Publication of the African and Afro-American Research Institute, no. 4. Austin: University of Texas.

———. 1980. Sixteen Cowries: Yoruba Divination from Africa to the New World. Bloomington: Indiana University Press.

Bastide, Roger. 1978. The African Religions of Brazil. Translated by Helen Sebba. Baltimore: Johns Hopkins University Press.

Bebey, Francis. 1975. African Music: A People's Art. Josephine Bennett, trans. New York: L. Hill.

Behague, Gerard, ed. 1994. Music and Black Ethnicity: The Caribbean and South America. New Brunswick, N.J.: Transaction.

Behrendt, Stephen D. 1997. The Annual Volume and Regional Distribution of the British Slave Trade, 1780–1807. Journal of African History 38(2):187–211.

ben-Jochannan, Yosef. 1991. New Dimensions in African History: The London lectures of Dr. Yosef ben-Jochannan and Dr. John Hendrik Clarke, edited with introduction by John Henrik Clarke. Trenton, N.J.: Africa World Press.

Berkman, Joyce Avrech. 1994. To Feel It Viscerally: Empathetic Knowing. Unpublished paper presented at Vermont Council on the Humanities, November.

Bermudez, Armando Andres. 1967. Notas para la historia del espiritismo en Cuba. Etnologia y Folklore 4:5–22.

Bernal, Martin. 1987. Black Athena: The Afro-Asiatic Roots of Classical Civilization. 2 vols. New Brunswick, N.J.: Rutgers University Press.

Biebuyck, David. 1973. Lega Culture: Art, Initiation, and Moral Philosophy among a Central African People. Berkeley: University of California Press.

Bilby, Kenneth, and Bunseki Fu-Kiau. 1983. Kumina: A Kongo-based Tradition in the New World. Brussels: Centre d'Études et de Documentation Africaines.

Blier, Suzanne. 1980. Africa's Cross River Art of the Nigerian Cameroon Border Redefined. New York: L. Kahan Gallery, African Arts. 3–26.

————. 1995. African Vodun: Art, Psychology, and Power. Chicago: University of Chicago Press.

Bloch, Maurice. 1974. Symbols, Songs, Dance, and Features of Articulation: Is Religion an Extreme Form of Authority? Archives Européennes de Sociologie 15:51–81.

Blum, Odette. 1973. Dance in Ghana. New York: Dance Perspectives Foundation.

Boatner, Clifford. n.d. Music Theory. Quincy, Massachusetts, manuscript.

Boggeman, Sally, Tom Hoerr, and Cristine Wallach, eds. 1996. Succeeding with Multiple Intelligences: Teaching through the Personal Intelligences. St. Louis: New City School.

Bolívar, Natalia. 1990. Los orichas en Cuba. Havana: Ediciones Union.

————. 1994, 1996. Unpublished lectures, summer. Banff, Canada: Banff Centre for the Arts.

Bourdieu, Pierre. 1984. Distinction: A Social Critique of the Judgment of Taste. Translation of original, 1979, by Richard Nice. Cambridge: Harvard University Press (Habitus and the Space of Life-Styles). 169–225.

Bourguignon, Erika. 1968. Trance Dance. New York: Dance Perspectives Foundation.

————. 1976. Possession. San Francisco: Chandler and Sharp.

Brandon, George. 1993. Santería from Africa to the New World: The Dead Sell Memories. Bloomington: Indiana University Press.

Brewer, Geovanni, producer, writer, translator. 1988. Bahia: Africa in the Americas [video recording]. Berkeley: University of California Extension Media Center.

Brown, Diane. 1986. Umbanda: Religion and Politics in Urban Brazil. Ann Arbor: UMI Research Press.

Brown, Karen McCarthy. 1989. Systematic Remembering, Systematic Forgetting: Ogou in Haiti. In Africa's Ogun. Sandra Barnes, ed. Bloomington: Indiana University Press. 65–89.

————. 1991. Mama Lola: A Voodoo Priestess in Brooklyn. Berkeley: University of California Press.

Browning, Barbara. 1995. Samba: Resistance in Motion. Bloomington: Indiana University Press.

————. 1998. Infectious Rhythm: Metaphors of Contagion and the Spread of Afro-American Culture. New York: Rutledge.

Burroughs, Joan. 1995. Haitian Ceremonial Dance on the Stage: The Contextual Transference and Transformation of Yanvalou. Ph.D. dissertation, New York University.

Cabrera, Lydia. 1940. Cuentos negros de Cuba. Havana: La Verónica.

———. 1957. Anagó: vocabulario Lucumí. Havana: Ediciones C.R.

———. 1970 (1958). La sociedad secreta Abakuá. Miami: Ediciones C.R.

———. 1974. Yemaya y Ochun. New York: Colección del Chichereku.

———. 1983 (1954). El monte. Miami: Colección del Chichereku.

———. 1986 (1979). Reglas de congo, Palo Monte Mayombe. Miami: Ediciones Universal.

Canizares, Raul. 1999. Cuban Santería. Rochester, Vt.: Destiny Books.

Carbonero, Graciela Chao. 1980. Bailes Yorubas de Cuba. Havana: Editorial Pueblo y Educación.

Carbonero, Graciela Chao, and Sara Lamerán. 1982. Folklore Cubano I, II, III, IV. Havana: Editorial Pueblo y Educación.

Carneiro, Edison. 1940. The Structure of African Cults in Bahia. Journal of American Folklore 53:271–78.

———. 1978. Candomblés a Bahia. Rio de Janeiro: Civilização Brasileira.

Carnet, Carlos. 1973. Lucumí. Religión de los Yorubas en Cuba. Miami: AIP Publications Center.

Carnoy, Martin. 1973. Education as Cultural Imperialism. New York: D. McKay Co.

Carpentier, Alejo. 1979 (1946). La música en Cuba. Mexico: Fondo de Cultura Económica.

Cashion, Susan. 1980. Educating the Dancer in Cuba. In Dance, Current Selected Research, Lynette Y. Overby and James H. Humphrey, eds. New York: AMS Press, vol. 1, pp. 165–85.

———. 1983. Dance Ritual and Cultural Values in a Mexican Village; Festival of Santo Santiago. Ph.D. dissertation, Ann Arbor: University Microfilms.

Chernoff, John Miller. 1979. African Rhythm and African Sensibility: Aesthetics and Social Action in African Musical Idioms. Chicago: University of Chicago Press.

Chipaumire, Nora. 2000. Danza contemporánea: African Influences and the Impact of Political Ideology on Cuban Modern Dance, master's thesis, Mills College.

Chomsky, Noam. 1999. Latin America: From Colonization to Globalization; Noam Chomsky in Conversation with Heinz Dieterich. Melbourne: Ocean Press.

Christ, William et al. 1966. Materials and Structure of Music. Englewood Cliffs, New Jersey: Prentice-Hall.

Christophe, Henning, and Hans Oberlander. 1996. Voodoo: Secret Power in Africa. Cologne: Taschen.

Chua, Daniel. 1999. Absolute Music and the Construction of Meaning. New York: Cambridge University Press.

Clark, Veve, and Margaret Wilkerson, eds. 1978. Kaiso! Katherine Dunham, an Anthology of Writings. Berkeley: Institute for the Study of Change, CCEW Women's Center, University of California.

Clifford, James. 1988. The Predicament of Culture: Twentieth-Century Ethnography, Literature, and Art. Cambridge: Harvard University Press.

Connerton, Paul. 1977. How Societies Remember. New York: Cambridge University Press.

Cosentino, Donald, ed. 1995. Sacred Arts of Haitian Vodou. Los Angeles: UCLA Fowler Museum of Cultural History.

298

Courlander, Harold. 1939. Haiti Singing. Chapel Hill: University of North Carolina Press.

———. 1955. The Loa of Haiti. *In* Miscelanea de estudios dedicados a Fernando Ortiz por sus discípulos, colegas y amigos. Havana.

———. 1973. The Drum and the Hoe. Berkeley: University of California Press.

Cowan, Jane. 1990. Dance and the Body Politic in Northern Greece. Princeton: Princeton University Press.

Crowell, Nathaniel. 2002. What Is Congo? *In* Caribbean Dance from Abakuá to Zouk. Susanna Sloat, ed. Gainesville: University of Florida Press. 11–20.

Crowley, Daniel J. 1984. African Myth and Black Reality in Bahian Carnaval. Los Angeles: Museum of Cultural History, UCLA.

Curtin, Phillip. 1969. The Atlantic Slave Trade: A Census. Madison: University of Wisconsin Press.

Dailey, Maurice Cecil. n.d. (c. 1950). Spiritism and the Christian Faith. Master's thesis, Union Theological Seminary, Department of Missions, Matanzas, Cuba.

Daniel, Yvonne. 1980. The Potency of Dance: A Haitian Examination. Black Scholar 11(8):61–73.

———. 1989. The Ethnography of Rumba: Dance and Social Change in Contemporary Cuba. Ph.D. dissertation, University of California, Berkeley.

———. 1992a. Cuban Dance Examples: A Glimpse of Cuba Through Dance [video recording]. New York: Insight Media.

———. 1992b. Cuban Rumba [video recording]. New York: Insight Media.

———. 1995. Rumba: Dance and Social Change in Contemporary Cuba. Bloomington: Indiana University Press.

———. 1996. Dance in Tourist Settings: Authenticity and Creativity. Annals of Tourism Research 23(4):780–97.

———. 1997a. In the Company of African American Dancers. In Dance Women: Living Legends. New York: Brooklyn Academy of Music (BAM), 6–10.

———. 1997b. Public Vodun Ceremonies of Haiti [video recording]. New York: Insight Media Distributors.

———. 2001. Embodied Knowledge in African American Dance Performance. *In* African Roots/American Cultures: Africa in the Creation of the Americas. Sheila Walker, ed. Lanham, Md.: Rowman and Littlefield. 352–61.

———. 2002a. Cuban Dance: An Orchard of Caribbean Creativity. *In* Caribbean Dance from Abakuá to Zouk. Susanna Sloat, ed. Gainesville: University Press of Florida. 23–55.

———. 2002b. Yet Another Praisesong [review of the Big Drum Ritual of Carriacou]. Canadian Journal of Latin American and Caribbean Studies 27(53):179–82.

———. 2004. Dance in the African Diaspora. In Encyclopedia of Diasporas: Immigrant and Refugee Cultures Around the World. C. Ember, M. Ember, and I. Skuggard, eds. New York: Springer Science and Business Media. vol.1, pp. 347–56.

Davis, Wade. 1985. Serpent and the Rainbow. New York: Simon and Schuster.

———. 1988. Passage into Darkness. Chapel Hill: University of North Carolina.

Dayan, Joan. 1995. Haiti, History, and the Gods. Berkeley: University of California Press.

de Andrade, Marilia, and Katia Canton. 1996. Overview of Dance Research and Publications in Brazil. Dance Research Journal 28(2):114–22.

de Azevedo Santos, Maria Stela. 1982. Meu tempo é agora. Curitiba: P. Centru.

Denbow, James. 1999. Heart and Soul: Glimpses of Ideology and Cosmology in the Iconography of Tombstones from the Loango Coast of Central Africa. Journal of American Folklore 112 (445):404–23.

Deren, Maya. 1953. Divine Horsemen: The Voodoo Gods of Haiti. New York: Thames and Hudson.

———. 1983. Divine Horsemen: The Living Gods of Haiti. New Paltz, N.Y.: McPherson and Company.

de Santana Rodrigué, Maria das Graça. 2001. Ori Apere O: O ritual das aguas de Oxalá. Salvador da Bahia: Selo Negro Ediçoes.

Deschamps Chapeaux, Pedro. 1971. El negro en la economía habanera del siglo XIX. Havana: Premio Unión de Escritores y Artistas de Cuba.

Desmangles, Leslie. 1992. Faces of the Gods. Chapel Hill: University of North Carolina Press.

de Souza, Martine. 2000. Regard sur Ouidah; A Bit of History. Ouidah, Benin: B.3.P.

DjeDje, Jacqueline Cogdell, ed. 1999. Turn Up the Volume! A Celebration of African Music. Los Angeles: UCLA Fowler Museum of Cultural History.

Dodson, Howard. 2001. The Transatlantic Slave Trade and the Making of the Modern World. In African Roots/American Cultures: Africa in the Creation of the Americas. Sheila Walker, ed. Lanham, Md.: Rowman and Littlefield. 118–22.

Dosser, Kenneth. 1992. Capoeira Angola: Dancing between Two Worlds. Afro-Hispanic Review 11(1–3):5–10.

Drewal, Henry, John Pemberton, III, and Roland Abiodun. 1989. Yoruba: Centuries of African Art and Thought. New York: Center for African Art.

Drewal, Henry, and Margaret Drewal. 1983. Gelede. Bloomington: Indiana University Press.

Drewal, Margaret Thompson. 1975. Symbols of Possession: A Study of Movement and Regalia in an Anago-Yoruba Ceremony. Dance Research Journal 7(2):15–24.

———. 1994. Yoruba Ritual and Thought: Play, Performance, Agency. Bloomington: Indiana University Press.

Du Bois, W. E. B. 1969. The Souls of Black Folk. New York: New American Library.

Dunham, Katherine. 1946. Journey to Accompong. New York: H. Holt.

———. 1947. The Dances of Haiti. Acta Anthropologica 2(4):1–64.

———. 1969. Island Possessed. Garden City, N.Y.: Doubleday.

———. 1983. Dances of Haiti. Los Angeles: Center for Afro-American Studies, UCLA.

Edwards, Gary, and John Mason. 1986. Black Gods: Orisa Studies in the New World. Brooklyn: Yoruba Theological Archministry.

Elbein dos Santos, Juana. 1986. Os Nágo e a morte: Páde, ásésé e o culto Égun na Bahia. Trans. from French. Rio de Janeiro: Coleçao Mestrado. 4.

———. 1998. Mestre Didi. Miami Beach: Bass Museum of Art.

Eltis, David, Stephen Behrendt, David Richardson, and Herbert Klein. 1999. The Trans-Atlantic Slave Trade: A Database on CD-ROM [electronic resource], http://www.cup.org/Eltis.html.

Eltis, David, and David Richardson. 1997. "Numbers Game" and Routes to Slavery. Slavery and Abolition 18(1):1–15.

———. 1997. West Africa and the Transatlantic Slave Trade: New Evidence of Long-Run Trends. Slavery and Abolition 18(1):16–35.

Emery, Lynne Fauley. 1985 (1972). Black Dance in the United States from 1619 to 1970. Palo Alto: National Press Books.

Feijo, Samuel. 1986. Mitología cubana. Havana: Editorial Letras Cubanas.

Feld, Steven. 1981. Sound and Sentiment. Philadelphia: University of Pennsylvania Press.

Fernandez, James W. 1965. Symbolic Consensus in a Fang Reformative Cult. American Anthropologist 67:902–27.

———. 1976. The Mission of Metaphor in Expressive Culture. Current Anthropology (June 15) (2):119–45.

Figueroa, Frank. 1994. Encyclopedia of Latin American Music in New York. St. Petersburg, Florida: Pillar Publications.

Fleming, Mali Michelle. 1995. Santería: Magic or Religion? Hispanic Magazine, 32–34.

Fleurant, Gerdès. 1996. Dancing Spirits: Rhythms and Rituals of Haitian Vodun, the Rada Rite. Westport, Conn.: Greenwood Press.

Fontenot, Wonda L. 1994. Secret Doors: Ethnomedicine of African Americans. Westport, Conn.: Bergin and Garvey.

Fouchard, Jean. 1988. La méringué, danse nationale d'Haiti. Port-au-Prince: Editions Henri Deschamps.

Freire, Paulo. 1970. Pedagogy of the Oppressed. Myra Bergman Ramos, trans. New York: Seabury Press.

Freyre, Gilberto. 1946. Masters and Slaves: A Study in the Development of Brazilian Evolution. Samuel Putnam, trans. New York: Knopf.

Friedman, Robert. 1982. Making an Abstract World Concrete: Knowledge, Competence, and Structural Dimensions of Performance among Bata Drummers in Santeria. Ph.D. dissertation, Indiana University.

Frigerio, Alejandro. 1988. Capoeira Angola, More than a Martial Art. Karate/Kung Fu Illustrated 19(8):38–42.

Fu-Kiau, Bunseki. 1980. African Book without Title. Cambridge: Fu-Kiau.

Funezalida, Edmundo. 1983. Dance as a Cultural Expression in an Interdependent World. Asociación Nacional de Grupos Folklóricos 6(1):24–27.

Galembo, Phyllis, et al. 1993. Divine Inspiration: From Benin to Bahia. Albuquerque: University of New Mexico Press.

Gardener, Howard. 1999. Intelligence Reframed: Multiple Intelligences for the 21st Century. New York: Basic Books.

Gardener, Howard, and Thomas Hatch. 1988. Multiple Intelligences Go to School: Educational Implications of the Theory of Multiple Intelligences. Educational Researcher 18(8):4–10.

Gerstin, Julian. 1998. Interaction and Improvisation between Dancers and Drummers in Martinican Bélè. Black Music Research Journal 18(1–2):121–65.

———. 2000. Musical Revivals and Social Movements in Contemporary Martinique: Ideology, Identity, and Ambiguity. In The African Diaspora: A Musical Perspective. Ingrid Monson, ed. Garland Press. 295–328.

Gilroy, Paul. 1993. The Black Atlantic: Modernity and Double Consciousness. Cambridge: Harvard University Press.

Glazier, Stephen D. 1991. Marchin' the Pilgrims Home: A Study of the Spiritual Baptists of Trinidad. Salem, Wis.: Sheffield Publishing Co.

Gleason, Judith. 1987. Oya, in Praise of the Goddess. Boston: Shambhala Publications.

Goins, Margaretta Bobo. 1971–72. African Retentions in the Dance of the Americas. *In* Dance Research Monograph 1, 1971–72. P. Rowe and E. Stodelle, eds. New York: CORD. 207–29.

Gonzalez-Wippler, Migene. 1973. Santería: African Magic in Latin America. New York: Julian Press.

———. 1989. Santería: The Religion; A Legacy of Faith, Rites, and Magic. New York: Harmony Books.

———. 1992. The Santería Experience: A Journey into the Miraculous. St. Paul, Minn.: Llewellyn Publications.

Gottschild, Brenda Dixon. 1996. Digging the Africanist Presence in American Performance: Dance and Other Contexts. Westport, Conn.: Praeger.

———. 2003. The Black Dancing Body: A Geography from Coon to Cool. New York: Palgrave Macmillan.

Graburn, Nelson, ed. 1976. Ethnic and Tourist Arts: Cultural Expressions from the Fourth World. Berkeley: University of California Press.

———. 1989. The Sacred Journey. *In* Hosts and Guests. Valene Smith, ed. Philadelphia: University of Pennsylvania Press. 21–36.

Graham, Martha. 1991. Blood Memory. New York: Washington Square.

Greenberg, Kim. 1996. Transformations: The Teaching of Afro-Cuban Sacred Dance. Master's thesis, Teachers College, Columbia University. 38–57.

Griaule, Marcel. 1965 (1948). Conversations with Ogotemmêli: An Introduction to Dogon Religious Ideas. London: Oxford University Press.

Guerra, Ramiro. 1990. Teatralización del folklore y otros ensayos. Havana: Editorial Letras Cubanas.

Guillermoprieto, Alma. 1990. Samba. New York: Knopf.

Gutheil, Emil A., Jay T. Wright, Vincent R. Fisichelli, Frances Paperte, and Alexander Capurso. 1952. Music and Your Emotions. New York: Liveright Publishing Company.

Halbwachs, Maurice. 1979. The Collective Memory. Francis and Vida Ditter, trans. New York: Harper and Row.

Hanna, Judith. 1979. To Dance Is Human. Austin: University of Texas Press.

Harber, Francis. 1980. The Gospel according to Allan Kardec. Brooklyn: Theo Gaus.

Harding, Rachel. 2000. A Refuge in Thunder: Candomblé and Alternative Spaces of Blackness. Bloomington: Indiana University Press.

Harris, Jessica B. 1988. Iron Pots and Wooden Spoons: Africa's Gifts to New World Cooking. New York: Atheneum.

———. 1993. The Welcome Table: African-American Heritage Cooking. New York: Simon and Schuster.

———. 2001. Same Boat, Different Stops: An African Atlantic Culinary Journey. *In* African Roots/American Cultures: Africa in the Creation of the Americas. Sheila Walker, ed. Lanham, Md.: Rowman and Littlefield. 169–82.

Harris, Joseph. 2001. The African Diaspora in World History and Politics. *In* African Roots/American Cultures: Africa in the Creation of the Americas. Sheila Walker, ed. Lanham, Md.: Rowman and Littlefield. 104–17.

Harrison, Faye, ed. 1991. Decolonizing Anthropology: Moving Further toward an Anthropology for Liberation. Washington, D.C.: Association of Black Anthropologists, American Anthropological Association.

Hazzard-Gordon, Katrina. 1990. Jookin': The Rise of Social Dance Formations in African-American Culture. Philadelphia: Temple University Press.

Hebb, Donald O. 1949. Organization of Behavior: A Neuropsychological Theory. New York: Wiley Publishing.

Hebdige, Dick. 1987. Cut 'n' Mix: Culture, Identity, and Caribbean Music. London: Methuen.

Hernandez, María del Carmen. 1980. Historia de la danza en Cuba. Havana: Editorial Pueblo y Educación.

Herskovits, Frances, ed. 1966. New World Negro. Bloomington: Indiana University Press.

Herskovits, Melville. 1975 (1937). Life in a Haitian Valley. New York: Octagon Books.

———. 1938. Dahomey, An Ancient West African Kingdom. New York: J. J. Augustin.

———. 1941. The Myth of the Negro Past. New York: Harper Brothers.

Herskovits, Melville, and Francis Herskovits. 1933. Outline of Dahomean Religious Belief. *In* Memoirs of the American Anthropological Association 4. 1934, 1937, 1966.

Heusch, Luc de. 2000. Le roi de Kongo et les monstres sacrés. Paris: Gallimard.

Hill, Donald. 1993. Calypso Calaloo: Early Carnival Music in Trinidad. Gainesville: University Press of Florida.

Hilliard, Asa. 1990. The Kingdom of Kemet. Atlanta: WASET Productions.

Honorat, Michel Lamartinière. 1955. Les danses folkloriques haitiennes. Port-au-Prince: Bureau d'ethnologie 2(11):3–153.

Horowitz, Michael, ed. 1971. Peoples and Cultures of the Caribbean. New York: Natural History Press.

Horton, Robin. 1993. Patterns of Thought in Africa and the West: Essays on Magic, Religion, and Science. Cambridge: Cambridge University Press.

Horton, Robin, and Ruth Finnegan. 1973. Modes of Thought: Essays on Thinking in Western and Non-Western Societies. London: Faber.

Hurbon, Laënnec. 1995. Voodoo: Search for the Spirit. Lory Frankel, trans. New York: Harry N. Abrams.

Hurston, Zora Neale. 1938. Tell My Horse. Philadelphia: J. P. Lippincott.

Idowu, E. B. 1962. Olodumare: God in Yoruba Belief. London: Longmans.

Inikori, Joseph. 2001. Africans and Economic Development in the Atlantic World, 1500–1870. *In* African Roots/American Cultures: Africa in the Creation of the Americas. Sheila Walker, ed. Lanham, Md.: Rowman and Littlefield. 123–38.

Inikori, Joseph, and Stanley Engerman, eds. 1992. The Atlantic Slave Trade: Effects on Economies, Societies, and People in Africa, the Americas and Europe. Durham: University of North Carolina Press.

Jahn, Janheinz. 1961. Muntu: The New African Culture. New York: Grove Press.

James, Joel, José Millet, and Alexis Alarcón. 1992. El Vodú en Cuba. República Domini-cana: Ediciones CEDEE/Casa del Caribe.

Janzen, John, and Wyatt MacGaffey. 1974. Anthology of Kongo Religion: Primary Texts from Lower Zaïre. Lawrence: University of Kansas.

Jones, Delmos. 1970. Toward a Native Anthropology. Human Organization 29(4):251–59.

Jordan, Stephanie, and Dave Allen, eds. 1993. Parallel Lines: Media Representations of Dance. London: J. Libbey.

Jules-Rosette, Bennetta. 1979. Symbols of Change: Urban Transition in a Zambian Community. Norwood, N.J.: Ablex Publishing.

———. 1984. The Messages of Tourist Art: An African Semiotic System in Comparative Perspective. New York: Plenum Press.

Jules-Rosette, Bennetta, ed. 1979. The New Religions of Africa. Norwood, N.J.: Ablex Publishing.

Kaeppler, Adrienne. 1967. The Structure of Tongan Dance. Ph.D. dissertation, University of Hawaii, Honolulu, Ann Arbor: University Microfilms.

Kealiinohomoku, Joann. 1975. A Comparative Study of Dance as a Constellation of Motor Behaviors among African and United States Negroes. In Dance Research Annual 7. New York: CORD. 1–181.

———. 1976. Theory and Methods for an Anthropological Study of Dance. Ph.D. dissertation, Indiana University. Ann Arbor: University Microfilms.

Kisliuk, Michelle. 1998. Seize the Dance! BaAka Musical Life and the Ethnography of Performance. New York: Oxford University Press.

Klein, Herbert. 1967. Slavery in the Americas: A Comparative Study of Virginia and Cuba. Chicago: University of Chicago Press.

———. 1986. African Slavery in Latin America and the Caribbean. New York: Oxford University Press.

Knight, Franklin. 1970. Slave Society in Cuba during the Nineteenth Century. Madison: University of Wisconsin Press.

———. 1990 (1978). The Caribbean: The Genesis of a Fragmented Nationalism. New York: Oxford University Press.

Kramer, Karen. 1981. To Serve the Gods [motion picture]. New York: Erzulie Films (35 min.).

———. 1985. Legacy of the Spirits [motion picture]. New York: Filmmakers Library (52 min.) [video recording, Franklin Lakes, N.J.: Karen Kramer, 1986].

———. 1988. Celebration! [video recording]. New York: Filmmakers Library (30 min.).

Kramer, Rita. 1991. Ed School Follies: The Mis-education of America's Teachers. New York: Free Press.

Kubik, Gerhard. 1954. Africa and the Blues. Jackson: University Press of Mississippi.

———. 1979. Angolan Traits in Black Music, Games and Dances of Brazil: A Study of African Cultural Extensions Overseas. Lisbon: Junta de Investigações Científicas de Ultramar.

Kurath, Gertrude. 1949. Dance: Folk and Primitive. In Dictionary of Folklore, Mythology, and Legend. Maria Leach and Jerome Fried, eds. New York: Funk and Wagnalls. 1:277–96.

———. 1975. Panorama of Dance Ethnology. Current Anthropology 1:233–54.

Labat, Jean Baptiste. 1724. Nouveau voyage aux isles de l'Amérique. Anthony Bliss, trans. The Hague.

Lachatánere, Rómulus. 1942. Manuel de Santería. Havana: Editorial Caribe.

———. 1961. Tipos étnicos africanos que concurrieron en la amálgama cubana. Actos del Folklore 1(3):5–12.

Laguerre, Michel S. 1974. Voodoo as Religious and Political Ideology. Freeing the Spirit 3(1):23–28.

———. 1980. Voodoo Heritage. Beverly Hills: Sage Publications.

———. 1987. Afro-Caribbean Folk Medicine. South Hadley, Mass.: Bergin and Garvey.

———. 1989. Voodoo and Politics in Haiti. New York: St. Martin's Press.

Landes, Ruth. 1994 (1947). The City of Women. Albuquerque: University of New Mexico Press.

LaRuffa, Anthony. 1971. San Cipriano: Life in a Puerto Rican Community. New York: Gordon and Breach.

Las FAR, Direción Política de. 1971. História de Cuba 1. Havana: Instituto Cubano del Libro.

Law, Robin. 1977. The Oyo Empire, c. 1600–1836: A West African Imperialism in the Era of the Atlantic Slave Trade. Oxford: Clarendon Press.

———. 2000. La cérémonie du Bois Caïman et le "pacte de sang" dahoméen. Maryse Villard, trans. In L'insurrection des esclaves de Saint-Domingue (22–23 août 1791). Laënnec Hurbon, ed. Paris: Éditions Karthala. 131–47.

Lawal, Babatunde. 1992. The Living Dead: Art and Immortality among the Yoruba of Nigeria. Africa 47(1):50–61.

Leacock, Seth, and Ruth Leacock. 1975. Spirits of the Deep: A Study of an Afro-Brazilian Cult. Garden City, N.Y.: Anchor Press.

León, Argeliers. 1984. Del canto y el tiempo. Havana: Editorial Letras Cubanas.

Lewis, John Lowell. 1992. Ring of Liberation. Chicago: University of Chicago Press.

Ligiero, Zeca. 2001. Iniciação ao Candomblé. Rio de Janeiro: Nova Era.

Linares, Maria Teresa. 1958. Ensayos sobre la influencia española en la música cubana. In Pro-Arte Musical. Havana.

———. 1970. El sucu-sucu de Isla de Piños. Havana: Instituto de Etnología y Folklore.

———. 1989 (1974). La música y el pueblo. Havana: Editorial Pueblo y Educación.

Lindsay, Arturo, ed. 1996. Santería Aesthetics in Contemporary Latin American Art. Washington, D.C.: Smithsonian Institution Press.

Locke, Alain. 1936. The Negro and His Music. Washington, D.C.: Associates in Negro Folk Education.

Lopez Valdés, Rafael. 1986. Hacia una periodización de la historia de la esclavitud en Cuba. In La Esclavitud en Cuba, Instituto de Ciencias Históricas. Havana: Editorial Académica.

———. 1988. Una nuestra de la composición étnica y el matrimonio de africanos en la Habana entre 1694 y 1714. Revista Cubana de Ciencias Sociales 17(1).

Lucas, Olumide. 1948. The Religion of the Yorubas. Lagos: CMS Bookshops.

MacCannell, Dean. 1976. The Tourist: A New Theory of the Leisure Class. New York: Schocken Books.

Macdonald, Annette. 1978–79. The Big Drum of Carriacou. Revista/Review Interamericana 8(4):570–76.

Macedo, Donaldo, ed. 2000. Chomsky on Mis-education. Lanham, Md.: Rowman and Littlefield.

MacGaffey, Wyatt. 1986. Religion and Society in Central Africa. Chicago: University of Chicago Press.

———. 1991. Art and Healing of the Bakongo, Commented by Themselves: Minkisi from the Laman Collection/Kikongo Texts Translated and Edited. Stockholm: Folkens museum—etnografiska; Bloomington: Indiana University Press.

———. 2000. Kongo Political Culture: The Conceptual Challenge of the Particular. Bloomington: Indiana University Press.

Manuel, Peter, ed. 1991. Essays on Cuban Music: North American and Cuban Perspectives. Lanham, Md.: University Press of America.

Manuel, Peter, with Kenneth Bilby and Michael Largey. 1995. Caribbean Currents: Caribbean Music from Rumba to Reggae. Philadelphia: Temple University Press.

Marglin, Frederique. 1989. Redefining the Body: Transformation of Emotion in Ritual Dance. In Divine Passions: The Social Construction of Emotion in India. Owen M. Lynch, ed. Berkeley: University of California Press. 212-36.

Marglin, Frederique, and Stephen A. Marglin, eds. 1996. Decolonizing Knowledge: From Development to Dialogue. New York: Oxford University Press.

Marks, Morton. 1987. Exploring El monte: Ethnobotany and the Afro-Cuban Science of the Concrete. In En Torno a Lydia Cabrera. Isabel Castellanos and J. Inclán, eds. Miami: Universal. 227-45.

Martinez, Joe. 1993. Physiological Psychology. Paper presented at the Ford Foundation Fellows' Conference, Washington, D.C., November.

Mason, John. 1981. Onje Fun Orisa: Foods for the Gods. New York: Yoruba Theological Archministry.

———. 1985. Four New World Yoruba Rituals. New York: Yoruba Theological Archministry.

———. 1992. Orin Orisa. New York: Yoruba Theological Archministry.

Matory, J. Lorand. 1994. The Empire That Is No More: Gender and the Politics of Metaphor in Oyo Yoruba Religion. Minneapolis: University of Minnesota Press.

———. 1999. Afro-Atlantic Culture: On the Live Dialogue Between Africa and the Americas. In Africana, The Encyclopedia of the African and African American Experience, Kwame Anthony Appiah and Henry Louis Gates, Jr., eds., New York: Basic Civitas Books, 36-44.

———. 1999. The English Professors of Brazil. Comparative Studies 41(1):72-103.

———. 2001a. Surpassing "Survival": On the Urbanity of "Traditional Religion" in the Afro-Atlantic World. Black Scholar 30(3-4):36-43.

———. 2001b. "The Cult of Nations" and the Ritualization of Their Purity. South Atlantic Quarterly 100(1):171-214.

Maximilien, Louis. 1945. Le Vodou Haitien: Rite Rada-Canzo. Port-au-Prince: Imprimerie de l'état.

Mazrui, Ali A., ed. 1993. Africa since 1935. London: Heinemann Educational, Berkeley: University of California Press.

Mbiti, John S. 1970. African Religion and Philosophy. New York: Doubleday.

McAlister, Elizabeth. 2002. Rara!: Vodou, Power, and Performance in Haiti and Its Diaspora. Berkeley: University of California Press.

McDaniel, Lorna. 1998. The Drum Ritual of Carriacou: Praisesongs in the Rememory of Flight. Gainesville: University Press of Florida.

Métraux, Alfred. 1972 (1959). Voodoo in Haiti. New York: Knopf.

Meyer, Leonard. 1956. Emotion and Meaning in Music. Chicago: University of Chicago Press.

Mintz, Sidney, and Richard Price. 1976. An Anthropological Approach to the Afro-American Past: A Caribbean Perspective. Philadelphia: Institute for the Study of Human Issues.

Moore, Carlos. 1988. Castro, the Blacks, and Africa. Los Angeles: Center for Afro-American Studies, University of California.

Moreau de Saint Méry, Médéric Louis Elie. 1976 (1796). Dance: An Article Drawn from the Work by M. L. E. Moreau de St.-Méry, entitled Repertory of Colonial Information. Lily and Baird Hastings, trans. Brooklyn: Dance Horizons.

Moreno Fraginals, Manuel, ed. 1984 (1977). Africa in Latin America: Essays on History, Culture, and Socialization. New York: Holmes and Meier.

Morgan, Marlo. 1994. Mutant Message from Down Under. New York: HarperCollins.

Morgan, Philip D. 1997. Cultural Implications of the Atlantic Slave Trade: African Regional Origins, American Destinations and New World Development. Slavery and Abolition 18(1): 122–45.

Morton-Williams, Peter. 1960. The Yoruba Ogboni Cult in Oyo. Africa 30(4):362–74.

Mosley, Albert, ed. 1995. African Philosophy: Selected Readings. Englewood Cliffs, N.J.: Prentice Hall.

Mufwene, Salikoko S., ed. 1993. Africanisms in Afro-American Language Varieties. Athens: University of Georgia Press.

Murphy, Joseph. 1988. Santería: An African Religion in America. Boston: Beacon Press.

———. 1994. Working the Spirit. Boston: Beacon Press.

Murphy, Joseph, and Mei-Mei Sanford, eds. 2001. Osun across the Waters: A Yoruba Goddess in Africa and the Americas. Bloomington: Indiana University Press.

Narmour, Eugene, and Ruth Solie, eds. 1988. Explorations in Music, the Arts, and Ideas: Essays in Honor of Leonard B. Meyer. Stuyvesant, N.Y.: Pendragon Press.

Ness, Sally. 1994. Body, Movement, and Culture. Philadelphia: University of Pennsylvania Press.

Nettleford, Rex. 1985. Dance Jamaica: Cultural Definition and Artistic Discovery: The National Dance Theater Company of Jamaica. New York: Grove.

Nketia, J. H. Kwabena. 1962. African Music in Ghana: A Survey of Traditional Forms. Accra: Longmans.

———. 1965. The Interrelations of African Music and Dance. Studia Musicologica 7:91–101.

Novack, Cynthia. 1990. Sharing the Dance: Contact Improvisation and American Culture. Madison: University of Wisconsin Press.

Olivera Chirimini, Tomas. 2001. Candombe, the African Nations, and the Africanity of Uruguay. In African Roots/American Cultures: Africa in the Creation of the Americas. Sheila Walker, ed. Lanham, Md.: Rowman and Littlefield. 256–74.

Omari, Mikelle. 1984. From the Inside to the Outside: The Art and Ritual of Bahian Candomblé. Los Angeles: Museum of Cultural History, UCLA.

Ortiz, Fernando. 1940. Contrapunteo cubano del tabaco y el azucar. Havana: J. Montero.

———. 1950. La africanía de la música folklórica de Cuba. Havana: Ministerio de Educación, Cárdenas y Cía.

———. 1985 (1951). Los bailes y el teatro de los negros en el folklore de Cuba. Havana: Editorial Letras Cubanas.

———. 1974. La música afrocubana. Madrid: Ediciones Jucar.

Ortiz, Renato. 1989. Ogum and the Umbandista Religión. In Africa's Ogun. Sandra Barnes, ed. Bloomington: Indiana University Press.

Pacini Hernandez, Deborah. 1995. Bachata: A Social History of a Dominican Popular Music. Philadelphia: Temple University Press.

Page, Helan. 1989. The Dialogic Principles of Interactive Learning. Journal of Anthropological Research 44(2):163–81.

Paquette, Robert L., and Stanley L. Engerman, eds. 1996. The Lesser Antilles in the Age of European Expansion. Gainesville: University Press of Florida.

Parrinder, George. 1962. African Traditional Religion. New York: Harper and Row.

Patterson, Orlando. 1969. The Sociology of Slavery: An Analysis of the Origins, Development, and Structure of Negro Slave Society in Jamaica. Rutherford, N.J.: Fairleigh Dickinson University Press.

Paul, Emmanuel. 1962. Panorama du folklore haïtien: Présence africaine en Haïti. Port-au-Prince: Imprimerie du l'état.

Pérez, Louis. 1988. Cuba: Between Reform and Revolution. New York: Oxford University Press.

———. 1995. Essays on Cuban History: Historiography and Research. Gainesville: University of Florida Press.

Perez Mena, Andres. 1977. Spiritualism as an Adaptive Mechanism among Puerto Ricans in the United States. Cornell Journal of Social Relations 12(2):125–36.

Perrone, Charles A., and Christopher Dunn, eds. 2001. Brazilian Popular Music and Globalization. Gainesville: University Press of Florida.

Pescatello, Ann, ed. 1975. The African in Latin America. New York: Knopf.

Phillips, John Edwards. 1991. African Heritage of White America. In Africanisms in the American Culture. Joseph Holloway, ed. 225–39.

Phillips, Miriam. 1987. Where the Spirit Roams: Toward an Understanding of Duende in Two Flamenco Dance Contexts. UCLA Journal of Dance Ethnology 11:45–63.

Polk, Patrick Arthur. 1997. Haitian Vodou Flags. Jackson: University Press of Mississippi.

Pressel, Esther. 1976. Umbanda in Sao Paolo: Religious Innovation in a Developing Society. In Religion, Altered States of Consciousness and Social Change. Erika Bourguignon, ed. Columbus: Ohio State University Press. 264–318.

Price-Mars, Jean. 1983. So Spoke the Uncle (Ainsi parla l'oncle). Magdaline Shannon, trans. Washington, D.C.: Three Continents Press.

Primus, Pearl. 1972. Life Crises: Dance from Birth to Death. In American Dance Therapy Association, Proceedings from the Fourth Annual Conference, Philadelphia. 1–13.

Raboteau, Albert. 1978. Slave Religion. New York: Oxford University Press.

Ramon y Cajal, Santiago. 1989. Recollections of My Life. E. Horne Craigie with Juan Cano, trans. Cambridge, Mass.: MIT Press.

Ramos, Arthur. 1935. O folklore negro do Brasil. Rio de Janeiro: Civiliação Brasileira.

Rego, Waldeloir. 1968. Capoeira Angola: Ensayo socio-etnográfico. Salvador da Bahia: Editora Itapoã.

Reis, Joao José. 1977. Identidade e diversidade étnicas nas irmandades as no tempo da escravidao. Tempo 2(3): 7–33. Florianópolis: Universidade Federal de Florianópolis.

Rigaud, Milo. 1953. La tradition Voudoo et le Voudoo Haitien. Paris: Editions Niclaus.

Robinson, Jenefer, ed. 1997. Music and Meaning. Ithaca: Cornell University Press.

Roberts, John Storm. 1972. Black Music of Two Worlds. Tivoli, New York: Original Music.

———. 1979. The Latin Tinge: The Impact of Latin American Music on the United States. Tivoli, New York: Original Music.

Rolando, Gloria. 1988. Oggún: An Eternal Presence [video recording]. Havana.

———. 1997. The Eyes of the Rainbow: Asada Shakur and Oya [video recording]. Havana.

———. 1999. The Scorpion: Comparsa El Alacrán [video recording]. Havana. Mundo Latino (distributed by Latin American Video Archives).

———. 2001. Huellas en Baraguá (Footsteps in Baraguá, video recording). Havana: Mundo Latino (distributed by Latin American Video Archives).

Royce, Anya. 1977. Anthropology of Dance. Bloomington: Indiana University Press.

Sandoval, Mercedes Cros. 1979 [1975]. La religión de los orichas. Hato Rey, Puerto Rico: Colección Estudios Afrocaribeños.

———. 1989. Santería as a Mental Health Care System: An Historical Overview. Social Science and Medicine 13B:137–51.

Savigliano, Marta. 1995. Tango and the Political Economy of Passion. Boulder: Westview Press.

Scheffler, Israel. 1965. Conditions of Knowledge: An Introduction to Epistemology and Education. Glenview, Ill.: Scott, Foresman.

Schieffelin, Edward. 1976. The Sorrow of the Lonely and the Burning of the Dancers. New York: St. Martin's Press.

Scott, Anna. 1995. It's All in the Timing: The Latest Moves, James Brown's Grooves and the 70s Race Consciousness Movement in Salvador, Bahia, Brazil. Graduate Research Award presentation, CORD Conference, Miami, November.

Serviat, Pedro. 1980. La discriminación racial en cuba, su origen, desarollo y terminación definitive. Islas 66 (May-August).

———. 1986. El problema negro en Cuba y su solución definitive. Havana:

Sieber, Roy, and Roslyn Adele Walker. 1987. African Art in the Cycle of Life. Washington, D.C.: Smithsonian Institution Press.

Simpson, George. 1980. Black Religions in the New World. New York: Columbia University Press.

Sklar, Deirdre. 1991. Invigorating Dance Ethnology. UCLA Journal of Dance Ethnology 15:4–15.

———. 1994. Can Bodylore Be Brought to Its Senses? Journal of American Folklore 107(423):9–22.

Sloat, Susanna. 2002. Caribbean Dance from Abakuá to Zouk: How Movement Shapes Identity. Gainesville: University Press of Florida.

Snyder, Allegra Fuller. 1981. The Dance Symbol. *In* Dance Research Annual. T. Comstock, ed. 6:213–24.

———. 1988. Levels of Event Patterns: A Theoretical Model Applied to the Yaqui Easter Ceremony. *In* The Dance Event: A Complex Phenomenon. Proceedings of the International Congress of Traditional Music Study Group for Ethnochoreology. Copenhagen, Denmark.

Sosa, Enrique. 1984. El Carabalí. Havana: Editorial Letras Cubanas.

Sowande, Fela. 1973. Black Folklore. Black Lines (special issue on folklore), Fall 2(1):5–21.

Stuckey, Sterling. 1994. Going through the Storm: The Influence of African American Art on History. New York: Oxford University Press.

Taylor, Patrick, ed. 2001. Nation Dance: Religion, Identity, and Cultural Difference in the Caribbean. Bloomington: Indiana University Press.

Tempels, Placide. 1959. Bantu Philosophy, translation by Colin King of the French translation by A. Rubbens of the original Tempels work. Paris: Presence africaine.

Thomas, Eudora. 1987. A History of the Shouter Baptists in Trinidad and Tobago. Ithaca, N.Y.: Calaloux.

Thompson, Robert Farris. 1971. Black Gods and Kings. Los Angeles: Museum of Ethnic Arts.

———. 1974. African Art in Motion. Berkeley: University of California Press.

———. 1983. Flash of the Spirit. New York: Random House.

———. 1995. From the Isle beneath the Sea: Haiti's Africanizing Vodou Art. *In* Sacred Arts of Haitian Vodou. Donald Cosentino, ed. Los Angeles: UCLA Fowler Museum of Cultural History. 91–121.

Thompson, Robert Farris, and Joseph Cornet. 1981. Four Moments of the Sun: Kongo Art in Two Worlds. Washington, D.C.: National Gallery of Art.

Thornton, John Kelly. 1998. Africans and African Americans in the Making of the Atlantic World. Cambridge: Cambridge University Press.

Thurman, Howard. 1967. Deep River [recording]. San Francisco: Howard Thurman Educational Trust Fund.

Trouillot, Michel. 1990. Haiti, State against Nation: The Origins and Legacy of Duvalierism. New York: Monthly Review Press.

———. 1995. Silencing the Past: Power and the Production of History. Boston: Beacon Press.

Turpin, John, and Blanca Martinez. 1980. Bata, the Sacred Drums of the Yoruba in Cuba, Selected from the Writings of Fernando Ortiz (2nd edition 1965 [1950]). John Turpin and B. E. Martinez, trans. Manuscript.

Van Gennep, Arnold. 1960 (1909). Rites of Passage. Monika Vizedom and Gabrielle Cafee, trans. Chicago: University of Chicago Press.

Vega, Marta. 2000. The Altar of My Soul. New York: Bantam Books.

Vega Drouet, Hector. 1979. Historical and Ethnological Survey on Probable African Origins of the Puerto Rican Bomba: Including a Description of Santiago Apostol Festivities at Loíza Aldea. Ph.D. dissertation, Wesleyan University.

Verger, Pierre (Fatumbi). 1957. Notes sur le culte des Orisa et Vodun à Bahia. Dakar: IFAN.

———. 1995. Ewé: Le verbe et le pouvoir des plantes chez les Yorùbá. Paris: Maison-neuve et Larose.

Vinueza, María Elena. 1988. Presencia Arará en la música folclórica de Matanzas. Havana: Casa de las Américas.

Voeks, Robert A. 1997. Sacred Leaves of Candomblé: African Magic, Medicine, and Re-ligion in Brazil. Austin: University of Texas Press.

Wafer, James William. 1991. The Taste of Blood: Spirit Possession in Brazilian Candom-blé. Philadelphia: University of Pennsylvania Press.

Walker, Sheila. 1972. Ceremonial Spirit Possession in Africa and Afro-America. Leiden, Holland: E. J. Brill.

———. 1980. African Gods in America: The Black Religious Continuum. Black Scholar 11(8):45–61.

———. 1990. Everyday and Esoteric Reality in the Afro-Brazilian Candomblé. History of Religions: An International Journal for Comparative Historical Studies 30 (No-vember 2):103–28.

———. 1991. A Choreography of the Universe: The Afro-Brazilian Candomblé as a Mi-crocosm of Yoruba Spiritual Geography. Anthropology and Humanism Quarterly 16(2):42–50.

———. 2001. African Roots/American Cultures: Africa in the Creation of the Americas. Lanham, Md.: Rowman and Littlefield.

———. 2002. Scattered Africa [video recording]. Berkeley: University of California Ex-tension Media.

Wexler, Anna. 1997. "I Am Going to See Where My Oungan Is": The Artistry of a Haitian Vodou Flagmaker. In Sacred Possessions: Vodou, Santería, and Obeah in the Carib-bean. Marguerite Fernández Olmos and Lizabeth Paravisini-Gebert, eds. Rutgers: Rutgers University Press. 59–78.

Wilcken, Lois. 1992. The Drums of Vodou. Featuring Frisner Augustin. Tempe, Ariz.: White Cliffs Media Company.

Williams, Drid. 1997. Anthropology and Human Movement. Boulder, Colo.: Scarecrow Press.

Williams, Eric. 1984 (1970). From Columbus to Castro: The History of the Caribbean. New York: Vintage Books.

Wilson, Olly. 1974. The Significance of the Relationship between Afro-American and West African Music. The Black Perspective in Music 2(1):3–22.

———. 1981. Association of Movement and Music as a Manifestation of a Black Concep-tual Approach to Music Making. In Essays on Afro-American Music and Musicians. Irene V. Jackson, ed. Westport, Conn.: Greenwood Press. 1–23.

———. 1983. Black Music as an Art Form. Black Music Research Journal, 1–22.

Wilson, Sule. 1992. The Drummer's Path: Moving the Spirit with the Ritual and Tradi-tional Drumming. Rochester, Vt.: Destiny Books.

Woodson, Carter. 1919. The Education of the Negro Prior to 1861. Washington, D.C.: Association for the Study of Negro Life and History.

———. 1933. The Mis-Education of the Negro. Washington, D.C.: Associated.

Yai, Olabiyi. 2001. African Diasporan Concepts and Practice of the Nation and Their Im-plications in the Modern World. In African Roots/American Cultures. Sheila Walker, ed. Lanham, Md.: Rowman and Littlefield. 244–55.

Yarborough, Lavinia Williams. 1958. Haiti-Dance. Frankfurt am Main: Bronners Druckerei.

———. 1980. Dunham Technique. *In* Katherine Dunham: Reflections on the Social and Political Contexts of Afro-American Dance. Joyce Aschenbrenner, ed. New York: CORD. 121–59.

Yudin, Linda. 1996. Divine Innovation: The Emergence of Contemporary Afro-Brazilian Dance from Salvador, Bahia. Paper presented at the American Anthropological Association meeting, San Francisco, November. Unpublished manuscript.

Zahan, Dominique. 1979. The Religion, Spirituality and Thought of Traditional Africa. Kate and Lawrence Martin, trans. Chicago: University of Chicago Press.

INDEX

Abakuá, Carabalí nación, 98 chart 3, 135–37. See also *Carabalí nación*
aberícula (unconsecrated drums), in Cuba, 155–56. *See also* drums, baptized
aberícula (uninitiated laypeople), in Cuba, 156
aché (divine life force), in Cuba, 81, 84–85, 232–33, 272–78. See also *axé; espri*
Adja (West African people), 96
aesthetic system as crosscutting domain, 54 fig. 1
affranchi (dances), in Cuba, 135; in Haiti, 107, 109, 117
Afoxé (popular music), in Bahia, 46
Africa and African Americas, continuous contacts, 68–69, 157
African Americas, 282n12
African Americas, religions, 2–4, 44–52, 96–103, 98 chart 3, 236–45, 254–55, 270–73; critique of scholarship, 45–46, 256–57, 285n3, 285n4; dance performance in, 51–56, 65, 160. *See also* syncretism
African Diaspora Dance Perspective, 51–56, 110–11, 276
African nation amalgams in the Americas, x, 1, 13, 44–49, 96–100, 98 chart 2.

See also *nação/nações; nación/naciones; nasyon/nasyons;* nations
Afro-Cuba (Cuban popular musical group), 241
Afro-Cuban religions, 14, 129. *See also* Cuban Yoruba
Afrogenic, 56, 284n8, 286–87n13
age, ritual calculation of, 31–32, 158–59
agogo (iron gong/bell), in Cuba, 128; *agogó,* in Haiti, 7, 181
aguardiente (raw white rum), in Cuba, 24
aguas de Oxalá (Oxalá's water ceremony), in Bahia, 39, 199–200
Agwé (Rada Divinity), in Haiti, 111, 113, 185
Ajayi, Omofolabo, 53
akpwon (lead singer), in Cuba, 20–22, 155, 206, 215–23
Aldamas, Benito, 290–91n1
alebê / alebês (Bahian Candomblé drummer/s), 40, 80, 195
Amado, Jorge, 45, 101–2
American Dance Performances, video (Dunham), 271
ancestors, 28, 54–55, 82 fig. 6, 82 fig. 7, 174, 251. See also *Eguns; ley mo*
Angola *nação,* in Bahia, 49, 98 chart 2, 98 chart 3

among African Americas nations, 160–61

conga (Kongo-Angola barrel-shaped drum), in Cuba, xvi, 128–29

conga (processional dance form), in Cuba, xvi, 128–29, 287n15

Congo (dance), in Haiti, 113, 117, 129–30

Congo (region in West Central Africa), xv, 97. *See also* Kongo (West Central African people); Kongo-Angola

Congo Minuet (dance), in Haiti, 107, 116, 285–86n3, 286n8

Congo rites, in Haitian Vodou, 13, 98 chart 2, 98 chart 3, 180–87

Conjunto Folklórico Nacional de Cuba (National Folkloric Company of Cuba), 16, 143, 238–39, 241–42, 244; *including* Sylvina Fabars, Nieves Fresneda, Fermin Nani, Juan "Petit" Ortiz, Amelia Pedroso, Jose Pilar

contas (beaded necklaces), in Bahia, 190. *See also* necklaces

contradança (European-derived dance), in Brazil, 144, 155

contredanse (European-derived dance), in Cuba and in Haiti, 108, 120–21

Conversation with Baba, 271–72

Conversation with Changó, 205–45

Conversation with Elegba, 95–96

Conversation with Ezili, 169–72

Conversation with Ogún, 97–103

Conversation with Oxalá, 274–75

Conversation with Oyá / Yansan, 188–90

coro (chorus), in Cuba, 15, 215–23

coro (two-line couplet refrain, Spanish), in Cuba, 122

coronal (front/back) plane of existence, realm of divinities, 82, 82 fig. 7, 83 fig. 8, 158, 252

counterclockwise circular dancing, 36, 81, 157, 159, 193–94, 201, 235

Creole, 106, 285n1

Cross-Cultural Model (African diaspora dance pedagogy), 240, 241, 243

Cruz, Celia, 46

Cuba J-Term, Smith College, 243–44

Cuba, history of, 47, 117–41

Cuban Dance Examples, video (Daniel), 299

Cuban educational policy, 264–65

Cuban *naciones* and their dances, 141–42 chart 5

Cuban Rumba, video (Daniel), 299

Cuban Yoruba (religion), 14–15, 19, 281n3; ceremony observed (1987), 14–27

cultural presentations of praise performances, 45, 47, 165. *See also* tourists, dance/music performances for

culture, 102

Cumina (Kongo-Angola dance and religion), in Jamaica, 287n16

damier (damye, martial art/dance), in Martinique, 287n17

dance, body orientation, 42, 160, 288n3

dance choreography, *On Beginning Again* (Daniel), 225–36

dance movement vocabulary, 15, 62, 105, 141

dance/music, as access to cultural knowledge, 12–13, 50, 60, 110–11

dance/music descriptions, colonial period, in Brazil, 144–45, 146 chart 6; in Cuba, 120–21, 126–28, 141–42 chart 5; in Haiti, 106–9, 117–18 chart 4

dance/music forms lost in the African Americas, 110

dance/music performance, open versus restricted participation, 39, 191

dance/music religious practices, 2, 28, 64, 272–73. *See also* African Americas, religions

Davis, Wade, 45, 283n5

de Andrade, Marilia, 143, 145

décima (Spanish lyric structure), 120

de Oviedo, Fernandez, 106

de Santana Rodrigué, Graça, 46, 275–76

Desmangles, Leslie, 46, 285n3, 289n3

devotional communities (worshipping congregations), 102–3. See also *casas; ounfos; terreiros*

Dia de los reyes (Three Kings Day), in Cuba, 92, 126–27, 141

disembodied knowledge, 57–59, 90–91, 237, 265

divination practices, 4, 33, 80, 284n9. *See also* Ifa divination diviner. See *babalawo, babaloricha, babalorixá, iyaloricha, iyalorixá, manbo, oungan*

divinities, 1, 15, 54–55, 82–83, 140, 232. See also *íremes; lwas; orichas; orixás; individual divinity*

divinities, associated body areas, 74–77, 75 fig. 3, 76 fig. 4, 76 fig. 5, 78–79 chart 1. *See also* individual divinity

divinities, associated colors, 24, 78–79 chart 1. *See also* individual divinity

divinities, associated with disease, 133, 140

dobale (ritual salutation), in Bahia, 31, 200–201; in Cuba, 25. *See also* salutations; *viré*

dressing, ritual, 23–24, 30–31, 104–5, 157, 165–66, 195–97

drum ensembles in Bahia, 88; in Cuba, 88; in Haiti, 88

drummers, ritual, 40, 87–89, 195; as librarians of codified knowledge, 66, 256. See also *alebês, batás*

drumming, 60, 86–92, 207–13 chart 12

drums, baptized (consecrated), 154–55. *See also* aberícula drums; *batás*

dry ritual (drumming without singing or dance), 15, 227. See also *oru seco*

Dunham, Katherine, 6, 107, 271, 293n12

Dunham technique, 7, 143

dwapo (Haitian Vodou flag), 228, 230

Easter, 107, 123. See also *Carnaval, Carnival*

ebomi (fully-initiated priest/healer), in Bahia, 30–31, 282n7

ebos. See *odus*

Efik (West African people), 96, 126

Egües, Richard, 241

Egunguns (spirits of dead ancestors in Yoruba Africa), 25

Eguns (spirits of dead ancestors), in Cuba and Bahia, 24, 28, 54, 250

Ejagham (West African people), 96

ekedi (ritual assistant), in Bahia, 37, 42, 43, 193, 282n7

Elbein dos Santos, Juana, 71

Elegba, divinity, 18–19, 69–71, 94–95, 138, 155; in Bahia: Echu, Elegba, Eleg-bara, Ena, Eshu, Exu; in Cuba: Echú, Elegba, Elegbara, Eleguá, Ena, Exú; in Haiti: Legba, Papa Legba

El Gato Gatell, Ernesto, 291n1

embodied knowledge, 4–5, 59, 60 fig. 2, 66, 256, 265–69, 274–76. *See also* specific disciplines

Emery, Lynne, 285n2

Encarnaçao, Antonio Carlos Silva, 72–73

enkríkamo (small, hand-held *Abakuá* drum), in Cuba, 128, 136

ere (boisterous, childlike character), in Bahia, 61, 158, 159 chart 9

Espiritismo. See Kardec, Allan

espri (vital energy), in Haiti, 81, 84–85, 232–33, 278. See also *nam; aché; axé*

Ewe (West African people), 96

Ezili, divinity, 10, 178, 230–31, 278, 286n6. *See also* Yemanja; Yemayá. *See also for* Ezili Danto: Oyá; Yansan. *See also for* Ezili Freda: Ochún; Oxun

Fa, Fon divination system, 2, 284n9

familias de santo (ritual families), in Bahia and Cuba, extended ritual families including worshipping congregations, ancestors and orichas, 28, 64, 64, 283n4

fanmis (ritual familes) in Haiti, extended ritual families including worshipping congregations, ancestors and lwas, 13, 28, 64, 174, 283n4, 287n21

fazem a cabeça (preparation for receiving a divinity), in Bahian Candomblé, 158

feint (dance posture), 88, 152–53, 267

feminine energy force, aspects expressed through Ochún, Oyá, and Yemayá, 252, 257–60, 266–68

filho/a do santo (son or daughter of the saints/orixás), in Bahia, 31, 101

Fleurant, Gerdès, 46, 116, 284n9, 286n8

flywhisk, ritual (íruke), 11, 23, 26, 139, 249

fodunes, Arará divinities, in Cuba 133, 134

FolkCuba Especial, 241–42

Fon (West African people), 2–4, 49, 96

Fon-derived nations, 49, 98, 98 chart 2, 104

food, communal, 115, 150, 155, 158, 250–51. *See also* sacrifices, animal

manman (lead Haitian Vodou drum), 88, 228

Marks, Morton, 72

martial art/dance forms of African Americas, in Brazil, 287n17; in Cuba, 130–31; in Haiti, 287n17; in Martinique, 287n17; in Trinidad, 286n4

Martinez-Furé, Rogelio, 256

masculine energy force, manifested in Changó, 262–63

mask performance in the African Americas, 127, 135–36

Mason, John, 247

Masters' Model (African diaspora dance pedagogy), 238–39, 240–42

Matanzas, Cuba, 14, 17–18, 125–26

mathematics, embodied, 19, 60, 86–91, 93; revealed in drum performance, 86–93. *See also* music

Matory, J. Lorand, 96–97

mayí (dance), in Haiti, 13, 88, 111, 112, 153

mazone (dance), in Haiti, 115, 178, 286n7

media sentada, limbo ritual status, 29, 35

Mestre King. *See* Bispo dos Santos, Raimundo

miseducation, 264–65. *See also* disembodied knowledge

Miss B. *See* Beckford, Ruth

modeling, as kinesthetic learning behavior, 17, 202–3

Moreau de St. Méry, Médéric Louis Elie, 106–10

mulatto cultures, 47

multisensory stimulation. *See* sensory stimulation

Muñiz, Harold, 291n1

muscle memory, 92, 110, 284n13

music, 60, 86–87, 91. *See also* drumming

nação (nation), *nações* (nations), African-amalgam allegiances in Bahia, 146 chart 6. *See also* nation, concept of

nación (nation), *naciones* (nations), African-amalgam allegiances in Cuba, 15–17, 126–28, 141–42 chart 5. *See also* nation, concept of

nações. See *nação*

Nago (Yoruba rites in Haitian Vodou), 13, 49, 98–99, 98 chart 2, 98 chart 3, 105, 111, 114

Nago/Ketu (Yoruba *naçao*), in Bahia, 44, 49, 98–99, 98 chart 3, 105, 157, 191

nam ("soul," vital energy), in Haiti, 81, 84–85. See also *espri*

nasyon (nation), *nasyons* (nations), African-amalgam allegiances in Haiti, 13, 110–17. *See also* nation, concept of

nasyons and dances in Haiti, 108–17, 117–18 chart 4, 151–53

nation, concept of simultaneous allegiance to multiple heritages, 2–4, 44, 46–49, 96–100. See also *nação; nación; nasyon*

National Folkloric Company of Cuba. See *Conjunto Folklórico Nacional de Cuba*

native peoples of the African Americas, dances of, 119–20, 143–44, 286n11. See also *caboclo*

necklaces, ritual, compared, 40–41; in Bahia, 40, 190; in Cuba, 23, 33, 40; in Haiti, 40

nkisis (Angola *nação* divinities), in Bahia, 157

nkisis (Palo *nación* divinities), in Cuba, 131–32

ñongo (medium-paced *batá* rhythm), in Cuba, 206, 207 chart 12, 248–49

Oba, divinity, 24, 77

Obatalá, divinity, 19, 24, 139, 234–35

Ochanla (Divinity), 227, 232–33. *See also* Supreme Divinity

Ochosi, divinity, 19, 24, 30, 138–39

Ochún, divinity, 24, 77, 121, 139, 234–35, 257–60, 277–78; *patakine* for, 214–15

Oddudua (Divinity), 227, 232. *See also* Supreme Divinity

odus (philosophical texts associated with the Ifa oracle), 80

odus (reciprocal ritual practices), 80, 158, 159 chart 10; also known as *ebos*

O'Farril, Alfredo, 241

ogan (ritual specialist), 40, 80

oggán (metal gong/bell and rhythmic pattern), in Cuba, 132; in Haiti, 153

Ogou, divinity, in Haiti, xv, 43, 63–64; *also known as* Ogoun. *See also* Ogun; Ogún

Ogun, divinity, in Bahia, xv, 43, 63–64; *also known as* Ogum, Ogú. *See also* Ogún; Ogou

Ogún, divinity, in Cuba, xv, 2, 19, 24, 43, 62–63, 138; *patakine* for, 214–15. *See also* Ogou; Ogun

Olofi (Divinity), 85, 227, 232–33. *See also* Supreme Divinity

Olokun (Divinity), 232. *See also* Supreme Divinity

Olorún (Divinity), 227, 232. *See also* Supreme Divinity

olubatá (lead *batá* drummer), in Cuba, 155. *See also batás*

Oludumare (Divinity), 227, 232–33. *See also* Supreme Divinity

Omolu, divinity, 133

Oracle stories, 197, 275–76. *See also* oral literature

oral history, 55

oral literature, moral and pedagogical roles of, 62, 80, 92, 203, 213–15, 275–76

ori (spiritual essence), 158

Oricha (popular music), in Cuba, 46

orichas (divinities), in Cuba, 1, 15, 54–55, 74–75, 76 fig. 4, 79 chart 1, 128, 141–42 chart 5

orikis (*orixá* parables), in Bahia, 80, 197, 213, 275–76. *See also* oral literature

Orixá religion, in Brazil, 30, 282n9

orixás (divinities), in Bahia, 1, 42, 54–55, 75–77, 76 fig. 5, 79 chart 1, 157, 146 chart 6

Orthographic Note, xii

Ortiz, Fernando, 89–90, 127

Oru de batá. See Oru seco

Oru de cantos (public music and dance ceremony), 14, 155, 207. See also *Oru de Eya Aranla*

Oru de Eya Aranla (public opening drumming with dancing at *wemilere* in Cuba), 14, 155

Orun, home of the Yoruba divinities, 158

Orúnmila, guardian of the Ifa Oracle, 95, 213; *oriki* for, 275–76

Oru seco (private opening drumming ritual at *wemilere* in Cuba), 15, 155

Ossein, divinity, in Bahia, 72

otan (divinity stone), 33

ouncis (community of initiates), in Haiti, 153

ounfo (temple), in Haitian Vodou, 58–59, 84, 116

oungan (priest, healer, leader), in Haiti, 7, 79–80, 153, 176. See also *manbo*

oungenikon (lead singer), in Haiti, 8, 9, 20, 153. See also *akwpon*

Oxalá, divinity, 38, 61, 201–3. See also *aguas de Oxalá*

Oxossi, divinity, 30, 44

Oxun, divinity, 195–96, 277–78. *See also* Ezili, Ochún

Oya / Yansan, names used interchangeably in Bahia, 188, 278

Oyá / Yansán, names used interchangeably in Cuba, 14

Oyá, divinity, 19–28, 32–33, 139–40, 247–50; *patakines* for, 214, 248. *See also* Ezili

Oyotunji Ojo settlement in South Carolina, 58, 102

Palo, Kongo-Angola-derived *nación* of Cuba, 15, 131–32; *also known as* Palo Monte

Papa Dambala (Rada divinity), in Haiti, 8, 77, 94, 111, 278. See also *yanvalu*

Papa Legba, 18, 71. *See also* Elegba

Papo Sterling, Victor, 29n1

parables. *See* oral literature

parrandas (storytelling parades), in Cuba, 126, 127

patakines (*oricha* parables), in Cuba, 80, 213. *See also* oral literature

Perez, Ana, 14–15, 17, 21, 29, 244, 290n1

peristil (interior space), in Haiti, 61, 116, 166

Petwo rites in Haitian Vodou, 13, 49, 75, 98 chart 2, 98 chart 3, 113–14, 130, 152

philosophy, embodied, 60, 79–80, 85, 93, 126, 162, 274; as positive community principles, 64, 252. *See also* oral literature

photography, 8, 179, 194, 289n8
physiology, embodied, 60, 74, 75 fig.
    3, 75 fig. 4, 76 fig. 5, 77–78, 81–83, 93,
    261–62. *See also* botany; divinities, as-
    sociated with disease
plane(s) of existence, 81–83, 82 fig. 6,
    82 fig. 7, 83 fig. 8, 233. *See also* coronal
    plane of existence; horizontal plane of
    existence; sagittal plane of existence
plante (*Abakuá* meeting place), in Cuba,
    135
playful dances, 115, 152
Popo (West African people), 96
possession. *See* manifestations of divini-
    ties
potomitan (center-post) in Haiti, 8, 166;
    as center of dance performance, 153; as
    center as ritual practice, 81; drawings
    on or at base of, 150, 181
pre savann, (Haitian Vodou reciter of
    Catholic prayers), 9, 101, 151, 168
Primus, Pearl, 271, 293n12
Priyé Guinen (African prayer), 151
psychology, embodied, 60, 77–78, 93
Public Vodun Ceremonies of Haiti, video
    (Daniel), 290n13, 299
puyas (insulting songs), 22

Quesada, Librada, 16, 241
Quessa, Sara, 289n3

Rada rites, in Haitian Vodou, 13, 49,
    74–75, 97, 98, 98 chart 2, 98 chart 3,
    104, 152
Rara (processional dance form), in Haiti,
    111, 116–17. See also *Gagá*
reading (consultation), 158, 165, 288n1
religion, 2. *See also* African Americas,
    religions
repetition, importance of, 5, 92, 249,
    265
research methods, 4, 48, 222, 269–70
rezo (prayer), in Cuba, 207, 215. *See also*
    chart 12, 207–13
ritual specialists, 155–56. See also *akp-
    won; babalawo; babalorixá; babloricha;
    ebomi; ekedi; iawo; iyakekere; iyaloricha;
    iyalorixá; manbo; ogan; oungan; ounge-
    nikon; santera / santero*

Rivera, Eduardo, 241
roça (natural grounds surrounding or in
    a *terreiro*), in Bahia, 30, 37, 282n9
Rodrigues, Xiomara, 242
Roman Catholic. *See* Catholic
Ros, Lázaro, 46
Royce, Anya, 52
rum, 166, 185; *aguardiente,* 24; *cachaça,*
    189; *kleren,* 11, 179, 181; *malafó,* 24
rumba columbia (popular dance form), in
    Cuba, 130

sacrifices, of animals, 36, 180–82
sagittal (vertical-left/right) plane of
    existence, ancestral realm, 82, 82 fig. 7,
    83 fig. 8, 251
Sagpana, Arará divinity, in Cuba, 133
salutations to worshipping community,
    11, 25–26, 31, 115, 133, 200–201. See
    also *dobale; viré*
samba (popular dance form), 130
santera / santero (ritual specialist), in
    Cuba, 14, 23, 80, 101, 282n7
Santería, in Cuba, 47, 101–2, 161, 281n3.
    See also Cuban Yoruba
Santiaguero dance style, in Cuba, 18
sarará (vibratory movements of mani-
    festing *orixá*), in Bahia, 42
Saro (West African people), 68
Scattered Africa, video (Walker), 282n13,
    311
scented water, 23, 178, 179, 233, 250
secrecy, role in religious traditions of
    African Americas, 31, 253–54
sensory elements, importance of, 52–53,
    103, 186
sensory stimulation, 102, 186, 250
Shack, William, 54
shoulder movements, 132–33. See also
    zépòl
siete potencies (seven powers), in Cuban
    Yoruba, 41
Sloss, Andrew, 240
Snyder, Allegra, 53
social medicine, 5, 55, 271, 273, 293n11
Soledade, Augusto, 290n1
songs, 22, 60, 190. *See also* chant; chants
Spanish Moors. See *Ladinos*
sphere, expressing three planes of

existence, 81; 82 fig. 7; metaphor of celestial orange, 81, 232

Yvonne Daniel is professor of dance and Afro-American studies at Smith College in Massachusetts.

The University of Illinois Press
is a founding member of the
Association of American University Presses.

UNIVERSITY OF ILLINOIS PRESS
1325 South Oak Street
Champaign, IL 61820-6903
www.press.uillinois.edu